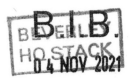

FOUR FIVE

FOUR FIVE

THE STORY OF
45 COMMANDO, ROYAL MARINES,
1943–1971

by
David Young

LEO COOPER LTD · LONDON

First published in Great Britain, 1972 by
LEO COOPER LTD,
196 Shaftesbury Avenue
London WC2H 8JL

Copyright © 1972 David Young

ISBN 0 85052 093 2

Printed in Great Britain at
The Pitman Press
Bath

CONTENTS

ILLUSTRATIONS

MAPS

FOREWORD

by the late Admiral Sir Michael Le Fanu,
G.C.B., D.S.C.

It is a great honour for me to be asked to write a foreword
to this fine record of 45 Commando's activities in peace and
war, ashore and afloat. Although, of course, I would not lead
with my chin by saying that Four Five are better than any other
Commando, I do happen to know them more closely. This is
because from 1965 to 1967, when they were serving in Aden
and the Radfan under the command successively of Robin
McGarel Groves, Clifford Bye and John Owen, I was the
unified Commander-in-Chief and naturally saw a lot of the
unit.

Although a unified Commander-in-Chief must lean over
backwards not to favour his own Service there is no harm in
his being pleased when a unit of his Service distinguishes
itself. So it was with Four Five. No Army unit performed
with more distinction, whether in the wild country round
Habilayn or in the Main Pass overlooking Crater. The Brigade
Commander, the Army Commander and I knew that we could
absolutely depend on the Marines to act with resolution, skill
and dash however disagreeable and dangerous the task.

I was grateful also to Four Five for much else: for providing
me with lively bodyguards, with a new pair of patrol boots
whenever I wanted them, and with a change from sweaty Aden
whenever I could manage a romp over the Jebel Jihaff.

Reading this book I see that the rest of their service has been
as gallant and devoted as during the time that I was lucky

ix

enough to serve with them. I'm sure their future achievements will be equally distinguished, because although, as I have explained, I would not care to be quoted as saying that Four Five are best, I am very happy to say that there isn't a better Commando in the business.

Good luck, Four Five, and thank you.

Michael Le F.

22 *November, 1970*

NOTE. *This Foreword was written a few days before the tragic and untimely death of Admiral Sir Michael Le Fanu. Lady Le Fanu has very kindly given her permission for us to use it.*

ACKNOWLEDGEMENTS

In a relatively small Corps such as ours the family spirit is ever-dominant and as a result, on this venture, the assistance and understanding I have had from both units and individuals have been enormous.

Firstly, I would like to thank General Sir Norman Tailyour and Col John Owen, who have kindly undertaken to read the entire manuscript and have been a constant source of counsel and encouragement. I am also deeply indebted to the editor of the *Globe and Laurel*, the Corps journal, for his generous permission to reprint numerous extracts from that magazine, and to the Royal Marines Historian and his staff who have provided invaluable help from the archives.

I am most grateful too to past Commanding Officers and the many officers and other ranks who have kindly loaned me documents, papers, photographs and material and have subsequently read and advised upon my drafts. The excellence of the maps and illustrations is entirely due to the skill of Sgts C. Ridgeway and R. Carr and Cpl B. W. Parry, the draughtsmen of Headquarters, Commando Forces, in Plymouth, who have devoted much of their spare time to complete this lengthy task. I should also like to express my gratitude to the Orderly Room Staff of 45 Commando, who have had to cope with an unending flow of correspondence and manuscripts from my office and in spite of their onerous operational commitments have never failed to meet my deadlines.

Finally, my sincere thanks go to the following who have helped enormously in my researches: The Records Officer and his staff, Ministry of Defence (Navy); The Records Officer and his staff, Drafting Pay and Records Office, Royal Marines; the Military Secretary and his staff, Department of the Commandant General, Royal Marines.

DAVID YOUNG
Leeds
October, 1971.

INTRODUCTION

Four Five tells the story of 45 Commando, Royal Marines, from its formation in 1943 to the present day.

The Commando's activities and travels have been widespread; successes and achievements have been numerous. It is for this reason that it has been impossible for me to mention every single episode or occurrence, however important it might have appeared to the participants at the time. I have, however, attempted to describe and enlarge upon single events typical of a campaign, of a theatre of operations or of the spirit and enterprise of the Unit.

Over the past twenty years it has been the privilege of Royal Marines to be engaged in nearly every important military activity which has affected this country overseas. The political implications, in many cases, have been far reaching. I have limited my observations to the factual events leading up to the particular situation and how they might have determined the Commando's subsequent actions. Political requirements have largely dictated day-to-day military tactics. These have sometimes caused restrictions, sometimes reappraisal. Where appropriate I have deliberately included the reactions these have caused to give a clearer picture of how officers and men of the Commando dealt with the problems and found the eventual solution.

Those who served with Four Five during the War may consider that I have not covered the events of this period in as great a length as those in subsequent and more recent periods. For this I make no apology. The wartime period has already been admirably covered in detail in two books: *The Story of 45*

Royal Marine Commando by Capt J. E. Day, formerly of B Troop, and published privately for members of the Unit, and *Commando Men* by Lt Bryan Samain, the Intelligence Officer, and published in 1948 by Stevens. Although I have referred to these works closely I have no wish to repeat verbatim all the various actions, but have included this important period so that the reader can get a complete view of the gallant deeds and developments of the Commando.

This is essentially the story of a Royal Marine Commando and the officers, non-commissioned officers and men who make it live, laugh and fight. I cannot mention everybody by name and I hope that the anonymous will bear with me. I feel confident, however, that past and present members of the Commando will be able to identify and relive their own important contribution to each action, and take pride in the fact that it is they, and they alone, who have made this story possible.

CHAPTER 1

The Birth and Development of Four Five

'Prime Minister to General Ismay 18.VI.40. There ought to be at least twenty thousand Storm Troops or "Leopards" (later named "Commandos") drawn from existing units, ready to spring at the throat of any small landing or descent.'*

The Commandos were born at the beginning of this century in the far off veldt of South Africa, for this was the name that the Boers gave to their shock troops, who 'operating as guerillas were few in numbers but harried a quarter of a million British troops with considerable success'. This name was now to be given to a new generation of superbly fit hand-picked men who were to prove at the time, and are still proving today, that they can both keep up to the traditions of their brave forbears and provide a match for any military force in the world.

This new name was to be added to the front line units of the British armed forces in 1940 soon after our magnificent withdrawal through Dunkirk. These Commando units were designed from the very outset to be aggressive formations and were not merely created from the surrounding 'bulldog' spirit which was so prevalent at the time. We wanted to oppose the Hun with something that could strike hard and effectively, both as an integral part of our major armies and independently, and the Commandos were to be the answer to this. The

* *The Second World War* by Winston S. Churchill. Volume II. Cassell and Company Limited.

success of the Boer horsemen, whom we still remember in the Royal Marines by the adoption of 'Sarie Marais' as the official Commando march and the naming of our sub-units in the Commandos as 'Troops', was due to several factors. If these factors are examined first of all we can then see how our more recent maxims compare. Determination heads the list coupled with the ability of the Boers to force home their surprise attacks and to make their presence a constant source of anxiety to the enemy; their flexibility which enabled them to fulfil a wide variety of different roles; and finally their speed and mobility—to strike and move quickly—thus tying down large and significant numbers of the relatively cumbersome troops in the guarding of supply routes and bases and diverting them from their rightful place in the front.

The wartime functions of Commando units again covered a broad field of activities. Primarily they were assault troops designed to be landed initially from the sea either as the spearhead of massive operations, such as D-Day, or on smaller raids like the Lofoten Islands, which forced the enemy to keep on the constant alert and denied him time to relax, even for a single moment, on every front. However, as we shall see later on in the case of Four Five, and for that matter any other Commando unit, it was not to be employed solely on given types of task, and many of those which it was to undertake would not be considered as the true Commando usage at all. For instance the Commando's unplanned long stand in the trenches at Le Plein in Normandy during June and July 1944, and some of the protracted campaigns after the War where Four Five fought alongside Army battalions employed in a conventional infantry role. Flexibility is perhaps a key word in the employment of Commandos. Primarily they must always be prepared to mobilize immediately for the classic raids—the night attacks of North West Europe, the assault river crossings in Germany, the daring and speedy helicopter landings at Suez and Dar Es Salaam—but they must also take their turn in the less glamourous type of duty, especially now that regrettably our armed forces have been so depleted in the post-war years and that the shortages, which were even apparent during the war, are even more acute.

The Commandos were first raised in Britain during the latter part of 1940 and were formed into independent companies manned by specially selected officers and men from Army regiments and the various associated Corps. The offensive spirit was now being fostered under the title of 'Combined Operations' ably directed by Lieutenant-General Sir Alan Bourne, Royal Marines—it was now being clearly realized that the independent operation of all the various arms in battle was an outdated method of winning a war of this magnitude and that three-Service unity was to become all-important. Sir Alan Bourne was succeeded as Director of Combined Operations by Admiral of the Fleet Sir Roger Keyes who described his appointment in these words: 'Among other executive responsibilities of office were included the raising, organizing and training of the special service troops now known as Commandos and of the ships, landing craft and naval personnel associated with them. I also had command of this splendid amphibious striking unit.' The next Chief of Combined Operations, as he was now called, was Vice-Admiral Lord Louis Mountbatten, and it was during his vigorous term of office which started on 19 October, 1941, that the Royal Marine Commandos first came into prominence and subsequently expanded rapidly. The first Royal Marine Commando was formed in February 1942 from volunteers from the Royal Marine Division and other units, and then, later that year, the second Commando was raised. Initially these two units were just known as 'A' and 'B' Commandos, but they were later given numbers—40 and 41 respectively.

Up to this date the 'per mare' functions of the Corps had been well defined and had been evolved through the years to meet the requirements of the detachments and landing parties in the Fleet where the contribution of the Marines was a positive and highly respected one. 'Per terram' the aims were not so clear and the stretched manpower was divided between the two major land formations of the Mobile Naval Base

Defence Organization (MNBDO) and the Royal Marine Division which had grown from a four battalion Royal Marine infantry brigade 'formed for seaborne raiding'. The task of the two MNBDOs was to seize and garrison advanced bases for the Fleet in time of war and for this they were equipped with coast and anti-aircraft artillery, searchlights, communications teams, landingcraft, transport and infantry units. A large proportion of MNBDO I (MNBDO II was formed in 1941) was to have been employed in establishing a naval base at Suda Bay in Crete in 1941, but soon after the advance elements, numbering some 2,000 out of a total of 8,000 ranks, had arrived the Germans mounted massive attacks on the island. Our troops were forced to withdraw and only half of the advance elements of the MNBDO, after much determined fighting and many brave deeds, returned unscathed. The remainder of this MNBDO was subsequently split up on various tasks of naval base defence which included Ceylon, Addu Attol, the Seychelles, and Bombay. Although there were no plans to use the MNBDO again in its entirety its members, spread around the globe, made a fine and distinguished contribution to the war effort in the bases in which they served. The formation was finally disbanded in Scotland later on in the War.

The Royal Marine Division was suffering similar difficulties of employment mainly because it was primarily carrying out an Army task but without the heavy backing and resources that a Division of this nature would require in battle or on a prolonged campaign. The death knell for this formation virtually came in 1942 whilst the General Officer Commanding the Division (Major-General "Bobbie" Sturges) was preparing for the assault on Madagascar. Initially it had been expected that the Royal Marines would provide the majority of the land forces for this operation, but in the end it was decided that Major-General Sturges and a small proportion of his staff would provide the Military Commander and Headquarters—as previously promised—but that the remainder of the attacking force would come from the Army (29th Independent Brigade Group and 17th Infantry Brigade). Although the operation

5

was a complete success the exclusion of the Royal Marine Battalions was a bitter disappointment to the Corps. It was during this time, the Earl Mountbatten of Burma later recalled,* that earnest consultations were in progress between the Royal Marine Office and the Combined Operations staff with a view to paving the way for an expansion of the Royal Marines' contribution to the Commandos as the Division could never really be a viable force on its own. This was a difficult decision for the Commandant General Royal Marines, General Sir Thomas Hunton, to make as it meant that although administrative control of these Commandos would still be retained by the Royal Marine Office, operational command would pass over entirely to the Chief of Combined Operations. In the event, and with the plans for the invasion of Europe gathering momentum, it was decided in the summer of 1943 to disband the two MNBDOs and the Division and from their ranks, and elsewhere, form Commando units, an Anti-Aircraft Brigade, an Armoured Support Group and crews for landing craft and beach organizations. Out of this reorganization six Royal Marine Commandos emerged—Numbers 42 to 47 to carry from 40 and 41. 48 Commando was later to be formed in 1944.

Surprisingly, at first, the Corps was reluctant to recognize the important and urgent needs of the Commandos in the early complicated process of forming. In some die-hard circles there was almost open hostility. Up until now the regular elements had been used to the more formal and deliberate life either afloat or in the military formations ashore and the rush to gather together new drafts and equipment for 'those men dressed in khaki battledress who wore the green beret' bemused the large numbers of those who were to wear the 'blue beret'† content with their relatively secure life in the big establishments. It was to be quite a few years before the Commandos, with a high proportion of 'Hostilities Only' ranks,

* On a visit to elements of Four Five at Stonehouse Barracks, Plymouth, on 23 June, 1970.

† Blue berets were introduced and worn by the 'non-Commando' elements of the Corps in November, 1943.

were to cease from being regarded as outsiders and accepted in their rightful place as an integral part of the Corps.

After the decision to disband the MNBDOs and the Division had been taken, the Royal Marine Commando units merged with the Army Special Service Brigade to form the Special Service Group, which was comparable in strength to an infantry division. The Group consisted of a combined Army and Royal Marines Headquarters and four Brigades, and by 1944 there were nine Royal Marine Commando units and eight Army Commandos. It was a great privilege for the Corps that Major-General Sturges, formerly of the Royal Marine Division, should be appointed to command this new Special Service Group, with Brigadier J. Durnford-Slater of the SS Brigade as his deputy. Each Brigade within the Group was designed to contain two Army Commandos and two Royal Marine Commandos, although this frequently varied, and their Headquarters were likewise organized on a joint basis.

Vice-Admiral Lord Louis Mountbatten, who had been instrumental in bringing about this momentous merger, and thus assuring the Royal Marines of a worthwhile land role after the War which it was to carry out with distinction and honour, handed over his duties to Major-General R. E. ('Lucky') Laycock in October 1943. Like his predecessor Major-General Laycock was to head Combined Operations during a historic period and be closely associated with Four Five in the years ahead.

Four Five, or to give it its official title, 45 Royal Marine Commando,* was born when the Division disbanded. A proportion of the ranks that had been in the original 5th Battalion (commanded by Lt-Col Kenneth Hunt) remained behind in the tented camp at Burley in the New Forest to form the nucleus of the new unit. At the time, on 1 August, 1943, it may have seemed a fairly routine parade on the grass between the neat lines of tents—for during those hectic wartime days military units were frequently forming or dispersing and the sense of history was perhaps not as strong as

* 45 Commando Royal Marines, after the War.

we might believe in retrospect. One wonders indeed how much those present, at this relatively inauspicious ceremony, realized that this was to be the beginning of a Commando whose contribution to world and military events in the forthcoming years was to be one in which all the ranks who participated could feel justly proud. The first Commanding Officer, Lt-Col N. C. Ries, a regular officer in the Corps, of smart military appearance and with a trimmed moustache, fully appreciated the difficult tasks that lay in the months ahead, and if these were to be anything to go by then the future was certainly going to be eventful. As he looked over his new charges Lt-Col Charles Ries no doubt wondered how they were going to shape up in the next few weeks, some would make it and some not, but at the end those who remained and stuck out the training were to form a battle-ready unit prepared for anything that came its way.

During these early days Four Five became part of No. 1 Special Service Brigade which was commanded by the famous Commando leader, Brigadier Lord Lovat, who in turn was to weld his units into a formidable fighting formation. The other three Commandos in the Brigade at the time were all combat hardened Army Commandos, so Four Five had special reason to keep its flag flying high! These units were: No. 3 Commando (Lt-Col Peter Young, Bedfordshire and Hertfordshire Regiment), No. 4 Commando (Lt-Col R. W. P. Dawson, the Loyal Regiment), and No. 6 Commando (Lt-Col Derek Mills-Roberts, Irish Guards).

On formation the battle strength of Four Five was approximately four hundred and fifty all ranks. There were five fighting Troops numbered A, B, C, D, and E, each of three officers and sixty two other ranks. A to D Troops were formed from the Companies bearing the same letters in the 5th Battalion. E Troop was an amalgamation of those not included in this redistribution. F Troop contained the Heavy Weapons such as three-inch mortars and medium machine guns. Headquarters, or H Troop, included the command element: signals and intelligence sections, plus the administrative departments:

orderly room staff, stores, victualling, motor transport and pay.

The medical section, for whom praise can never be too high, consisted of Royal Army Medical Corps personnel, but after the War, in 1947, this responsibility was taken over by the Royal Navy. The Navy also provided Chaplains for Royal Marine Commando units and again, at the end of the War, Royal Navy Instructor Officers, 'Schoolies', were attached for educational duties and to augment the Intelligence section in times of active service.

The nomenclature of the Troops within the Commando changed in January 1947, whilst the unit was in Hong Kong. A and B Troops remained—B Troop was in fact non-existent at the time due to a shortage of reinforcements—and C, D and E were renumbered X, Y and Z respectively.* F Troop was renamed S for Sugar, but more recently known has been as Support. The Commando reduced to three rifle Troops later in 1947 and when the fourth Troop was reformed it was named 'B'. Y Troop was never reformed, but in 1951, during the Malayan Emergency, when the fifth Troop was raised again, it was named 'E'. This nomenclature (A, B, E, X and Z) lasted until September 1962 when Four Five, along with other Commando units in the Corps, adopted the new organization similar to that of an infantry battalion. E and X Troops became X Company, A and B Troops formed Y Company and Z Troop was enlarged to form Z Company.† Support and Headquarters Troops were renamed Companies. The three 'platoons' of each rifle Company were called Troops and numbered from one to nine.

The greater independence with which Commando units have had to operate and the ever-increasing sophistication of

* The letters 'X' and 'Y' were adopted for use by Royal Marine Commandos because traditionally, the Royal Marines always manned X and Y turrets in ships of the Fleet.

† Whereas before Troops were given the same letters in each Commando the new lettering of Companies was such that no letter (apart from S for Support) is now repeated throughout the units of the Corps.

weapons has meant an expansion in size of Commando units since the War, especially in the Headquarters and Support elements, so that today the total war establishment number is some six hundred and eighty men.

The changes in Support Company have been significant and the only Troop that has survived is the Mortar Troop but of course with weapons of a higher calibre and accuracy. The first addition to Support was the Assault Pioneer Section (now known as Assault Engineers) which became an integral part of the organization in Malta in 1947 when the Brigade Engineer Troop was dispersed amongst the units of the Commando Brigade. Next to arrive was the Anti-Tank gun Troop. Sections were first formed in Four Five in October 1956 and when 106 mm. guns were issued in preparation for the Suez landings. These weapons stayed in service until 1959 when the Mobat was introduced to the Commando. This weapon has now been superseded by the Wombat.

The MMG Troop has also had a chequered career. The Vickers machine guns were originally phased out in 1948 but as there was no suitable replacement at the time they were brought back into service much to the delight of the 'older warriors'. The Vickers was eventually replaced by the General Purpose Machine Gun which combined its capabilities with that of the Bren. These GPMGs were introduced in the early 1960s and distributed at section level within the rifle Troops. The MMG Troop was finally disbanded in Four Five in 1963 and formed the nucleus of the new Reconnaissance (Recce) Troop, whose task was to carry out the pathfinding and forward observation duties. The 'eyes' and mobility of the Commando were further supplemented in 1966 by the formation of the Air Troop, with an establishment of three Sioux light helicopters.

These changes give some idea of the development of post-War tactics. The task of the front line rifleman remains essentially the same, but the support which he can expect from within the unit to achieve these aims has improved considerably. These additions make the problem of command and control far more complex and have resulted in big expansions within the signals, transport, supply and victualling departments.

Having examined the development of the composition of Four Five let us turn briefly and take a look at the dress and distinctive badges of the Commando. In the War years Commandos, which consisted of a large number of Hostilities Only ranks, were normally only issued with the shore service khaki battledress. The shoulder flashes were red on navy blue and in the case of Four Five, sewn on to each sleeve, was: '45' (on top) 'COMMANDO' (curved flash), 'ROYAL MARINES' (straight flash). Underneath was the Combined Operations emblem: wings over an automatic rifle superimposed on an anchor. In addition to these badges each Troop within the Commando wore different coloured epaulette tapes. The headdress, even in battle, was of course the much prided green beret awarded on completion of Commando training. After the War, when the Commando Brigade was reorganized purely on a Royal Marine basis, each unit was allocated its own colour. Four Five was given red which was worn as a lanyard on the right shoulder on certain uniforms. The '45' flash was dropped with the introduction of the lanyard and the Combined Operations badge replaced with that of a Commando dagger. By the time Four Five had returned to the United Kingdom from Aden in 1967 battledress had been replaced by lovat uniform throughout the Royal Marines and the Commando and dagger flashes disappeared with it. The colour red was also used for garter tabs—worn with tropical uniform—and incorporated in the gold tassels attached to the Commando's Colours which were first presented in 1952. Distinctive badges or lanyards are not worn with ceremonial uniforms or whilst on operations although it was a custom to wear flashes during the War.

The unit flag, introduced after the War, is dark green with a red dagger in the centre and the numbers '45' on either side of it. In addition to the Commando flag each Troop or Company has always had its own flag or sign. These first came into prominence in early 1945 and were used to mark the Troop offices and sometimes, in action, the headquarters. A Troop had for its sign the famous figure of Leslie Charteris' 'Saint'. B Troop, nicknamed 'Butcher' Troop, appropriately adopted a white cleaver, the sign of the trade. Its motto, sewn on to their Troop flag was 'Bash On, Regardless'. C Troop, being more conservative, contented itself with a large Union Flag in the centre of which was embroidered the Globe and Laurel and the various Commando 'Battle Honours'. This flag is still preserved and displayed in the Corps Museum at Eastney. D Troop, usually known as 'Dog' Troop, had a colourful painting of Walt Disney's 'Pluto' complete with green beret on his head and Commando dagger between his teeth. E Troop, whose ranks were all parachute trained soon after its formation, sported the Combined Operations sign with parachute wings. F Troop had obtained a former German SS Battalion Flag consisting of a white lightning flash against a black background, which rapidly found its way to the top of its Troop flagpole! The design of Troop signs and flags has altered considerably since the War. Most of the changes and developments have not been recorded although it appears that the Saint and SS flags survived the longest. When E Troop reformed in 1951 it adopted a fierce looking Eagle as its emblem, and in 1960 it is recorded that the various Troops of Support Troop sported their own triangular red pennants with the appropriate military symbols of their various weapons marked on them. When the Companies were formed in 1962 they adopted the international letter code for their flags.

Lastly let us meet the most important ingredient of Four Five, the men. It has always seemed difficult to establish the true public image of the Commando. In the early years of the War when many of the Commando exploits were shrouded in secrecy and the channels of communication were not as sophisticated as we experience today, a sort of mystique was built up around these troops and imagination ran wild—the Commandos were often likened either to supermen or swash-buckling killers and many variations in between. Nothing could have been farther from the truth, and the men, as in virtually every other occupation, came in all shapes and sizes. Commandos are essentially truly representative of the society from which they emerge and one of the most apt descriptions of the type of man serving in Four Five was: 'Ordinary men doing extraordinary deeds'.* The training, of course, helps to develop the qualities which the Commando must possess, but even these cannot be categorized into neat little compartments. Ideally the man should have the basic old-fashioned soldierly virtues so that upon these can be built some of the more specialized Commando techniques.

On the physical side endurance is probably the most important attribute. The Commando tests at Achnacarry were designed with this very much in the forefront. The ability to keep running or marching when lesser mortals would slow down, to make the mind concentrate on shooting to kill whilst the body was completely exhausted, to overcome the natural fear of heights and danger so that all obstacles could be crossed to reach the target. These were not tests solely of strength but ones designed to bring out qualities latent in the majority of us. Attached to fitness is skill. The skill of unarmed combat, stealthy movement, handling weapons under all conditions, operating by night and even the use of the fearsome Commando dagger—the emblem of the Commando Brigade. Interwoven into all these subjects were the essential ingredients of teamwork and spirit. The boastful, complaining or ill-disciplined man will soon prove to be a liability to his comrades in war where ones life so frequently depends on the person alongside. Time and time again, we see how, that in moments of adversity or in everday life, these brave men have resorted to humour or seen the funny side of an incident, which has been so instrumental in building up a bond of friendship and spirit which has been carried on through the years despite the change of faces. The spirit of Four Five can perhaps be embodied in the phrase 'firmness with a smile'.

* These words were spoken by the Reverend Ray Roberts RN at a Remembrance Service in November 1969. Reverend Roberts was Chaplain to Four Five during the last days in Aden.

One of the most difficult tasks in writing this story has been getting the true facts, not because of lack of memory, but because of the belief that the countless acts of bravery and heroism committed by all the various individuals were in reality just everyday events undertaken by an overriding sense of duty. This humility is a quality which emerges repeatedly and is an essential ingredient of our 'Commando Men', who are really just ordinary people but with an exceptionally important and responsible job to do.

For over twenty-five years the words Four Five have been used affectionately by thousands of Royal Marines to describe their parent unit. The factors of determination, flexibility, mobility and spirit have been repeated in countless operations and actions both during and after the War. The winning by ranks serving in the Commando, of over one hundred and fifty awards for gallantry and distinguished service throughout these years is ample testimony of this. Evidence can only suggest that this fine record will be upheld and surpassed in the years to come.

CHAPTER 2

Formation and Battle Baptism

In preparation for its transition into a Commando the 5th Battalion had trained hard. From the outset Four Five trained even harder. The other units of No. 1 Special Service Brigade had already seen action and the new arrivals were rapidly christened 'the virgin soldiers', but this title was not to stick for long. Within ten months Four Five was to be equipped, trained and sent into battle for the first time. In the years ahead this unit was to prove that it was equal to the many varied, difficult and important tasks that it had to undertake.

The details and movements of these élite Commando units were cloaked in secrecy in the wartime years and thus the initial formation of Four Five, in the first week of August 1943, was highly classified. Even the training programmes, which today would be considered commonplace, were marked 'Secret'. The reason for this, although not apparent to every-body at the time, was the systematic work up of all the spearhead troops in readiness for the assault on Europe. A cover story even had to be provided for the Commando's later presence on the south coast—the unit was merely described as 'part of the local coastal defence forces' and was 'attached' to the nearest Army Headquarters.

The early days of Four Five's training were later recalled in *The Globe and Laurel* (the journal of the Royal Marines) by Sgt. 'Abdul' Harvey. Sgt. Harvey wrote under the pseudo-nymn of 'Sandpiper' and was a frequent contributor to this journal and was later editor of the unit's magazine, 'Tiger Times', when the Commando was in Malaya. 'Sandpiper' remembers that the words 'Speed March' appeared frequently in these early programmes so that individual fitness and stamina could be developed in preparation for the more rigorous courses that lay ahead. Even at this stage some men could not stand the pace and fitter and more suitable ranks took their place. After the formation of Troops from the Companies of the 5th Battalion, Four Five moved down to Hilsea Barracks, on the northern outskirts of Portsmouth, and soon long lines of khaki-clad figures could be seen sweating their way up Portsdown Hill in the August heat.

The next move was up to Ayr, in September, and for the first time the men moved into civilian billets. The occupation of billets was a privilege normally given to Commando or specialized units and saved headquarters from considerable administrative burdens, as well as being a slight reward to the troops for the hazardous work and training being undertaken. This system also gave the individual additional self-reliance, in that all ranks had to parade at the various Troop offices at specified times and carry out other duties independently, rather than adhere rigidly to a barrack-type routine. Another attraction of billets was the Special Subsistence Allowance, over and above the normal pay, given to cover the accommodation expenses. The daily rate was thirteen shillings and fourpence for officers and six shillings and eightpence for the other ranks. The Administrative Officer, who normally travelled in advance of the unit on a move of this nature, had a formidable task on his hands arranging lodgings for several hundred men and trying to convince anxious landladies that their homes were not going to be broken up by the 'sweepings of the southern gaols'.

The training at Ayr was spent in preparation for the Commando Course at the Commando Depot at Achnacarry, which was commanded by the legendary Lt-Col Charles Vaughan. On 26 November, Four Five entrained for Spean Bridge and, like all other units, faced the seven mile march to 'Castle Commando'. There was only enough transport for the baggage. For four weeks the 500-or-so-men braved the snow, sleet and mist of the Scottish Highlands. The facilities were rudimentary—

chilly Nissen huts and leaking bell tents. Shaving water was cold. In spite of these conditions turnout had to be immaculate, weapons and equipment spotless. The routine was tough. Speed marches, assault and 'Tarzan' courses, and bivouacking out on the damp moors were the order of the day. The curriculum also included the basic Commando skills, cooking and living in the field, unarmed combat and small arms handling— German as well as our own weapons. The fear and disgrace of being Returned to Unit (RTU) loomed high over everybody and the determination to succeed, instilled into all by the Achnacarry instructors, soon became apparent. Thus Four Five became a composite battle trained Commando unit; morale was high and the coveted green berets had been well earned in time for Christmas leave 1943.

On 2 January, Four Five was on the move again. This time it was to Dorlin, on the coast of Argyllshire near the Point of Ardnamurchan. Here, at the Combined Training Centre, more advanced assault training was carried out in LCAs. Beaching and other drills were rehearsed and re-rehearsed for many long hours in the tempestuous seas whipped up by the winter gales. To add realism, and in preparation for the operations that lay ahead, live ammunition was used as the craft approached for their beach attacks and many thoughts still linger on those practice raids made at Kentra Bay. The Chief Instructor at Dorlin was Major W. N. (Nicol) Gray, and for him this was the beginning of a partnership that was to last for eighteen memorable months. Later, in 1944, Major Gray took over as Second-in-Command from Major A. R. Wooley, and on D-Day became Commanding Officer and subsequently led Four Five from Normandy in the advance across North-West Europe.

The trip back from Dorlin was almost as adventurous as the training itself. For this journey the Commando embarked in the Belgian ferry *Prins Leopold* and set sail for the next base, Eastbourne. Whilst passing through the Irish Sea the vessel ran into a Force 9 gale, and turned to seek shelter at Milford Haven. This was found to be impossible and the *Prins Leopold* then headed for Liverpool, dodging a minefield en route. Such was the ferocity of the storm that the duty officer, Capt Salmon, slipped and broke a leg whilst doing rounds of the troop decks, thus excluding him from future operations. The *Prins Leopold* eventually reached Liverpool and left the somewhat relieved Commando to continue its interrupted journey—this time in the comparative safety of the railways.

At Eastbourne civilian billets were again occupied and advanced invasion training continued apace. Emphasis was laid on sub-unit teamwork—Troop and section drills and field firing. These manoeuvres were rehearsed time and time again until perfection was reached, so that implicit understanding and mutual trust was built up at all levels. Night patrols and beach landings became more frequent, but on quieter days there was still time for marching. Sandpiper recalls that Four Five adopted, and adapted, several tunes that were popular at the time. . . . 'Lt-Col Ries' favourite was *Passengers Will Please Refrain* that lasted as a Sergeants' Mess ditty into the Malayan days, whilst *Sambo was a Lazy Coon* and *You'll Never go to Heaven* were also favourites. . . .' More specialist training followed in March 1944, but this time the Troops were detached so that each one could carry out a particular role should the need arise in the future. E Troop (Capt I. N. N. Beadle) went up to the Parachute Training School at Ringway, Manchester, and qualified as parachutists. B (Capt N. G. Michell), C (Capt J. N. Rushforth) and D (Capt A. A. B. Scott) Troops went down at various times to the Commando Mountain Warfare Centre at St. Ives in Cornwall to learn the skills of cliff climbing and practice amphibious landings on the rocky shoreline. In April all the elements returned to the fold and the scope of training widened even further. Naturally units had not yet received any details about forthcoming operations but it was fully realized that these painstaking rehearsals would lead to something. To this end each Troop had to have its own assault task which could be adapted to meet any contingency. Consequently every Troop began to train in the carriage of specific loads. These loads varied in weight and size, often over a hundred pounds, but it was not uncommon to see men advancing with bicycles, scaling ladders or even large bundles containing rubber dinghies. The men with the heaviest loads were usually those of the Heavy Weapons Troop (Capt A. W. Neaves) who were normally selected for their physique and ability to carry the fantastic weights of the machine guns and mortars over long distances.

To the present day observer many of these loads might seem to have been excessive, especially as men had to negotiate narrow ramps and catwalks on landing craft, move through sometimes deep water and then fight their way to an objective. This picture of 'lightly equipped mobile troops' probably seemed rather incongruous at the time especially as, in the event, most of these stores were not used and only impeded the initial advance. However, in many cases it was not known beforehand exactly what was going to be encountered and commanders had to stay on the safe side.

As April progressed Troop and sub-unit training gave way to Commando and Brigade exercises. By now military activities began to slacken as the climax of preparations had almost been reached. No. 1 Special Service Brigade, and in particular Four Five, was ready for action.

The events of May, a gloriously sunny month, included a review of the Brigade by His Majesty King George VI, and sporting and social activities with units of the 6th Airborne Division—comrades-to-be in Normandy. This was all part of the programme to build up full integration between combat elements, but some of this goodwill might have been temporarily undone when Four Five beat No. 3 Commando in the Brigade football final.

Although an air of relaxation may have been apparent at Troop level, Commando Headquarters worked harder than ever. The Commanding Officer found that he was unable to devote as much time as he might have wished on internal matters and began to disappear 'up the line' more frequently. The Adjutant (Capt B. G. White) likewise was becoming heavily involved in planning at a unit level and more often than not was locked in his office with a 'Not available' notice on the outside of the door. Suddenly censorship came into force. After months of waiting and rumour something was in the air—this time it must surely be for real.

The momentous journey eventually began at four a.m. on 26 May when Four Five travelled by train from Eastbourne to Southampton, where the enormous invasion force was beginning to assemble. For the next ten days or so the Commando was sealed in a tented staging camp, soon christened the 'Stalag'. Here Intelligence and other staffs revealed the plans for the great task ahead—Operation Overlord. For days and nights the men were briefed incessantly on maps, models and air photographs so that each rank knew by heart both the overall plan and the individual part which he had to play. Kit, special stores and other battle items were checked, inspected, and packed ready for the big day. The Chief of Combined Operations came down to visit the Special Service troops before their departure. It was now just a question of waiting.

On 5 June, after rumours of further postponements, Four Five eventually found itself on the move again to the embarkation point. This was Warsash, a small village on the quiet estuary of the Hamble River, which flows into Southampton Water. Here the unit boarded five LCIs, which formed part of Force S, and at five o'clock that evening the flotilla proceeded down the tree-lined estuary and out into the Solent, to join up with the vast armada which was shortly to cross the English Channel to assault Hitler's Fortress of Europe.

Four Five was about to go into action for the first time, appropriately enough on the biggest invasion of all time. The feelings of the men were naturally apprehensive. Training had been hard and realistic, but only a few were veterans, and for most this was the first time into battle. There was little time for private thought as the flat-bottomed craft began to wallow in the open sea. The living quarters were cramped. There were still last minute briefings to be attended. Security, which all along had been very tight, was still maintained on some

2

subjects. Maps, codes and the precise objective could now be released. This was Queen Red Beach, two miles west of Ouistreham in Normandy. The unit was to land with No. 3 Commando at H + 90 (ten minutes past nine) in the follow up wave.

6 June, 1944. The thoughts and actions of all those who landed on this historic day are still vividly remembered. The first signs of enemy action were the flashes of shore batteries replying to the heavy bombardment of the naval task force. Fighters circled overhead, and above these our troops could see the bombers as they returned from their objectives. As the LCIs started their 'run in' a mile offshore, shells began to fall around the long column of craft—even after ninety minutes the Boche still seemed pretty active. Landmarks, studied carefully beforehand, could be identified on the shoreline. Now there was only fifty or so yards to go and underwater wire and concrete obstacles began to scrape the bottoms of the craft. Anti-tank guns opened up from a flank and hit two of the flotilla. The LCI carrying B Troop (Capt N. G. Michell) was hit twice, killing all the seamen, who were preparing to lower the ramps for landing. In spite of the flames and flying debris Lt P. M. (Piers) Dunkerley, assisted by Cpls W. Noakes and J. Bastable, managed to clear the smouldering woodwork and get the ramps down.

It was now H hour for Four Five and the Commandos surged forward down the catwalks and ramps. The wreckage of war could be seen everywhere, smashed landing craft, drowned tanks, wounded men, and the dead.

Some got ashore dry footed, but the majority had to try and swim, wade or struggle through five feet of water with enormous loads on their backs and holding their weapons up high to keep them dry. The implications of these heavy loads now became apparent. The Troops fanned out and pressed forward across the mined beach. Coastal guns, some not yet silenced, boomed out spasmodically, sending their shells towards the offshore fleet. German artillery and mortars, a few miles behind the beach-head, were still engaging our advancing forces. A flanking pillbox raked the beach with machine gun fire, sending spurts of sand up and down the line. For many of Four Five their sodden clothes added to their already heavy burdens, nevertheless steady progress was made towards the dunes on the edge of the beach. Here the wounded, who had been helped across the more open ground by their comrades, were left behind what scant cover could be provided. The remainder made their way to the beach exits. Barbed wire blocked many of these but they were soon bypassed and the men moved inland to the first objective.

This objective was the Brigade check point, a wood on a small hillock surrounded by deep swamp and about 1,000 yards away. The nature of the ground slowed down the rate of advance and many of the men needed assistance with their loads. By now the Commando had become a long, winding snake of men staggering along with mortar bombs thudding down on either side. Luckily the boggy terrain rendered most of them harmless. Suddenly, above the din of battle, the clear sound of a hunting horn could be heard. The Adjutant was blowing the Headquarters rallying signal—'Gone Away'.* The Commando re-organized and the casualties and missing so far were added up. These amounted to twelve or so ranks and included the Intelligence Officer, Lt Bill Kennedy, Royal Fusiliers, one of the first to be killed when Four Five landed at Queen Red Beach.

It was now ten o'clock and just over half a mile had been covered in three-quarters of an hour. The next task was to advance another two miles to link up with and relieve the Fifth Parachute Brigade, which had dropped some seven hours previously, and captured the strategically important bridges over the Caen Canal and River Orne. Up until now No. 1 Special Service Brigade had been under command of the Third British Division, but for the next phases allegiance was transferred to the Sixth Airborne Division, with whom, it will be remembered such close ties had been established earlier.

* This horn is still preserved in the Commando's Officers' Mess.

Whilst waiting at the check point some of the stragglers, who had been separated from their Troops, rejoined, but the enemy still continued to be very active. No. 6 Commando had to be detached to silence a German strongpoint and an ever-increasing hail of mortar bombs made life exceedingly unpleasant. Orders were then received to move forward and the advance went ahead as planned. At a quarter past twelve the bridges were reached. The parachutists had successfully achieved all their objectives and captured the bridges intact, thus precluding the use of the bulky rubber boats which had been carried for such a long distance by E Troop.

The meeting of the red and green berets was a famous one. The Brigade was led over the bridges by Lord Lovat, characteristically accompanied by a piper playing a lilting Highland march. As the parachutists cheered evidence of a previous contest in the form of dead Germans, lay sprawled around them. The transport for the raid, a camouflaged glider, was left abandoned a few yards away. These celebrations, however, were short-lived. Snipers, in a château some 800 yards away on the west bank of the canal, were bringing down a steady fire on the bridges and one burst caught Lt-Col Ries as he was returning from visiting the forward Troops. He was wounded in the thigh and had to be evacuated. It was later learnt that the Commanding Officer was shot a second time in the legs, by enemy aircraft, whilst lying on a stretcher on the beaches.

It was during this critical period that Major W. N. Gray had to assume command. Major Gray recalls that, as was customary, he was some way back along the column and his first task as he moved forward was to order the Machine Gun Troop Commander (Lt Colin Fletcher) to mount his Vickers and counter the fire from the château. The enemy were quickly and effectively silenced, the whole proceedings being watched by a jubilant French café owner, standing outside his premises oblivious to the battle being waged around him!

Once ashore No. 1 Special Service Brigade had two main tasks. The first was to secure the high ground in the area of Hauger, Le Plein and Amfréville, which would help to both hold the vital bridges and safeguard the entire invasion force's left flank. The second task was to capture Franceville Plage and 'infest' the coastal area eastwards towards Cabourg. Four Five was ordered to assist in this secondary task. Before this could be accomplished the German coastal battery near Merville, which dominated the whole area, had to be captured. The initial plans had given this task to the 9th Battalion Parachute Regiment, but at this stage it was not yet clear whether the battery was in our hands or not. Major Gray was therefore told to take the Commando and move at a fast pace, independently from the Brigade, and seek out this information. C Troop (Major J. N. Rushforth), who were equipped with bicycles, acted as advance guard. They were followed by A Troop (Capt E. E. D. Grewcock), the Reconnaissance Group—consisting of the Commanding Officer and the remaining Troop Commanders—and finally the rest of the Commando.

When they had passed through the village of Sallanelles the two leading Troops turned off to the east. Due to a sharp bend in the road this move was not seen by the Reconnaissance Group and they prepared to continue along the main coast road. The Germans were still present in strength in some parts of the area and were holding a strongpoint two hundred and fifty yards away. This was spotted by Four Five—but too late. Both sides opened fire simultaneously and Marine Irving, of E Troop's leading section, bravely stood his ground in the open and hit a running German at 200 yards range with a rifle shot fired from the standing position—a splendid piece of marksmanship. The enemy defences were well sited and the Reconnaissance Group and part of E Troop were pinned down in a roadside ditch. Those not caught in the fire had to withdraw back to Sallanelles. Some, in more exposed positions, faced a long and painful crawl; others had to make a quick dash back to the shelter of the houses. Those who could not be extricated had to be left behind and faced a very uncomfortable time until the mantle of darkness came to their rescue.

Major Gray now ordered the Mortar Troop (Capt A. W. Neaves) into action. This delighted the mortar crews who had been carrying their heavy weapons and bombs ever since landing. The first contribution of the three-inch mortars to the battle was a reassuring one, and within minutes the stronghold was engaged and thirty bombs dropped in and around the position. Under cover of this fire Four Five moved back on to the right route and continued its original advance towards the Merville Battery which, it was now learnt, had been silenced by the parachutists earlier that morning. However, the Germans had returned in strength and the leading Troop was greeted by a hail of fire. The Commando was halted as the Commanding Officer made plans for an assault on the battery but this was forestalled by Brigade who ordered Four Five to bypass the position and hold the village of Merville for the night. The advance to Franceville Plage was to be postponed.

The village of Merville was largely in ruins as a result of heavy pre-invasion bombing by the RAF. The civilian population had departed but their place was taken by German snipers who hid amongst the rubble. These had to be carefully winkled out and it wasn't until seven o'clock that evening that the village was finally cleared. Even then the men couldn't relax as the Troops had to be deployed and defences prepared in case of a counter-attack. Commando Headquarters were established in two broken down cottages. Longing eyes were cast at a big undamaged farmhouse nearby, but it was decided to sacrifice comfort for safety—this was a fortunate decision as the house was demolished later that evening by an enemy self-propelled gun.

When the defences had been constructed there was, at last, a chance for a brief respite, and time for a quick 'brew up'—the first hot drink since landing. Four Five's first day at war was almost over and as the evening passed relatively quietly the Adjutant was given the opportunity of adding up the cost of D-Day. Four ranks including the Intelligence Officer had been killed; sixteen including the Commanding Officer and Signals Officer (Lt Peter Nelson) had been wounded and twenty were reported missing. Many of the latter were still pinned down near Sallanelles and were to rejoin the next day having carried out their own private war against the strongpoint and inflicted more casualties. Another of those missing was Lt Peter Winston, a tall young officer who had jumped with the 9th Battalion Parachute Regiment as the unit's liaison officer. 6 June had been his 20th birthday. His adventures over the next few weeks were truly remarkable and will be recounted later.

Four Five had to make an early start on the next morning—7 June. At three o'clock Major Gray was given a signal ordering the Commando to withdraw to the Brigade's defensive position in the area of Le Plein, and by four the unit was on the march, moving stealthily through the half light. The only noise was the muttered curses from the unfortunate members of the Cycle Troop who had to negotiate deep bomb craters made all along the road by the RAF. Sallanelles seemed to be deserted as Four Five moved through the village for the second time. The silence was suddenly shattered by Major Rushforth, the leading Troop Commander. 'Come out—I've got you covered!' he yelled, as he poked his rifle through an open window behind which he had seen something move. Much to his surprise he was greeted by an elderly Madame, looking equally warlike in her curlers, who merely exclaimed 'Ah, ces Anglais!'

After this exchange the remainder of the three-mile journey passed relatively uneventfully, and for the rest of the morning the unit dug in next to No. 4 Commando who had just returned from Ouistreham where they had been fiercely engaged in capturing a battery there. During this period the stragglers of the Reconnaissance Group began to return as the Commanding Officer was summoned to Brigade Headquarters for briefings. Another welcome arrival was the Commando's jeeps, last seen at Eastbourne a fortnight ago. The jeeps were loaded with much needed ammunition, signal stores, medical supplies and spare weapons. These were rapidly unloaded and the wounded put on board for the return journey. By now the Germans had located our positions making life exceedingly unpleasant with their mortar fire. Our own mortars returned this but a direct hit on one of our pits caused delays as the guns had to be moved.

When Major Gray returned he brought news of a Commando attack on Franceville Plage. The Orders Group was assembled and the scene was later described by Lt-Col Young of No. 3 Commando.* 'No. 45 Commando was now commanded by its rugged Second-in-Command, Nicol Gray. . . . Nicol gave out his orders in a field not far from Sallanelles, and I went along to see what task was to be given to my detachment, and to ensure that, as far as possible they had everything needed for the job. . . . Halfway through Nicol's orders the Germans began to mortar our group which was rather large. At first he took no notice, but after a few salvoes he said lightly: 'The Bad Men are getting more accurate'—to him the Germans were always the Bad Men—and we withdrew to a neighbouring ditch.' The initial preparations and rehearsals for an attack on Franceville Plage had already been carried out at Eastbourne. Models and air photographs were then carefully studied during the briefing period at the 'Stalag' so that each man was fully acquainted with the ground and conversant with his own task.

Franceville Plage was a small coastal resort, consisting of small detached villas and divided in two by a long straight road, codenamed Piccadilly, which was to be the axis. C Troop was to attack enemy posts to the west and also give flank protection. A and D Troops were to follow up the axis and then take enemy positions to the east. C Troop's objective was nicknamed 'Freeman', E Troop's 'Hardy' and A Troop's 'Willis'.

Four Five moved down the main street of Sallanelles for the third time. The Germans continued to mortar and shell with increased intensity. All around shells exploded and masonry tumbled to the ground. The Commando's own machine guns joined in the battle and kept the Germans' heads down thus reducing our own casualties, but the enemy did achieve some success and scored a direct hit on a jeep carrying a mortar and its ammunition. Two men were killed and as Four Five were progressing deeper into occupied territory it became

* *Storm from the Sea*. William Kimber and Co, 1958.

increasingly impossible for replacement supplies to be despatched from Brigade—the Commando was now virtually isolated. At four o'clock the Merville Battery opened up and a Troop was detached to engage it. Final orders were issued in Merville where the Commando had spent the previous night. Whilst the unit was forming up the objective was subjected to a heavy bombardment by two cruisers and two destroyers whose fire was directed by the two FOBs* attached to Four Five and No. 3 Commando.

The advance started at five minutes past five, the distance between Merville and Franceville being some 500 yards across flat open country The edge of the town was reached and cleared without incident, and so C Troop swung left to occupy a wood so that it could cover the final assault. The wood was full of slit trenches, but most of these had been hastily evacuated. Those which weren't soon had their residents cleared by hand grenades. C Troop then settled down into their slits to observe the attack and prevent any outside interference. They could see E and B Troops picking their way down Piccadilly and see the naval gunfire landing on enemy positions to the east of the town. This was being directed by the FOB (Capt J. A. Goodall, RA) who had positioned himself in a tree top in Sallanelles which had been conveniently constructed as an observation post by the Germans and afforded an excellent view of the battlefield. Further firing could be heard from the Merville direction, but as both wireless sets and signallers had become casualties, no news of how the two Troops of No. 3 Commando were faring could be obtained. Likewise communications with Brigade Headquarters were severed. Four Five was now completely cut off.

By this time E and B Troops had made their way up to a strong German pillbox at the northern end of Piccadilly. A Troop was following in their wake. Heavy mortar fire was raining down on the two leading Troops forcing them to seek cover in nearby buildings. So that Four Five could regain the

* Forward Officer Bombardment—A Royal Artillery officer who directs Naval supporting guns.

initiative Capt Beadle moved forward with the E Troop PIAT* group, L/Cpl Davis and Marines Lee and Lowe, in a gallant attempt to fire a bomb through one of the pillbox slits. After one bomb had been fired the group came under heavy attack. Davis was killed and Lowe wounded, but despite this Capt Beadle and Lee dashed back into the open and managed to rescue the wounded man and the weapon. Major Gray decided to move forward at this stage as radio contact had been lost and he wanted to find out what was going on in the forward area. His patrol, which was advancing up Piccadilly, received a direct hit from an anti-tank gun which killed the Regimental Sergeant-Major (RSM Grimsey) and the Pay Corporal (Cpl Watson). German resistance was becoming stiffer and A and D Troops moved up on either side of Piccadilly to join the battle. A Troop (Capt E. E. D. Grewcock) were met by heavy fire from houses on the eastern side of the town, where the enemy seemed to be concentrating in strength, and had to fan out clearing each house as they went. The enemy were eventually forced back to near the beach on this sector, but it was becoming a desperate struggle.

It was decided by Major Gray at this juncture that Four Five should consolidate on their existing positions and Pte Arnold of No. 10 (Inter-Allied)† Commando was sent forward with a white flag advising the enemy to surrender 'as we had three divisions behind us and it was useless to fight on'. The

* Projectile Infantry Anti Tank.

† No. 10 (Inter-Allied) Commando was formed in 1942 and consisted largely of men belonging to the nations overrun by Germany. In Operation Overlord Nos. 1 and 8 Troops (composed of Frenchmen) were under command of No. 4 Commando and played a decisive part in the fighting for the capture of the German battery at Ouistreham. Due to their expert local knowledge many of the ranks of No. 10 Commando were used for intelligence or interpreting duties on operations on their parent soil. Special precautions were taken to conceal their true identity and they were given false names. Elaborate measures were also taken to provide these brave men with false regiments, personal histories and service records. German-speaking ranks of No. 10 (Inter-Allied) Commando were attached to Four Five for Operation Overlord.

Germans had already begun to counter-attack and their only reaction to this suggestion was heavy machine gun and mortar fire which sent Arnold racing for cover. It was apparent that the 'Bad Men' were trying to cut the Commando off and force it back onto their own beach defences. After another attack the Commanding Officer appreciated that the best solution was for the unit to fight its way out of the vice being created by an exceedingly strong force and take up new positions on the south side of Franceville.

During the withdrawal there was hard and confused close quarter fighting, and those who were present at this action remembered that as dusk was fast approaching it was often difficult to identify friend from foe. The Commanding Officer, now with A Troop, took up position on a sandy knoll on the outskirts of the village which dominated the surrounding area, but the Germans were beginning to work their way round to the rear and close in on this knoll. C Troop, which was still protecting the left flank in the slit trenches in the wood, was now in wireless contact and ordered to counter-attack and clear the right flank. The unit was beginning to rendezvous on the knoll and patrols were being sent out to collect the stragglers and wounded left behind after the bitter fighting. Few of those guarding the knoll will ever forget the next hour or so.

Soon after receiving their orders C Troop came into the attack led by Major Rushforth and after fifteen fierce minutes they captured a large school building which completely dominated the Commando's rear. Major Rushforth was wounded whilst leading this assault and was wheeled to safety in a wheelbarrow, conveniently found nearby. Lt G. T. Jackson took over command of the Troop just as the Germans were making a strong counter-attack. The school was held with great courage and Four Five was saved from being cut off. Major Rushforth was later awarded the Military Cross for his bravery, and Sgt R. Stuart and Cpl T. Harrison received Military Medals for their gallantry in this particular battle.

It was now eleven o'clock and darkness had set in. Ammunition was alarmingly low and there was a large number of missing and wounded men. Major Gray decided to re-occupy Merville that night, so B and E Troops were sent ahead to clear out any Huns who might have moved into the positions. The Troops finally moved into Merville just before midnight. A Troop found that they had to overcome some opposition before they could settle in and C Troop surprised some Germans who were digging their former homes even deeper— they were allowed to continue under armed supervision.

Radio communications with Brigade still proved to be very tenuous. The only outside link was via the FOB's set to the HQ ship and then to Brigade. It was still not yet known how the two Troops of No. 3 Commando had fared against the Merville Battery.

As Four Five settled down for what was left of the night the cost of the day's fighting was counted. Casualties were heavy. Sixteen killed, thirty-nine wounded (many more still bravely carried on fighting) and twenty-four missing,* which included Lt Piers Dunkerley. This brought the total casualties after two day's fighting to over a quarter of the strength of the Commando—many of them key personnel. It was a great tribute to the team spirit of the newly-blooded unit that it continued to fight such a decisive battle despite the many changes and improvisations that were necessary.

These hectic first days also imposed a great strain on the Medical Section who had to attend to the wounded in full view of the enemy and under heavy fire. It was characteristic of their devotion that L/Cpls Relf and Dunlop, both of the Royal Army Medical Corps, volunteered to remain behind with the badly injured who were left in German hands in Franceville Plage. The medical team was led by Capt H. N. Smith and Sgt Curren. Capt Smith later received a Military Cross for his courage on this day.

That night the enemy, like Four Five, was exhausted, but everyone had to remain fully alert—just in case. There was little activity except for a three-man patrol of C Troop which

* Most of these were wounded and later reported as prisoners of war.

was sent through enemy lines to Brigade Headquarters at Le Plein. The patrol was led by Sgt Hemmings and soon after it had departed it met up with six members of D Troop who had become detached at Franceville. They followed on behind but half a mile further on the patrol ran slap into a German position. There was quite a scrap for a few minutes but the sergeant and one other managed to escape and reach their objective. The patrol returned soon after dawn with relief signalmen and spare sets. This successful mission ensured that the vital communications could be restored and important signals traffic passed.

That morning Brigade signalled that another attack was expected and that Merville was to be held at all costs. Orders were given to tighten the defences and ammunition, now extremely short, had to be redistributed. Commando Headquarters gave up most of theirs to the Troops. As this was in progress enemy patrols and sniping had increased, and Four Five's own snipers found themselves exceptionally busy. Cpls Emuss and Bartholomew of E and C Troops respectively were both reported to have had particularly good 'bags'. At half-past nine heavy mortar fire was opened as a prelude to an attack from the direction of the Merville Battery. The brunt of this was borne by A and C Troops and was beaten off after some close range fighting, but the rest of the morning continued with spasmodic mortaring and continuous sniping.

The shortage of ammunition meant that the return fire had to be strictly controlled, and as a result casualties were beginning to mount up and some eight stretcher cases now needed evacuation from the beleagured village. The answer was soon provided. Two Renault ambulances drove in to Merville, their German drivers unaware of the fact that British troops were in occupation. L/Cpl G. V. Saunders of No. 10 (Inter-Allied) Commando, who was himself slightly wounded in the leg, volunteered to lead the party in an ingenious attempt to get back to the Brigade lines. In addition to the eight casualties a badly wounded German prisoner was loaded into the ambulance. This operation was done under cover of a

Red Cross flag and involved a long carry across an orchard which had been under constant sniper fire. The enemy respected our wishes and the loading was completed without interference. Only a few minutes afterwards, however, the barn where the loading took place and the nearby RAP* were shelled and had to be evacuated. L/Cpl Saunders' journey was short-lived. Despite frantic explanations from the German drivers, at gunpoint, the ambulances were recaptured. Fortunately Saunders escaped, his treatment in enemy hands would probably have been exceptionally harsh, and reported on his return the next day that the wounded were receiving proper medical attention.

At this time fire had to be brought down to check the continuous mortar fire. The FOB called for fire from a destroyer to silence positions at Franceville. The Navy's salvoes were most effective and the firing soon subsided from that area. In reply the German mortars opened up from the Merville Battery, but this time their target was their own positions on the south of Franceville. Four Five watched this brief exchange with amusement, but the humour did not last for long. The ammunition had almost been expended, as had the two days' food ration. Small patrols were sent out to recover secret dumps of ammunition that had been left during the street fighting at Franceville the day before. These patrols were carried out with success but increasing enemy surveillance made further sorties impossible.

Just before noon the Germans attacked Merville from both the east and the south in a determined effort to dislodge Four Five. Despite more heavy shelling and mortaring the attackers were repulsed with heavy losses. A man taken prisoner later confessed that only eighteen had survived from one of the attacking companies.† This shows a remarkable standard of marksmanship and determination from a unit which was completely surrounded and desperately short of ammunition. During the course of this attack Major Gray found that he

* Regimental Aid Post.
† Probably a total of one hundred men.

had to conduct his own private duel with the Huns. He was going round the Troop positions when he suddenly bumped into two Germans, lying in a ditch, who were preparing to open fire with a Spandau machine gun. Surprise was equal on both sides but Major Gray recovered first. He shot one with his rifle, which then jammed at the crucial moment, and he had to swiftly despatch the other with his .45 Colt automatic.

By midday there was a brief lull in the fighting and the Troop Commanders came into Commando Headquarters to report the state of their Troops. Much to the joy of all present the Adjutant (Capt White) had unearthed a bottle of champagne and each visitor received a sip. The Commanding Officer was heard to complain of its quality, but, doubtless because of his recent experiences, it was observed that he still insisted on his share!

After the Troop Commanders had left there were only two officers remaining to man the Headquarters, and the Adjutant took but a few seconds to produce the Duty Officers' Roster:

To: CO
From: Adjutant

Duty Officers
You
Me
You
Me

The afternoon was hot. The German mortars and snipers continued to plug away at Merville, but thankfully caused no further damage to Four Five. At one stage Sgt Stewart and Cpl Shelley, both of No. 10 (Inter-Allied) Commando, spotted a small enemy party which had worked their way up behind a barn in the eastern sector. Stewart and Shelley managed to crawl along our side of the building and lobbed grenades over the roof. The grenades landed with complete accuracy and the Germans fled before they could do any harm, leaving their wounded behind.

A couple of hours later, at about half past four, more heavy firing was heard, this time from the direction of Franceville. This was followed by a lot of activity and commotion from a house about four hundred yards in front of E Troop's position. The Germans were shouting and gesticulating wildly. Lt J. E. Day of E Troop and Pte Hepworth of No. 10 (Inter-Allied) Commando moved forward in the open, thinking that the enemy might wish to surrender. This was clearly a diversion and fire was rapidly opened from another German position, causing Day and Hepworth to withdraw to the safety of their own trenches. It was obviously an inopportune moment for any further discussions.

At five o'clock Brigade Headquarters signalled Four Five, saying that all attempts to effect a relief had failed and that the unit was to rejoin the Brigade at Le Plein after dark. The Commando's plight was now desperate as over five hours still remained until darkness was due to fall and a determined foe lay all around. This seemed an interminable length of time to the men, for their ammunition was virtually exhausted and the Germans were bound to continue their attacks. Sure enough the next onslaught came half an hour later. This was supported by self-propelled guns which soon reduced many of the houses of Merville to rubble. Some of the ruins in the east end of the village began to burn fiercely in the dry atmosphere and as the dark smoke began to drift over the men in their trenches reports came in that all the two-inch mortar and PIAT ammunition had been exhausted. It now became apparent that Four Five might be in a very dangerous position should the Germans attack Merville with any vigour, and Major Gray decided that the time to withdraw had now come. This was a difficult and daring decision, especially as it was still broad daylight and a distance of some four miles had to be covered through enemy-dominated territory.

It was nearly six o'clock when the unit set out on its brave mission to reach Le Plein. C Troop covered the rear as the remainder of the Commando, led by E Troop, thankfully pulled out of the besieged village. The Germans did not wait for long and as Four Five moved away from Merville they entered from the other side, hoping to cut off stragglers. Naval gunfire helped to keep the Hun at bay, and the FOB controlled fire from a destroyer on to the village only minutes after C Troop had evacuated it, so that the enemy would be reluctant to advance any further and carry on a running fight.

Four Five advanced for about a mile without incident, then E Troop came under fire from German machine gun posts and were forced to go to ground. Major Gray was now faced with another critical decision. The present axis of advance was blocked by machine gun posts. The right flank was open and thought to be mined. On the left was a wood known to contain enemy emplacements, and beyond that the German-held Merville Battery. Keeping one section of E Troop holding its present line, Major Gray decided to move the remainder of the unit under the cover of hedgerows down the left.

As the Commando advanced Capt Beadle bravely moved out from behind cover and, undeterred by the heavy enemy fire, personally sited his automatic weapons. Sgt J. Brown of E Troop also courageously came out into the open, in front of the machine gun posts, and calmly engaged them with 68 Grenades—fired from a discharger on a specially strengthened rifle. One of the enemy positions was completely silenced. Marine N. Green, realizing that the advance would be seriously jeopardized by this continued firing, forsook the safety of a ditch so that he could engage the machine guns with greater accuracy. Spare magazines for his Bren gun were filled and flung to him by his comrades lying nearby. Green continued his diversionary action although the magazines on his gun were twice hit by German fire. Both Sgt Brown and Green were later decorated for their fearlessness, which undoubtedly saved many lives.

Whilst this action of E Troop's leading section was in progress the Commando continued to move forward stealthily, unopposed. Capt Beadle decided that the time had now come to assault the remaining positions, as their fire was beginning to decrease. Capt Beadle led the assault section accompanied by his Troop Sergeant Major, TSM H. J. Caiger who, despite being wounded two days earlier, characteristically elected to stay with the Troop. The dash of E Troop soon convinced the Germans that further delay might prove unwise, and they were chased from their defences leaving behind two 81 mm mortars, two machine guns and a motor cycle. The citation for Capt Beadle, who was later awarded the Military Cross, stated that 'This action restored a critical situation and its success was primarily due to Capt I. N. N. Beadle's sound judgement, intrepid gallantry and devotion to duty, which was an inspiration to all ranks.'

Four Five, joined by E Troop, was now able to return back to the original axis and withdraw without further opposition. Dusk was beginning to set in and it was with considerable relief that the unit reached the comparative safety of Le Plein. It was here that the Administrative Officer (Capt F. E. Derbyshire) and his staff were waiting with the first hot meal that Four Five had had since the landings at Ouistreham sixty hours previously. Then the Commando moved into the village church at Le Plein and due to the fatigued state of most of the troops, who had been almost continuously in action since their arrival in Normandy, the Brigade Commander decreed that all the necessary guards that night would be provided by Brigade Headquarters. Although the other three Commandos of the Brigade were still engaged in heavy fighting against the persistent enemy, Four Five was not recalled into action that night.

Much of the success of the Commando's exploits was due to the inspiration and tactical decisions of Major Nicol Gray. While most of the unit had managed to snatch a bit of sleep here and there, Major Gray had worked and fought without rest since he unexpectedly assumed command at the Orne Bridges, and he had brought the Commando through a period during which it was fighting for its very existence. He was later awarded the Distinguished Service Order and the following is an extract from the official citation: 'He continued to fight his unit for the next thirty-six hours until almost out of ammunition, when he received the order to withdraw. This he achieved successfully, and under difficult circumstances brought his unit back to our lines intact.

Major Gray's tireless energy, devotion to duty and unfailing cheeerfulness throughout all difficulties has been an example to all and it is largely through his fine leadership that his unit has inflicted such heavy casualties upon the enemy.'

The battle for Franceville Plage and the gallant stand at Merville were by far the most ferocious actions the Commando ever had to fight in its history. Indeed one observer later wrote 'My guess is that it was about as tough or tougher assignment than any of the Commandos immediately after D-Day. Probably a good bit tougher, too, than Montforterbeek because in June, especially the first day or two after the 6th, we weren't sure we were going to win.' Not only did Four Five suffer twenty per cent casualties but the Germans had to divert a vastly superior force in a desperate bid to defend this vital hinge on the front. The enemy, on all sectors, was putting up a stiff resistance to the initial invasion and hoped to contain the Allied Forces where they were and then drive them back on to the beachhead. This diversion caused by Four Five had the effect of considerably weakening the assault on No. 1 Special Service Brigade who were, at the time, holding a position which was to prove of outstanding strategic importance during the remainder of the campaign.

Four Five had now been tested in the fiercest of battles and shown that it was equal to any of the demands placed upon it.

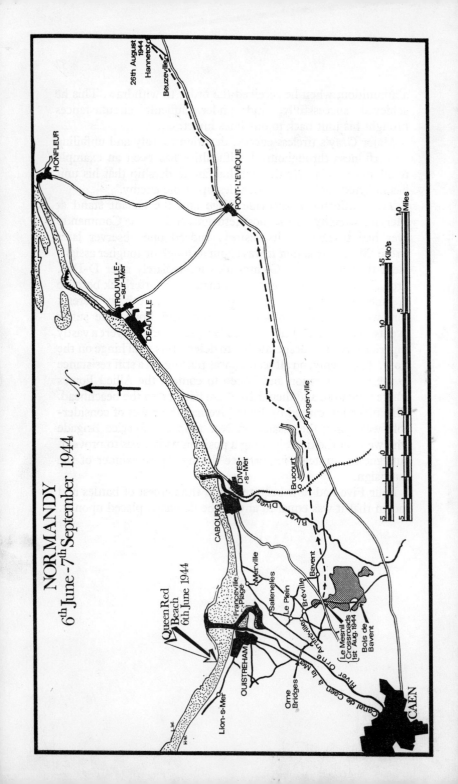

NORMANDY
6th June – 7th September 1944

CHAPTER 3

France.
9 June to 7 September, 1944—
The Left Flank and the
Pursuit

The overnight rest in the church was more than welcome and Four Five was not required to move in to the front line until ten o'clock on the morning of 9 June. The tower of the church at Le Plein, where the Commando had sought shelter, had in fact been used as a refuge for a German sniper for a long time and this sniper had been a source of constant annoyance. It was not until an observant member of the Brigade had spotted the hands of the clock moving unusually quickly that the offender was eventually dealt with. A gaping hole in the clock face bore testimony to the accuracy of the Commando marksman.

Four Five moved up to take a defensive position on the right of No. 6 Commando, a position that was to be held for over six weeks, and which resulted in a strong bond of friendship between the two units that lasted throughout the war. In the original briefings for Overlord the Commando had been led to believe that it would be employed in the traditional role and be withdrawn from the beach-head for operations elsewhere after forty-eight hours, or, at the most, a week or so. This was not to be, however, due to the general shortage of reinforcements and the stiff resistance of the Germans, who had not only checked the general advance, but then carried out a skilful delaying withdrawal.

The countryside surrounding the Orne was a mixture of wide rolling fields studded with woods, as experienced in the coastal area, or closer country known as the *bocage* which was more typical of the region surrounding Le Plein, and further south nearer Caen. The *bocage* consisted of a patchwork of tiny fields flanked by steep banks surmounted by hedges. Sunken lanes abounded, effectively dividing the area into innumerable small sectors making it ideal terrain for defence. The fighting here was carried out at extremely close quarters as long-range visibility and observation were usually limited. This placed a great burden on the listening posts, who had to guard against sudden attack, and the snipers who had to crawl stealthily up to their targets.

Although the villages of Le Plein and Amfréville had both been badly damaged many of the inhabitants elected to remain behind, and for their bravery won a strong place in the hearts of the Brigade. The men acted as guides to the French troops of No. 10 (Inter-Allied) Commando, and helped to bring in German prisoners. The women played their part as well and assisted in the domestic chores such as laundry and cooking. These civilians had to pay a heavy price for their outstanding loyalty and many were killed by fire from both sides. A further bond between Le Plein and No. 1 Special Service Brigade was the consecration, by the village priest, of a stone cross on 14 July, 1944, which served as a memorial to those men of the Brigade who had died in the liberation of France. The cross was constructed by the local stonemasons, aided by members of the Brigade, and was erected on the village green at Le Plein in front of the church. The ceremony was followed by a march past of detachments from each Commando in the Brigade and a party of *Les Anciens Combattants* of the village. Brigadier J. F. Durnford-Slater, Deputy Commander of the Special Service Group, took the salute. This ceremony was closely followed by a show of German strength when a formation of twenty bombers flew low over the village just after the march had ended. Fortunately they did not release any of their weaponry.

The first five days, from 9 to 13 June were, the busiest at Le Plein. The Germans were still intent on forcing our troops back on to the beaches. However, the longer the Allies were able to hold on to and consolidate their positions, then the more remote the likelihood of a concerted enemy counter-attack became.

9 June was a reasonably quiet day for Four Five, and the Commando was able to busy itself in constructing defences and getting to know, in detail, its new surroundings. The only nuisance was caused by snipers, and patrols had to be sent out to deal with these. Enemy activity increased on the 10th and it now became clear that strong offensive action would be needed by both sides to decide who was to dominate the area. It seems likely that the lull on the previous day was due to the Germans regrouping for the attack. Soon after dawn enemy aircraft machine gunned the nearby dropping zone of the 6th Airborne Division, where supplies were still being received. At eight o'clock the Germans turned their attention to the area of No. 6 Commando and E Troop, who were on the left flank of Four Five. Under a barrage of shelling the Germans attacked these positions, not realizing that Four Five had been brought up to reinforce this sector—the enemy's probing fire on the previous day had failed to draw any reply and they must have assumed that the area was clear. In the close countryside, at some thirty yards range, Four Five were able to inflict heavy casualties as the enemy thundered into the forward locations. Then, after being repulsed by No. 6 Commando, the enemy again moved across the front offering easy targets.

That afternoon a patrol from E Troop was despatched to pick up stragglers from this abortive attack and it returned less than two hours later with a dozen prisoners. On the way they spotted a concentration of enemy troops in a wood less than a mile away, and when they came back the patrol reported these details so that our mortars could go quickly into action. Capt Grewcock of A Troop took out another patrol to investigate and was able to bring back the welcome news that many Germans had been killed, and that a direct hit had been scored on a half-tracked vehicle on which a gun was mounted.

The patchwork of fields meant that the front line was frequently difficult to discern. Bréville, a village less than a mile from Le Plein, was still occupied by the enemy, who became a constant source of worry by their harassing raids and sniping. In order to put the Germans on their guard a fighting patrol, led by Capt Beadle of E Troop, raided the village at two o'clock in the morning of 11 June. In the darkness a short, bitter exchange took place amongst the buildings, and both sides suffered casualties. TSM Caiger again distinguished himself, and despite being wounded for a second time in the leg, led a successful assault on a machine gun position. The tired patrol returned to its lines before dawn, bringing back the wounded with them—tragically two of these later died in the RAP. The men could get little rest, however, as less than two hours later, at a quarter-past five, the E Troop trenches were heavily mortared. This was the prelude to an enemy attack from Amfréville supported by self-propelled guns. At the same time the German infantry tried to probe the forward positions of No. 6 Commando. The lines of enemy approach to E Troop's position were difficult to cover because of the close nature of the ground. One of these axes was a sunken road and Marine Lee, armed with a PIAT, repeated the bravery he had shown at Franceville Plage and managed to keep many of the attackers at bay. Four enemy dead were later recovered from within ten yards of E Troops' position. Although the infantry withdrew after this attack the Commando was harassed spasmodically throughout the remainder of the day. Capt Neaves' mortar detachments were called in to put down a heavy concentration on Amfréville and succeeded in silencing the offending 20 mm cannon. Lt Day of E Troop went out later to check on the effects of this shoot and found eighteen dead, identified as belonging to the crack 21st Panzer Division, and also two 81 mm mortars and two 20 mm cannons mounted on half-tracked vehicles. This was proof of the accuracy and skill of Four Five's mortar teams.

It is very difficult to put life under these tough conditions into its right perspective. In spite of the many deeds of bravery and the constant action, most of the Marines treated their daily tasks with the hardened attitude common to all true professionals. One participant modestly described this period as 'merely boiling down to a routine and acting out our parts which we had so carefully rehearsed in England for many weeks beforehand.' This description came from Marine J. K. Crooks who, if the following incident is anything to go by, led anything but a routine life.

Whilst serving with F Troop in the Amfréville area Crooks was ordered to drive his Sergeant-Major down to the beach landing area to collect some Vickers machine gun spares. This was soon accomplished, but on the return journey Crooks got lost in the maze of narrow lanes and ran into a German sentry. The sentry promptly 'vented his spleen' and opened fire at the offending jeep. Crooks accelerated, jammed the wheel hard over, negotiated a ditch, hurtled through a hedge, crossed a field, demolished a fence and coasted to safety—still followed by a fusillade of shots. When the jeep eventually came to a standstill the three breathless occupants looked at each other. The silence was broken by the Sergeant-Major. 'Crooks. I don't know what effect you have on the enemy, but by God you scare the hell out of me!' The ensuing laughter quite obliterated the terror that had been felt only seconds beforehand.

This episode shows how close the forward troops of each army were to each other and by now it was apparent that the strong German stand at nearby Merville, at such proximity to the Brigade, would have to be countered. On the morning of 12 June a Warning Order was received stating that the 12th Battalion, The Parachute Regiment would be attacking Bréville at ten o'clock that night. In conjunction with this raid Four Five was to provide a patrol to capture a big house beside the road on the outskirts of the village. This house was known to be occupied by a large number of Germans who might otherwise have impeded the main assault. Throughout the day preparations were made for this important operation. The first sign of increased activity was the arrival of supporting Sherman tanks soon after midday. These rumbled into the forward area and a patrol of E Troop went out to join up with the tank Squadron Commander, so that he could reconnoitre the route forward through Amfréville.

Throughout the day a heavy exchange of artillery and mortars, as a prelude to the battle, was made by both sides. Four Five's patrol consisted of twenty men of A Troop led by Capt Grewcock, and they had a long wait until dusk eventually fell and they could move off to their objective. Soon after this the parachutists took up their allotted positions and the Shermans began to advance. As the attack was getting under way the Germans chose this moment to open up on Le Plein with a heavy barrage of guns and mortars. The forward area suddenly became an inferno of explosions. Shells screamed overhead and buildings burned.

Those of Four Five who were in a position to observe watched anxiously as the A Troop patrol advanced steadily towards Bréville. Their silhouettes could be seen against the flash of gunfire ahead. The Germans were raking A Troop's axis, a sunken road, with murderous machine gun fire. The parachutists followed behind, amidst the explosions of artillery and mortars.

The battle for Bréville raged throughout the night, and eventually, after a tough struggle, the village was taken. Our losses were considerable. Out of the brave patrol of A Troop only nine returned unscathed. Four were killed, including Capt E. E. D. Grewcock, and seven others wounded. As the conflict continued up front, a macabre procession of wounded returned through the Commando's lines—some 160 casualties from the Parachute Battalion were evacuated through Four Five's position alone, which gives an indication of the ferocity of the struggle. It was later estimated that during the last year of the war hardly a man survived in the front line without being wounded at some stage or other, and that between D-Day and 30 September, 1944, some 100,000 casualties were evacuated back to the United Kingdom from the Normandy battlefield.

The action was not confined to Bréville alone. The remainder of Four Five, standing-to in their dug-outs, also suffered from the heavy artillery fire. Thirty-three shells landed in the immediate area of Commando Headquarters killing two and wounding three. Because of the damage sustained to the roof this Headquarters was later nicknamed 'the colander' by its visitors! E Troop also suffered casualties during this bombardment. Two were killed and nine wounded, including Capt Beadle and Lt Day. The RAP, which was shared with No. 6 Commando, was hit twice and set on fire. The Royal Army Medical Corps personnel bravely carried on despite the enormous difficulties and most of the casualties were evacuated safely. In addition the Brigade jeep drivers were having a busy time. All the surrounding roads were under constant fire but they managed to dodge the craters and shells to get the injured back from the front line to the Airborne Dressing Station.

It was a night of many heroic deeds and both No. 6 Commando and Four Five bore the brunt of the artillery onslaught. The wounded also included the Brigade Commander, Brigadier the Lord Lovat, and as he was carried from the battlefield he sent the following message to the brave men of his Brigade still remaining in the conflict: 'I have become a casualty, but I can rely on you not to take one step back. You are making history.'* Lt-Col D. Mills-Roberts, Irish Guards, Commanding Officer of No. 6 Commando, who himself had been wounded in the action, took Lord Lovat's place and was to remain in command of the Brigade until the end of the war.

After the noise of the previous night the morning of 13 June was comparatively quiet, both sides being obviously content to lick their wounds. Four Five set about reorganizing itself. Casualties, especially amongst officers and senior non-commissioned officers, had been heavy and so it was therefore

* *The Green Beret* by Hilary St George Saunders, Michael Joseph, 1949. Copyright Curtis Brown Ltd.

reluctantly decided to disperse D Troop, which had no officers left, and use it to reinforce the four other Rifle Troops. D Troop was not reformed until the Commando returned to England in September.

From 14 June until the end of July, Four Five remained entrenched in their positions at Le Plein. Mortar and artillery attacks were constant, but fortunately did comparatively little damage. After the furious events of the first week in Normandy, the holding of a static position with the ever-present threat of attack became wearisome. One of the greatest enemies during this period was battle strain, and even some of the bravest succumbed to this and had to be evacuated for a rest. However, the offensive spirit of the battle still had to be maintained by the Brigade and nearly every night each Commando took it in turn to provide a patrol of Troop strength to harass the enemy lines. These patrols had the effect of both lowering the German morale and keeping up our offensive outlook.

Typical of these raids was 'Operation Vixen', which took place in the early hours of 29 June. Lt T. Thomas, SAUDF, led a raiding party of twenty men from A Troop from a forward base positioned in front of our own lines. This base was in a wood and for much of the day they laid low until it was time to attack. When it was time to move they were supported by a mortar and artillery barrage and, as the fire lifted, they charged the German forward slit trenches with fixed bayonets and grenades, and then continued on to the main objective—two houses which contained the enemy headquarters of that sector. Fighting was hard and at close quarters, but the patrol did not sustain any serious casualties and wiped out the opposition and set the buildings on fire. In the glow of the flames Lt Thomas decided to lead his party still further into enemy-held territory, although the Germans were by now fully alerted. Another strong-point was overcome and the occupants all killed.

As the enemy was now beginning to rally Lt Thomas decided to lead his group back, and had to conduct a fighting withdrawal to save themselves from being cut off and surrounded.

Despite its adventures the patrol returned in good order with only light casualties. One of the only injuries was to Lt Thomas, who, earlier on in the operation, had been slightly wounded by a grenade, but gallantly carried on. He was later awarded the Military Cross for his brave leadership. The success of 'Operation Vixen' caused the Divisional Commander, Major-General R. N. Gale, to send a congratulatory signal praising Four Five for the raid, which he described as a 'first class piece of enterprise'.

In fact, prior to the return of the patrol Major-General Gale had not been too pleased with Four Five. As the countryside was particularly close Lt-Col Gray was not unnaturally worried about German interference from the flanks after and during the attack. In addition to the bombardment he ordered the unit's machine guns to drop back and angle up so that they had a clear 'beaten zone' of some two thousand yards. This they did and chose a position close to Divisional Headquarters. When the Vickers opened up during the action Major-General Gale thought that he and his staff were under attack and ordered an immediate stand-to, little realizing that it was 'friendly forces'!

The Germans carried out retaliatory action in an attempt to lower our spirits. In addition to direct military offensive they also distributed propaganda leaflets, either from aircraft or by leaving them at 'convenient spots' in No Man's Land. An example of this literature, retained from the trenches of Le Plein by Cpl Lynn of C Troop, is reproduced below:—

CAUGHT LIKE FOXES IN A TRAP

English and American soldiers!

Why has Jerry waited ten days after the landings to use his so called secret weapon behind your back? Doesn't that strike you as queer?

It looks very much as though after waiting for you to cross the Channel, he has set a TRAP for you.

You're fighting at present on a very narrow strip of coast, the extent of which has so far been regulated by the Germans.

You are using up an enormous number of men and huge quantities of material.

Mean while the Robot-planes, flying low, scatter over London and Southern England explosives, the power and incendiary efficiency of which are without precedent. They spread death and destruction in the towns and harbours, which should be sending you much needed supplies.

THEY ARE CUTTING
THE BRIDGE TO YOUR BASES

In addition to the destruction and panic at home, traffic is disorganised, ships, even hospital ships, are held up.

How long can you keep up this foolish 'invasion' in those circumstances?

It's up to you to think of the best way to get out of the TRAP in which you are CAUGHT.

Time is precious. To-morrow may be too late.

On the reverse of this crude leaflet was printed several 'press clippings' attributed to various newspapers. One stated: 'Pauseless attacks with the new German weapon. The South Coast has been shrouded for days in light and fire'. Another claimed: 'According to a London report, King George has left London for an unknown destination with a view to greater personal safety'. The final boast was that 'No shelter affords protection against the terrific effects of the new German Weapon'.

This form of warfare was particularly unpleasant and would be described by purists as 'not cricket'. However, although these documents had a slightly unsettling affect, which was obviously the aim, there was no evidence that they seriously undermined the morale of our men in the front line.

Apart from these distractions July passed by relatively quietly. Life in the dug-out positions was hot and tedious, although the only thing that seemed to bother the weary Commandos was the occasional shelling and the ever-present mosquitoes. One of the most profitable pastimes during the daylight hours was sniping, and during these weeks Four Five frequently sent out small parties to carry out this task. These men were dressed in heavily-camouflaged suits, and on occasions were able to crawl to within a hundred yards or less of the enemy positions and lie in wait for suitable targets. Marine Cakebread was reported to be one of the unit's most outstanding marksmen and, in the Normandy campaign alone accounted for over thirty Germans in this manner. In contrast, the Commando's nocturnal activities had to be greatly curtailed as the enemy had put down strong minefields around its locations and had also laid numerous booby traps.

During June and July, with the arrival of reinforcements, various changes took place in Commando Headquarters and amongst the Troop Commanders. Major W. N. Gray was promoted to lieutenant-colonel and Major I. D. De'Ath joined as Second-in-Command. Major De'Ath, who was an out-standing leader and a very able officer in every respect, was to have a close association with the Commando over the next decade. Other changes included a move for Capt A. W. Neaves, from F Troop to Adjutant, whilst Capt B. G. White went to command A Troop. Capt I. N. N. Beadle (E Troop) was promoted major and Lt B. (Bryan) C. Samain joined as Intelligence Officer.

The primitive surroundings do not appear to have unduly cramped the routine administration of Four Five. Typewritten orders and directives were still being issued to Troops under these very basic conditions, although 'shortages prevented more than one copy being sent to each location'. One of Major De'Ath's first instructions, signed on 12 July, 1944, aptly reminded everyone that 'the top cover on trenches is primarily designed to give protection from splinters and not from the elements'. Another feature of life at this time, intro-duced on 16 July, was periodic Brains' Trusts. These were aimed at giving the Troop Commanders and officers in Com-mando Headquarters a chance to meet and discuss current mutual problems, both tactical and administrative.

Life at Le Plein could never be described as pleasant, but

two anecdotes concerning ranks of Four Five were recorded during this long occupation, and although the participants must remain anonymous, they are reported to have caused much amusement in the Brigade at the time.

One is of a marine who after breakfast was sitting quietly on the latrine having a smoke and meditating. Without warning the Hun, 'crude fellow that he is', opened up with his mortars and 'stonked' the latrine area. As the bombs were falling pretty close, the marine, without a moment's hesitation, kicked the latrine bucket aside and dived into the pit! From that day on he was a marked man.

The other story is of two off-duty marines who were trying to sleep in their slit trench through a night air raid. A very heavy thud indicated that something had dropped near them. One man, a Scotsman, got up to investigate and bumped his head on what appeared to be the biggest bomb in the world lying across the trench. In a rather hesitant voice he informed his pal, who bravely, and from the bottom of the trench, suggested that the other might push it aside. 'Not ruddy likely, chum,' was the reply. 'It might go off!' Thereupon the two marines sweated it out in the bottom of their trench until dawn, when further investigation proved the bomb merely to be a jett-isoned petrol tank!

These lines occupied for such a relatively long period of time by the Special Service Brigades and the 6th Airborne Division had been described by some as the 'phoney front'. By defending this left flank against bitter opposition—originally it had been assessed that it would only take a week or so to break out from the Normandy beach-head—our troops had prevented the Germans from moving round to the north, and had thus retained this vital position that was eventually to form the pivot for the final advance eastwards.

The long awaited break-out started towards the end of July when the British Second Army began to advance, albeit slowly, to the south-east of Caen. On 1 August, having been there for seven weeks, Four Five was relieved at Le Plein by a unit from No. 4 Special Service Brigade, and moved forward to Le Mesnil with No. 3 Commando to take over from the 5th Parachute Brigade. Although the move offered a change of surroundings it was by no means a rest cure.

Four Five's new domain was in the area east of Le Mesnil cross-roads and here again the countryside was close. The distance between the opposing forces varied from 150 yards to as little as fifty yards in some places. No Man's Land was heavily mined and booby-trapped, thus precluding any large scale forward patrolling activity. The Commando's front positions were well dug-in in a bank behind a hedgerow and overlooking a field, on the far side of which lay the enemy. The left flank at Le Mesnil was formed by a road which went forward into the German lines and was covered by their guns. A hessian screen was rigged across this lane so that we could cross in comparative safety and communicate with the parachutists on the far side. Lt-Col Gray remembers that a large pig appeared in No Man's Land near this spot, closely pursued by a group of Boche, doubtless wishing to add the poor animal to their dinner table. Four Five got the best of this encounter and captured both the Germans and the pig! However, the Commanding Officer does not recollect being offered a share of the feast.

Heavy and persistent enemy mortaring severely restricted movement throughout the front and our casualties, which had dwindled in previous weeks, began to mount up again. At night, to lessen the noise, the men in the front trenches would change from boots into light rubber shoes and move cautiously forward to repair our wire defences and place booby traps. It was soon discovered that the Germans, despite being at the early stages of a withdrawal, usually appeared to be in high spirits, as on most nights the marines could hear singing and on many occasions women's voices. The opposition's front-line facilities appeared to be well organized. The rendezvous, a farmhouse, was soon identified and our supporting artillery conducted a special shoot, after the Germans had had time to get 'settled in'. Several direct hits were recorded which forced the Hun to continue his amorous pursuits at a greater distance from our lines in the future!

3

Commando Headquarters, which was sited in a large brick-works near the cross-roads, experienced some of the worst shelling and mortaring. Protection was constructed from anything that became available and ample use was made of the kilns reinforced by sandbags. At first many people were caught unawares by the mortars, but after a time it was soon learnt that after the initial 'pop' of the bomb leaving the barrel there was about half a minute until the time of impact. A special sentry was posted to listen for the 'pops' and he would then give warning blasts on his whistle so that everyone could dive for cover. In spite of these precautions however, casualties still rose, especially amongst the ration parties who had to leave the protection of their slits and carry the heavy laods of food up to the two Troops out in front. Communications also suffered and the telephone lines were often severed and wireless sets damaged by splinters. This meant that the line repairing team, led by L/Cpl T. M. Cordon, often had to move out in the open whilst these shoots were in progress and bravely ensure that these links were not broken for long.

One visitor to this dangerous spot was the Chief of Combined Operations, Major-General Laycock. It was discovered that the factory, in addition to making bricks, was also engaged in the manufacture of china ornaments. As the General was about to clamber into his jeep at the end of his tour Lt-Col Gray presented him with a black cat as a memento of his visit to Four Five. Major-General Laycock flew back to London that night and the souvenir was immediately put in a prominent place on the mantelpiece of his club!

For over a week Four Five remained pinned down by this increasing barrage of fire.* The only means of retaliation was our own mortars and the snipers, who notched up several kills. One of the most serious setbacks to the Commando was a German attack on a three-man listening post some fifty yards forward of A Troop's front-line position. The post was caught completely by surprise and one man was killed and another

* A daily average of 400 bombs was reported to have been fired at the Brigade front during this period.

wounded. This outburst was in fact a prelude to the German withdrawal, for on 16 August there was an eerie calm over the area. The stout resistance of the Brigade at Le Mesnil over the past fortnight had broken the back of what, for the Hun, was a last ditch stand before he had to pull back on the long retreat which lasted until May, 1945.

The pre-arranged plan for the pursuit, 'Operation Paddle', was about to begin. The Germans were known to have withdrawn to a line east of the River Dives. Their area was dominated by the Brucourt feature, some five miles behind their front line, which overlooked all crossings of the river on the Brigade front. The low-lying area had been flooded by the enemy—they had broken the sea walls to swamp the reclaimed marshland—so as to provide an obstacle for infantry and tanks.

Immediately to the east of Le Mesnil cross-roads lay the Bois de Bavent, a large wooded area, and on 17 August, Four Five moved cautiously through these woods, but the enemy was well clear. However, detailed information was still required on dispositions on the Brucourt feature ahead and the Brigade Commander ordered the unit to carry out this reconnaissance. The patrol consisted of B Troop (now commanded by Capt H. E. K. Burge) and was led by Major De'Ath. The patrol left at ten o'clock on the morning of 18 August and had to cross the Dives by a partly demolished bridge and then move northwards. Progress was slow in the wet and muddy conditions, but by 'judicious exposure' the patrol drew enough fire to determine the outline of the German defences. The return journey was even more uncomfortable as the German artillery fire became increasingly close and the shells rained down, sending up great columns of spray. It was not until nearly eight o'clock that evening that the patrol returned to Bavent, fortunately without sustaining casualties.

The following morning (the 19th) Major De'Ath led out a second patrol to confirm potential crossing places of the subsidiary streams east of the Dives. These two patrols were the prelude to a full-scale Brigade night infiltration and attack which was planned, mounted and successfully executed in just over twelve hours. Brigadier Mills-Roberts did not receive his final orders until late afternoon and had to make his plans on the return journey from Divisional to Brigade Headquarters. At six o'clock that evening Four Five, along with the other units of the Brigade, crossed the Dives and moved into a forming-up area where the Brigade Commander gave his confirmatory orders. There was little time for last minute preparations. No. 4 Commando set off first for a separate objective whilst the remainder of the Brigade moved soon after midnight. The objective was the 300-foot high Brucourt–Angerville feature behind the enemy front lines. The order of march was No. 3 Commando, Four Five and No. 6 Commando.

The countryside at first was low lying and marshy but improved as the units follows a railway line and after that crossed a canal on an improvised bridge. Lt H. Muir Beddall of A Troop still remembers this approach march vividly:

> 'The entire Brigade was advancing slowly in single file. The advance guard had laid white tape to ease direction finding—this was the first of many occasions on which this successful form of navigation was used. The night was pitch black and the Commandos, exhausted by weeks of action, stumbled and groped their way forward for what seemed an endless period of time.'

And so, No. 1 Special Service Brigade continued in this manner throughout the night. The first warning that the Germans had of this occupation was at about six in the morning when their headquarters was taken by surprise by a group from No. 3 Commando. Hilary St George Saunders described the operation thus:

> 'The tactical handling of the Brigade had been perfect; it had slipped through all the lines of the enemy and reached the heart of his position undetected, although every man had had at one moment to cross a bridge covered by a German machine gun post less than 150 yards away.'*

* *The Green Beret*, Hilary St George Saunders.

Once the Angerville feature had been reached the units began to dig-in frantically in preparation for the inevitable German counter-attack. Despite the tired condition of the troops and accurate enemy fire, Four Five's positions were almost complete within an hour.

It was at this stage of the battle that A Troop (Capt B. G. White) was given the task of linking up with No. 4 Commando—who had moved off independently—so that a supply route could be opened up for food, ammunition and for the evacuation of casualties. Lt Beddall continues with the story:

'The route was through territory still held by the Germans. We had to open it up and get supplies through as at that time in the morning the whole Brigade only had what they carried on their backs. I was in the leading section and we were approaching some farm buildings, which were on the far side of a bridge. Suddenly I spotted a German looking over a low wall. Brian White came forward and ordered me to take my section to the left and come in at the rear as he charged down the road with the rest of the Troop. There was a stream or ditch on either side of this road. The Germans then opened up with a self-propelled anti-tank gun, and the first shell killed Brian White, as he bravely directed operations from the centre of the bridge, and two others.'

It seemed pointless to risk further valuable lives against this strongpoint and so under cover of a smoke screen the remainder of the patrol was safely withdrawn.

Throughout the rest of the morning the Brigade resolutely held on to its positions. Nos. 3 and 6 Commandos repulsed strong counter-attacks and E Troop successfully beat off an onslaught without loss. In the afternoon A Troop (now commanded by Lt Tommy Thomas), who were covering the rear of the Commando, inflicted heavy casualties on a suicidal German attack. As the day wore on the shelling and mortaring became more intermittent and the weary troops were glad of the respite. At eleven o'clock that night, under cover of a smoke barrage, a convoy of jeeps at last got through to the beleaguered Brigade positions bringing with it food and ammunition. The vehicles were quickly unloaded and raced back on the return journey with forty or so wounded. The rest of the night passed without harassment, but not particularly restfully, for it rained incessantly until dawn.

For the loss of one officer and eleven other ranks killed the Brigade had captured and held a position that was later described as 'one which the enemy might with justice have regarded as impregnable'.

The Germans were now in full retreat and their great columns of transport and infantry blocked the roads eastwards heading towards the Seine. Their resistance was dwindling fast. Paris had fallen (the Germans had surrendered there on 25 August) and those bewildered stragglers who had been left behind in the path of the Brigade were usually quite willing to give themselves up. The Brigade was now in the van of the pursuit which was being continued unrelentlessly on all sectors, and during an eight day period some thirty miles were covered and an axis cleared from Le Mesnil to Beuzeville. To speed up the advance at this stage Four Five was ferried forward by vehicle—great luxury!—but there were still frequent occasions on which stealth was all-important and movement would then have to be made on foot. On the nights of 24 and 26 August two more night infiltration marches were made, although on a smaller scale than the famous one on to the Brucourt feature. The first was done in company with No. 6 Commando and the second by C Troop (Capt Peter Barnard, Gordon Highlanders) with a Troop of each of the other Commandos. Both marches were over long distances, to outflank the enemy's rearguard, and were again extremely tiring. Complete success was achieved on both occasions.

All of a sudden the momentum of the last few days was checked and the Brigade was given forty-eight hours rest. For the Commando this was to be the first time for eighty-three days that it had been out of range of enemy mortar and small arms fire. Full advantage was taken of the break and the rest period developed into a week. All ranks were reported to have joyfully 'sampled the delights' of nearby Beuzeville, Trouville and Honfleur.

One of the few who could not afford to relax was Lt-Col Nicol Gray. His thoughts were on the next move which he assumed to be the continuation of the advance. Unbeknown to anybody else he set off with Lt Tommy Thomas and two Marines to scout the route ahead to Paris. Although the Germans had officially surrendered they were still much in evidence and the delighted Maquis warned the Commanding Officer and his party in the staff car to be on their guard in case of trouble. Lt-Col Gray recalls that this group was one of the first of our army to enter the city and they were mobbed wherever they went. At one stage they had to leave the car in a back yard, remove their green berets and run the gauntlet to the Bristol Hotel. Here the management welcomed the battle-dress clad Commandos with open arms and gave them a free lunch complete with pink champagne, much to the anger of the senior German officers still resident at the hotel!

However, Four Five was not to be employed in the advance to Paris and the only purpose their visit subsequently achieved was to cement a long friendship. For the waiting men of the Commando more than welcome news was received on 2 September, when it was learnt that the Brigade would be returning to England to refit. The steps that had been fought for so tenaciously over the past weeks were soon retraced and on 7 September the unit was at Arromanches, near the original beach-head, ready to sail for Southampton.

For Four Five the first stage of their war was now over.

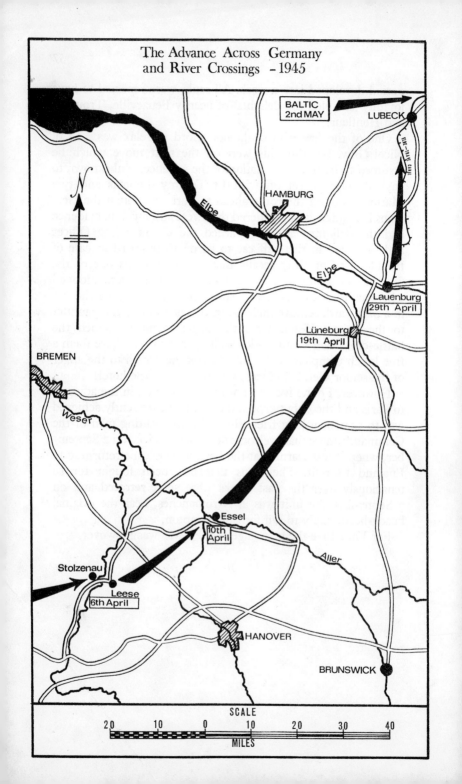

The Advance Across Germany
and River Crossings – 1945

BALTIC
2nd MAY

LUBECK

ELBE-TRAVE CANAL

Elbe

HAMBURG

Elbe

Lauenburg
29th April

Lüneburg
19th April

BREMEN

Weser

Essel
10th
April

Aller

Stolzenau

Leese
6th April

HANOVER

BRUNSWICK

SCALE

20   10   0   10   20   30   40
MILES

CHAPTER 4

Return to England
and an Escape Story

Four Five returned to Southampton nearly three months after it had departed, but this time it was a very different Commando. The rigours of the Battle of Normandy had taken their toll. Nearly a half of the original 400 or so who had left on that memorable June evening had become the victims of the desperate hard-fought German withdrawal, either as killed, wounded or prisoners of war. Those who were left and the reinforcements who had joined on the battle front had now been welded into a well-drilled and experienced team worthy of the heavy wartime responsibilities thrust upon it. The strain of action was apparent on the faces of many, but this was soon to be dispelled with the good news of well-earned leave.

The formalities of the reception camp at Petworth were soon over—perhaps the greatest need, apart from pay and railway warrants, was new uniforms. The khaki battledresses had, for many, been the only outer clothing since June, and these bore testimony to the weeks of hard struggle and rough conditions.

Leave passed all too quickly and Four Five set about re-organizing itself. Many of those wounded in Normandy rejoined from convalescent leave and about eighty reinforcements were received from the Holding Commando at Wrexham. Such was the reputation of Four Five that when volunteers were called to serve with Commando units the rush to its particular marker flag was considerable.

Among those who rejoined was Lt Peter Winston, reported

missing on D-Day. His travels since then demonstrated outstanding initiative and daring. Showing typical reticence,
Peter Winston was unwilling, at first, to say anything. However,
after persistent questioning from his inquisitive comrades
he relented and gave a full account to the Intelligence Officer
(Lt B. C. Samain). Here it is in Winston's own words:

'Three weeks before D-Day I was told that I would accompany
the Sixth Airborne Division as liaison officer in the assault on
Normandy. My fears of possible failure (it would be my first
operational jump) were somewhat quietened when I learned that
I would be jumping in the distinguished company of war reporters
and B.B.C. commentators. I felt that they were just as much
amateurs as myself!

The weeks went quickly enough, with their incessant briefings
and rehearsals, and before we knew where we were the time had
come. We were waiting on the airfield, loaded with sixty pounds
of equipment, tense, expectant. Waiting to go.

We took off from the airfield at dusk, some ten hours before
the seaborne assault. As we glided low over the Channel we could
see the landing-craft, silhouetted in the moonlight, putting out to
sea. Thousands of tiny specks in the water, each speck representing
a vessel crammed with men who had trained for four years to make
the greatest operation of this war a success.

England was soon left behind us, however, and for the next
three hours there was nothing but sea below. Nearing the French
coast, we ran into a tornado of flak from the enemy's coastal defences.
We were only five hundred feet up and could see very plainly the
curving tracer and 20-millimetre shellfire as it came towards us,
then zipped past, missing our Dakota by a miracle.

We were crossing the French coast now. My adventures had
begun.

In the swaying Dakota the red light suddenly flashed on. We
knew when we saw it that we had exactly ten seconds to go before
we jumped. As we all stood up to get ready the green light flashed
on with equal suddenness. From then on it was pandemonium.
Every man was trying to beat his comrades to the door. The next
thing I knew was that I was in space . . . jumping . . . just a
madly swirling body at the mercy of the slipstream; then my
parachute opened: down, down, down . . .

I landed in a clump of large treees and within five minutes or so
succeeded in disentangling myself from the 'chute. I looked about

me, and everything seemed peaceful after the turmoil preceding the jump. Just trees and fields on all sides.

I looked around for my comrades but couldn't see anyone. There was not a single living thing to be seen. Nothing but trees and fields. Where was everyone else who jumped with me?

Then the horrible truth gradually dawned upon me. I was alone.

Ten minutes later a solitary glider passed overhead, about two hundred feet up. Its sides were ripped with flak, but it went on. Apart from two other aircraft which passed over a little later, I saw nothing. Everything was deathly quiet.

To the east the sudden sound of firing broke the silence. It seemed very near—possibly only three or four hundred yards away. I learned later that in actual fact it was nearer a mile. I hurried towards the sound, hoping to find some of our own troops. As I walked along a path running along the side of a field a figure suddenly loomed out of a nearby hedgerow. My fingers stiffened on the trigger of my Sten, but instead of firing I gave the password. A voice replied with the countersign in low, relieved tones. It was the voice of a parachutist corporal, lost like myself.

We exchanged handshakes, held a rapid consultation, and decided to head north for the French coast. We started to move rapidly across country which was completely unrecognisable from the air photographs we carried. Our aim was to make contact with the seaborne troops, as we had obviously lost touch with our own airborne comrades.

We trudged across the countryside for an hour in this manner. As we neared a main road running across our line of march we suddenly heard the sound of movement on the road. Feverishly we threw ourselves into a ditch, and from our hiding-place saw a Germany party of cyclist troops about 100 strong go by. As soon as they had passed us we moved on.

Daylight came, and we had picked up three other parachutists in the meantime, all of them victims of circumstances similar to our own. The five of us hid for a short time in a thick copse, until we saw an old Frenchwoman walking across the fields. I got up and approached her, telling her that I was British. She didn't seem the least bit interested. Then I asked her, in halting French, where we were. I gathered from her reply that we were somewhere near Trouville, fifty miles east of our original objective!

This was not the most depressing news she gave us. Apparently we were surrounded by the enemy, who were fully alive to the fact that the invasion of the Continent had begun.

For the next five days we hid by day and only moved in the hours of darkness. The 24-hour rations we had dropped with were eked out with supplies of milk bought from the old Frenchwoman. During this period of hiding four more parachutists and a glider pilot joined our ranks. Our total number was now ten, including myself.

On the afternoon of the sixth day, just as we were preparing to move, we heard someone softly whistling "Tipperary" nearby. Looking out, I saw a Frenchman walking towards us. He introduced himself as Paul, spoke good English and, having heard our story, implored us to let him take us to his nearby house, where he could feed and hide us. We were only too glad to take advantage of his offer and that night he guided us there.

During the week Paul brought in five Canadian parachutists and a wounded glider pilot. Despite his entreaties to the contrary, I decided to try and slip through the German lines and reach our own troops. A route was planned involving a lengthy detour to the south. This was highly necessary, as we wished to avoid Dozulé, a small French town packed with German reserves at the time. We could only move short distances by night and were obliged to hide by day. Paul proved invaluable throughout, providing us with all the information we required regarding enemy movements and positions. In addition to this, he was able (as a civilian) to move ahead of us unhindered, selecting hiding-places for us and obtaining food from friends.

We travelled some twenty minutes in this fashion without incident. During this time we learned of another party of parachutists who were in precisely the same straits as ourselves but were believed to be in direct contact with our own troops. We therefore decided to try and find them. When we found them, however, they were no better off than we were. Amongst their party was a French-Canadian rear-gunner from a crashed Lancaster, who had made his way from the other side of Paris.

The two parties, now numbering forty strong, joined forces, camping a mile or so apart for the purpose of safety. We were approximately three miles from the scene of battle now, and although it had been unanimously decided to try and re-join our own troops rather than wait for the advance to liberate us, the difficulties to be overcome were immense. In the first place we did not definitely know where our own troops were. We could only guess. Secondly, if we moved off and failed to make contact within two days or so, we should be cut off without food. Careful reconnaissance of the proposed route was therefore highly necessary, and this was carried out by a local member of the Resistance Movement, the French-Canadian and myself. (I had by now succeeded in obtaining a suit of civilian clothes and the requisite papers. These had been carefully faked, my father's photograph passing as my own.)

Our position was now one mile south-west of Troarn. Two days previously a squadron-leader who had crashed near Falaise and an American pilot of a Thunderbolt which had crashed near Dozulé joined us. We still lay hidden, and after a further four days' reconnaissance (which revealed that it would be quite definitely impossible to get a party of our size back to the British lines) decided upon a change in plan. This seemed highly expedient, especially as a considerable body of German troops had suddenly encamped in the neighbouring field.

We held a Council of War, at which everyone was given an opportunity to state their views and decide what they wanted to do. About fifteen were prepared to make a dash for the British lines, moving in pairs. Eight decided to head for Spain, whilst the remainder were now either for staying where they were until the advance caught up with them or working their way round to the American sector, which might provide an easier route for escape.

All the available maps, compasses, money and food were accordingly pooled and divided. Civilian clothes were found for those heading for Spain (of which I was one) and such weapons as we had were given to those making a dash to the British and American lines in uniform.

On the evening of 4 July, having been together for almost one month, we split up into our various parties. In many ways it was a dramatic moment, for obviously none of us knew which party would be successful, or which would fail. We therefore solemnly promised to contact each other's next-of-kin should any of us get through.

Of the parties heading south for Spain, all had members who spoke French. Our party consisted of the squardon-leader and myself. The danger lay, as far as we were concerned, in that he had no identity papers. Consequently we kept well clear of the roads for the first day, looking innocent enough in our guise as farmhands, or *cultivateurs*.

At four o'clock that afternoon we reached the town of Mezidon and spent the night in a large double bed which we found in a bombed-out house. It was the first bed we'd slept in since D-Day.

The next day we pushed on towards Argentan, twenty-five miles away, following the line of the railway. We had to make frequent detours to avoid the huge craters on the line caused by the R.A.F. A mile and a half outside Argentan we found a hayloft by a farm and spent the night there. At ten o'clock the next morning we passed through the town itself on our way to Alençon, which was the next town on our route.

There was not a single living thing in Argentan. The railway sidings and marshalling yards were completely wrecked; the station was almost unrecognisable as such, except for a battered, twisted sign which bore the town's name in faded letters.

The R.A.F. had reduced Argentan to dust and ashes.

We continued along the railway line into Alençon. At Sees we were stopped by a German sentry who sprang out upon us suddenly from a small house beside a level-crossing and demanded, in perfect French, where we were going. I explained that we were refugees from Falaise, and that we were trying to reach relatives in Alençon. After examining our papers (the squadron-leader had been fitted out with these by the Resistance at Mezidon) the sentry allowed us to proceed, warning us to keep off the railway line. This we weren't at all sorry to do, as we had covered about sixty miles in this manner, moving along the line of the track from sleeper to sleeper.

That night, by great good fortune, we stumbled across a member of the local Resistance, who put us up for the night. He insisted upon taking us the next morning to see four Allied airmen who were hidden in a wood five miles away. One of these turned out to be a member of the same squadron as the squadron-leader. He had been shot down a week previously and the squadron-leader had thought him killed in action.

However, it was impossible to move with any degree of safety through enemy territory if we increased the party in numbers, so rather reluctantly we left the four airmen in the wood and continued the journey to Alençon alone.

We arrived in the town without further mishap and there met the leader of the local Resistance, who promised transport to help us on our way. The transport turned out to be a fire-engine, the only vehicle which could be run under the noses of the Germans without arousing suspicion. Donning firemen's helmets and ringing the fire-bell somewhat loudly and unnecessarily, we proceeded for some thrity miles along the main highway. The only upsetting factor throughout the whole of this was the number of inquisitive R.A.F. fighters overhead.

By pre-arranged plan the fire-engine dropped us at a house five miles outside Le Mans, which was the next town running due south. The occupants of the house supplied us with two bicycles to continue our journey. We passed through Le Mans that afternoon whilst an air-raid was in progress and pushed on towards Le Flêche, which we reached just before nightfall, spending the night in a farmhouse on the outskirts.

The next two days were comparatively uneventful. Progress was slowed down considerably owing to the excessive number of punctures which our bicycles received. As we had no repair outfit with us, this necessitated frequent hunts for *mechaniciens*, who more often than not were many miles off our route.

In this way we moved through Saumur to Poitiers. It was now 15 July and we had already covered nearly 300 miles of our journey to Spain.

Once past Poitiers, we began to enter the Maquis country. We were stopped at frequent intervals by German patrols, who proved to be by far the most suspicious we had yet encountered. That night, as was our custom, we approached a house and asked for water. This was always our preliminary when seeking a bed for the night. As I was talking to the occupant of the house, an old man, on the doorstep I could hear the B.B.C. news in French coming through very faintly from London. I immediately disclosed our identities. The old Frenchman was extremely suspicious, however, and we had to spend the rest of the evening convincing him that we were British. Once satisfied, however, he put us up for the night and the next morning directed us, through devious channels, to the headquarters of the local Maquis. But our troubles were not yet over. Most of the local inhabitants (themselves members of the Maquis) suspected us of being Gestapo agents. We eventually succeeded in convincing them and found ourselves in the local Maquis headquarters. Here we were obliged to stay for seven days, for the Maquis insisted on providing a guide (who had to be summoned from Bordeaux) to conduct us on the remainder of our journey.

The guide duly arrived after a week, and we departed by train, in brand new suits of civilian clothes, to Bordeaux. Our instructions were to feign sleep whilst in the train and to do whatever our guide did. All went well until we were some thirty miles from Bordeaux, where everyone was ordered to change trains. To our dismay we found that the new train was nothing more than a German troop train on which civilians had been permitted to travel! However, apart from an attempt by the Maquis to wreck the train on the way, we arrived at Bordeaux quite safely and followed our guide on to a tram which took us into the suburbs of the city. Here we were obliged to stay until we could catch another train running south to the Spanish border.

We learned later, however, that the railway line had been sabotaged (again by the Maquis) and so had to prolong our stay. The local Resistance eventually decided to move us by car to a point twenty miles south of Bordeaux, where we could pick up the train. Accordingly, on the morning of 4 August we met the car at a pre-arranged rendezvous and started on our journey. We reached the centre of the town and were proceeding along one of the main streets when a cordon of Gestapo agents (armed mostly with British Stens and automatics) was suddenly thrown across the road. Without further ado we were stopped, unceremoniously bundled out of the car, thoroughly searched, then marched off to Gestapo headquarters with our hands above our heads.

We had been trapped. Unfortunately, as we afterwards learned, the head of the local Resistance was also head of the Bordeaux Gestapo.

At Gestapo headquarters we were grilled with typical German thoroughness and ingenuity. The usual tricks were employed— face-slapping, refusal to recognise us as prisoners of war, threats of death if we didn't talk, statements waved in our faces purporting to have been signed by our accomplices which revealed our "true" identity.

We revealed no information. The Gestapo accordingly placed us in solitary confinement, and we each found ourselves in small cells some twenty feet underground.

Further interrogation followed, after which we were transferred to Bordeaux goal. Here we were later joined by six American fliers, tricked into capture by exactly the same ruse as we had been.

We spent nearly three weeks in the gaol. Our food during this period consisted mainly of bread and soup. Every day Allied airmen who had been shot down in the area were being brought in, and by 12 August Allied prisoners totalled nineteen.

Thanks to the American break-through at Nantes and the crossing of the Loire, however, the Germans started to evacuate the goal, handing us over to the Luftwaffe at Bordeaux-Merignac aerodrome. We stayed another five days here and the treatment we received at the hands of the Luftwaffe was infinitely better.

But on the night of the 26th, having completely wrecked the aerodrome, the Luftwaffe evacuated Bordeaux and headed for Germany, taking us with them. For three days and nights we travelled in lorries, and covered a distance of almost one hundred miles inland. During this period one of the prisoners fell sick and was placed in the civilian hospital at Angoulême. The next day we all feigned sickness, claiming that we had contracted ptomaine poisoning. To our amazement the German doctor believed us, placing us all in the same hospital as the prisoner who had fallen sick the day before.

That night the Luftwaffe's lorries moved out and the following morning we contacted the local Maquis. By this time half the town had been liberated and was under their control. We were still far from home, however, for a retreating German army lay between us and the Allied forces. On the night of 2 September help came at last from an unexpected quarter. Without warning the Maquis transported us to an unknown point in the surrounding countryside where two American supply planes operating in conjunction with the Maquis were expected to land. At two in the morning they arrived.

Four and a half hours later the squadron-leader and myself touched down on an airfield.

England was beneath our feet'.

Returning to the more normal activities of day to day life within the Commando, several officer changes took place after this September leave. Capt H. E. K. Burge (B Troop) and Capt E. Lee Smith, South Wales Borderers, who had commanded A Troop for the last days in Normandy, left the Commando for staff appointments. Capt J. Tulloch, RAMC joined as Medical Officer. He was a quiet and unassuming officer but was to prove in the days ahead that he had all the brave qualities needed by a doctor working in the field under tough front-line conditions. Lt L. W. (Len) Bridger came in as Signals Officer and Major B. W. De Courcy-Ireland joined as commander of the re-formed D Troop.

Just before Four Five left Sussex, No. 4 Commando departed from the Brigade and went to join No. 4 Special Service Brigade in Belgium. The Brigade subsequently took part in the famous raid to sieze the formidable island of Walcheren, on 1 November, 1944. The place of No. 4 Commando was taken by 46 Royal Marine Commando which was commanded by Lt-Col C. R. Hardy. Col Hardy's association with Four Five was to be a close one in future years. He was Brigade Commander of the 3rd Commando Brigade when the unit was serving in the Malayan Emergency during the period 1950–52 and also, as Commandant General, landed by helicopter with the Commando at Suez in November, 1956.

Early in October the Commando moved to Southsea where it was stationed at the Royal Marines Barracks, Eastney, a spacious establishment overlooking the Solent. Here life was in sharp contrast to that normally experienced within a Commando unit, and for many members of Four Five this was the first ever visit to a Royal Marine Division. Here the unit was able to complete a lot of much-needed re-kitting and basic training in addition to getting acquainted with the 'per mare' side of the Corps. The Commanding Officer was very keen that the unit should not be regarded as 'a private army' and wisely decided to adhere rigidly to the barrack routine although, of course, Four Five carried out its own separate programme. A special Guest Night was arranged in honour of Four Five in the fine Officers' Mess and although the high spirits afterwards were said to have lasted far into the night, the rivalry was a friendly one and there was complete harmony between the khaki-clad officers of the Commando and their counterparts at Eastney in blue.

At the end of the month it was back to Bexhill and civilian billets. After the rigours and tensions of war the routine life back in England was becoming somewhat irksome. Rumours of a move abroad in the near future were rife. It was originally thought that Four Five would be going out to the Far East to join No. 3 Commando Brigade, and in anticipation of this some ranks even underwent jungle training in the New Forest! To give authenticity to this 'buzz' someone in the know had seen the Medical Officer's store cupboard full of 'tropical injections'. For the time being this move was not to be. The news of the raid on Walcheren was read with admiration. November and December wore on without any more news of a re-deployment and field training continued apace on the Downs in the crisp winter weather. The reinforcements had to be integrated into their Troops, and the battle procedures polished up before the next call into action. Lt-Col Gray remembers one form of training designed to sharpen up the accuracy of the two-inch mortar teams—these weapons were issued at Troop level. 'Golf' competitions were introduced here at Bexhill and with tin cans representing the 'holes' at some two hundred yards range each Troop team was soon vieing for the lowest round. Needless to say holes-in-one were not uncommon.

An important change in the nomenclature of the Special Service Group came into force on 6 November when the title was altered to that of Commando Group. Although several explanations were offered at the time one of the most likely reasons for this change was Europe's hatred of 'SS' troops, and a more favourable impression would undoubtedly be created if the term 'Special Service' was dropped.

Shortly before Christmas leave Major De'Ath left Four Five, having already won a fine reputation both within and outside the Commando. He was later to rejoin the unit at the end of the war for a brief period as Commanding Officer, and then again some eleven years later when he became Staff Officer Operations during the critical period of the Suez and Cyprus operations. Major De Courcy-Ireland, formerly of D Troop, took over as Second-in-Command. Leave started in mid-December, but for Brigadier Mills-Roberts this fortnight merely afforded him an opportunity to go on a 'busman's holiday'—to visit Second Army Head-quarters in Holland. The purpose of this trip was not revealed until the New Year and the first news Four Five received was when it was called together at the end of a training session on the Downs and told to stand by to proceed overseas. The months of waiting were now drawing to a close and the Commando was going to enter the fray again. Baggage and stores were quickly packed, farewells to many friends in the neighbourhood were made and orders for the move given.

The Brigade left Bexhill on 13 January, 1945, embarked at Tilbury on the 14th and arrived at Ostend on the following day. This time, however, it was not straight into action and for two days the relative boredom of a transit camp had to be fought. The only pastime seems to have been watching the leave parties passing through on their way back to England with some hopeful members of Four Five wondering when their turn would come!

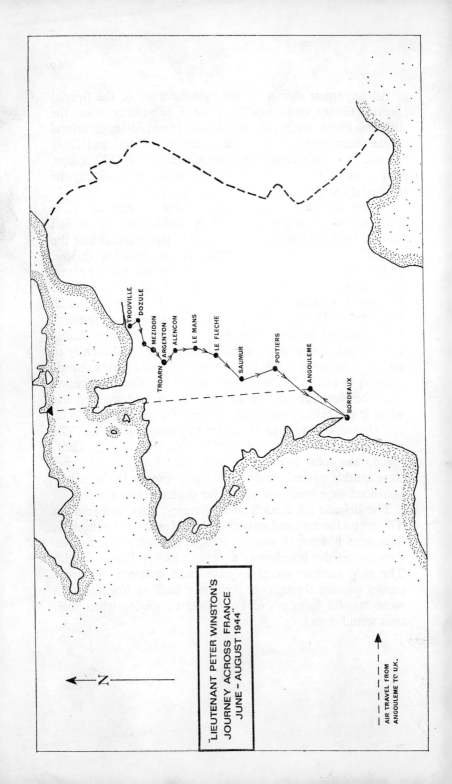

TROUVILLE
DOZULE
MEZIDON
TROARN ARGENTON
ALENCON
LE MANS
LE FLECHE
SAUMUR
POITIERS
ANGOULEME
BORDEAUX

← N

"LIEUTENANT PETER WINSTON'S
JOURNEY ACROSS FRANCE
JUNE – AUGUST 1944"

--- AIR TRAVEL FROM
ANGOULEME TO U.K.

CHAPTER 5

Holland.
Montforterbeek and Belle
Isle, January, 1945

The weather in the Low Countries was bitterly cold, and snow lay thick on the ground. After the short stay in Ostend Four Five was glad of the move some 130 miles eastwards, by train, to Helmond in Holland. No. 1 Commando Brigade was by now split under various commands. Brigade Headquarters, No. 6 Commando and Four Five were under command of the 15th (Scottish) Division. No. 3 Commando was operating under the 11th Armoured Division and 46 Royal Marine Commando, now commanded by Lt-Col T. M. Gray, the brother of Four Five's Commanding Officer, was sent to Antwerp for anti-sabotage duties. Lt-Col T. M. Gray was later to command Four Five in 1946—an interesting family association. Within Four Five there had been many internal changes as a result of reorganization in England so before we continue on our historic journey let us briefly re-examine the key officer appointments. A Troop, Capt. E. D. W. Coventry, East Lancashire Regiment; B Troop, Capt J. E. Day; C Troop, Capt P. D. Barnard, Gordon Highlanders; D Troop, Major R. H. W. Kirkby; E Troop, still the redoubtable Major I. N. N. Beadle; F Troop (Heavy Weapons) Capt C. E. Fletcher, previously the Machine Gun Officer. Capt A. W. Neaves, formerly of F Troop, became Adjutant.

Four Five reassumed its rightful positions at the spearhead of the Second Army's advance across the continent on 19

January when it was moved forward with No. 6 Commando to the area of Baarlo. This sector of the front was bordered by the river Maas to the east of which lay the German positions. The 'Bad Men' seemed unwilling to give any trouble and the only evidence of token resistance was some occasional mortaring. The freezing conditions limited activities on both sides, and the standing patrols, patiently waiting and watching the possible crossing positions throughout the long cold nights, had a most uncomfortable time. For four days both sides appeared to be content with the primary task of keeping themselves warm.

This static existence was not to last for long. Early in the morning of the 22nd both Commandos were unexpectedly relieved and moved south to Echt, some twenty miles away on the same front. Echt is on the eastern side of the Maas in the narrow strategic south-west strip of Holland, only a few miles wide, which lies between Belgium and Germany. Signs of a recent battle as part of our overall advance were much in evidence. The white background was blackened by shell-damaged buildings, burning houses and wrecked tanks. Four Five settled into the ruins of Echt for an uncomfortable night but was warned that the stop was only to be a brief one. The Commando would be going into the attack at dawn the next day.

This advance was to be part of the 12 Corps (Lieutenant-General Ritchie) offensive east of the River Mass which was aimed at pushing the Hun back into Germany behind the River Roer and thus clearing the area between the two rivers. More infantry was required to consolidate the successes of the 7th Armoured Division—'The Desert Rats'—and so No. 1 Commando Brigade was placed under command.

The Brigade was required to clear the Division's left flank between the railway—Echt to Roermond—and the Maas, and to capture Maasbracht, Brachterbeek and Linne as a prelude to the capture of Montfort by the 7th Armoured Division. The whole of this sector formed part of the much-vaunted Siegfried Switch Line, and was thought to be virtually impregnable.

No. 3 Commando, now commanded by Lt-Col A. G. Komrower, Lancashire Fusiliers, was to rejoin the Brigade the following day, and it was planned that Four Five and No. 6 Commando should start the advance on the morning of 23 January. A Squadron, Royal Tank Regiment, was under command for this operation.

In the dim half-light Four Five formed up to move off at a quarter to eight in the morning. No. 6 Commando (Lt-Col A. D. Lewis, Dorset Regiment) led the Brigade advance with Four Five following, and by nine forty-five they had reached Maasbracht without incident. It was a bright clear morning by now, but still bitterly cold, and the long file of men moved forward silently, their footsteps being muffled by the crisp dazzling snow. Even the supporting tanks fitted into the landscape as they were either painted white or covered with sheets.

At ten o'clock the Brigade Commander ordered Four Five to move into the lead and search Brachterbeek. No opposition was encountered here either and by ten thirty the leading Troop, A Troop, was clear of the straggling houses. According to the jubilant Dutch inhabitants, many of whom were lining the route to welcome the liberators, the Germans had pulled out the night before. Even the policeman seemed to be joining in the fun and was excitedly handing out apples to the troops as they marched by. A Troop was then told to head for the next objective—St Joostbrug and the area of the station. The countryside was flat and open. Between the Troop and its objective was a small village lying astride a wide, straight, tree-lined road. Running north from this village for about 600 yards, was a dyke containing a frozen canal. This dyke, several feet below the surrounding area, was known as the Montforterbeek and at its northern end it was joined by a small stream which meandered through a wooded valley to the hamlet of De Villa. A windmill stood on the eastern bank of the canal where it met the gully, and at this point there was also a small bridge carrying a lane which ran from Brachterbeek to Linne.

The leading section of A Troop was led by Lt Tommy

Thomas and as it approached some buildings near the village it came under heavy fire from small arms. The Commandos rushed the buildings in front of them but could progress no further. The section Bren gunner, Marine N. J. Patrick, who was later awarded the Military Medal, courageously stayed out in the open. His bursts of fire helped to protect his comrades as they dashed across the snow-covered ground and as a result they did not sustain any casualties. A Troop's second section under Lt R. C. E. Cory fared little better. This too was caught out in the open by machine gun fire from the direction of the Montforterbeek, and was forced to keep on going to reach the comparative shelter of the houses. Unfortunately not everbody made it and Cory and three other ranks, including Marines F. Wales and A. Wheeler, were left lying wounded in the snow. The remainder of A Troop, together with a jeep-borne machine gun section was also caught out in this featureless terrain behind the front two sections and had to scramble for what cover they could find.

The Commando had become a victim of the clever delaying tactics of the Germans. The whole of the line of the Montforterbeek and eastwards was in enemy hands and Four Five found itself in an exceptionally exposed piece of ground confronted by several positions which were able to sweep their front at will. A Troop, now virtually cut off, was still in the lead and the rest of the Commando was trapped in Brachterbeek by a heavy artillery and mortar barrage. Our own artillery twice laid down smoke screens in an attempt to extricate A Troop, but on both occasions the Germans intensified their fire, making it impossible for the men to move. The tanks also tried to come to the rescue but the accuracy of the enemy's mobile anti-tank guns forestalled their attempt.

In A Troop Headquarters, behind the front two sections, the Troop Medical Orderly, L/Cpl H. E. Harden, RAMC, was one of the first to be told of the casualties lying out in the open and instinctively made preparations to go out and administer first aid. He did this in spite of the fact that the distance was 120 yards, devoid of any cover, and was being shelled, mortared and raked by small arms fire from at least four known German positions. On his first journey Harden went out to look at the casualties and dress their wounds. He then returned to Troop Headquarters, reported the condition of the wounded, and then went out to the nearest man again, Marine Wheeler, who was badly wounded in the leg and unable to move unaided. He carried Wheeler back, zig-zagging all the way to avoid the bullets which were striking the snow beside him and sending up sprays of fine powder. When he got back to Troop Headquarters after this sortie it was noticed that Harden had got bullet holes in his smock and was bleeding from a wound in the side.

Regardless of these discomforts, Harden remained un-daunted. Capt Dudley Coventry ordered the Medical Orderly not to got out again until tanks had been arranged to support the evacuation of these casualties. Harden, however, insisted that the wounded should be brought in immediately as with every minute spent in the freezing cold their chances of survival were slimmer. He went off and organized two volunteer stretcher bearers, Marines R. Mason and J. Haville, to go out with him to collect Wales, whose condition was the most serious and who was haemorrhaging badly. By now the fire from the Hun was increasing in intensity but in spite of this Harden walked coolly beside the stretcher apparently oblivious of the opposition—his only preoccupation on this return journey was to render aid to the badly injured Wales, who was tragically hit again and later died of his wounds. With his thoughts only on the bullet-swept field with its wounded men in jeopardy Harden went out for a third time to bring back Lt Cory who was lying the farthest away. The stretcher party reached Lt Cory safely and, having picked him up, started on the perilous return journey. It was then, with only fifty yards to go, that fate struck a cruel blow. L/Cpl Harden was hit in the head by a bullet and killed instantly, just a short distance from safety.

The Troop Sergeant Major, TSM H. Bennett, dashed out to give what assistance he could to the stretcher party in those final yards and later gave his account of the action: 'During the time leading to his death, L/Cpl Harden spoke to me and laid emphasis on the fact that the the casualties must be got in from the extreme cold to have a chance to survive. During my conversations with him, he gave no thought to his own safety provided the wounded could be got in, and was cool and calm in dealing with his patients even though he had himself been hit on one of his journeys.'

L/Cpl Eric Harden, later described as a 'fearless soldier' was posthumously awarded the Victoria Cross. An extract from his citation reads: '. . . The magnificent example he set of cool courage and determination will never be forgotten by those who saw it.' Harden also made history within his own admirable Corps for he is the only member of the rank and file who, since the RAMC's formation, has ever been awarded the Victoria Cross—all the other fifteen recipients have been officers.

As was customary on such occasions the Commanding Officer later sat down to write a letter of condolence to the next-of-kin, in this case Harden's young widow.

'His death has hit us all very hard for he was trusted, loved and respected by all ranks of the Commando. He lost or rather gave his life to save the lives of our wounded . . . I shall always be proud of having had him in my unit. He was a very brave and gallant man and his devotion to duty and to his comrades was a fine example to us all. I have recommended him for the Victoria Cross and hope he will be granted it.'

It is, of course, virtually without precedent to intimate to a relative that such an award has been recommended as citations of this nature are always treated in the strictest confidence. However, Lt-Col Nicol Gray was desperately tired after the day's bitter fighting and as it was his policy to write as quickly as possible it is understandable to see how the slip-up occurred. All was well as the award was subsequently confirmed on 8 March, 1945, although the press did get hold of the story.

Ex-Marine Richard Haville, who was Mentioned in Despatches for his part in this drama, added his praises to the host already given when he wrote after the war: '. . . L/Cpl Harden was a very courageous man, not only in battle but in normal life. I can say this as I spent a lot of time with Harden, and saw some of his fine spirit and strength, which he shared with us all. One instance, we had done a very hard march over rough ground and pebbled beach and most of us needed first aid for our feet. Although needing more attention than any of us he treated all of the Troop before attending to himself. . . . May I say that L/Cpl Harden won his Victoria Cross not by rash deeds but by courage and loyalty to the RAMC in bringing help to the wounded. He was a great loss to us all in the Troop and loved by us all. . . .'

The act of valour also prompted the Secretary of State for War, the Rt Hon Sir James Grigg, to say, on the floor of the House of Commons on 13 March when referring to the award: 'I do not remember ever reading anything more heroic.'*

Harden's brave deeds were afterwards recorded on three memorials. The first was on the bridge over the Monforterbeek by the windmill. Two plaques, one in Dutch and the other in English have been placed on opposite sides of the bridge to commemorate the courage shown nearby. A second memorial was placed at his home church, All Saints', at Northfleet in Kent, where part of the altar setting, consisting of four golden angels, was dedicated to his memory at a service attended by his family and representatives of many public bodies from the neighbourhood. At this service, on 23 April, 1949, the Representative Colonel Commandant of the Royal Marines, Sir William MacArthur, unveiled a memorial plaque. The final commemoration was a house that was named after L/Cpl Harden at the Royal Army Medical Corps Apprentices' School at Mytchett, Ash Vale, near Aldershot.

Let us now return to the scene of the fighting near the Montforterbeek. By now, midday, all efforts to extricate A

* *Hansard* Vol. 409 page 195.

Troop had failed and Lt-Col Gray was forced to issue orders to Capt Coventry to hold his present position and then withdraw after dark—still some hours away. One person, however, was able to make a dash up to the stricken front line, and that was Capt John Tulloch, RAMC, the new Medical Officer. He was later awarded the Military Cross for the courageous way in which he personally led a convoy of jeeps across the bullet-swept ground to A Troop Headquarters just before one o'clock, to evacuate the many wounded.

So that we could gain a foothold on the Montforterbeek Lt-Col Gray ordered E and B Troops to advance along the line of the embankment which ran between Brachterbeek and the gully at the north of the dyke and dislodge the enemy from there. E Troop were in front and their leading section came under heavy fire as it passed a small copse on the way to the objective. Cpl Cocks and Marine Russell were killed by this burst of fire and three others wounded. Sgt Ahern, one of the injured, later died of his wounds. It was clear that the Hun was making a fierce effort to check our advance.

One of the ranks on this perilous move forward of E Troop was 'Marine' R. W. Merry. Merry was in fact an Army Commando from the West Yorkshire Regiment who had been temporarily attached to Four Five with five others. These ranks were in the unusual position of having been 'transferred' to the Royal Marines for a six-month period—they were given Royal Marine Regimental numbers although basically Army personnel. At the end of hostilities these six men were returned to their parent regiments proud, no doubt of their service with Four Five during such a critical period.

By now B Troop was moving up and, determined to keep up the momentum of the advance, Capt Day decided to probe forward further to the left over an area of frozen marsh. Initially, Capt Day was only willing to commit Lt H. G. Riley's section to this important task as he was uncertain as to the firmness of this marsh and naturally did not wish that the whole Troop should become bogged down. Soon after Riley had gone on ahead the sounds of heavy firing could be heard.

It is probable that Riley had caught the group that had originally inflicted such heavy losses on E Troop and were now pulling back to their next line of defence. As Riley and his men exchanged fire with the Germans the tanks were brought into the fray and with timely accuracy directed their shells on to the known enemy positions on the flanks. The leading section of B Troop was now in what was later to be known within the Commando as 'Riley's Gully'. Lt Riley and his section sergeant, Sgt W. J. Noakes, were leading an attack against two machine gun posts which lay on the far side of the stream. The Germans soon withdrew under the pressure of the Commandos but when the remainder of B Troop arrived on the scene they found that the enemy, showing typical tenacity, was putting in a counter-attack. This attack was repulsed, and as wireless communications had failed, Capt Day remembers telling TSM B. M. Aylett to throw his green beret in the air to indicate to E Troop that the position had been taken. Now that the Germans had plotted our front line in their old trenches it was not long before mortar fire rained down on the newly captured area, causing several casualties. One of these was Major Beadle who was wounded in the head, but displaying the fortitude for which he had now become renowned within the Commando, he refused to relinquish the leadership of his men, who were still under heavy and accurate fire. In order that the bridgehead on the Montforterbeek should be consolidated D Troop was sent forward and took up a defensive position on the left. The time by now was nearly three thirty and as D Troop came up the gloom of the northern dusk was beginning to set in.

Throughout the day, however, the fighting had not merely been confined to the front line. Both C and D Troops had been heavily shelled at Brachterbeek and Capt Barnard of C Troop was wounded in the left foot whilst having discussions with the Commanding Officer and had to be evacuated. Capt M. C. Brockbank then assumed command of the Troop. Another casualty was the Commanding Officer's wireless operator, Marine F. Burton, who was badly hit by a splinter in the right arm. With this useless limb and obviously in great pain he continued on his hazardous journey with the Commanding Officer, who was visiting the forward Troops at the height of the battle, 'giving a shining example of a signaller's devotion to duty and loyalty to the unit'. Burton, who was later awarded the Military Medal, continued to maintain vital communications and pass orders for supporting fire to aid the forward Troops, and refused to go to the RAP until a relief had been obtained. So exacting and dangerous was the duty of Commanding Officer's signaller that the Adjutant later commented to Lt-Col Gray 'that demand frequently outstripped supply'. Amongst other awards made for gallantry on the Montforterbeek were the Military Cross and Military Medal to Lt Riley and Sgt Noakes respectively for their outstanding part in gaining the decisive initial bridgehead.

As evening approached the tired men of Four Five began to feel the effects of a long day's fighting in the bitter cold. The most uncomfortable, of course, were the members of A Troop, trapped on the outskirts of St Joostbrug for over six hours in a temperature of some fifteen degrees below freezing. However, much had been achieved by the Commando and when the news had been received in the higher echelons that a foothold had been gained on the enemy's strong front line along the Montforterbeek the Brigade Commander, Brigadier Mills-Roberts, forwarded the following Special Order of the Day, which was received by Four Five that evening.

'To all ranks of 45 R.M. Commando. The Divisional Commander* congratulates 45 R.M. Commando on their valuable work to-day which has been of great importance in driving back the enemy on the Divisional front. Well done, Royal Marines. You put up a fine show to-day and I am very proud of you.'

There could be no higher praise for Four Five than contained in this historic signal, but this was no moment to reflect on

* Major-General Lyne of the 7th Armoured Division.

past success. Although darkness had now set in A Troop had still to be withdrawn—this was achieved by eight o'clock—and the Montforterbeek guarded against surprise attack. During this period of early evening a patrol drawn from C Troop, who had been guarding Commando Headquarters at Brachterbeek all the day, was sent forward to the gully to re-supply the three leading Troops with much needed ammunition. One of the members of this patrol, Cpl E. P. Lynn of C Troop, still vividly remembers the tension as the Commandos stole forward stealthily on this bright crisp night, heavily laden and expecting the Hun to launch an attack without warning. Lynn had joined Four Five in early 1944 and had been in C Troop for all its operations during the North-West Europe campaign. This truly remarkable veteran then served in the Commando on three later occasions, in Malta, Cyprus and Aden, as a specialist Assault Engineer, and at the celebrations to mark the twenty-fifth anniversary of Montforterbeek Lynn was the only rank who had fought in the battle still on the active list of the Royal Marines. Another member of this brave night patrol to 'Riley's Gully' was the Rev Reginald Haw, RNVR, the Commando's Chaplain. He had shown by his calmness that both a sense of dignity and reassurance could be brought to what might seem to many to be a purposeless holocaust. Throughout the day the Rev Haw quietly continued to minister to the wounded and dying under the most frightful and danger-ous conditions in the forward areas of the battlefield, and in full view of the enemy. In recognition of this selfless display of devotion to his faith he was later awarded the Distinguished Service Cross.

The patrol managed to complete its mission without hin-drance and all remained relatively quiet until nine thirty when the Germans started shelling 'Riley's Gully' again, killing Marine Lyons and wounding TSM Hanes, who had been the stalwart Sergeant-Major of D Troop for such a long time. This appeared to be the prelude to an enemy counter-attack and put our men very much on guard. Shortly after this artillery outburst B Troop, well entrenched in the old enemy positions to the southern end of the gully, spotted some white-clad German soldiers approaching from the direction of the windmill to the south. However, it was not just a simple case of a frontal assault as sounds of movement were also heard in the gully itself—the Hun was trying to move in from all directions. Capt Day now describes what must have been a very dramatic few minutes in his own simple words:

'The Troop stood-to and every man was waiting for my order to open fire. When the Hun was within certain killing distance B Troop opened fire with all available machine guns and tommy guns—even the Troop PIAT. One or two white-clad Huns ran away, the remainder remained very still. I then brought down our own artillery fire right on the Montforterbeek, less than forty yards from our trenches, to check the enemy who were infiltrating into the gully. Even though I caused one or two casualties to my own Troop I felt that my decision was justified as some of the enemy there were killed by this artillery fire.'

The results of this tough encounter could not be reckoned until the following morning when twelve dead were found in front of B Troop's positions and a further three in the Montforterbeek. A German prisoner captured later revealed that out of the forty or so men who had attacked the gully only two had escaped unhurt—a very pleasing success for Four Five.

After this setback the Hun seemed reluctant to make any more sorties and receive further punishment from us. The rest of this cold night passed quietly and at six o'clock the welcome news was received that No. 6 Commando were coming forward to relieve B, D and E Troops. As dawn broke the incoming and outgoing units exchanged the normal goodwills and banter when the trenches were being handed over, but these were especially heartfelt as Four Five and No. 6 Commando had always been on the best of terms. The unit reorganized at Brachterbeck later that morning and began to count the cost of the previous day's fighting. Although the figures were not nearly as high as at the gallant stand at Merville

1. King George VI with Brigadier the Lord Lovat meets the commanding officers of No. 1 Special Service Brigade. Lt-Col Charles Ries is in the background. (Imperial War Museum)

2. Major-General 'Lucky' Laycock, accompanied by Lt-Col Ries and Major Nicol Gray, inspects Four Five at Southampton, 31 May, 1944. (Imperial War Museum)

3. 'A' Troop prior to the invasion of Europe. L/Cpl Eric Harden is seated at the far right of the picture. (Imperial War Museum)

4. 'Hitler here we come!' D-Day, 1944. (Imperial War Museum)

and Franceville Plage, when over eighty casualties were suffered, the losses in the fight to sieze the Montforterbeek were considerable—thirty-six (six killed and thirty wounded). Most of these casualties had come from A Troop and its machine gun section which had borne the brunt of the earlier fighting, and from E Troop on their advance in the afternoon. Against this the Germans had lost their hold on the line of the Montforterbeek and had suffered many more killed. The Germans had held the initial advantage of surprise and strong defences but were forced to continue their withdrawal by the sheer perseverance and determination of Four Five under these most appalling conditions. This action is recognized as an official memorable date for Four Five and every year, on 23 January, a citation recalling the brave deeds of this battle is read out to all the assembled troops.

Nowadays this area, which must be indelibly imprinted on the minds of the participants, is vastly changed. The wide open spaces, which took so many hours to cross, are dwarfed by an *autobahn* which runs from north to south and bisects Massbracht and Brachterbeek. A new giant generating station, built between the Beek and Roermond, now dominates the formerly more open eastern sector. The area, little more than a mile square, can be passed in a matter of seconds but the brave deeds, recorded on Harden's Bridge, will be remembered for years to come.

Four Five remained in reserve in Brachterbeek throughout 24 January and was moved forward again on the 25th to Linne, which had by now been evacuated, to assist No. 3 Commando in the occupation of the town. A and C Troops remained in Linne while B and E Troops were moved to Weerd, overlooking the Maas and the inhospitable marshes that lay on either side of it. D Troop and Commando Headquarters moved into the hamlet of De Villa. Opposite B and E Troops lay a small bell-shaped island, which was, apart from its obvious outline, appropriately nicknamed 'Belle Isle' after the island of that name off Brittany, which the Royal Marines helped to capture from the French in 1761. It was as a

4

result of this earlier action that the Corps was privileged to wear the laurel wreath surrounding its badge of the globe. Like its predecessor, Belle Isle was observed to be occupied, but the precise strength of the enemy was not known. Lt Tommy Thomas and three ranks of A Troop were given the task of finding out this information and set out on what was to be a short-lived 'Operation Belle Isle I'. When the patrol was half way across the fast-flowing river it was spotted by the Germans and fired on. Thus forced to retire, the men could only come back confirming the previous information that there was believed to be one platoon concentrated on the western end of the island, near the lock.

Later that morning Lt-Col Gray received orders that information was required about enemy forces in the Merum area, which was on the far side of the Maas from Belle Isle. Plans were therefore drawn up for the next operation, which was to be known as 'Operation Belle Isle II'. The aim of the operation, as given by Divisional Headquarters, was as follows: '45 Royal Marine Commando will capture Belle Isle with a view to making a raid on the Merum area.' This ambitious operation was to be conducted in two phases. Phase I of this carefully prepared plan was to be the capture of Belle Isle. The assault was to be led by D Troop (Major R. H. W. Kirby) with a section of A Troop, commanded by Lt Tommy Thomas, which was to raid the adjoining Anchor Isle at the same time. The entire crossing was to be covered by E Troop who were also to provide a small party, commanded by Lt A. Tate, to hold the bridge-head on Belle Isle. Phase II was to be the raid on the Merum area which was to be carried out by B Troop who were to capture a prisoner from Drift, on the far bank of the Maas, for interrogation and intelligence purposes. To assist in the interrogation task, B Troop was to be accompanied by a detachment of 3 Troop No. 10 (Inter-Allied) Commando who were commanded by Capt J. Griffiths, Royal West Kents. Capt Griffiths was a fierce anti-Nazi and was described thus: 'He was without fear . . . and revelled in danger'.* The

* *The Green Beret*, Hilary St. George Saunders.

boat parties for the river crossing were to be supplied by I Troop, Engineer Commando, Royal Marines, who were experts in this field of activity, and the artillery support for the operation was to be provided by no less than four regiments, showing the importance that was attached to Four Five's dangerous mission. It was, however, hoped to complete Phase I without this heavy support, so that the raid on Merum could be undertaken without the enemy being alerted beforehand. As the terrain was so flat and open additional backing was to be provided by a machine gun detachment from No. 6 Commando and of course, Four Five's own heavy weapons, who could rake the river over to the island in case trouble arose. H hour for Belle Isle II was fixed at nine-thrity on the night of 27 January and the whole operation was planned to be completed by seven o'clock on the following morning.

In the bitter cold of winter all the participants rehearsed and were briefed on every aspect of the forthcoming raid. The supply organization was fully stretched to get in the special stores and equipment. Four Five had a foretaste of things to come in the years ahead when special snow suits were issued to the raiding and assault parties, and the Brigade Engineer Troop constructed sledges on which the boats would be hauled across Belle Isle. By the evening of 27 January all the intricate preparations were complete. As the gloom of dusk gave way to darkness it soon became apparent that conditions were not going to be easy. The almost full moon reflected brilliantly off the still white landscape, making visibility too good and thus putting the attacker at a disadvantage. A further setback occurred later on, while the marines were moving silently about their final appointed tasks on the south bank, H hour had to be delayed owing to a breakdown in the all-too-important wireless communications with the supporting artillery. The men, keyed up and ready to go, just had to crouch impatiently in their positions waiting for the executive order. Communications were restored just before ten and soon afterwards Belle Isle II got under way. Without a sound D Troop and the bridge-head party of E Troop crossed the Maas.

This in itself was a difficult task, as the strong current, six and a half knots, was continually pushing the assault boats downstream and the strength of every man on board was needed to operate the especially long steering paddles provided with the boat.

Once ashore, each Commando carried out the routine which had been so painstakingly rehearsed beforehand—there was hardly any need for verbal orders. Lt Tate gathered his group around him to cover the crossing point and the white shadows of D Troop moved off westwards in a long line. In a matter of minutes heavy firing broke out, shattering the still of this freezing night. D Troop appeared to be engaged in a fierce battle, but, hard as all the other unit signallers could try, they could not raise them and everyone was in ignorance as to what was going on at the western end of Belle Isle. Our own artillery and mortar fire was brought down on known enemy positions but still the battle seemed to rage and the Troops on the south bank could only wait helplessly, sensing that something was going desperately wrong across the fast flowing and icy water.

Capt Day, waiting with B Troop for their mission to Merum, was told that as surprise had obviously been lost it would be suicidal to continue to try and snatch a prisoner, and that Phase II was therefore cancelled. Instead the Troop should reinforce the bridge-head party prior to helping D Troop, of whom no news had yet been received. The first job for B Troop was to get a line across the river so that a ferry system could be implemented to build up a force on the northern bank. The river at this point was a hundred yards wide, but the current so fast that it was impossible to get a boat back without a full load to paddle it, thus it was imperative that this line should be fixed with all speed. Capt Day set out in two assault boats on this task—they seemed pitifully small as they paddled with all energy across this vast expanse of water. TSM Aylett, in command of the first boat, got across safely, but the second boat with Capt Day and the detachment of No. 10 (Inter-Allied) Commando soon found itself in difficulties.

The all-important rope, which had already been secured to the south bank, was on board this boat which had been swept 400 yards downstream by the strong current in spite of the superhuman efforts of all on board to get the boat straight across. This distance was in excess of the length of the rope, and after three gallant attempts against the overwhelming elements it was found to be impossible to fix this vital life-line.

Whilst these efforts were in progress some of the wounded and other survivors of D Troop were able to make their way painfully back through the snow to the bridge-head party, and give their account of what had happened. Near the lock at the western end of Belle Isle was a long line of trees where the enemy positions were known to be. D Troop was approaching this area cautiously, but the Germans had presumably been able to see them long beforehand silhouetted against the barren landscape in the bright moonlight, and had skilfully laid an ambush at very close quarters from which, tragically, only a few were to survive unscathed although, as was learned later, they were able to inflict as many casualties on the enemy in what can only be described as a violent battle. As the first few survivors of D Troop began to make their way through, the Germans made a desperate attempt to make their success absolute and cut off the remainder from the bridge-head. Our guns, however, which were well sited on the south bank, were able to check this infiltration and gave some most effective covering fire which checked the Germans in their tracks.

It was by now after midnight and up until this time Lt-Col Gray had still hoped to overcome the position at the western end of Belle Isle using reinforcements, but because of the strong current it had been proved impossible to push any great numbers of men across the Maas. Reluctantly, the Commanding Officer decided to abandon the operation and evacuate as many as possible from the island in good order. Much of the responsibility for this task rested with Lt Tate and his bridge-head party who started to carry the more seriously-wounded members of D Troop down the slippery bank to the water's edge, where an assault boat was waiting. As soon as this had been despatched the small group on the northern bank found themselves under attack—the Germans had managed to crawl up and were hoping to cut off Four Five's last remaining link with its own territory. However, the section Bren gunner, Marine J. Clarke, who was covering the bridge-head, soon observed the approaching Hun and almost single-handedly beat off the attack with cool and accurate fire which wrought havoc amongst the enemy. After this unwelcome diversion Lt Tate began to evacuate the remainder of those of his party and D Troop who were in the checkpoint. It was perhaps during this part of the withdrawal, that some of the greatest displays of courage and unselfishness were shown typical of the Commando spirit that had been instilled at Achnacarry. There was not enough room in the small assault boats due to the many wounded and some of the bridge-head party, who had been lying in the snow since soon after ten o'clock, bravely forsook their places and elected to swim alongside the boats in the icy and fast flowing water. Fortunately they were not molested by the Germans as we put down a heavy barrage of supporting fire, but for the men in the water it was a truly nightmare trip, with little thought of the shells screaming overhead, as they clung on to their comrades and to the sides of the boats, their bodies completely numbed by the freezing water, watching the shoreline and anxiously praying that they would make those last few yards to safety. When the bank was reached the Medical Section, with their traditional efficiency and sympathy, soon took care of the battle casualties and those others, soaked to the skin, who were suffering from exhaustion and exposure.

As the injured were being evacuated in the darkness the noise of gunfire began to die down and an eerie silence began to fall over Belle Isle, still harbouring many mysteries of the previous few hours. The Commanding Officer was still keen to clarify the situation and complete the initial aim of capturing a prisoner, and, therefore, Major Beadle and six of his ranks from E Troop with Capt Griffiths were ordered back across the

Maas at four o'clock in the morning. This time they landed without interruptions and paid their first visit to the area of the old bridge-head where they found five dead Germans— sure testimony to the skill of Clarke and his friends. The journey was not in vain, for one of the bodies was that of an artillery officer and contained a map giving invaluable information of the German dispositions in the area south-west of Roermond. Most important of all, a prisoner was taken, a German corporal, and Major Beadle's party was able to return safely having been able to achieve part of the original mission.

The time was now approaching to pull back altogether from the banks of the Maas and as dawn was getting near the Troops began to prepare to return to De Villa. The boats were hauled out of the water and the special stores for the operation packed. One of the groups by the riverside suddenly heard a shout. For a few moments there was silence. The voice was heard again: 'I'm Sgt Fenwick of D Troop and I've got a wounded man with me'. There was little time to be wasted and so Capt Day took five ranks from B Troop and crossed the river where they met the sergeant, who led the patrol to the wounded man, Marine Hannah, who was in such a serious condition that he was unable to move unaided. Slowly they carried Hannah back to the river but as they were going down the steep bank a machine gun post opened fire hitting one of the rescue party, Marine Ogle, twice. The Marines managed to scramble on board safely and as they drew out from the lee of the bank the gun opened up again. Fortunately no one else was hurt and Capt Day later remarked: 'Never has an assault boat manned by so few moved so fast!'

Although the rumours of what had happened were now being passed throughout the unit it was not until later on the morning of 28 January that the final number of casualties could be counted. Three officers and fourteen other ranks were listed as missing and thirteen, who had already been ferried back, were known to have been wounded. All of these were from the three Troops, B, D and E, who had taken part in the operation. Some of those missing were believed to have been wounded and probably in enemy hands. The loss of so many fine men and their relatively unknown fate was a shattering blow to the Commando and the look of disbelief could soon be discerned on the faces of many, coupled with a feeling of numbness at this first major setback for the unit. Perhaps those who suffered most were the gallant men of 'Dog' Troop who had so recently reformed and had now lost over half their comrades, including all their officers.

There was little time to dwell on 'what might have beens' and Four Five had to embark on the task of trying to secure the release of the prisoners. Under flags of truce Capt Griffiths and his Sergeant Major, TSM Howarth, went forward on to the exposed river bank to try and persuade the enemy to hand over the wounded. The Germans allowed Four Five to cross over the Maas to retrieve the dead but would not hand over any prisoners. The fearsome business of ferrying back and identifying the corpses took many hours, and it was with great distress that it was learnt that one of the ten dead was the brave and well-liked Peter Winston, who had travelled so many miles and survived Gestapo imprisonment to rejoin Four Five, only to die on this tragic mission. The remainder, previously reported missing, were now known to be wounded and in enemy hands. They included Major Kirby, who was hit in the arm and ankle by German bullets, and carried to a factory in Merum which was their headquarters, Lt Jack Alvey, one of his subalterns, and four other ranks.

Throughout these negotiations, which lasted for over two days, Capt Griffiths tried to persuade the Germans to surrender, but they were adamant in their brave insistence to carry on in spite of the fact that they had suffered heavier casualties than we had. The German commander was now a young cadet officer of the Muller Parachute Regiment who assumed command after his senior officer had been killed—his body was the one found by the bridge-head with the map. Interrogation of the prisoner and other sources had revealed that the garrison of Belle Isle was some fifty strong and that they had lost at least twenty men killed during the raid—evidence of D Troop's tenacity. For two days the uneasy respite continued as the slow process of bargaining and messages went on. The negotiations eventually broke down and it was back to hostilities.

There were many contributory factors to the failure of Operation Belle Isle II. The inability of the initial reconnaissance party to get across the River Maas and get additional information about the enemy dispositions made D Troop's task that much harder. The two-phase plan, in these circumstances, was too ambitious and would possibly have been modified if it had been known that the opposition on Belle Isle to Phase I would be so determined. Finally, the climatic and geographical conditions which hampered one of the most important items of any military operation—the reserve. The exceptionally strong currents of the Maas in flood prevented the follow up Troops being landed and of course the bright moonlight reflected off the snow-covered surface greatly favoured the defender. Despite these setbacks Four Five displayed, even in adversity, the qualities of a highly trained and disciplined Commando unit. The withdrawal under constant harassment and fire was carried out efficiently and calmly, and it is fitting that two members of the bridge-head party, Lt Tate and Marine Clarke, should have been decorated for their actions on this night. The last tribute, during these hours of many outstanding deeds, must be paid to those selfless individuals, whose names may never be recorded, who gave up the relative comfort of the interiors of their boats to face certain injury, if not death, in the icy waters of the Maas.

After the activities of the past week the next three weeks in the De Villa area were comparatively uneventful. Reinforcements helped to swell the numbers of the much-depleted D Troop which was now commanded by Capt H. G. Riley, who had led the attack which wrested the gully from the Germans on the Montforterbeek. The Commando's Second-in-Command also changed during this period. Major B. W. D. Courcy-

Ireland left the unit and his place was taken by Major A. L. Blake, MC.*

Much of the story of Four Five up until now has dealt with the Rifle Troops, who naturally reap much of the glory in battle, but the final results achieved by any unit are, of course, dependent upon the overall effort contributed by the various elements. Much of the credit for Four Five's success on the battlefield is due to the little-publicized activities of the headquarters and administrative elements who had to carry out their normal duties under the most appalling conditions and were rarely safe from attack, even if they were not in the front line of action. We have already heard of the bravery of the medical staff whose exploits always aroused well-earned admiration. The signallers, burdened with cumbersome radio sets and passing essential operational traffic, played a very important part, especially when the Commando was spread out over a broad front or extended during the advance. The ranks of the Signals Troop, commanded by Lt Len Bridger, were also liable to suffer high casualties as their wireless aerials made them easier targets for the enemy and their heavier loads restricted mobility. One is also apt to forget too one of the unit's smallest sections, the Intelligence Section, under Lt Bryan Samain. Although only six or so in number this team would always be working in the forward zone, manning headquarters round the clock seeing that the Troops were supplied with maps, air photographs and information about the enemy and at the same time passing back and receiving details from Brigade. Finally, let us meet the supply and administrative organization commanded by Capt 'Bob' Armstrong. This tall, cheerful north countryman was a highly respected figure and

* Major A. L. Blake was Lord Mayor of Portsmouth when the Freedom of that city was granted to the Royal Marines on 14 May, 1959. In his reply to the Lord Mayor's speech the Captain General, HRH Prince Philip, Duke of Edinburgh, stated: 'That this honour (the Freedom) and happy distinction should come from the hands of one who served his country with gallantry as a member of the Corps, is an added pleasure and a symbol of the very close ties which exist between the Corps and the citizens of Portsmouth.'

had been one of the founder members of the Commando when it was formed from the 5th Battalion. Capt Armstrong had landed as a Troop subaltern with A Troop on D-Day and was to hold his post of Administrative Officer for many years after the War. His responsibilities were widespread and it was virtually a question of 'you name it and I'll get it'—and he rarely failed! The supply team had to bring up hot food to the men in battle, usually after dark to minimize the chance of detection; carry dangerous cargoes of ammunition forward; replace the numerous items of stores, weapons and equipment damaged in action; look after the transport section in their vulnerable jeeps and also supervise the pay and clerical departments. One of the most eagerly awaited items on the re-supply runs was drink. Under these conditions it was strictly limited to the frugal ration of one bottle of beer per man per week, although officers were given a concession of a bottle of gin and a half a bottle of whisky which had to last for a month. It is hardly surprising that any stocks found en route were quickly devoured.

After the rigours of the Belle Isle operation the days up to 19 February, spent in the line, were relatively uneventful. Shelling and mortaring were intermittent and there was the occasional clash with a German patrol in No Man's Land, near the station, to relieve the monotomy. E Troop, covering the Maas flank, contrived to make life miserable for the enemy still left on the island and gain some revenge for the events of the night of the 27th. With the aid of tanks, artillery and their own weapons they would conduct shoots on the Germans in their trenches with considerable accuracy. In fact, both sides had a pretty trying time. It was still bitterly cold—one outpost was given the appropriate title of the 'Ice Box'—but as the temperatures rose slightly the snows began to melt and turned this white-clad terrain into a muddy quagmire interrupted by sheets of water over the low-lying marshes.

Units of the United States Army relieved the Brigade in the Linne area on 19 February and later that day Four Five found itself on the way to Venray, some thirty miles to the north.

Two days rest were spent here, the Commando being conveniently housed in a monastery! Then it was back to the front with a battalion of Dutch troops under command to look after an eight-mile stretch of the Maas for a week. On 1 March the Brigade was again split up and Four Five joined No. 6 Commando, under command of the 52nd (Lowland) Division, to take part in a sweep down the eastern side of the Maas in the narrow corridor between Holland and Germany to chase the withdrawing Hun. The advance started on 1 March and progress was frequently impeded by mines of all descriptions, which the Germans had liberally distributed in their wake at strategic points such as track and road junctions. This sweep was supported by tanks of the Guards Armoured Division and on 2 March Lt-Col Gray went on one of the probes forward on the back of a tank. It was not long before they caught up with the fleeing enemy and were able to bring back a prisoner—a wretched stores Corporal who had overslept when his comrades withdrew and had been left behind! That afternoon, after this 'minor success', Four Five was ordered to move by night to a small village called Well, opposite 46 Commando's area. Although the distance of the approach was not particularly long, five miles, it was a particularly unpleasant march described as 'the most hateful that the unit ever undertook'. There was no direct opposition from the enemy but for twelve hours the men of Four Five, many of whom had not slept for two days, picked their way forward along a nightmare route 'of mines laid every foot of the way'. Added to this the night was bitterly cold, and the men further back in the column could only wait patiently doing their best to keep warm in the biting wind. The unit arrived in Well just before dawn in a chilled and tired state but spirits were soon aroused when 46 Commando, on the western banks of the Maas, ferried over a hot breakfast which was not only more than welcome but provided an excellent prelude to the exhausted men for their rest period. A witness recorded: 'and with their (46 Commando's) patrols now in front of us, we slept and slept'.

After four days in Well the Commando was withdrawn to

Venray again for rest and retraining. Preparations were now in their final stages for a major offensive into the Reich and it was Four Five that was to be one of the units that was to have the privilege of being in the van on this historic thrust.

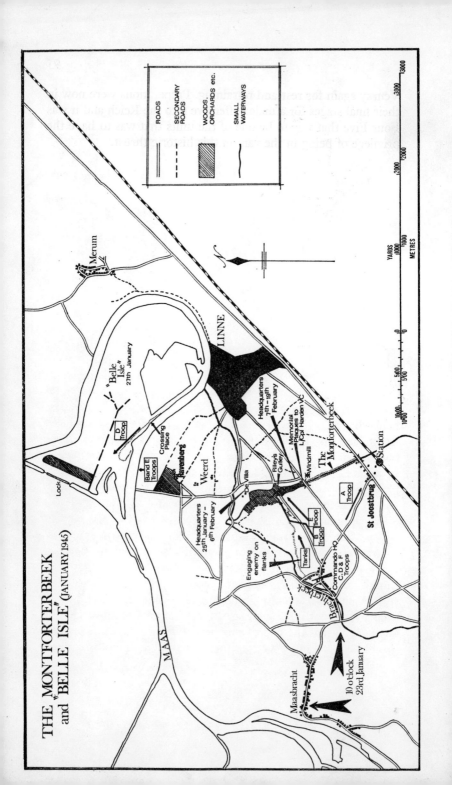

THE MONTFORTERBEEK
and "BELLE ISLE" (JANUARY 1945)

ROADS
SECONDARY ROADS
WOODS, ORCHARDS etc.
SMALL WATERWAYS

N

YARDS
METRES

Merum

MAAS

LINNE

"Belle Isle" 27th January

D Troop

Crossing Place

B and E Troops

Ravenberg

Weerd

De Villa

Lock

Headquarters 25th January – 6th February

Engaging enemy on flanks

Tanks

Commando HO C, D & F Troops

Brachterbeek

Maasbracht

10 o'clock 23rd January

Rileys Gulley

Windmill

Memorial Plaques to L/Cpl Harden v.C

Headquarters 7th–19th February

The Montforterbeek

A Troop

E Troop

St Joosbrug

Station

CHAPTER 6

The Advance into Germany— The River Crossings and Occupation

For nearly a fortnight Four Five stayed in billets with Dutch families who made the new arrivals more than welcome. The luxuries of home living such as hot baths and regular meals were a wonderful contrast to the cold and uncertainty of the battlefield. For the previous month or so up until now parties of a dozen had been fortunate in getting forty-eight hours Brussels leave. These groups were reported as 'usually having left the Commando in the front line dirty and tired, but invariably returning cleaner but even more tired!' These Brussels leave periods ended during the time at Venray and the Commando began to concentrate on its forthcoming task, one of the more traditional roles of the Royal Marines, that of the approaching amphibious river crossings the majority of which were to be bitterly opposed. The daily programme at Venray was filled with arduous watermanship training. Various types of craft were used, including dories, storm boats and Buffaloes.* The exact objective for the next raid was kept secret, but a creek running into the River Maas at Wansum was used by the entire Brigade as a rehearsal area to simulate the target. Towards the end of this period, training with Buffaloes (in the case of Four Five) was intensified by both day and night

*Armoured Amphibious Troop Carriers.

so that drills became second nature and that 'no man felt that any river was an obstacle for him'. Other aspects such as street fighting and weapon training were not neglected either; these were to prove to be of vital importance in the days ahead.

While Four Five was at Venray, the Second British Army Commander, Lieutenant-General Sir Miles Dempsey, paid a visit to watch this training and the other preparations. It was he who later wrote the foreword to the war-time history of the Commando and paid tribute to Four Five as follows: '. . . They fought many battles . . . with that skill, tenacity and courage, for which they became so well known. They built up a great tradition for themselves in the space of eleven months, and amongst those who gave their lives for victory was one who gained the most coveted honour in the world. A splendid fighting unit, whose great achievements will never be forgotten.'

On 20 March the Commando left Venray at the end of their training and crossed into Germany. The final phase of the pursuit was about to begin. The honour of being the first Commando unit to enter the Third Reich had, in fact, already fallen to 46 Commando who had sent a Troop patrol into the Well area of Germany earlier in March and had returned after penetrating a few miles without meeting opposition. Four Five, with the remainder of the Brigade, was now sent forward some fifteen miles into Germany to the village of Birten which was to be the forward base for 'Operation Widgeon', the crossing of the great natural barrier of the Rhine and the subsequent capture of Wesel. For three days the unit was to remain at Birten for incessant briefings and further rehearsals. The magnitude of the operation soon became apparent. Wesel contained some 24,000 inhabitants and was the chief centre of communications on the Second Army front. The Rhine at this point was 300 yards wide and flanked by twenty foot-high dykes, or *bunds*, to prevent flood-ing. In spite of these there was a lot of water on the low ground, similar to the later days by the Maas, as a result of the recent thaw.

Enemy dispositions on the far side were not known precisely, but it was assessed that there were about 2,000 troops and their main lines of defence would probably be in the wooded country to the west of the town which forms the lip of the saucer in which Wesel stands. From the outset all planning was based on the gigantic bombing raid to be made by the RAF on the night of the assault. To achieve surprise it was planned that the initial crossing of the Rhine, on flat muddy ground about two miles downstream from Wesel, should precede the heavy air bombardment, and that the Brigade should then assault the town while it was still reeling from the effects. It was considered to be too adventurous to capture the entire town in one blow as the Germans would be likely to counter-attack, so it was therefore planned that the Brigade should just hold a compact area on the northern edge of the town. In this sector there was a large factory, to the north of the station, which was a vital point as it dominated the area and controlled the main routes into Wesel. One of the key factors of this daring raid was going to be surprise and throughout all the planning stages thought had been given to methods of concealing the strength and whereabouts of the Brigade once it had crossed. To achieve this it was decided to remove all traces of the Commandos at the initial crossing place, Grav Insel, during the daylight hours after the raid and this meant that there would be no immediate back-up sorties of reinforcements or stores and that the troops had to carry all their own supplies.

Brigadier Mills-Roberts therefore made the following plan: 46 Commando was to cross first and establish the initial bridge-head at Grav Insel. The remainder of the Brigade was then to pass through the bridge-head in the order No. 6 Commando, Four Five, and finally No. 3 Commando (now commanded by Lt-Col P. I. Bartholomew, Somerset Light Infantry). The Brigade would then wait until the completion of the heavy air bombardment and then advance, still in darkness, towards Wesel. The Brigade Commander then decided to adopt the method that he had so successfully used in 'Operation Paddle' in Normandy, and ordered that No. 6 Commando should mark the route to Wesel with white tape and that the remainder of the Brigade should follow in Indian file. While the other units were consolidating their sectors on the northern edge of the town, Four Five was to press on to capture and hold the strategically placed factory. It was calculated that it would take until dawn to consolidate these positions. After that the Brigade was to move south to exploit through the town and establish a ferry route so that the 1st Battalion the Cheshire Regiment, who were being held in reserve, could be brought across at a later time to reinforce the operation. The final phase of Widgeon was to be the dropping of the 17th US Airborne Division, who were to drop to the north of the town and then move south to link up with the Brigade. During this drop, which it was estimated would take four hours, there could be no artillery support from the west banks of the Rhine, and so it was vital that Wesel should be held at all costs throughout this long period without any outside assistance at all. H hour was fixed at ten o'clock on the night of 23 March, and the heavy air bombardment was due to start at ten thirty.

Friday, 23 March 1945 dawned bright and clear—a perfect spring day which contrasted sharply with the sounds of battle later on. The briefings of Four Five were by now almost complete and each man knew the details of the plan and the part which he had to play in it. Although the attack on Wesel, as part of the overall offensive on the Rhine front, was essentially a Brigade-sized raid its fufilment was not entirely dependent upon the success of each unit carrying out its own task, but upon the individual, whose contribution on an occasion such as this must never be glossed over in favour of a seemingly broader sense of achievement. In addition to its briefings, the Commando had two other visitors on that sunny morning. The first was Lieutenant-General Ritchie, the commander of 8 Corps, who said: 'I think, although my knowledge of history is a little rusty, that you will be the first British troops ever to have crossed this river. Not even Marlborough attempted it.'

The second visitor was Brigadier Mills-Roberts, admired by
every man in the 1st Commando Brigade, who explained to
his captive audience all the details of the plan, and stressed
that the Brigade during this historic night was going to be
supported by one of the biggest air and artillery bombardments
ever known. The Brigadier also added, in a lighter vein, that
although Hannibal crossed the Alps on elephants the Commandos could tell their grandchildren that they crossed the
Rhine by Buffalo!

For the remainder of the day Four Five waited in the
marshalling area well back from the crossing point. Weapons
and ammunition were checked, and checked again. Vehicles and
troops were moving everywhere. To hide this activity, a thick
smoke screen had been laid and the effects of the acrid fumes,
when the wind blew in the wrong direction, were most uncomfortable. That afternoon the unit was told that a preliminary
air bombardment on Wesel was going to take place and at
half-past five all eyes turned skywards as wave upon wave of
Lancasters droned overhead. The waiting men watched with
satisfaction as a hundred of them dropped their lethal loads in
a quarter of an hour and then turned homewards. Soon afterwards the deafening roar of the supporting artillery opened up.
This continuous blast was to form the background for the
assault throughout the night. Eventually, as darkness fell,
Four Five moved off towards their forming up position near
the river bank. 46 Commando rumbled past in their Buffaloes,
but most attention was still being paid to the horizon ahead
which was a continual red glow of burning buildings and
exploding shells. Perhaps some of the troops even felt pity for
the citizens and garrison of Wesel who were receiving this
merciless pounding and were wondering how anyone could
survive to oppose the Brigade. A few hundred yards short of
the river, Four Five, the faces of the men now blackened out in
the true Commando raiding style, was halted by a small
farm. Here tea laced with rum was served out to the unit by the
supply team, although some of the luckier ones later confessed
that they had received rum laced with tea! Mail was also issued

and the troops huddled around what meagre lights they could find to read the welcome letters and messages from home before they were plunged into battle. By now H hour was approaching and Four Five was on its way forward again on foot. The men passed near to the guns which were firing on to the bridge-head—46 Commando's objective. As the unit got near to the crossing point it fanned out and the Troops formed up, lying on the grass behind the bunds, in readiness for the Buffaloes which would return after their first sortie. The tenseness of the situation was temporarily relieved by the voice of a Commando, inside a Buffalo, which could be heard above the noise of the engines. An eager BBC commentator was moving amongst the vehicles, microphone in hand, recording battlefield impressions. 'Do you think you'll be first across?' he asked one individual as he thrust his microphone towards him. 'Not if I can bloody well help it, mate!' The commentator disappeared. Royal Marine humour had prevailed.

Precisely on H hour 46 Commando moved forward and landed on the far bank in two waves. It was nearly ten thirty when the Buffaloes arrived at Four Five's forming up area and the heavily laden men scrambled on board in the manner which they had rehearsed innumerable times before at Birten. The Buffaloes revved up and roared off, moving up over the high dykes and then lurching downwards before they plunged into the fast flowing water. The time was just after half-past ten and the Commando's first wave was now crossing the Rhine, heading for the bridge-head held by 46 Commando. The air bombardment had just started and this is how Capt Day of B Troop described the scene:

'The night was almost beyond description. To our right Wesel was being annihilated; to our front we could see the angry red glow of the supporting barrage; to the left one Buffalo on the far bank was ablaze; overhead we could hear the rushing wind of the long range shells, and at short intervals the bark of Bofors guns firing tracer to mark the flanks'.

Four Five reached the far side safely and began to form up
for the night march. No. 6 Commando, who had been landed
further downstream in storm boats, passed through the bridge-
head and moved on silently to carry out their task of laying
out the tape on the route to Wesel. Four Five followed on
behind moving stealthily in single file. The Brigade was described as looking 'purposeful and sinister'* as it advanced
across the plain where the moonlight was being reflected off
the flooded fields. There was very little opposition on this part
of the advance except from a few frightened stragglers who
were taken on the way. The first of our troops to come under
fire were the men of the leading Troop of No. 6 Commando
and they soon dealt with their dazed opponents and continued
to their appointed sector. It was now the turn of Four Five to
enter what was left of Wesel, which was very aptly described as
looking like 'Dante's Inferno'. Progress was slowed down by
huge craters and the destruction and desolation everywhere
were unbelievable. All that remained of Wesel were large
heaps of smouldering rubble and the occasional burning shells
of buildings.

Four Five halted briefly in No. 6 Commando's area and then
moved off, at about one o'clock in the morning, towards the
factory. Almost immediately B Troop came under fire. It
seemed incredible that anyone could have survived the bombardment of the previous few hours, but even so there were
several Germans who were still hiding in the ruins and prepared
to put up a stiff fight. B Troop quickly disposed of their
opposition but one of the 'corpses', believed to be the garrison
commander or a member of his staff, unfortunately came to
life and fired a *Panzerfaust*† at very close range which severely
wounded Lt-Col Gray in the arm and six members of B Troop.
Seeing that his Commanding Officer had been wounded one
of the medical orderlies rushed forward to give assistance,
and started to cut away the trouser leg where he saw a lot of
blood. Lt-Col Gray was furious at this intrusion, firstly because

* *The Green Beret*, Hilary St. George Saunders.
† German Anti-Tank Rocket Launcher.

he had not been injured in that limb at all and secondly because under these severe combat conditions it was his only pair of trousers and he was unwilling to part with these at any cost! He was then taken to the RAP and after being patched up in one of the ruined buildings bravely rejoined the battle and continued the advance later with the forward Troops. Progress was painfully slow and the men had to pick their way cautiously through the rubble and debris. No more opposition was encountered and to speed things up Major Beadle was detached with E Troop and ordered to advance towards the factory following the route of the railway, or rather what was left of it. This was a slightly easier route to follow than through the town, where all the streets had been virtually obliterated, even so the railway was hardly recognizable as such except by the rails which had been twisted into grotesque shapes and were jutting out of the innumerable craters at odd angles. Compared with its surrounds the factory was still fairly intact, although the Commanding Officer had asked that it should be completely demolished by the prior bombardment. It was an enormous building encircled by stout high walls and Major Beadle led his men on the formidable task of clearing it before the remainder of Four Five arrived. Every part of these large premises was systematically searched, no chances could now be taken, and as it was a strategic key point the chances of a counterattack was very high indeed.

Lt-Col Gray, still in great pain, returned to co-ordinate the plans for the defence of the perimeter where the Troops were now being spread out. E, B and C Troops held the northern fringe while A and C Troops looked after the flanks. Commando Headquarters and the other elements remained inside the building but their domain wasn't without its hazards. The only entrance was through a dark doorway and as the first men scrambled through they stopped abruptly in their tracks when confronted by a large gaping hole. Closer inspection revealed an unexploded bomb in the bottom which acted as sentinel to this doorway for the next twenty four hours. Once inside the Commandos busily engaged themselves in erecting hasty defences. One marine, Harry Sullivan of E Troop, remembers that the factory had been employed in the manufacture of lavatory pans and these were hanging from the roof on overhead rails in the process of drying. For the next hour or so the men of Four Five inside the factory had to brave the dangers of shattering porcelain as German bullets ripped into the ceiling. These lavatory pans also came in useful in the construction of barricades to block up windows and other holes. The defensive positions were consolidated just before dawn and soon afterwards the Commando received its first visitors. A cyclist patrol, eight strong, approached the front door of D Troop's position, obviously on a reconnaissance in search of information. This they soon received from the hands of Lt Alan Tate and his men, who calmly waited until the Germans came right up close and then disposed of the lot. Soon afterwards E Troop, who were in the right corner facing east, were visited by another patrol who suffered a similar fate. In both cases it seems that the Germans were taken completely by surprise and unaware of our presence, proof of the really effective and speedy penetration of the Commandos during the night.

There were also some more German civilians hidden in an air raid shelter within the unit's perimeter, but this time the Commando's presence was not resented as our green berets were considered to be preferable to the dress of the Russian soldiers.

The only supporting vehicles that had come in Wesel so far that day were eleven Weasels* under the command of Capt H. Muir Beddall, formerly of E and A Troops. During the night they had ferried the casualties back from the bridge-head to the marshalling area and one of the initial twelve had been damaged on these crossings, but the remainder had come forward before dawn so as to be in the town before their movement could be detected. Initially movement from the bridge-head had been slow for them as they were the first Brigade vehicles to move into Wesel and there was a risk of mining.

* Light Armoured Amphibious vehicles.

However, they arrived intact amongst the debris with their medical teams and stores who could then set about treating the wounded that had not been taken back previously.

As ten o'clock approached on the morning of 24 March, our artillery barrage abated in preparation to the drop of the 17th US Airborne Division and elements of our own Sixth Airborne Division. All eyes instinctively turned northward as the gliders swooped towards their landing zones and the parachutes with their welcome reinforcements floated gracefully towards the ground. The Hun chose this moment to launch his counter-attack to try and gain control of the all-important factory. Taking advantage of the respite in the bombardment, the enemy was able to advance across the open ground with tanks and infantry supported by his own spasmodic artillery fire. Lt-Col Gray decided at this juncture to adopt another ingenious ruse and ordered that the PIAT's should be used in the 'mortar' role. Angled up, these weapons had a range of some 300 yards—at the receiving end the effect was very similar to that of an artillery barrage. The demoralized German infantry were soon beaten off, but one tank, more resolute than the remainder, started to pump shell's into E Troop's area from almost point-blank range. E Troop suffered six or seven casualties during this fierce onslaught and were in many ways at a disadvantage because of an earlier decision, made at higher headquarters, not to bring the heavier anti-tank guns with the assault troops as 'there wasn't a significant tank threat'. Because of the mounting number of wounded in E Troop's area the Troop Commander was told that he could withdraw from his exposed position on the outer wall to the comparative safety of the factory building. However, Major Beadle characteristically refused to move back and instead bravely elected to hold his ground, raked by gunfire, in case the German infantry attempted to advance even further forward and thus gain a foothold on the Commando's perimeter. Fortune was on Four Five's side and the offending tank, for some reason best known to itself, withdrew, and soon afterwards, as the 'no fire' limit had expired, E Troop was able to call for gunfire. The 3.7 inch Howitzers of the 52nd (Lowland) Division Light Regiment were one of the units in direct support for Operation Widgeon and their timely and accurate response quickly scattered any of the German infantry who had unwisely chosen to remain in the open countryside in front of E Troop's sector. There was little doubt that the Hun had been determined to dislodge Four Five from their important position, although the attacks were spasmodic and ill-coordinated, but after his rough reception he became less enthusiastic and the rest of the day passed fairly quietly, except for B and D Troops' front, which was still occasionally pestered by self-propelled guns. To strengthen the open flanks along this long open wall reinforcements were sent up to Four Five later on in the day and A Troop of No. 3 Commando moved into a position next to D Troop, covering what was left of a level crossing.

Throughout the remainder of the day the Brigade programme went according to plan. The other Commandos, assisted by the 1st Battalion of the Cheshire Regiment, were sucessfully clearing the rest of this shattered town and winkling out the odd prisoner from amongst the debris. For once the deep bomb craters came in useful—as collection areas for captured Germans—and only one or two Commando guards were necessary to keep watch from the rim as many more times their number of bewildered enemy sat crouched in the bottom trying to keep out the northern chill. As the green berets continued through the ruins they found one group of Germans, or rather their leader, who was very reluctant to surrender. This was later discovered to be General Deutsch, the Garrison Commander of Wesel, whose party had inflicted so many casualties upon B Troop with whom the Commanding Officer was moving at the time. The General had tried to shoot it out with a patrol of No. 6 Commando led by Regimental Sergeant-Major Woodcock, but was soon killed by a burst of tommy-gun fire. The rest of his staff wisely decided to give themselves up.

That afternoon the Commanding Officer, despite all his

fervent protests, was evacuated from the factory.* The wounds in Lt-Col Gray's arm were of a serious nature and he was in great pain. The medical evacuation line back across the Rhine had now been re-opened and Capt Tulloch recommended more intensive treatment than could be provided in the temporary dressing stations of the front line. Major Blake assumed command in very similar circumstances as the leadership of Four Five had changed at the Orne Bridges in June 1944 for the Commandos and the paratroopers—of the United Airborne Division—were beginning to link up. At five o'clock that afternoon the Marines watched with interest as an American patrol came into the factory, still 'guarded' by its unexploded bomb, to give Four Five details of their dispositions, their nearest unit being about a mile away. After this brief union with the paratroopers the Commando returned to its grim task of holding on to the factory, still very much alone. German resistance was waning but had not yet been completely overcome. That night, at about ten o'clock, after hours of waiting patiently in the dark sounds of movement could be detected on the far side of the railway lines about a hundred yards from B and D Troops' positions. The men, as they stood to, could hear the rumble and clatter of the German tanks as they approached the defences. Artillery fire, accurate as ever, was brought down and the attack petered out to the accompaniment of the screams and shouts of pain of those unfortunates caught in the open. One tank, however, appeared to be very persistent in its efforts and continued, as an eye witness put it, 'moving rather ominously towards D Troop'. The Troop Sergeant-Major, TSM H. F. G. Beavan, gallantly volunteered to stalk it and, leaving the safety of his shelter, grabbed a PIAT and moved stealthily out into the night across the twisted railway lines. Soon afterwards the welcome sound of two shots was heard by those waiting anxiously back at the factory. The Sergeant-Major recalls: 'It was impossible to

* Lt-Col Nicol Gray was awarded a bar to the Distinguished Service Order for his gallantry and leadership of Four Five during the Rhine crossings and the subsequent occupation of Wesel.

see whether direct hits were scored or not, but there was no doubt about the Hun's reaction. With a roar of its engine the vehicle shot off into the night and did not return'.

Even this brave episode did not seem to deter the Germans who started to shell B and D Troops again remorselessly, causing even more casualties. Infantry could be heard as well—this seemed to be the prelude to yet another attack. Capt Day decided to repeat his favourite tactic, which he had so successfully employed on the Montforterbeek, and called for artillery fire right in front of his own position. The response was so rapid and accurate that a badly shaken Capt Day barely had time to dive into his bunker. The attack subsided and Four Five remained unmolested for the remainder of the night.

The morning of 25 March was reasonably uneventful apart from the rather unwelcome attentions of one or two self-propelled guns, and a patrol of B Troop. This patrol was ordered to clear some houses on the far side of the railway as a prelude to an attack on the German barracks, one of the last bastions of resistance. The patrol commander, Lt E. Y. McDonald, with his section cleared the first buildings without difficulty, but further progress was checked by the Germans who were still occupying strong defences nearer their barracks. The patrol was withdrawn when it was learnt that this phase was to be undertaken by a larger force—an American parachute battalion. B and D Troops had a ringside view as they watched with relish the paratroopers storming into the assault, supported by British self-propelled guns.

Wesel was now in our hands and completely cleared. To assist in our build up, a bridge across the Rhine enabling heavy equipment and stores to be brought over, was almost finished. German losses to defend this strong town had been heavy, several hundred dead and 850 prisoners. Against this the Brigade had lost only nine killed, sixty-eight wounded and sixteen missing. Four Five's share of these, in the bitter struggle for the strategic factory, had been four killed and sixteen wounded, fantastically light casualties considering the magnitude of the operation and the almost numerical equality of the opposition. The heavy pre-bombardment undoubtedly reduced the likelihood of losses to ourselves, and it is, of course, arguable as to what level of destruction is acceptable for the achievement of the military aim, because in this case virtually every building in the town of Wesel was left a total ruin. Even so, the Brigade met with stiff and spirited resistance. 46 Commando had to overcome strong defences before it could secure the initial bridge-head, and it took another two days before the town was completely cleared. The success of the raid lay, however, in the daring Brigade plan and its brilliant and speedy execution by all participants who gained such convincing results. It was appropriate that one of the first visitors to Wesel on the night of 25 March, to offer his congratulations to the weary Commandos, was the General Officer Commanding the Commando Group, Major-General R. Sturges.

After two days' rest Four Five was not sorry to leave the gloomy surroundings of Wesel. American Engineer Battalions had moved in with bulldozers and trucks to fill in the craters and clear the roads of debris. There was now a thick cloud of dust, which as a result of this activity hung over the town and made the sight even more depressing. The unit departed thankfully on 27 March and continued the advance eastwards, in the wake of the fast-moving forward columns who were pursuing the fleeing Hun. Although the majority of the Commando was on foot a variety of methods were used to speed up progress. Bicycles, hand-carts, prams and, for the lucky few, one or two commandeered cars. The rate of movement for the unit was relatively slow, and it was a very unhappy sight, so soon after the splendid Rhine crossings, to see the other formations rush by—'even RAF ground crews passed us!'—and be left so far in the rear. However, Four Five was soon to re-assume its rightful place in the column and after two days the unit gave up its motley collection of vehicles, which were gladly exchanged for a convoy of Royal Army Service Corps trucks which sped the Commando north-eastwards through the battle-scarred countryside towards Munster. The next big objective in the line of advance was Osnabrück, so far the biggest town to be attacked by our forces, and this task was appropriately given to the 1st Commando Brigade on the night of 2 April. By now speed was essential and there were few opportunities for long drawn-out, deliberate plans. The Commando left its base, the small town of Greven ten miles north of Munster, early the next morning and for the next nineteen hours the convoy lurched and bumped over a series of rough roads. In fact the distance was only some sixty miles but interminable delays and hold-ups soon changed this into a never-to-be-forgotten trip. The winter cold had given way to spring rains, and the intermittent drizzle did little to ease the tedium or gloominess. It was a weary day, for the men were given neither hot food nor drink, and it was with some feeling of relief that the trucks eventually came to a halt at one o'clock in the morning, in a hamlet some four miles short of Osnabrück.

The reconnaissance party consisting of Lt-Col Blake, the Intelligence Officer, now Lt Geoffrey Boardley, the Troop Commanders plus about a dozen drivers and orderlies, had arrived during the previous evening and had already had a few brushes with the enemy as this particular sector had been by-passed by our forward troops. However, this party had had some successful hunting and had collected about thirty prisoners to show off to the remainder of the unit. Again there was little time for delay before the attack was to be launched. Brigadier Mills-Roberts had observed that the outskirts of the town were strongly held by snipers and to minimize their effect decided that the Brigade should enter Osnabrück before dawn. A more than welcome hot meal was quickly gulped down followed by confirmatory briefings. At three o'clock on the morning of 4 April, after only two hours respite, the now familiar 'snake' moved silently off into the black night. No. 3 Commando led, followed by Four Five, then No. 6 Commando and 46 Commando taking up the rear. This time the approach march was not so bad as the nightmare journey to Well. Most of the men were probably glad to stretch their legs after the cramped conditions of the draughty trucks and it was reported that 'As always when stimulated by active operations, fatigue seemed to vanish'. No. 3 Commando entered the town without meeting any serious opposition, but by the time Four Five reached its sector, the uncertain shadows of dawn were giving way to full light and the defenders were able to pick out their targets with greater accuracy and put up a positive resistance. Snipers, hidden behind windows and on rooftops, and 'suicide' machine gun posts were able to inflict quite a few casualties and Four Five had to conduct the only really serious fighting of the day. Although the action was over by ten-thirty that morning the unit incurred more casualties at the hands of the marksmen here than in the inferno of Wesel— four killed and twenty-nine wounded. C Troop lost two men during the assault on one position—Marines Keogh and Clarke —and A Troop lost Lt Trevor Wright who was covering his section during their advance. The section soon avenged their leader's death, for 'they went on to annihilate the enemy in the position which had held them up'.

These losses were, in part, compensated by the total of over 450 prisoners taken by the Brigade in those few hours, and such was the speed of the advance of the Commandos that the town had been virtually left intact by the fleeing civilian populace—the last train of refugees had departed at seven o'clock on the previous evening. No. 3 Commando were particularly fortunate in this respect and their Head-quarters was served with an excellent breakfast, which included champagne and strawberries, by the housekeeper of a mill owner. Other Troops of that Commando were lucky to find themselves in a brewery and doubtless soon set the wheels of production into motion. The particular celebrations of Four Five are not officially recorded!

Four Five was off to an early start on 6 April, at half-past four, this time by itself. It was intended that the Commando should undertake a one-unit operation which would entail its second river crossing, the Weser, and passing through a weak bridge-head, held by two companies of the Rifle Brigade. Beyond this bridge-head there was a village named Leese which was reputed to contain two companies of pioneers and was to be the eventual target. The Commando was under the direct command of the 11th Armoured Division—this was to be another 'instant' operation.

The men debussed at Stolzenau, on the western bank of the Weser, five hours after leaving Osnabrück, and almost immediately were being briefed and making preparations. Leese was a mile and a half from the far bank and, apart from a railway embankment near the village, the ground which separated the village from the river was completely flat. In broad daylight this was going to be an extremely hazardous operation necessitated by the urgent need to build a bridge across the Weser, the construction of which was being held up by continuous shellfire. By one-fifteen the hasty preliminaries were complete and nine assault boats started to ferry the Commando across the wide Weser, supported by our own artillery and machine gun fire. Even so the Germans shelled this small armada ceaselessly throughout the crossing, but fortunately did not inflict any casualties. Although the Commandos did not know it at the time this was going to be probably the most fiercely opposed of all the four major river crossings undertaken by the unit.

Once ashore on the eastern bank Four Five advanced southwards, in the lee of the steep sides of the river, led by D Troop under Capt H. G. Riley. The Germans were well dug-in some hundred yards back from the river bank and had an excellent 'killing ground'. This meant that it was impossible to carry out any flanking attacks which involved leaving the protection of the river banks, and much of the force was pinned down by an extremely accurate barrage of fire which rapidly, and 'nearly always through the eye', cut down anyone unwise enough to expose himself to the view of the enemy. Undeterred by this stiff opposition, D Troop pressed on doggedly and after some grim hand-to-hand fighting secured the trenches in their immediate area nearest the river. It was now that the real strength of the Germans at Leese became apparent. From some of the prisoners that the brave D

Troop had captured it was discovered that they were part of the 12th SS Training Battalion and, although they were youthful, they were still showing much of the tough fighting tradition and flair of their regiment. There was no trace of the expected Pioneer Companies! The Germans were obviously resorting in desperation to newly-recruited youths to defend their fatherland.

Four Five had now gained a foothold, albeit tenuous, on the far side of the Weser and A Troop was able to pass through D Troop's position and move farther along the river bank. Resistance was still fanatically stiff and the Troop Commander of A Troop, Capt Dudley Coventry, was credited with killing a German with one blow of his fist. The German, a young SS trainee, leapt out at the Troop Commander from behind a hedgerow. For a brief moment the two opponents confronted each other in sheer disbelief and then Capt Coventry felled the startled youth with a mighty punch on the jaw. The Chaplain, who was characteristically moving with the forward Troops, rushed up to render first aid but found the body was lifeless. While A Troop was engaged in its action, B Troop and a section of E tried to press on in an attempt to reach the more certain cover of the railway embankment. The Luftwaffe, so far conspicous by its absence, then decided to intervene in the action and FW 190s* and Stukas started to bomb the Engineers working feverishly on the bridge further upstream. It was an awesome sight watching the dead and wounded plummeting into the deep waters below, but it was not long before these aircraft turned their attention towards the troops crouched beside the river banks. They raked the area with cannon and machine gun fire before finally flying off, much to the relief of all those on the ground. By now it was nearly four o'clock and movement forward was painfully slow. The bulk of the Commando was still pinned down, and it was becoming increasingly difficult to even hold the present lines under the constant surveillance of the Germans, who were strategically placed across the open ground only a few yards away.

* Focke-Wulf.

5. *Harden's Bridge over the Montforterbeek. The windmill in the background was a German OP. (Heemkunde-Vereniging, Roerstreek, Netherlands)*

6. *The Bicycle Commandos, Warsash, 5 June, 1944. (Imperial War Museum)*

7. *The pursuit of the Germans to the Seine; Four Five enters Pont l'Evêque.*
24 August, 1944. (Imperial War Museum)

8. *On the look-out for snipers in Osnabruck, 4 April, 1945. (Imperial War*
Museum)

Reluctantly, Lt-Col Blake recalled those ranks of B and E Troops who had ventured on ahead and ordered that the Commando should dig in and consolidate its positions. The attack on Leese would have to be a Brigade task.

Four Five was not to remain unmolested for long and just before dark the Hun tried to come round on the right (southern) flank and put in an attack, but our artillery, which had remained close at hand throughout the battle, came to the rescue with an accurate concentration which dissuaded the enemy from making a further sortie for the time being. For the next eight hours, in the darkness, Four Five was imprisoned in a tight ring beside the river bank being constantly harassed by shellfire. After what seemed an endless time more unwelcome news was received when it was announced that there were insufficient assault boats for a reinforcement by the remainder of the Brigade, which was by now moving forward. It was after midnight and Four Five was ordered to return back to the bridge-head area, which was still being held by the Rifle Brigade. At three o'clock in the morning, whilst this reinforcement was taking place, the Germans decided to launch yet another of their spirited attacks. The forward section of B Troop, commanded by Lt E. Y. McDonald, bore the brunt of this attack on the right flank. The enemy rushed the trenches in an attempt to overthrow the Commandos who resolutely stood their ground. The brave young SS recruits were forced to withdraw, leaving many casualties behind them. Four Five was now firmly entrenched in the bridge-head and, with the assistance of No. 3 Commando, who arrived just before dawn on 7 April, was able to hold the position for the rest of a fairly quiet day. The Germans did not seem keen to repeat their attempts of the previous night.

The Brigade advance that night on Leese bore Brigadier Mills-Robert's traditional stamp of success. The remaining two Commandos were ferried across the Weser under cover of darkness, and at ten o'clock that night the entire Brigade set off in file with the object of entering Leese at dawn. To gain surprise the Brigade Commander chose a circuitous route approaching the village from the south-east. Compared with the approach to Osnabrück the march was long and tedious. Firstly down the river bank, where Four Five had fought with with such determination the day before, and then across railway embankments, marshes ditches, hedges and other sundry obstacles. The end was an anti-climax to these men, keyed up as they were for a fierce struggle against the SS. The bulk of the enemy had fled some two hours before rather than face the Commandos, and the village was now virtually deserted. No. 3 Commando, however, had better luck and shortly afterwards were detached to capture a large factory a mile or so north of the village. The objective was seized only after a fierce battle and it was then discovered what the defenders were guarding so diligently—the site for the manufacture of V2 rockets. This was a really valuable haul as some of the weapons were found, with fully armed warheads, on railway wagons awaiting despatch to their launching sites. The entire area was well concealed as all the roofs of the buildings were planted with trees, and inside, as well as all the equipment, No. 3 Commando found the entire staff of scientists.

There was not now much time to reflect on past successes as the Germans were being pursued with vigour on all sectors. The types of operations involved were ideal for specially trained Commando troops. Within two days of the capture of Leese the dash and tenacity of the Brigade was again put to the test on its third river crossing in as many weeks. This time it was to be the River Aller, on the night of 10 April.

The eventual aim of the assault crossing was to capture the road bridge which ran over the Aller at Essel intact, as intelligence sources had confirmed that this had not yet been destroyed by the Germans in the course of their retreat. To achieve this the Brigade conceived another bold plan; the Commando were to infiltrate, in file, across a railway bridge a mile north of the town and then attack the road bridge, before it was blown, from the enemy's side. The Germans, realizing that a crossing was imminent, blew up the railway bridge, but this hardly acted as a deterrent as most of the charges failed to explode and only the first span, on our side of the river, was damaged. No. 3 Commando was in the lead and had little difficulty in negotiating this span as it ran across flat meadowland and was resting on the ground for some of the distance. The leading Troop of No. 3 Commando, 6 Troop, were the first to meet with any opposition—from a guard post on the eastern end of the bridge, although it put down a heavy shield of machine gun fire the Commandos were in no mood to be held up and quickly overran it, despite casualties. The initial bridge-head was now secure.

Thanks to the efficient work of the advance guard Four Five, the second unit to cross, had an uneventful passage across the bridge and by half-past three in the morning was digging-in at its consolidation area—a small knoll about half a mile from the river. This knoll was one of the few outstanding features in an otherwise thickly wooded area where visibility rarely exceeded fifty yards. It was going to be a difficult area to defend. All was quiet on Four Five's front during the morning, but nearby the sound of heavy firing could be heard as No. 3 Commando and Brigade Headquarters defended their locations against the Germans who were crawling up through the thick undergrowth. At times it seemed unreal, waiting in these vast woods hearing the noises of battle all around and trying to gauge the progress of one's friends but without being able to see anything but dense foliage. At half-past eleven a tremendous cheer was heard from the south. This was No. 6 Commando who, with bayonets fixed doubled 400 yards through the trees in the most frightening manner, unceremoniously clearing all opposition from their path. Unfortunately, much of their dash was of little avail as their target was the road bridge, which, when they got there they found had already been blown by the Germans.

This strong determination did not seem to weaken the Germans, who still offered a stiff resistance. The reason soon became apparent; the foe was in far greater strength than had first been expected and the majority of them, identified from dead and prisoners, came from the seasoned 2nd Marines

Fusilier Battalion—the counterparts of Four Five and 46 Commando—who had been drafted into the area from the ports in the north to counter the advance of the Allies. The Germans were systematically trying to surround the 1st Commando Brigade and force it back from the bridge-head. Consequently the Brigade Commander decided to tighten the perimeter and withdraw Four Five back from its knoll to a position between No. 3 Commando and 46 Commando. As always seemed to happen, the unit was attacked just as it was settling in. C and D Troops bore the brunt of this fighting along with two companies of the King's Shropshire Light Infantry who were reinforcing this sector. The attack was beaten off, and in the ensuing calm B Troop was detached to guard the railway bridge, so that the Royal Engineers building another bridge nearby did not suffer a fate similar to that of their comrades near Leese.

After a quiet night it was considered that the time was ripe for the Brigade to widen its front again and strike out to re-occupy its old positions. Four Five's task was a particularly difficult one as the Germans had now infiltrated into the trenches on the knoll and would be hard to dislodge. In addition the German Marines had been reinforced in a desperate attempt to stop the Brigade breaking out and were on full alert for any such moves. C Troop were leading the advance and as they cautiously moved into one clearing, which had been the home of the Commando only the day before, they were caught in a horrifyingly accurate burst of fire at close range which killed five, including the Troop Commander, Capt M. C. Brockbank, and wounded six more. The advance of Four Five was planned to coincide with a similar move forward by 46 Commando but as both units had met with heavier opposition than expected the two Commanding Officers decided to pull back a short distance. Whilst this move was in progress the wounded of C Troop were still lying in a perilous condition in the clearing. Major Beadle, as ever an inspiration to those around him, went back into the enemy dominated territory and although in grave danger and under the most close surveillance he and his patrol managed to evacuate the casualties back to our own lines.

Major Beadle went back into the same area on the following morning to find out what the Hun was doing and this time he came back with the welcome news that the Commando's old positions had now been left vacant, and that the enemy had pulled back to the nearby railway line and was preparing positions with which to continue the fierce fighting. Lt-Col T. M. Gray then commanded both the Royal Marine Commando units on an advance back through the woods clearing either side of a road. This was done without opposition. Four Five re-occupied its former positions surrounding the knoll and 46 Commando went on to capture the village of Hademsdorf which lay about a mile further on beyond the woods. German resistance in this village was again strong and the forward Troop of 46 Commando, Y Troops suffered heavy casualties. A bitter fight ensued and as the other Troops darted in to the rescue, the defences finally crumbled and the Germans fled. One German officer was so ashamed at the action of his countrymen that he was seen to shoot himself as the troops ran from the battlefield.

The ring of encircling troops had now been smashed and the 1st Commando Brigade had been saved from the setback caused by a numerically superior and remarkably resolute enemy. The Aller was bridged successfully and Four Five was able to remain in its now peaceful position for four days, waiting for further orders to advance.

As the tanks and heavy equipment of the 11th Armoured Division streamed over the newly completed bridge the Brigade was ordered to move out of the woods and act as mobile flank protection force for the advance of 8 Corps to the River Elbe. By 19 April another sixty miles had been covered to reach the picturesque old town of Luneburg, largely saved from the destruction so evident up until now. For a week the Commando was put into comfortable billets and one of the first sights that the men noticed was streets full of German soldiers, certainly more than the occupying force. The reason for this was because the town was full of hospitals and convalescent homes, but such was the discipline of our troops that there were no incidents.

During this week Lt-Col Nicol Gray rejoined Four Five having recovered from his wounds. To celebrate their Colonel's return, the officers decided to give a party and thought it most appropriate that the services of the German town band should be provided to mark this joyful occasion. An official of the British Military Government in Luneburg, upon hearing this request, seemed insulted that such a triviality should ever reach his ears. 'The town band! Don't you fellows realize that there's a war on!' With the persistence for which it was now becoming renowned Four Five eventually got its own way. Later that evening the musicians were duly picked up by an armed escort, as instructions at the time dictated, but the players were obviously under the mistaken impression that if their efforts failed to please they would meet with instant death. It was reported that they played with considerable fervour long into the night!

All those present at this dinner were most anxious to learn what had befallen Lt-Col Gray during the past three weeks and they soon appreciated that his adventures had been equally as tense as those experienced by the unit. After he had been evacuated from Wesel the hard-pressed doctors along the line all took one look at his badly shattered arm and pronounced that amputation was the only answer. The Colonel then employed several ruses to get himself back to England, where less abrupt treatment was given which enabled him to return to Germany and re-enter the fray within a remarkably short space of time.

The week in Luneburg passed all too quickly. Cinemas, Service variety shows and football soon filled in the spare hours, although there was a constant reminder that war was not far away. A steady stream of guns, bridging equipment, tanks and stores was rolling past towards the front—the River Elbe—which was a mere ten miles away.

The crossing of the Elbe, on the night of 28 April, was to be the fourth and last classic operation of this nature undertaken by the Brigade. Similar to the Rhine crossings, this operation was to be preceded by a heavy artillery bombardment and then the Brigade was to cross the Elbe by boat and enter the town of Lauenburg from the rear. Again the task was going to be a formidable one as the river was difficult to approach on the western side—there was a wide open plain—and on the enemy side thickly wooded slopes rose sharply to a height of between fifty and a hundred feet just near the crossing point. Undaunted, the Commandos waited patiently in the assembly area. The artillery of 8 Corps pounded the enemy on the far bank for two hours, but there seemed to be little response. It was a miserable night and for a long time most thoughts were preoccupied with keeping dry as the shells whined overhead. At last, at two o'clock in the morning, No. 6 Commando reported that they had stormed the far bank and that the bridge-head was secure. Four Five then crossed in Buffaloes and just before dawn found itself entering the town with 46 Commando. B Troop was in the lead and opposition at this time could only be described as 'slight'. Within minutes the Troop was in possession of its objective, the Furstengarten, and such was the complete surprise that the Commandos achieved that the Troop Sergeant-Major, TSM B. M. Aylett, caught one German soldier, blissfully unaware of what was happening, creeping across the courtyard of a house in order to wake the cook up in time for breakfast!

Over 300 frightened and startled Germans were dragged out of buildings and cellars that morning—a considerable haul for Four Five. The only interference which came later that day, was from German aircraft which were employing their favourite tactic of trying to prevent the Royal Engineers from building their bridge to replace the ones previously destroyed. The speed with which these Engineers worked is worthy of the highest praise as in many cases they were able to bridge some of the most difficult of rivers, sometimes in a matter of hours, up in the front line and often under direct fire from an ever-vigilant enemy. To counter the German aircraft fire at

Lauenburg, Four Five manned a battery of light flak guns kindly left intact by the enemy in his haste to withdraw. These were quickly brought into action against their own aircraft and Capt H. A. Evans, RA, the Commando's Forward Observation Officer, achieved perhaps the greatest success of the day when he recorded a direct hit on a FW 190 which sent it crashing to the ground. Capt Evans was from the 1st Mountain Regiment RA who had been supporting the Commando on many of the operations during the advance across Germany, and their skill and fast reaction on many occasions were outstanding and prevented several German attacks from getting under way.

Four Five was now only some fifty miles away from its final objective, the Baltic, and the end of its heroic journey was almost in sight. The day after the Elbe crossing the Commando advanced another five miles to the town of Lutau, which had just been captured from an SS Battalion. However, orders were received to keep moving for a further three miles to the village of Wangelau, still in enemy hands. The attack was preceded by a short artillery bombardment and then E and A Troops headed the Commando in the charge into the village. It was most fitting that E Troop should be in the lead in this, the last action of the war for Four Five, as the Troop Commander, Major Ian Beadle, had been in virtually every engagement with the Commando since it had landed near Ouistreham. He had survived some of the fiercest of battles, and shrugged off injury, to remain throughout in command of the Troop in which his name was a byword—a proud achievement indeed. Wangelau was not taken without cost, although the battle conducted by the two leading Troops was a brief one. Sgt W. A. Wilson of E Troop was tragically killed whilst his section was overcoming a machine gun post. Such is the fate of war, especially so near to the end and to final victory.

As Four Five pressed on towards the Baltic with all speed the signs of the defeat of Germany were manifest. The roads were crowded with long lines of haggard, dispirited and battle-weary German soldiers who had been harried across Europe for the past eleven months. The civilians, who were in a similar state, just stood and stared with soulless expressions at the advancing columns, wondering what their fate would be and whether things were to be as bad as many of their misguided leaders had made out. The sight of a defeated nation was not a pleasant one and much of the sense of elation which one might have expected amongst the victors was dispelled by this scene of complete apathy and bewilderment. At last, on 2 May, the Brigade reached its objective on the Baltic, the small port of Neustadt. Here, for the first time, Four Five came face to face with the real atrocities and the evils of war which the Commando had helped to suppress. On the whole the conduct on the battlefield, between similar armies, had been based on a fairly straightforward code and there had been little evidence of acrimony between the opposing forces. But now, well behind the original front line, could be seen some of the sinister brutalities perpetuated in a cause actively supported by only a fanatical few. The first sight to greet the Commandos was a concentration camp which was perhaps rather mildly described as being '. . . grossly over-crowded; its inmates were unfed and badly treated'. In the harbour even greater horrors could be seen, the notorious 'hell ships' which contained many hundreds of political prisoners virtually abandoned and left to a cruel fate. Pathetically, most of the citizens of Neustadt seemed to be indifferent to the plight of their fellow human beings and when questioned either professed complete ignorance of just regarded these unfortunates as another species.

Only a week was spent in this unhappy town before the unit moved to its occupation area on VE Day, 8 May, 1945. This was Kries Eutin, a portion of Schleswig-Holstein about the size of a large English county. Based in the town of Eutin, Four Five immediately set about restoring order out of chaos, and was to prove its versatility in an exceptionally short space of time. Only days beforehand these gallant men had been fighting the toughest of wars and now, almost overnight, they were to act as peacemakers in an attempt to get civilian life back to normal. Lt-Col Gray established himself as Military Governor of the region and immediately embarked upon an ambitious programme of bringing back normal life to this shattered community. Being an army of occupation is never a pleasant task, but Four Five adapted to its new and strange role with traditional good humour, and as a result very little resentment was apparent during this period, which bears excellent testimony for these outstanding men. By the first evening the Commanding Officer had issued his outline plan:

1 The round-up of Nazi officials still at large, and appointing a town council from screened officials.

2 Restoring public services—electricity, gas and railways.

3 Setting up of emergency food centres.

4 Collecting food produce from outlying farm districts.

5 Temporary rehabilitation of thousands of displaced persons.

6 Restarting the local police force.

7 Organizing the reception of ten thousand German prisoners who were to be bivouacked in the Eutin Forest.

8 Re-housing of thousands of German family refugees who had concentrated in the area.

9 Re-opening of churches for undirected public worship.

The speed with which this challenging and all-embracing plan was carried out can be judged by the fact that objective 1 was implemented by the second day and objectives 2, 3 and 4 were functioning by 13 May. This says much for the ability and drive of Lt-Col Gray in reorganizing this area after such a short space of time, especially as everything previously had come to a complete standstill. To accomplish this rapid transition, Col Gray recalled that he summoned a conference so that administration of the various domains could be delegated to local officials. A *Landraat* was appointed as county administrator and the senior German Army and Naval officers took over their respective commands, although one of these gentlemen saw fit to open the conference by holding up a Nazi flag!

The police, who were to be the backbone in restoring law and order, presented their own peculiar problem as they had been largely taken over by pro-Hitler elements. These were replaced by members of the old school who soon proved their worth and won much public admiration, especially for the way in which they marshalled the hundreds of people queueing outside municipal offices with requests. Some of these requests showed how many restrictions the populace had been subjected to under the Nazi régime—permission to move house, get married and even light fires.

This new role was not without its problems and called for great flexibility on the part of the Marines. How to deal with 300 prisoners a day; how to provide shelter for thousands of refugees, how to get the farming cycle re-started so that the spring crops could be sown in time. E Troop had their moment of excitement when a group of railway enthusiasts was able to take the first post-war train steaming out of the station.

The region, like many others in Germany at the time, had large numbers of East Europeans who had been drafted in as forced labour. These individuals were overjoyed to have been liberated and in many cases the exuberance being shown was starting to cause trouble. The different races were quickly formed into communities and head men appointed, responsible for keeping discipline and other matters. The head of the Polish nationals started off by taking a very strict line and was advocating death by shooting for some wrongdoers—until persuaded by the Commanding Officer that perhaps he was going too far. The German prisoners were also catered for satisfactorily. Despite being a defeated army they behaved well and were put under command of their own officers. One of the most prized possessions of the Commando at the time was a couple of chargers from the German national stud. These were duly used by Col Gray on some of his official visits and on two occasions, with the Adjutant, Capt Neaves, he went out to see the German troops camped in the forest. The soldiers were reported to have received their visitors, mounted on these magnificent beasts, with every respect. 'Saluting was marked, as was the expert adaptation at living out, with the maximum of comfort afforded by nature'. True praise indeed for a former adversary.

Four Five's days in this 'beautiful district' were drawing to a close. Not all the plans had reached complete fruition, but at least a very solid and worthwhile foundation had been laid upon which future peace and prosperity could be built, largely due to the efforts and foresightedness of Lt-Col Gray, who had proved himself both a warrior and a peacemaker. Perhaps one of the greatest tributes to Four Five came from the inhabitants of Eutin themselves. On the Commando's last Sunday in the region, in early June, a ceremonial Church Parade was held in Eutin Cathedral. Religion had paid an important part in this rehabilitation programme, but because of the previous persecution many of the local population had been reluctant to attend church services. Col Gray held long discussions with the German bishop who was told that all would be welcome at this and other services. The Unit's own Chaplain, the Rev Haw, conducted the service and the salute at the march past was taken by Major-General R. G. Sturges, who was relinquishing his command of the Commando Group. There could have been no better farewell as the whole town turned out to watch Four Five, immaculate in their khaki battledress and green berets, as they were inspected and subsequently marched through the streets to the cathedral. It was a moving service conducted against a background of wreaths, in memory of the countless German fallen from the district. One witness commented '. . . judging by the emotion shown by these people they were relieved to be free'. Four Five could have rendered no greater service and this was a truly memorable end to their stay in North-West Europe, which finished on 9 June.

One can never hope, or wish, to condone a war of this magnitude, for the scars it leaves on both sides take many years to heal. However, the Second World War, for ourselves, proved to the the birthplace of a new military formation—the Commando unit. Within the space of less than two years the officers and men of Four Five had already established a proud and formidable tradition, and the men of the 1st Commando Brigade, in which the unit was so privileged to serve, were described by Hilary St George Saunders as being '. . . among the most expert soldiers the war has produced'. There were, of course, moments of failure and disappointment, but Four Five was able to overcome these with its spirit and determination—essential ingredients of the 'Commando Men'. Many tactics, which were to become indelible for operations and training in the years to come, were fashioned during this campaign: the daring night infiltration raids deep into enemy lines; the rapid deployment to seize key positions; the bringing down of close fire support on forward areas; the opposed crossing of large water obstacles. None of these goals could ever have been achieved without the most vital ingredient, the individual marine. It was his bravery, dash, fitness and perseverance which brought success to all these plans.

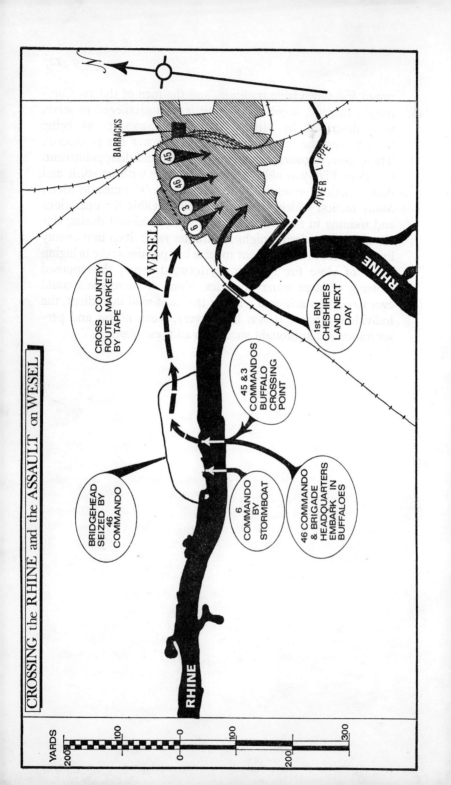

CROSSING the RHINE and the ASSAULT on WESEL

YARDS

200
100
0
100
200
300

RHINE

BRIDGEHEAD SEIZED BY 46 COMMANDO

CROSS COUNTRY ROUTE MARKED BY TAPE

6 COMMANDO BY STORMBOAT

45 & 3 COMMANDOS BUFFALO CROSSING POINT

46 COMMANDO & BRIGADE HEADQUARTERS EMBARK IN BUFFALOES

WESEL

45 46 3 6

BARRACKS

RIVER LIPPE

RHINE

RHINE

1st BN CHESHIRES LAND NEXT DAY

CHAPTER 7

Hong Kong.
Peace Keeping Duties
in the Far East

An uneasy calm had now been restored to Europe but there was still conflict in the Far East. The rumours that had been rife in Four Five at the beginning of 1945 began to take an air of reality again and the unit started to train for operations in Burma, where 3 Commando Brigade was still actively engaged. The dropping of atomic bombs on Hiroshima and Nagasaki brought an abrupt end to Japanese participation in the war and to Four Five's hopes of moving to that particular area. Once again the move was postponed.

The sudden lull in activity created an uncertain vacuum for a unit whose diet for the past two years had been one of combat punctuated by intensive training for specific operations. Since returning from Germany in June, Four Five had enjoyed the luxury of billets in Bexhill and Eastbourne, but in November, 1945, these had to be forsaken for the damp of a somewhat indifferent hutted camp near Horsham. Many of the Hostilities Only ranks, who up until how had formed the bulk of the Commando and rendered such sterling service, began to trickle away during this month and readjust themselves to the comparative safety of civilian life. Lt-Col Gray, however, was not going to enjoy the fruits of peacetime for some years to come. Soon after the war he was appointed Inspector General of the Palestine Police, and in 1948, after the British evacuation of Palestine, was selected as Commissioner of Police in Malaya.

These were both important posts in countries whose political development at the time attracted world wide interest and called for large scale British military intervention. It is also interesting to note that Four Five subsequently served in both campaigns and Col Nicol Gray was able to watch with pride and special interest the unit in which he had been so instrumental in moulding.

Capt John Day, lately of B Troop, also had an interesting appointment soon after the war. With a small team of British Commandos, which included TSM H. F. G. Beavan (D Troop), he went out to Algiers to help train our French counterparts, the *Fusiliers Marins*, in Commando methods. Here he was able to pass on the lessons learnt in the cooler and wetter surrounds of Achnacarry and in the more arduous conditions of the battlefields of North-West Europe. Even in the desert wastes there were some familiar faces as some of the French instructors had landed on D-Day with No. 10 (Inter-Allied) Commando, and then served alongside No. 1 Special Service Brigade in Normandy.

Major Ian De'Ath, who had been Second-in-Command for a period in 1944 and had by now been promoted to lieutenant-colonel, returned to command Four Five in July, 1945. This was a critical time for the unit as the numbers in the Commando had been drastically depleted by many departures and the Troops had to be largely reformed and retrained in preparation for whatever might lie ahead. The ranks soon swelled as Four Five was augmented by personnel from 46 Commando, which had been disbanded recently, and from 2 Commando Brigade (40 and 43 Commandos) which was also in the process of being dispersed, having fought outstandingly in the Italian and Dalmatian Coast Campaigns. Four Five had thus escaped the post-war 'axe' and was combining the skills and experience of many Royal Marine Commando units. The prospects for the future became even brighter later on in the year when it was learnt that the Commando was going to be on active service again—this time it was the Far East—in Hong Kong where 3 Commando Brigade had moved in September from Burma.

Special training continued apace throughout December under the watchful eye of Lt-Col R. D. Houghton who had formerly been Second-in-Command of 40 Commando and had been taken prisoner during the fierce, but ill-fated Dieppe raid of 1942. Command changed again in January, 1946, when Lt-Col Tim Gray arrived at Horsham to take over the reins. As the brother of Col Nicol Gray he was no stranger to the unit and to the ex-46 Commando ranks who had fought alongside Four Five during the many heroic battles of the previous year.

The long awaited trip to the Far East started from Chatham on 31 January in the aircraft carrier HMS *Rajah*. The process of trooping in those seemingly far off days appears slow compared with the present methods of speedy global reinforcement and the voyage, which now takes a day by air, lasted for over five weeks. One witness recalled . . . 'The voyage out was a novelty to many of us, but we soon got used to the ship's routine. Naturally we suffered from seasickness whilst crossing the Bay. Most of us managed to get pretty bronzed on the way out through continual sunbathing. Others got somewhat burnt and retired to the sick-bay for treatment! However, we managed to keep pretty fit playing lots of deck-hockey, tug o'war and other peculiar games which the PTI thought up for us.'

One of the first ports of call on this 'cruise' was Port Said on 11 February. The Commando had a foretaste of things to come here as Anglo-Egyptian relations were beginning to become strained and, as this visit coincided with King Farouk's birthday, it was thought that the political situation might be further aggravated by a large number of British troops. Shore leave was therefore cancelled and the Commandos had to content themselves with watching the persuasive sales talk of the bum-boat boys hawking their wares.

At Singapore, on 1 March, HMS *Rajah* was more welcome and one of the first visitors on board was the Supreme Allied Commander, South-East Asia Command, Admiral Lord Louis Mountbatten who was directly concerned with the massive expansion of the Royal Marine Commandos during his term of office as Chief of Combined Operations. The unit was formed up in a half circle on the flight deck of HMS *Rajah* to hear the Supremo's address and he started off by welcoming Four Five to the theatre and wished the men the best of luck in their new job. At one point Lord Mountbatten's words were drowned by an aircraft which seemed intent on 'buzzing' the carrier. The persistent and tactless pilot repeated this manoeuvre twice before he eventually disappeared. The Supremo waited in impatient silence whilst these interruptions were in progress and then when the offending aircraft became a mere speck on the horizon he observed after the pilot: 'Helpful B . . . !' and turned to finish speaking to his attentive audience.

The 'Rajah Draft', as it was to be known for many months ahead, eventually arrived at Kowloon on the morning of 7 March. In addition to the unit there were many other reinforcements on board which included the Brigade Engineer and Signals Troops. The first impressions of this magnificent harbour were mixed ones of wonderment at the beautiful surrounds and bitterness towards the reminder that the Japanese had left of their presence, for dominating this otherwise colourful setting was an enormously tall and austere monument built on to the steep wooded hillsides erected as a memorial to the Japanese dead. To the British, however, this construction served as an ever-present perpetuation of Japanese atrocities in the Far East and was soon dismantled. The task of our troops out there at the time was to erase the unhappy memories of the past few years and restore the civil life of the Colony. One of the Commando's first tasks was to organize a formal parade for the Commander-in-Chief, Hong Kong, Vice Admiral Sir Cecil Harcourt, who was shortly to hand over to Sir Mark Young, when the civil government returned to office. Sir Cecil was able to tell Four Five what difficult problems it was likely to encounter in the future, but perhaps as a background it is best to summarize in his own words what the Brigade had done up to this date. This letter was written to the Commandant General shortly before his retirement.

My dear Hunton,

I hear with regret from Fellowes* that you are retiring at the end of next month. Before you lay down your office I should very much like to take the opportunity of telling you how well the Royal Marine Commandos have done here in Hong Kong. They, together with No. 5 Commando, which is drawn from all regiments of the Army, have very much enhanced the reputation of the British Services in this part of the world, both by their smart appearance, and also by their good sense and good humour, which has been apparent in the excellent way in which they have handled the many problems with which they have been faced during the rehabilitation of the Colony. Ever since we arrived the maintenace of law and order in the Colony, both in Victoria and Kowloon, and more particularly in the New Territories, has been done chiefly by the men of the three Services, as the police force has had to be reorganized and still has only taken over a small part of the police work. In the New Territories this work has been done entirely by the Commandos and they have handled their many problems most excellently. I have been very proud of them and I can assure you that you can also be proud of them.

With every good wish.

Yours sincerely, Cecil Harcourt.

With this reputation to live up to Four Five soon set about its duties with customary vigour. The unit had already had experience of establishing a military government in Schleswig-Holstein less than a year previously but now only a few of the original wartime ranks were left. Many lessons had to be re-learnt, but with traditional adaptability the unit soon mastered the intricacies of its new tasks. In addition to police work these duties included civil documentation and administration, the distribution of food, medical treatment and patrolling and visiting the many scattered villages. The main problems in the Colony in these months were the general shortage of food and

* The Commander 3 Commando Brigade, Brigadier H. D. Fellowes.

materials, which resulted in a flourishing black market for the profiteers, and an influx of Chinese at the rate of nearly a hundred thousand a month—in early 1946. With these huge numbers flocking across the border a major task was to prevent smuggling, otherwise the economy of the Colony would have been completely undermined. The import of foodstuffs was strictly controlled and other imports such as opium, guns, Chinese liquor and tobacco, which usually found their way into the vice rings, were banned altogether. Exports were also restricted, again food headed this list and other items included motor accessories and rubber which were some of the most important industrial supplies. The task of regulating this flow fell almost entirely on our forces and it was indeed a formidable problem. The inhabitants of this region are renowned for their prowess and ingenuity in smuggling and their choice of illicit trade routes for the various commodities was a wide one— either the rugged mountainous border area with China or the hundreds of miles of coastline provided by the mass of offshore islands.

There was little time for the unit to settle down as the rehabilitation work had to be tackled immediately and after an initial fortnight spent in a temporary home—the Diocesian Boys School in Kowloon—Four Five moved up to take over its new operational responsibilities in the New Territories from 44 Commando. The Commando's Troops were dispersed over a wide area and occupied varying billets which ranged from spacious European and Chinese houses to more cramped quarters in police stations and Nissen huts. This diversification of tasks and independent siting of Troops was to start a trend that was to become a common feature of many post-war campaigns. In addition to building up a corporate Troop spirit, it provided a splendid opportunity for the junior leaders—both officers and NCOs—to exercise their command and initiative away from the more overshadowing environment of the larger organization.

One of the biggest responsibilities was the manning of the islands and two Troops were allocated to manning these outposts. One Troop was split up between Cheung Chau, Ping

Chau and Silvermine Bay—on the eastern end of Lan Tao, whilst the other Troop was responsible for the remainder of Lan Tao with detachments at Tai O and Tung Chung. B Troop (Capt John Sturgis) was the first to be based on Lan Tao and the first to be at Cheung Chau was A Troop (Capt Ian Gourlay). The Troop Headquarters, of A Troop, was sited in a large residence above the town of Cheung Chau which was huddled round a small harbour packed with junks, and with the pungent odour of fish clinging oppressively to the whole neighbourhood. Life here was typical of the island locations and TSM 'Wiggy' Bennett, veteran of Montforterbeek and numerous other actions, now found himself acting in the more peaceful role of registrar of births and deaths for the district, in addition to his normal administrative work in the Troop office. The Royal Army Medical Corps team under Capt John Tulloch found that they had a very large parish and cemented good relationships by carrying out countless medical patrols and treating a seemingly endless procession of Chinese patients who had been denied much-needed attention under the previous régime. On Cheung Chau cholera was one of the major threats to health and Cpl O'Hara, RAMC, found that the market place was one of the best places to do business, and judging by the number of 'clients' who were queueing up for their injections he was keen competition for the adjoining traders.

The first major incident which occurred on Cheung Chau, proving that the Commandos have to be diplomats in addition to carrying out their other exacting duties, was on 25 March, 1946, only four days after A Troop had arrived. Capt Gourlay still remembers the day vividly and recalls that he was up in his Troop Headquarters at the time when a tremendous 'woomph' from the direction of the harbour, suddenly shattered the morning calm. Realizing that there was something seriously amiss he waited for the inevitable news. This was not long in arriving and sure enough, a few minutes later, the sound of running footsteps could be discerned approaching up the hill. There was a frenzied knock on the door and it opened, filling the room with the bright spring sunshine. 'Sir, the boat's blown up,' gasped the messenger. Capt Gourlay grabbed his green beret and ran down the hill. The boat was the first of three brand new Motor Fishing Vessels which had just been brought into service by the Brigade for anti-smuggling patrols around the island and was, of course, the pride of the Cheung Chau detachment.

A thick pall of smoke was now rising over the town and the commotion soon attracted a large crowd. The Troop Commander had to force his way through the masses of Chinese, all chattering excitedly, who crammed the jetty and when he eventually reached the muddy water's edge he found to his horror that the MFV was ablaze from stem to stern. A fireboat was summoned from Hong Kong but this took nearly two hours to arrive so that the audience had good value for their money. When the fireboat eventually appeared the MFV was burning at the water level, and any chances of salvage were soon dismissed. With great gusto the firemen directed every hose they could bring to bear on the stricken vessel and sent it straight to the bottom! With nothing now left of his maritime force Capt Gourlay had to send a signal to Commando Headquarters— it was brief and informative: 'From A Troop to 45 Commando. MFV 777 gutted and sunk 1030 today.' The sheer disbelief with which this message was received can well be imagined and even the subsequent inquiry could not uncover all the facts behind this remarkable episode, which still remains an inscrutable 'mystery of the Orient'

Apparently, a local gold merchant had previously asked Capt Gourlay to take the body of his dead son over to the mainland in the MFV because the ferry captain had refused as this might bring bad luck to his boat. The military commander, always willing to foster good relationships with the local populace, gave his permission. The coxswain of the MFV had no objections—he was a Christian—but it seemed that one or two members of the crew did not share his thoughts and were not too happy about having the corpse on board. In the event the body was taken across but on the fateful morning some of the crew were conveniently not on board, although one who was there ended up in hospital as the result of his injuries, so that it could not have been a general plot. The conclusions of the inquiry could only be largely guesswork and so it was assumed that a deliberate petrol explosion by 'a person or persons unknown' was started in order to appease the spirits and avoid, perhaps, sailing in an unlucky ship. In any case, in their own way, the Chinese proved the superstition! 'Joss', local parlance for luck, certainly played its part.

Returning from the islands let us now visit the Troops on the mainland which were spread out between Castle Peak (Commando Headquarters) and Kowloon, where C Troop occupied Tungslo House on the northern outskirts of the city. The other two Troop locations, in March, were Yuen Long, which housed E Troop (Capt Bob Loudoun) and Tsun Wan where F Troop (Capt Cedric Walker) and D Troop (Capt Johnny Buscall) resided.

C Troop (Capt Derek Pounds) had a large and active area of responsibility and soon won fame within the Colony for their skill in discovering opium dens in the unfriendly maze of backstreets. Fortunately many of their adventures are still preserved through their Troop Diary and their busy life must have been typical of that experienced by the other Troops in that area at the time. Immediately on arrival, on 21 March, C Troop sent out one section to man a permanent road block and another was detached to the nearby police station to carry out mobile patrols throughout the district. Such was the intensity of these law and order duties that most of the Troop could not enjoy a full night's sleep until 13 April because of the heavy watchkeeping rota which had to be maintained round the clock. The first arrests were made by the Troop on the 22nd, when the Commandos discovered two trucks trying to leave the city with illegal exports—flour and barbed wire. The Troop's efforts were so keen that the police had to issue a plea two days later saying that the jail was already full and that they could not accommodate, or feed, any more prisoners! This vigilance soon resulted in a marked decrease in the amount of attempted smuggling, but Capt Pounds was not over-optimistic and knowing his 'enemy' guessed that 'they must be using alternative means'. One of the most frequent nocturnal activities in this district was the raiding of opium dens. At four o'clock on the morning of 26 March, Capt Pounds, Lt Terence O'Connell and Marine Miller carried out two raids in the darkness and on one of them dashed into one dimly lit parlour to find a group of startled addicts huddled round earthenware crucibles. Their long session was brought to an abrupt close and fourteen pipes and half a pound of raw opium were confiscated. These efforts were well rewarded and the owner of the den was fined 200 dollars and deported. By day the programme for those not on guard or patrol was equally well filled. Weapon training, physical training, firing on the thirty metres range and educational classes occupied the mornings, whilst Troop games ensured that the afternoons were not idle either. 'Troop morale is high and everyone very keen' often appeared in the diary and other records proving, as ever, that the Marine is usually happiest under these, the most strenuous and tiring of conditions, and as a result can enhance both the spirit of his Troop and the reputation of his unit.

Entertainment at these locations was always of a very rudimentary nature and many an evening was whiled away with the inevitable game of cards and a glass of beer nearby. One innovation, which broke the peace at Tungslo House for a short time, was a twin turntable gramophone with two speakers which was loaned by F Troop. The generous selection of records meant that the machine was played in the Marines' two rooms almost incessantly sending the noise reverberating round the building. The music soon attracted a large crowd of Chinese who were content to gather round outside and listen for hours on end—such were the numbers that Capt Pounds thought of levying a charge. One mother even blamed this decadent western pastime for the loss of her daughter and came to the guarded front gate to demand her return! A thorough search of the area, however, revealed that the unfortunate girl was not there. The next morning the Troop Commander attempted to arouse his braves at half-past six to the strains of the regimental march *A Life on the Ocean Wave*, this was met with 'derisive catcalls' and probably prompted him to give a lecture on musical appreciation later that day! The offending machine was returned to its owners the following morning and the relief and silence was appreciated by everyone inside the compound.

In spite of these diversions the operational patrolling continued in earnest and on many occasions danger was not far away for the men of Four Five. Some of the C Troop patrols had to break up a gang fight in Nathan Street (Kowloon), on the night of 30 March, between two rival groups who were hacking it out with butchers cleavers, of all weapons, and Marine Ross narrowly escaped injury, on 11 April, when a dissident shot at him whilst he was searching four men for contraband. Less fortunate was the driver of the Troop's 15 cwt truck who was hit by a horseshoe earlier that day whilst he was driving out with a reserve section. This section was going to support a section under Sgt Ridge that had to disperse a hostile mob who had collected to support members of the Chinese Nationalist Army. C Troop's burst of activity was not to last for long as in mid-April the Troops rotated to give them a change of scenery. Doubtless TSM Bennett was glad to hand over his duties of registrar on Cheung Chau to the much respected TSM 'Jimmy' Baines of C Troop, especially as a death had recently occurred and had to be recorded within the first half-hour.

One of Four Five's visitors at the end of April was Brigadier B. W. Leicester, the Commander, Commando Group, who was amongst the foremost Commando leaders during the war and had commanded 4 Commando Brigade during their bitterly contested, but successful, raid on Walcheren late in 1944. He was a much liked and admired figure and always made a special point of talking to nearly all individuals during his tours of inspection. Brigadier Leicester made no exception to his custom whilst at Cheung Chau—'Galley and latrines and everything possible was whitewashed, the place looked quite smart when it was ready'—where he spoke to each man and dined later that evening in the town with the local elders before spending the remainder of the night on this island.

The Administrative Officer throughout this period was still the redoubtable Capt Bob Armstrong, and amongst his charges he remembers that he had a group of about 120 Japanese prisoners of war under a Capt Muri. These prisoners were allocated to the Troop locations and acted as general working parties until they were eventually shipped back to their homeland. The Japanese propaganda machine had indoctrinated its armies into believing that the British commandos shot all prisoners in the same manner as we were alleged to have shot the Germans. Capt Muri and his men started off their days with Four Five in fear and trepidation but were soon more than surpised at their just treatment. The Commando Brigade also had the less pleasant task of guarding suspected Japanese war criminals in Stanley Gaol. On one occasion, in later months, when Four Five was carrying out this duty the inmates gave a display of traditional wrestling. The eager audience expected a spirited show from what were, after all, the recognized masters of this sport. The subsequent disappointment of the spectators after a somewhat restrained performance was later attributed to the fact that some of the participants were under sentence of death and probably had other preoccupations!

For a brief while let us turn our thoughts from the tropical heat of Hong Kong to the cold damp mists of the Scottish Highlands. Until now the rugged Commando training, the passing of which had resulted in the award of the coveted green beret, had taken place at Achnacarry. At the end of May, 1946, this establishment closed and with it an era of British Commando history. To mark this closure, the *Globe and Laurel* included these few apt paragraphs:*

'Achnacarry has seen 30,000 men in six years—men of all Services and all Regiments, from all over Europe and from a dozen Allied nations.

* June, 1946.

All Royal Marine Commandos, and most of their reinforce-ments, passed through. Some came as hastily-collected individuals, not quite sure of themselves; they marched over the hills, doubled along the twisting roads, shivered in wet bivouacs, swarmed in the trees, climbed the cliffs, struggled through the mud, fell in the lochs, and seldom ceased cursing. Some enjoyed their stay—many did not; all left with added confidence in themselves and their comrades, born of mutual exertion and discomfort. Their experience stood them in good stead on battle-fields throughout the world, and what they did made history.'

Four Five, which had trained as a unit at Achnacarry in November, 1943, justifiably felt indebted to the invaluable contribution this establishment made to its early development and the bond that this training created was to weld the Com-mando together and form a spirit that was to be handed down through the succeeding years. Although the veterans may have mourned Achnacarry's passing and insisted that 'it would never be the same again', the same tests and high traditions were transferred to the Commando Training Unit Royal Marines in North Wales. In September, 1947, this unit, now renamed the Commando School, moved to Bickleigh, just outside Plymouth on the edge of Dartmoor, before settling at another West Country base, Lympstone, near Exeter. Here all recruits and other attached personnel undergo their strenuous Commando Courses before they join active units or the Commando Brigade.

Returning from the process which turns the ordinary man into a Commando let us rejoin Four Five in Hong Kong during the summer months of 1946. In June, after three months of peacekeeping duties in Victoria, Kowloon and the Islands, we find that the unit is on the move again—to the New Territories to man the frontier with China, a frontier that had to be guarded with great vigilance and where any incident, however trivial, could flare up into a major issue. The border here is some twenty miles long and largely runs along the line of the Sam Chun River which meanders through rugged hills and mountains

rising to 2,000 feet. At that time this region required intensive patrolling from the Troop and section outposts to check
smuggling across some of the more inaccessible and inhospitable
points. The problem was made more difficult because away
from the river line the actual border, in some places, was hard
to identify, but in others recognition was simplified by E
Troop (Capt Bob Loudoun) whose progress along the frontier
could easily be traced by generous daubings of yellow paint—
the Troop colour!

There were four main Troop locations on the border, Cha
Tau Kok, Ta Ku Ling, Lo Wu and Lok Ma Chau, all of which
were to be remembered by the occupants for many years to
come and at the time were household names for those serving in
the Commandos, although with the passing of the years their
fame within the Corps has diminished somewhat. Some of these
locations had small frontier guard posts away from the main
position and every month or so, as on the islands, the Troops
would rotate so as to prevent staleness and to give them a
change of scenery. There were only four Rifle Troops in the
Commando at this stage as B Troop had been disbanded—
the effect of the immediate post-war cuts were now being
severely felt in the front line and the size of drafts taking the
'time expired' and Hostilities Only ranks back to 'Blighty'
were usually much larger than those coming out with the badly
needed reinforcements.

Cha Tau Kok was situated near the village bearing the
same name and always presented plenty of problems as the
international border ran down the main street. The sleeping
accommodation here was under canvas—an uncomfortable
experience during the wet season—and the remainder of the
camp was described as looking 'rather like a shanty town with
scattered corrugated iron offices and stores deployed on a small
hill overlooking the Fan Ling–Cha Tau Kok road.' A section
outpost, a lonely but responsible command, at Ma Hang was
attached to this base. The location at Ta Ku Ling, the next
along the line, was a more permanent structure, but its outpost
was perhaps the most famous of them all, the Chick's Bridge

detachment—one section strong and living in Nissen huts beside this important border customs post. Chick's Bridge was on the main exit and entrance point to the Colony by road and the old bridge, which had been blown during the war, was now replaced by a Bailey bridge, which had been built over the Sam Chun River. The other locations occupied by the Commando were at Lo Wu, the border customs station on the main Hong Kong—Canton railway, and at Lok Ma Chau on the eastern end of the border.

Life at these border outposts was full and interesting. Day and night patrols had to be on the constant alert for trains of coolies trying to smuggle flour, rice and sugar into China at remote crossing places. Smuggling was organized on an enormous scale and trains of thirty or forty coolies trekking across the lonely hillsides were not uncommon. The capture of these could lead to the confiscation of as much as two and a half tons of flour. Most of the coolies carried sticks which were greatly treasued by their owners. The reason for this close attachment soon became apparent as the centre of many of these sticks were hollowed out to enable opium to be transported; their confiscation usually led to heated, but thankfully incomprehensible, abuse from their owners.

Throughout the summer the green berets of the Commando patrolling the border were augmented by the blue ones belonging to the Marines' counterparts of the detachments on the cruisers HMS *Blake* and HMS *Bermuda*.* The detachments were split up into small parties and the groups were able to participate in welfare and anti-smuggling patrols, thus enabling them to enjoy a break from maritime duties and giving them an insight into the tactical and training problems ashore.

The year which Four Five spent in Hong Kong was an important one for the internal affairs of China, where the Communist and Nationalist armies were struggling for supremacy. Hong Kong fell within the area of military operations

* Nowadays all Royal Marines are Commando trained as part of their initial training and wear the green beret whether serving afloat or ashore.

controlled by Chiang Kai Shek, and Chinese troops remained in the Colony until May, 1946. Even after that date the Chinese Nationalist Army was allowed access through the New Territories and on occasions took advantage of this free passage for the smuggling of prohibited goods. On 12 July, Sgt Stuart and his section of C Troop were alertly patrolling near a ford on the frontier. In the valley below they spotted a group of CNA, about forty strong, preparing to cross into mainland China. Before they could do so, however, they were stopped by the Marines who discovered that they were carrying no less than 160,000 cigarettes! The Troop Commander, Capt Derek Pounds, and a strong detachment from the remainder of the Troop rushed from Ta Ku Ling and diverted the shamefaced soldiers, including two colonels, to the Chick's Bridge customs post where they were soon divested of their booty. Another incident with the CNA occurred about two weeks previously when E Troop, near their post at Lo Wu, captured a quantity of flour from a coolie train. The sacks were then loaded on to a native sampan in preparation for the trip down river to Troop Headquarters. The reaction of the CNA was pretty speedy and within a short space of time they set up a machine-gun post and when the boat sailed they forced the native crew, at gunpoint, on to the far bank of the river and re-confiscated the cargo! Further intervention by our troops would have doubtless sparked off an international incident and although there were some red faces at Commando Headquarters, in Fan Ling, political expediency dictated that the matter had to rest there. There are many similar instances when Four Five was involved in brushes with the CNA and Capt Bob Loudoun remembers one episode when a CNA soldier leapt on to a sampan loaded with contraband brandishing a primed hand-grenade. The soldier then threatened the startled onlookers of E Troop with instant extermination, but on this occasion the CNA were willingly left to their own devices. There were enough problems just controlling smuggling without adding to the confusion by engaging in hostilities with the troops across the border.

Surprisingly enough there were hidden advantages of being

based so near to China, especially at Lo Wu. One famous figure in the area at this time was 'Knocker' White who had for many years served in various messes throughout the Colony and had then transferred to the Chinese Customs Service and lived on the 'other side' of the border. In those days it was considered to be more profitable to employ British customs officials because of their traditional honesty—at least some of the dues reached the Government's coffers! Mr White was renowned for his Chinese chow parties to which he frequently invited our troops. It was not uncommon to see members of the Lo Wu detachment creeping back along the railway lines to their location after enjoying a good night out in Mainland China!

In addition to the CNA and coolie trains, Four Five also had to contend with extremes of weather. Typhoons and torrential rain were not uncommon in the summer months in Hong Kong and one of the fiercest typhoons on record struck on 18 July, 1946, whilst Four Five was up on the border. A typhoon warning was received on the afternoon of Wednesday, 17 July and as a result of this all windows were battened down, tents struck and vehicles ordered off the roads. The 18th was a day of apprehension. High winds had already started during the previous evening but they did not reach their maximum intensity, 128 m.p.h., until later on the 18th. The Troops could do little else except sit huddled in their locations waiting for the storm to pass. C Troop, however, were not all able to remain under shelter as that evening an urgent message came in from the detachment at Lin Ma Hang asking for a hot meal as the winds had extinguished their cooking facilities. The Royal Army Service Corps cook at Ta Ku Ling, Pte Kennedy, duly prepared the food and a patrol staggered through the gale in the darkness with the hot refreshment. After the winds the men had to endure another day indoors because of torrential rains—an aftermath of the typhoon. This twenty-four-hour period was a miserable one for those unfortunates at Chick's Bridge as their Nissen huts leaked badly and they could get little rest. Unlike their comrades at Lin Ma Hang, the Chick's Bridge detachment managed to keep their stove going so were able to cook some hot food to counteract the dampness. Thankfully the rains abated on the morning of the 20th and the pale sunlight illuminated the damp and glistening terrain as the Troops re-emerged. Fortunately there were no casualties within the unit, although the high winds had shattered many of the windows and sent glass flying about inside the buildings, and all that remained to do was to pick up the debris lying around the locations and repair the broken telephone lines.

During these exacting months in Hong Kong the Commando Brigade had been commanded by Brigadier H. D. Fellowes and in October he handed over to Brigadier J. H. G. Wills. Within Four Five too there had been some officer changes. Major Peter Matters, who had come out in HMS *Rajah* as Second-in-Command was promoted lieutenant-colonel and took over 44 Commando. Capt Freddie Clifford, formerly of Headquarters Troop, succeeded Major Matters. Capt Ian Gourlay had become Adjutant soon after the MFV incident (although he assures the author that the two events were purely coincidental!), and the former Adjutant, Capt 'Tosh' Jewers, succeeded him in A Troop.

It was whilst A Troop were responsible for the detachment at Chick's Bridge, later on in the year, that a major incident occurred which had world wide repercussions at the time. At about two o'clock on the afternoon of Thursday, 3 December the detachment was carrying out its normal duties of checking individuals and any stores that they might be taking across the frontier. For several days feeling had been running high, on the Chinese side of the border, over alleged rough methods used by our troops to discover and search for illegal goods. It should be stressed, however, that the Chinese were employing every ruse possible to smuggle food and cigarettes and in addition there was an exceptionally high proportion of 'pregnant' ladies crossing the frontier. On the afternoon in question, the 3rd, one particular youth seemed to take exception to being searched and having goods confiscated. This youth was then released and crossed into the village of Man Kam To on the Chinese side of the border where he doubtless gave his friends a very colourful version of what had just happened to him, thus adding fuel to an already smouldering fire.

Within minutes an angry crowd had gathered at the Chinese end of the bridge shouting abuse and blocking the roadway. The detachment commander bravely went forward in an attempt to resolve the situation, but after being threatened at revolver point appreciated that discretion was preferable to valour and returned to the Customs post. The detachment was then ordered to 'stand to'. One of the emplacements, on the right hand side of the road, contained a Vickers machine gun kept primarily as a show of force and whilst this was being cocked in readiness by a marine one round was accidently discharged. A hush fell over the Chinese crowd and soon afterwards a Chinese official rushed across the bridge and said that a bystander, Mr Cheung Tim-Cheong, had been killed by the bullet. The Troop Commander, Capt Jewers, was immediately informed and arrived soon afterwards with reinforcements from Ta Ku Ling. Chinese troops could be seen to be manning positions on their side of the border and for a time open conflict seemed to be threatened. When he heard the news Lt-Col Tim Gray accompanied by his Intelligence Officer, Lt Tony Mould, rushed up to Chick's Bridge to see how matters were progressing. On arrival the Commanding Officer astutely realized that the first thing he had to do was to calm the heated atmosphere down. Ignoring the excited gesticulations of the Chinese he nonchalantly sat down in full view of all the onlookers and commenced to play a quiet game of dice! This action seemed to have the desired effect and although Four Five had to maintain a lot of men on the alert throughout the night there were no further incidents.

Naturally there were strong protests from the Chinese on the diplomatic side and a translation from an official report from the Pao On District* claimed that '. . . Commando soldiers on guard were chasing after them (two boys) over the border and seized them. . . . A party of six or seven fully armed English soldiers was then sent out and fired at the bystanders. . . .'

* The district of the Chinese side of Chick's Bridge.

6

This incident was soon labelled 'The Hong Kong Border Affair' in many newspaper reports and received prominent coverage. The Chinese and British versions varied considerably and one account even suggested that the officer in charge was so enraged at the behaviour of the youths that he went back and ordered his men to fire on the watching crowd. The officer was then alleged to have attempted to take over the body 'but the Chinese would not allow the removal'. Nevertheless, the British military authorities accepted the Chinese statement that the one round fired was the cause of death, and the Hong Kong Government paid handsome compensation to the relatives of the unfortunate Cheung Tim-Cheong, much of which was believed to have been spent on an imposing memorial erected near the scene of the incident.

The official communique, issued a week later, ended as follows: 'Although British officers were not allowed to view the body the British military authorities have accepted the statement that the one round fired was the cause of death of a bystander and have expressed deep regret at this unfortunate accident.

It should be mentioned that, owing to recent reports of armed Chinese bandits, believed to be operating in Chinese territory near Cha Tau Kok and elsewhere, instructions had to be given that a high state of alertness of men and weapons should be adopted on the border.

Finally incontrovertible proof exists that only one round was fired and that entirely accidentally.'

Officially the matter was now closed but the whole affair remained another of those mysteries of the Orient and to this day no one in Four Five really knows whether or not it was one of our bullets that killed Cheung Tim-Cheong.

This dramatic incident was, perhaps, a fitting finale to the Commando's six-month tour of duty on the frontier which ended, as planned, on 11 December, 1946. The unit's first Christmas of twenty-one consecutive ones to be spent abroad was to be celebrated in a manner which was soon to become tradition. Four Five's new home, back in the Colony, was in Murray Barracks, Victoria, and the festivities started on Christmas Eve with a concert party produced by the Instructor Officer, Instructor Lt Ian Roach RN, which provided excellent entertainment and relaxation for the troops who had recently returned. Christmas Day started with the senior NCOs serving tea (plus rum?) to those lucky marines in bed, and then at lunch time roles were reversed as the officers took over guard duties (inspected by the youngest marine) and served lunch in the Main Galley. In the afternoon, those still with the ability, engaged in a fierce round of Inter-Troop and Inter-Mess sports. As some marines put it, away from war-time restrictions, 'The best Christmas we've had in years'.

The year 1947 saw important changes in the structure of the Commando Brigade in Hong Kong and it is, perhaps, worth examining these in some detail as they were to form the basis for the Commando organization in the years to come. After the war the necessary run-down of the British forces left a vacuum in some spheres of our defence structure and there was considerable re-shaping of existing formations. Although there was no question of disbanding the relatively recently formed Commandos there was considerable discussion as to whether the Army or the Navy should assume overall responsibility for this commitment. At the end of the war the Army Commandos had been run down considerably as their ranks had either been demobilized or returned to their parent regiments. On the other hand it will be remembered that the war had seen a considerable upheaval in the '*per terram*' functions of the Royal Marines and with the passing of the Division and the Mobile Naval Base Defence Organizations the Commandos were the only major land formations left in the Corps. Therefore, in late 1946, the Royal Marines were given the sole privilege and responsibility of furnishing Britain's Commandos as being 'one for which they are fully qualified by their long tradition and history'. As a result of these decisions the 3rd Commando Brigade was reorganized on a purely Royal Marine basis of three units.

In early 1946 the Brigade, in Hong Kong, had consisted of Nos. 1 and 5 Army Commandos and 42 and 44 Royal Marine Commandos. Due to the shortage of officers and administrative personnel Nos. 1 and 5 Commandos amalgamated to form No. 1/5 Commando. Four Five then came out to join the Brigade to bring the strength up to four units again. No. 1/5 Commando, the last Army Commando in existence, was finally, disbanded at the end of February, 1947, and on 16 March, 44 Commando, Royal Marines, changed its nomenclature to 40 Commando, Royal Marines. Thus the 3rd Commando Brigade now consisted of 40, 42 and 45 Commandos, and the history of each Special Service (Commando) Brigade was continued. 40 Commando represented 2 Commando Brigade which fought in Sicily, the Dalmatian Coast and Italy; 42 Commando represented 3 Commando Brigade which had fought in Burma; Four Five, of course, represented 1 Commando Brigade. In 1948, when the Royal Marines Forces Volunteer Reserve* was created in the United Kingdom, the formation was called 4 (Reserve) Commando Brigade, thus continuing the name of the Brigade that had fought so gallantly in North-West Europe and in particular at Walcheren.

This 'change of ownership' meant that important changes were about to take place within the Medical Sections of the Brigade. At the end of January, 1946, having completed Commando training, the first of the Naval doctors and Sick Berth ratings sailed for Hong Kong in the *Ranchi* to relieve the Royal Army Medical Corps personnel. This changeover took place in March, and in Four Five, in particular, it will be remembered that the Royal Army Medical Corps had given both loyal and valiant service to the Commando during the war and had been awarded a posthumous Victoria Cross and two Military Crosses for their bravery. In subsequent years (up to 1970) the unit's Royal Navy Medical Section was to keep up this proud record and was to be awarded one George Medal two Mentions in Despatches and four Commendations for Brave Conduct—an excellent record for such a small

* Later Royal Marines Reserve.

department. The first Royal Navy Medical Officer in the unit was Surg-Lt Ken Stewart.

After only a short stay in Victoria Four Five moved to the rambling Gun Club Hill Barracks in Kowloon, on 20 January, 1947, where the unit was responsible for guarding buildings and installations of key strategic importance. In general the intensity of military operations in the Colony was decreasing. The solid groundwork of previous months was now paying dividends and the resultant stability had allowed the civilian authorities to resume their pre-war strengths and duties. This respite allowed the Commando to get in some much needed retraining and Support Troop and others soon found themselves up near the frontier again, this time in a different capacity, on the Lo Wu field-firing and exercise areas.

This lull in active operations gave the Commando the chance to prove its prowess in another sphere, that of football. In these last few months in the Colony the unit team distinguished itself by reaching the semi-final of the Hong Kong Senior Challenge Shield competition. The opponents were the Colony's premier side, Sing Tao, and in the struggle to reach the final Four Five was the only white team left in the final stages of the competition and thus had a very heavy burden to carry. The first match between these two rival teams ended in a draw, after extra time, and the game had to be replayed four days later on Wednesday, 26 February, 1947. The venue for this replay was the Causeway Bay ground (near Happy Valley Race Course) and like the first game proved to be so popular that it was witnessed by a record crowd for the Colony of over 10,000 spectators. The packed stadium (the gates had to be locked before the kick-off on both occasions) created a typical English cup tie atmosphere for this tough encounter.

Four Five lost this replay by the odd goal of three, but the team's display was so determined that it brought glowing reports from the local press the following day. 'The teams, old rivals as chief representatives of Chinese and Services football in the Colony, gave the crowd plenty of thrills and each piece of individual brilliance met with immediate applause from a crowd which had decided to make it a red letter day in local football. Even the most biased Sing Tao supporter will admit that the Chinese side were decidedly lucky to win for there were periods in the game when the Commandos were far superior. The sides were meeting for the second time within a week for they shared four goals on Saturday and a replay was necessitated despite extra time on that occasion. There were long queues outside all entrances when the game began and the crowd extended right to the edge of the touchlines.' Sing Tao took the lead after fourteen minutes but shortly before half time Marine Reynolds, the Commando's inside left, equalized with a spectacular header. The winner, for Sing Tao, came midway through the second half and although Four Five doggedly stormed their opponents' goal (four corners were forced in the closing minutes) they were unable to get the equalizer for their loyal and by now hoarse, supporters. The team for these historic matches was: Cpl Taylor; Sgt Burnage, RAMC, Cpl Dear; Marine Humble, Lt Partington, Cpl Nicholson; Sgt Neale, Marine Didcott, Marine Goldthorpe, Marine Reynolds, Marine Broadhead.

Sing Tao went on to win the competition and in addition to winning the shield this victorious team also secured an exhibition tour of the United Kingdom. It is interesting to speculate the additional sporting fame that the Commando night have achieved if the scores had been reversed. Much of success of this team was due to the thorough and painstaking coaching of Sgt L. J. Causley who later recalls in appreciation of the Commando's great efforts to promote football in the Colony the team was treated to a 'slap up' Chinese dinner by the sponsor of Sing Tao, a Mr Hoe, who was one of the millionaire brothers who owned 'Tiger Balm', the popular Chinese cure for almost everything.

The quietening down of events in Hong Kong lead to much speculation as to where Four Five's next move was going to be. Rumour was rife and only the super-optimistic put the United Kingdom at the top of their lists! Eventually the news came through that the Brigade was going to move to Malta in May.

This was not received with undue sorrow as the frontier posts had been handed back to the police and the routine guard duties, although important, were never a pleasure. In addition Four Five was severely overstretched in its commitments as the numbers going home were not being compensated by outcoming drafts and the strength of the unit had been reduced to three fighting Troops in addition to Support—A, X and Z (B and Y had been disbanded out of the five Troops now renamed A, B, X, Y and Z).

On 11 April, 1947, the Brigade received a very signal honour. On that date the Brigade Commander, Brigadier Wills, received a silver salver from the Governor of Hong Kong, Sir Mark Young, bearing the following inscription. 'Presented by the Government of Hong Kong to 3 Commando Brigade, Royal Marines: In grateful recognition of the valuable services rendered to the Colony during the period, September, 1945–April, 1947.' Sir Mark Young, in making the presentation, spoke the following words: 'In my opinion the work of the Brigade will live long in the memory of the Colony and your departure will be an irreplaceable loss. . . . I congratulate every officer, Non-Commissioned Officer and marine.' This honour was an exceptional one, as rarely before had a military formation received such a presentation from the Government of a country or a colony in honour of its services.

As Four Five sailed from Hong Kong in HMT *Strathnaver* on 17 May, 1947, the unit could feel justly proud that its first tour outside Europe had received such glowing recognition and praise and that the transition from war to peacetime soldiering had been accomplished with the undertaking of such purposeful task.

The restoration of Civil Government to Hong Kong was not the end of the Colony's immediate post-war problems. In 1949 world attention turned to the Far East when the civil war in China flared up with renewed intensity, resulting in victory for the Communists. The armies of the People's Republic began to appear on the border and incidents in local territorial waters increased alarmingly. Fears for both internal and external stability in the Colony rose and massive moves were launched to bring the strength of the British garrison up to some 40,000 troops. The Commando Brigade, deployed in the Mediterranean at the time, was alerted in early June and on 13 August, 1949, the main bodies of the three units disembarked at Kowloon, from HMT *Georgic*, to the strains of the pipe band of the 1st Battalion the Argyll and Sutherland Highlanders.* BBC 'Radio Newsreel' was there to record the event and this is part of their account:

'It was not just the arrival of another troopship when the liner *Georgic* drew alongside Kowloon Wharf this morning, for the arrival of a troopship is almost a weekly event in Hong Kong these days. But there was something special about the *Georgic*. For one thing she was the largest liner to visit the Colony since the war, but more important she had aboard the green-bereted and suntanned men of 40, 42 and 45 Royal Marine Commandos, together with the Headquarters' staff of the 3rd Royal Marine Commando Brigade. . . .

The pipes of the Argyll and Sutherland Highlanders, kilts swinging as they marched, played the ship in, while the Commandos' own band on the upper deck of the *Georgic* answered with the Royal Marines' march *A Life on the*

* Although the Royal Marines and the Argyll and Sutherland Highlanders have fought alongside each other in such varied parts of the world as South Africa, the Crimea and India an official association was not brought about until after the Second World War. During these years the 8th Battalion, the Argyll and Sutherland Highlanders, was attached to the Royal Marine Brigade in Devon when that brigade was amongst formations responsible for the defence of the country after the fall of Dunkirk. More famous ties with the Argylls, however, were made in January, 1942, when survivors of the Royal Marines detachments of HM Ships *Prince of Wales* and *Repulse* formed a composite battalion with the remnants of the 2nd Battalion the Argyll and Sutherland Highlanders for the defence of Singapore. As the 'Royals' hailed from the Plymouth Division the battalion was nick-named the 'Plymouth Argylls'.

Ocean Wave. The *Georgic* had made a fast and comfortable trip out from Malta picking up Four Five at Suez. *Georgic* had been fitted out chiefly for the emigrant run to Australia and was only on loan to the British Government for one trooping voyage. Everyone had been in cabins, instead of the usual troop decks.'

The rapid strengthening of the garrison meant that accommodation in Hong Kong was at a premium and for the first fortnight Four Five lived in buildings owned by the Hong Kong Jockey Club at Happy Valley Race Course. In four days, miracles which normally take 'a little longer' happened at the Commando's new home. The Quartermaster's requisitioning eye was soon cast far and wide and within hardly any time at all accommodation plans were being drawn up; a field kitchen complete with roof erected by the Royal Engineers; 400 double-tiered bunks were hammered together with the aid of the Hong Kong Chinese Training Unit, and load after load of various other stores rumbled in. This hasty move in was necessitated by the fact that the Argylls were prevented from moving out of Stanley Barracks as their new location had been washed out by torrential rainfall. Four Five had to stay in tented accommodation for three weeks, but this state of affairs admirably suited the punters in the Commando who were able to lean against the railings studying form as they watched the horses being put through their early morning paces! These somewhat idyllic conditions were sacrificed in early September for the more spacious empire of Stanley Barracks, but even here some improvisation was necessary as the typhoons which had struck earlier came again and shattered many of the windows and caused widespread flooding.

However, all these administrative discomforts had to be put in the background as preparations for the operational role went ahead. Externally the Chinese Communist armies were sweeping forward and there was a distinct possibility that they would keep progressing in to the Colony. Inside Hong Kong the Brigade was to take over responsibility for internal security in

Kowloon and Victoria on 1 September, and this only left a fortnight to get ready. There was also the additional task of supplying amphibious or conventional support should an invasion take place. Thus the month of September was a hectic one for Four Five which had to carry out ambitious and comprehensive exercises throughout the Colony in preparation for these contingencies. Concurrent with this, shades of the last tour, there was an operational commitment of manning a Troop patrol base on the island of Lan Tao. Those who had not been here before were soon to get to know the island well as it formed the centre for much of the unit's assault and landing craft training.

The first threat of disturbances came on the Double Tenth (10 October). This festival passed quietly in 1949, although it acted as a good prelude to violence. It seems hardly co-incidental that this day was set aside for a Colony-wide internal security exercise witnessed by the General Officer Commanding-in-Chief Far East Land Forces, Lieutenant-General Sir John Harding, who was to see a lot of the Commandos in the years ahead. The Double Tenth is celebrated annually as a Nationalist Government ceremony and in 1949 local Communist elements were not keen to encourage the festivities, thus allowing the day to pass fairly peacefully. Apart from the patrols on Lan Tao, the only other major call for operational duty for Four Five came on 30 January, 1950, when elements were standing by in Victoria during rioting by strikers of the Hong Kong Tramworkers Union. The incidents fortunately did not become more widespread and everything returned back to normal the following day.

The early months of 1950 passed peacefully and the expected troubles never came so that Four Five was able to take full advantage of Hong Kong's varied facilities and attractions. However, a peacetime situation was no place for Commandos in the troubled post-war years of the Far East. There was a job to be done elsewhere.

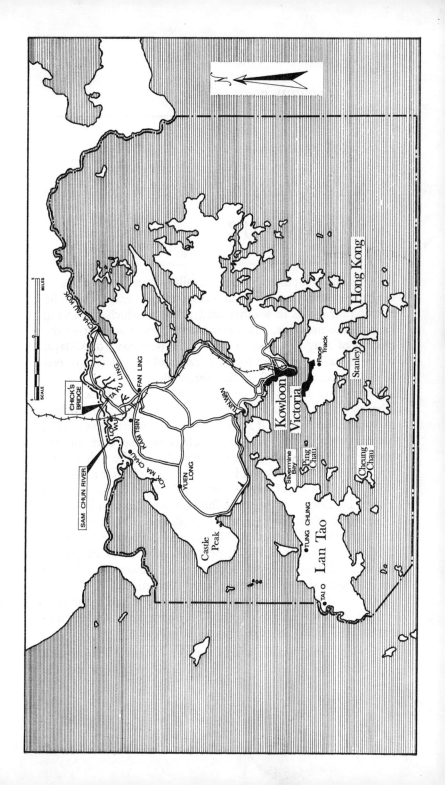

CHAPTER 8

Malaya.
The Jungle Emergency
1950—1952

The comparative calm prevailing over Hong Kong at the time meant that the 3rd Commando Brigade could be released for duties in another land; Malaya, which was facing its own internal crisis. The Brigade left Hong Kong during the months of May and June to sail for the west coast of Malaya, where it was to be based for two years and to achieve a record of success equalled by few other formations.

Four Five, under the command of Lt-Col Charles Ries, who had been the Commando's first ever commanding officer in 1943, disembarked off Penang from the *Empire Trooper* on a heavy, sultry day in early June. There was no time for any respite and immediately after disembarkation the unit moved up to Sungei (River) Patani in the State of Kedah for a month's training in the art of jungle warfare. Based in a tented camp, Four Five discarded the more formal khaki uniform in favour of the lightweight olive green, designed especially for operating in these tropical jungles. Perhaps the most popular feature of this new uniform was the 'floppy hat', which was frequently adorned with humourous slogans by its various owners and could also be shaped into many weird contortions.

The training programme was a rigorous one and at the time a participant was able to record vividly how the unit adapted to the skills of living in its new surroundings.

'Here (in Sungei Patani), in the swamp, belukar and rubber, the Marines, now garbed in green, learned the

finer points of Boy Scouting from the cadre of Non-Commissioned Officers who had the fortune to attend the Jungle
School in Johore. They learned how to prepare their meals
without making smoke, how to follow barely visible trails
through undergrowth of tangled thorn and bramble, how to
move noiselessly through the trees. With the assistance of the
wily Ibans, they learned to construct *bashas* of attap to
keep out the torrential rainfall, learned to do without smoking
and, most valuable of all, learned the secret of perpetual
silence. It is strange how discordant a human voice sounds,
even amid the jangle and clatter of birds and insects along
the jungle fringes, and how the smell of tobacco hangs in the
still, lifeless air long after the smokers have finished. Long
hours were spent lying cramped in damp, leech-ridden,
mosquito-haunted swamps. Melting into the vegetation at a
given signal became an art. We came to know the uses and
skills of those strange, dark little men with long hair and
distorted ears, the Ibans. They, in turn, grew to know us
and our peculiarities.'

In addition to training, the Commando was given long and
detailed briefings on the Emergency, how it arose, and possible
future trends. The background to this situation has already
been admirably described by Col A. J. Crockett, who was
serving in 42 Commando at the time, in his book *Green
Beret, Red Star**, and his account is reprinted below in full:

'During the war against the Japanese the struggle was
continued on behalf of the Allies by a number of underground
organizations. One of the most powerful and better organized
of these was the Malaya People's Anti-Japanese Army
(MPAJA). This was composed largely of Chinese, and much
of the success which it achieved was due to the administrative
ability, the skill, energy and closely knit fabric of the Malayan
Communist Party. The latter had been outlawed in the
Federated Malay States before the war but, on the entry of

* Eyre and Spottiswood. Copyright, Christy and Moore Ltd.

the Japanese, a truce was patched up between it and the Government and it was loyally supported by the British throughout the occupation.

The support thus given took the form of the introduction of certain British officers into the country and the setting up of precarious communications with them and with others who had remained behind after the surrender. These brave and devoted men did all they could do to organize the resistance and to weld the large and scattered underground groups into a cohesive whole, carrying out a concerted plan. Later, numbers of weapons and ammunition, largely small arms, and wireless sets were supplied to these forces, mostly in air drops.

Once the war was over and our forces and regular government had returned to Malaya and Singapore, the need for the MPAJA came to an end, and steps were taken to disband it honourably and to collect the arms and ammunition still in its possession. This, however was exactly what the Communist party least wanted, for like its fellows in other countries, its intention was to seize control of the government for its own ends. So the hard core of the MPAJA went underground and took with it or hid any of the weapons and ammunition it could lay hands on.

The main and immediate object of the party was to secure a large enough section of territory, preferably containing at least one sizeable town, and there set up its own government. Once this was achieved the party could then lay claim to a certain amount of popular support and could reasonably hope to widen both this and the area under its domination. The successes of Communism in other parts of the world, particularly in French Indo-China, might then be counted upon to draw more waverers to the cause.

With their efficient undergound organization, their propaganda and their experience gained in the war against Japan, the Communists met with a certain amount of success in the early stages. Out of the remanants of the MPAJA was forged the Malayan Races Liberation Army

(MRLA), a uniformed force, organized into loose, military formations. Its tactics were based on fear, intimidation, terrorization, murder, arson, abduction, threats and blackmail.

Its efforts were aimed at winning over the Asiatic population of Malaya, principally the Chinese, by propaganda and persuasion and by disrupting the machinery of government, the public services and the large European-owned concerns, such as tin mines and rubber estates.

The Communist organization was split into three more or less independent bodies, which were yet closely interrelated; the armed and uniformed bandits, who were formed in military units and were the MRLA proper; The Min Yuen, who were its plain clothes workers, living in the towns and villages; and the Lie Ton Ten, or Killer Squads, who corresponded very much to the strong arm thugs of gangsterdom, charged with the "rubbing out" of elements undesirable to the Communists and with minor operations such as the slashing of rubber trees, cutting of telephone wires and so on.

To keep their organization going and, in fact, to exist at all, the Communists needed money, food, arms and ammunition. The last two they already had in fair amounts at the end of the war and had added to them since by raids on police posts and from what they had been able to salvage from the dead bodies of armed men they had killed. For money and food they relied largely on what they could extort from the local population. This extortion they had worked out to a fine art. The Chinese have a saying in which they liken themselves to bamboo. When the storm comes, they say, the straight, tall tree stands proudly in his resistance to it and when he can resist no longer he breaks. But the humble bamboo bends his head, bows before the storm—and survives.

The Communists made every small community responsible for supplying a quota of money from its weekly pay packets, and each and every family was bound to provide food under arrangements laid down for them. This system of supply was greatly facilitated by the presence of a vast population of "squatters", nearly all of whom were Chinese. The Chinese, or their forebears, had entered Malaya, most of them illegally, and had settled down quite arbitrarily on a patch of ground where they had built a shack and then proceeded to cultivate the ground around it. Some of these people lived on the very fringes of the jungle, where their isolated homes formed ideal staging posts for money and food destined for the bandits living in it. Others of them lived in squatter villages which had grown in the course of time and which were far enough away from the main populated areas to make them only too accessible to the bandits.

In order to strangle this almost inexhaustible pipeline a vast system of resettlement was undertaken by the civil authorities. All isolated squatters were concentrated into villages defended by barbed wire, protected by police posts and provided with such facilities as medical and welfare centres and schools. These measures not only protected the squatters from the easy depredations of the bandits, but afforded them such an extent of security that they began to lose some of their initial fears and to pass information to the police . . .'

The 3rd Commando Brigade took over military responsibility for the State of Perak in July, 1950. Perak is similar in area to Wales, but at that time not more than a quarter of the State had been opened up. The majority of the terrain consisted of primary rain forest, with trees up to 250 feet in height, except for areas which had been temporarily cleared for shifting cultivation, where a dense secondary growth had sprung up. The cleared area of land was made up of neat rubber plantations, tin mines with their open cut workings and corrugated iron buildings, and the small holdings of Chinese squatters.

The inhabitants of Perak numbered about a million— fifty per cent Chinese, forty per cent Malay and ten per cent Indians, chiefly Tamil. There were also about 17,000 aborigines. Four Five's area in South Perak had a population of about a quarter of a million. When the Brigade arrived in the State, a squatter settlement, involving some 90,000 Chinese, had just begun. The number of known bandits was estimated to be about 1,500, 1,000 of which were formed into units of the MRLA.

Four Five relieved the 2nd Battalion Coldstream Guards, in the Tapah District in the southern part of the State, in early August. The Guards had acted as hosts to a Royal Marine Battalion, engaged in ceremonial duties in London, fifteen years previously. Despite this lapse of time the Commando had a very cordial reception, and the relief went smoothly. Entertainment was reported to be lavish, although operations continued in earnest, and on the day of departure the Commando Brigade Band played the packed troop train out of Tapah Road Station, to the delight of the cheering Guardsmen.

Tapah is a small town on the Sungei Batang Padang, set in the heart of rubber estates at the foot of the central highland region. It is the road head for access into the highlands, and in former times the town acted as staging post for those disembarking at the nearby Tapah Road Station, or motoring up to the hills to seek a cooler climate during the hot season. There were few local attractions for the Marines apart from the rest house, club and local cafes, and the peace of this normally quiet town was disturbed only by canned music which reputedly blared continuously from the Chinese laundry whilst the workers went busily about their tasks.

Four Five's camp consisted of long attap huts and was situated on the east of the town on Temoh Hill and acted, initially, as the base for Headquarters and two Troops, B (Capt Nick Carter) and Support Troop (Capt Jimmy Wild). Headquarters Troop, at that time, was commanded by Major 'General' Allenby. Later on E (Eagle) Troop was reformed here (the Commando's fifth Rifle Troop had been disbanded in Hong Kong in 1951) under command of Capt Neville Michell who had formerly been the founder Troop Commander of B Troop during the war. The Adjutant for much of the time at Temoh Hill was Capt David Smith, who like his commanding officer, had had an exceptionally varied and active commission which was to lead to the title, for those in similar circumstances, 'the last of the Aqabites'. As the Commando's area of responsibility in South Perak was over 1,900 square miles, about the size of Northumberland, it was necessary to have three other Troop locations to dominate this vast terrain. The first was in the Cameron Highlands, some thirty-four miles north-east of Tapah, the home of X Troop (Capt David Hunter). The second location was at Kampar, a village twelve miles north of Tapah, where Z Troop (Capt Tony Crawford) were based. Sungkai was the third location, seventeen miles south of Tapah, but this was not occupied until October, 1950. The first Troop at Sungkai was A Troop (Capt Bob Farquarson Roberts).

A description of Kampar is included elsewhere in this chapter, and before we examine the specific tasks of Four Five in Malaya, let us make a brief visit to one of the other Troop locations—the Cameron Highlands. This base was some 5,000 feet up in the mountains at the end of a forty mile-long road from Tapah which was completed in the early thirties. By 1940 there were three hotels, a golf course and about a hundred houses, surrounded by fruits and flowers which gave the general impression to all visitors that they were 'back home in England'. The climate was an unusual one for this region as whilst the plains, barely twenty miles away, one would swelter in the steamy heat, up here those on holiday would wear thick tweeds by night and enjoy the comforts of blankets and fires. The Cameron Highlands, however, was no rest centre for Four Five's garrison. Like their European counterparts the bandits would use the hills for their leave periods and each gang, refreshed by a two or three weeks' stay would commit some fresh nuisance as a parting gesture before they returned to their stamping grounds below. The bandits in the hills could not, of course, survive without supplies, and a major problem for the Troop up here was to track down the squatters —the terrorists' quartermasters. No description of the Highlands would be complete without reference to the Sakai, those timid aborigines who move from *ladang* (clearing) to *ladang* dressed in little more than their birthday suits and with faces reddened from chewing betel. Their principal weapon was the blowpipe and the Marines up in the Camerons were reported to have given up playing darts—'now one sees them playing "301-up" with a blowpipe!'

The first task of the Commando in the Tapah District was the assistance in the resettlement of squatters as part of the overall Briggs Plan—devised by the Director of Operations, General Sir Harold Briggs. Although it could never be claimed that resettlement in itself was the complete answer to the bandit problem, it did force the terrorists out of their jungle hideouts. This sometimes had alarming consequences as there were occasions when out of necessity they raided police posts and guarded villages in the search for food. Nevertheless, the traditional versatility of the Marines enabled them to participate in this tedious and often boring business without further alienation of the population. This project was carried out in conjunction with the police and local authorities, and the Marines normally acted as cordon parties whilst families were being moved, and then subsequently searched the buildings and destroyed anything that could be used by the bandits. Naturally these moves created great social problems, although these were in part alleviated by the 'Hearts and Minds' campaign. This campaign was aimed at giving welfare assistance to the local population, normally in the form of minor engineering projects such as the construction of wells. Four Five spent a total of eight months on resettlement work, and co-ordinated the construction of eighteen villages.

In August, 1950, Four Five had a change in Commanding Officers, Lt-Col Ries returned to the United Kingdom after a varied commission which had ranged from the sands of Aqaba to the mountains of the New Territories, and from the bare rocks of Malta to the hot jungle of the Malay Peninsular. In his place Lt-Col R. C. de Mussenden Leathes who, like his predecessor, had been a founder commanding officer of a Commando during the war—42 Commando in 1943. The drive and energy of Lt-Col Leathes in the following months not only contributed towards the great operational successes of Four Five, but also to a close and friendly working partnership with the local police (Mr Derek Winn was the Officer Commanding the Police District, Tapah) and civilian authorities. He was subsequently awarded an OBE for his work in Malaya.

British strategy, and indeed British tactics, at the start of the Malayan campaign in 1949/50 were based on the re-settlement plan which has already been described. By the time, therefore, that Four Five had arrived and took over the unit was committed to a pattern of operations already in train. In preventing the bandits from obtaining supplies there was a direct military aim, but it did mean that the numbers of troops available for more aggressive operations were very limited. The troop that were available from Four Five were in the most part deployed on numerous small patrols under young officers or senior NCOs, operating independently over a widely dispersed area. The local bandit leader, in South Perak, was one Yong Hoi,* commander of the 39th Platoon and was known to be the master mind behind the raids and murders in the neighbourhood. His victims, during his reign of terror, were estimated to have numbered some one hundred persons.

In addition to the formidable terrain, which greatly helped in the concealment of the bandits, the lack of intelligence in the initial stages restricted severely action that could be taken by ourselves. The police and other government agencies were, of course, able to give much useful information but 'hot intelligence' which could only come from the local population was almost totally lacking due to the fear of the inevitable reprisals from the bandits if anyone dared to make contact with the administration. This confidence in the Security Forces could only be built as the result of visible successes, and this could take months or even years; patrolling against

* 'It is believed that a fellow bandit eventually murdered both Yong Hoi and two of his compatriots. This bandit then surrendered to the Police at Kampar.' (*Globe and Laurel*, 1953.)

the elusive enemy had to continue relentlessly, and every lead, however fruitless or out of date, had to be followed up.

Concurrent with the re-settlement programme there was a substantial and rapid increase in the Malayan Police Force. Previously it had been a small Colonial force organized on strictly police lines, but now it found itself acting in the role of a para-military force as well. Its expansion was so rapid that understandably many of its new recruits lacked experience in the numerous duties which they had to perform. As a result, in these formative months, the force was both a prey to the bandits and to the local populace, who were hesitant in coming forward with intelligence.† On the military side local army and Commando units made a valuable contribution and Four Five, like many others, played its part by sending teams out to visit the special constables and kampong (village) guards to assist in weapon training, elementary tactics and the siting and repair of defences. This policy proved to be a considerable morale booster, which in time began slowly, but surely, to be reflected in increased confidence on the part of the local population. So much so that by the end of 1951 there was a steady trickle of information and intelligence where previously there had been hardly any. At the same time there was a noticeable increase in the size and scale of military operations that were being mounted. The earlier pattern of lots of small independent patrols was being replaced by Troop, Commando and at times even Brigade operations. It was, in fact, and end to that era of the campaign that had been called the 'Subalterns' War'.

This trend towards more co-ordinated operations had, to some extent, already been evolved by Four Five due to the very nature of the task which confronted the unit. The Commando was faced with an enormous area and only 600 men to patrol it, so it was impossible to dominate the whole territory at any one time. Equally obvious was the futility of waiting to act until the enemy had disclosed his presence, by some act of

† Language and racial difficulties were experienced too, as Malays were used as kampong guards in the predominantly Chinese villages.

terrorism, because he would never stand up and fight if he could avoid it and so he invariably withdrew to some secure hiding place until the storm had blown over. Accordingly Four Five had already taken steps to play the leading hand, as Lt-Col Leathes later wrote: 'The first lesson of guerilla warfare is that success goes to the side that has the initiative.' The unit's technique, in the main, was to take a relatively small part of its area, in which bandit activity was prevalent, and saturate it with troops to the point that supply lines were completely disrupted and the enemy just had to move to another area. In forcing them to do this against their will there was a good chance that the bandits would give their position away as they would have to re-establish supply routes and contacts in their new area. Of course this policy of saturating one specific region meant that other areas had to be denuded of troops, but this was a risk that had to be acknowledged.

Deception also played a large part in the Commando's tactics and there was a constant battle to outwit the enemy's intelligence system, which like his supply organization depended largely upon local sources in kampongs and squatter areas. Before an operation, 'ostentation' orders groups would be held in a different areas, bogus ammunition dumps (boxes filled with sand) were established and false rumours circulated, all in an effort to confuse. Troops were withdrawn at night from their normal locations and on one occasion they even moved into an operation dressed in football clothes! It has to be remembered that roads were few and as nearly every Troop location was near some form of habitation or other the word of movement soon got passed around. Field Artillery also played its part in this deception game. Programmes of firing were arranged to cover wide areas so as to simulate military activity, where, in fact, there was none. Fuses would be set to go off in the tree tops and using a single gun an effective pattern of noise was established sufficient to worry any bandit troops in the area and keep them guessing.

The bandits scored their first success against Four Five on 14 September, 1950, when Marines Ernest Nevard and David

Keyes were ambushed and killed as they were returning in a vehicle to the unit along the lonely Tapah road with despatches. Yong Hoi had shown his hand at last and the search for his killer gang and associates was about to begin in earnest, despite the distractions of the re-settlement programme. At the same time the bandits were adopting other nuisance tactics throughout the neighbourhood, such as ambushing and burning civilian buses, hanging their red flags on the outskirts of rubber *kongsis*, pinning up their propaganda and slashing rubber trees.

The Commando used many methods to check these outbursts. As a counter against road ambushes a troop of scout cars of the Queen's Own 4th Hussars* was permanently attached to Four Five to act as convoy escorts, and patrol the jungle fringed roads. The largest convoys formed were those taking children up to the Cameron Highlands School, and the Slim Army School which was moved up to the Highlands during the emergency. The security arrangements for these convoys were enormous. The students travelled in vehicles protected by armour plate, and in addition to extra escorts, constant air cover was provided throughout the journey. Fortunately the bandits were never able to inflict any casualties on the school children due to these stringent precautions.

In addition to jungle and road patrols Four Five was able to protect another form of communication—the railway. This task was carried out with the assistance of a small shunting engine, nicknamed the 'Caliban', and four armoured freight wagons. It was reported that this contraption could steam at a maximum speed of twenty knots, if the native stoker was feeling energetic! Lt John McCrae, the Assault Engineer Officer, remembers patrolling the railway in 'Caliban' checking for any sabotage attempts. The limited protection afforded by the freight wagons also meant that the 'Caliban' could transport three-inch mortars for day and night shoots, and carry supplies for troops on extensive operations.

Towards the end of 1950 events took a serious turn for the

* Relieved by 12th Royal Lancers, September, 1951.

worse in South Perak and Four Five suffered two reverses during a fortnight, on 28 December, Marines Turner and Parr were killed between Gopeng and Kampar and on 10 January, 1951, the unit incurred seven casualties. A joint patrol of A and X Troops (this was the advance party of A Troop which was to take over the Cameron Highlands area later that month) was ambushed in the Cameron Highlands by a force of some thirty bandits. Sgt George Westwood, Cpl John Henry and Marine Leslie Miller were killed and four others wounded, including Lt Jasper Bacon and an Iban. Air support was called for and the RAF responded with speed and bombed the river valley thought to contain the bandit camp. One Brigand on this sortie developed engine trouble and crashed, although one of the crew was reported to have baled out—in thick jungle over twenty miles from the populated area. Capt Mark Nunns set out almost immediately with a rescue party into this inhospitable terrain. One of the first mishaps occurred when Capt Nunns badly injured a leg. It was impossible to evacuate him on foot and axes had to be dropped on to a pin point target from a Dakota so that a big enough clearing could be made for a rescue helicopter—one of the first rescues by helicopter from really difficult country in this campaign. Once this evacuation had been completed Lt Ralph Davison took over the patrol. The going was so rough, over mountains and swollen rivers, with no view apart from the endless jungle canopy, that it took three days to cover the twenty miles. As a result of faultless navigation the wreck was found, but no trace of the aircrew. The trackers then went to work, speed was now of paramount importance. The airman was eventually found two miles away in a deserted aborigine hut, but had tragically died of his wounds. It was assumed that he had been seriously wounded whilst making a low-level descent, and although he had managed to salvage a first-aid kit from the aircraft was unable to survive without medical attention. This sad ending after so many days of superhuman effort was of course a bitter blow to the patrol, which now had to retrace its weary steps back to camp.

The fine work by Four Five prompted the Commander, Royal Air Force Malaya, Air Vice Marshal Sir Francis Melleish, to send the following signal to the unit: 'I would like to send you, on behalf of the RAF in Malaya, our appreciation and thanks for the magnificent effort put up by your patrol in fighting your way through the jungle in an attempt to rescue one of our aircrew who had baled out when a Brigand crashed last Thursday. We all fully realize what a fine show they have put up and can only regret that the airman was dead on arrival.'

The Royal Air Force provided invaluable support for operations at all times. Air strikes were made on likely enemy camps and on the jungle fringes, to drive the bandits out into the open, but perhaps the greatest morale booster of all was the 'resupply drop'. These were made to patrols in the more inaccessible and remote areas and the use of aircraft meant that the range of operations could be extended as hitherto distances patrolled depended solely on the amount of supplies that could be carried by each individual. The only time that the Royal Air Force were unpopular with the Marines during an air drop was when a crate of soap was delivered instead of soup! Another form of air support was the emergency evacuation of casualties. These were either made from the regular landing sites at Troop locations, or, on some occasions as we have just seen, from hastily constructed clearings in the heart of the jungle. The immensity of the Royal Air Force's support can be gauged by the fact that in the first three months of 1951 no less than 205 sorties were flown on behalf of Four Five.

These latest bandit outbursts led to Four Five's resources being stretched severely as the bulk of the unit was still engaged in the re-settlement policy and every available man had to be called forward for active patrolling. One such body was the 'Headquarters Ramblers'—cooks, clerks and buglers— who after a full week's work on their normal duties found themselves out in the jungle during their week-ends and half-days. The enemy during this period of patrolling did not always come in bandit form and one of the most extraordinary stories came from Support Troop who were attacked by Sakai aborigines using blowpipes. The patrol was engaged in an operation to arrest and move Sakai who were suspected of aiding the bandits. The patrol commander, Capt Jimmy Wild, received a dart in the shoulder and Marine Jack Blythe was pierced in the throat. Fortunately the poison was of the mild, anti-bird type and not of the anti-human variety which would have caused far greater damage.

The description of jungle patrolling, in retrospect, can be both impersonal and over dramatized. The story really belongs to the marine in his Troop location who spent his time either on guard catching up on lost sleep or out with his section for hours on end. Fortunately two ranks in Malaya at the time recorded their impressions of Troop life and tell us of a typical Troop area—Kampar. Marine Tooms of X Troop sets the scene:

'Our operational area consisted of the Kampar Hills, rising over 4,000 feet, and part of the Kinta Valley, the richest tin and rubber producing area in the world. The hills are fringed by rubber plantations on the lower slopes, but the majority is covered with thick jungle, and it is here that the bandits live. As for the Valley, it is mainly swampland, dotted with rubber estates and tin mines, with the railway running through the centre, and the main north road running up the eastern edge, at the base of the hills.

As for the bandits, they are organized in regiments, companies and platoons, although there are no fixed numbers of men in a unit. When the 27th platoon, MRLA, moved into the Kampar Hills* they were twenty strong, but when we left, they had been whittled down considerably. X Troop killed five and an ambush party from Headquarters got four, and four surrendered. . . .'

Marine 'Don' Stone, who was in Kampar (with Z Troop) earlier, continues the story.

* September, 1951.

'Z Troop consisted of a captain, two lieutenants and about sixty Non-Commissioned Officers and Marines and they were all living in a large house lying just off the main road running north from Kampar. It was a bit crowded in there; but it was good fun because the Troop was all on its own and we had a swimming pool and a decent canteen of our own.

As I was already a marksman with the Bren light machine gun, I was made a Bren-gunner in one of the sub-sections. The Troop was organized as a headquarters and four sub-sections, each commanded by a sergeant. We used to patrol pretty hard in our sub-section and I cursed that Bren gun of mine sometimes at first; but I changed my mind about her afterwards. There was a lance-corporal in charge of the Bren group, which consisted of myself and my number two, a young "Geordie", and we used to carry twelve loaded magazines between us, besides the one on the gun.

The weather was hot and sticky and I used to sweat pints. We all took salt tablets every morning before going on patrol and also a paludrine tablet; for there were always swarms of mosquitoes on the rubber estates and I used to get bitten to death by them while lying out on night ambushes. Another bit of discomfort was the rain. Every afternoon at about four o'clock there would be a sharp torrential downpour. Sometimes we would be caught out in the open and everything would be a sodden mass in a few minutes, and everyone would curse and swear silently as jungle boots slipped and slithered on the muddy path. I did not mind getting wet myself; but I did not like getting the Bren wet; because all the other lads seemed to put so much faith in the Bren and me, although they were carrying some pretty handy looking automatics, such as carbines and Owen guns, themselves.

Our patrols were usually uneventful; but I remember once how we had a fleeting contact with three bandits on the jungle fringed border of a rubber estate. I had a brief vision of three khaki clad figures streaking into the jungle and I just had enough time to fire a long burst from the hip.

We followed up and found some bloody trails; but although our little Iban tracker kept on the trail for several hours, it eventually petered out and we had to withdraw before dark.

Once or twice Z Troop left Kampar to take part in a unit operation and I found myself in more hilly country. Here I got used to finding leeches clinging to various parts of my body and practised burning them off with my cigarette end, which was the best way of dealing with them. I was always glad to get back to Kampar, and our swimming pool made up for all the sweat and dirt of each day's patrolling. I used to enjoy drinking my "Tiger" beer in the canteen in the evening and sometimes we would have a film or, if a bandit had been killed, one of the Ibans would do a war dance with his parang.

Occasionally one of the other sub-sections would kill a bandit in the chance encounters among the rubber trees or in the jungle, or perhaps the leading scout of the patrol would find a fresh path leading to a bandit camp, sometimes a recently used one and sometimes quite old. We had our own casualties as well once or twice. I always remember how two of the lads were killed in a nasty road ambush. We all felt pretty bad about that and the patrolling continued relentlessly.

I think that of all the incidents that took place during my twenty-one months in Malaya the most exciting was a night attack on a bandit camp.* A bandit surrendered early one evening to the Malay sergeant in charge of a police post not very far from Kampar. It was during the Easter weekend and quite a few of the lads were away on leave at Telok Anson. Suddenly the Sergeant-Major (QMS Lang) dashed into our room and said that a patrol was required in five minutes' time to go out on some really good "Information". Everyone volunteered to go, from the cook downwards. A Bren-gunner from one of the other sub-sections came along with me. It only took a few minutes to put my equipment on,

* 23 March, 1951.

grab my Bren, and jump into the transport. We drove first to the police post and picked up the surrendered Chinese bandit. Our interpreter took charge of him and he promised to lead us to the camp. The road that we followed soon narrowed to a track and we jumped out of the trucks and continued on foot. The track gradually led towards marshy ground and eventually we reached the banks of a small river. The bandit pointed to a sampan secured alongside and we jumped in. It was now dusk and we paddled along the river with the reeds brushing against us on either side. The short twilight deepened into night. On one occasion we saw a dark blur on the bank ahead and trained our weapons upon it instinctively, then when we were closer we recognized it as a water buffalo, standing motionless and staring. It was a long journey with those short paddles. Later, when we crossed a much larger and faster flowing river, we had to paddle hard to gain the opening to our small river on the other side. After about an hour we approached a widening of the river and saw a rough landing stage with a waterlogged sampan beside it. The bandit told the interpreter to stop the sampan and get out here. The camp was apparently one half hour's walk away. After leaving a guard with our sampan, we walked in single file along a narrow track surrounded on either side by high grass or lallang. The moon had now risen and we could see around us quite clearly. After walking for about twenty minutes we stopped. The bandit was whispering excitedly to the interpreter who was translating to the patrol commander. Very briefly we were told that the camp was only about 400 yards ahead, a little way off the path on the left hand side. It consisted of two small bashas built below a small tree, up which was a sentry post. The patrol commander moved the Bren-gunner and myself up behind him and sent the bandit and the interpreter to the rear of the patrol. As we moved forward cautiously my heart began to beat furiously. The action of my gun was cocked and all I had to do was ease the change lever forward. A dark mass began to loom up on the left, and took shape as a tree. We came in line with it and saw movement just beyond it. The patrol commander signalled us to kneel behind the cover of the grass. Suddenly someone shouted a nervous challenge in Chinese from the direction of the base of the tree. We remained deadly silent. The voice came again and against the light of the moon we saw a shape climbing to a sentry position in the tree. My safety lever was forward now and the order to fire came in a quiet voice. The silence was rent suddenly by the staccato roar of two Brens. The dark form dropped like a stone from his perch. I then fired low into where I thought the bashas would be. I managed to whip on a fresh magazine and fire that before the order came to stop firing and advance. It made all those weary patrols worthwhile to be able to squeeze the trigger of the Bren and listen to her music.

As we walked through the bushes I saw two small bashas made of attap (a form of jungle creeper). One body lay at the base of a roughly made ladder which was nailed to the tree and another lay inside one of the bashas. There was a well dug outside and the remains of a small fire. We went through the camp quickly and searched the far side, but it ended in deep swamp. A more thorough search produced a number of green coloured packs containing documents and clothing. The two dead bandits were dressed in khaki drill and were carrying '36' grenades.

The patrol commander had the documents collected together to return to Police Headquarters. The dead men were lashed on to carrying poles and after setting fire to the two bashas and contaminating the well, we moved off along the path with our burdens. When some of the lads said "Well done, Stonie. You did your stuff with your Bren tonight", I felt pretty good. . . .'

The Ibans which Stone mentioned were natives of Sarawak and were expert trackers. They were attached to units in Malaya during the emergency and were employed with patrols in the jungle. Lt Derek Oakley, formerly the Assault

Engineer Officer, remembered times when the Ibans went out on patrol unaccompanied by interpreters. All conversation was carried out in sign language. One of the more familiar actions was that of lifting their hair with one hand and making a slicing motion with the other. This was demonstrated on one occasion when the intended victim was an officer who had forgotten to draw their pay. However, a frantic rush to the bank before it closed saved his scalp!

In all bandit operations the most important factor, as we have just seen, was naturally the 'kill', and these could only be officially recorded if the body had been recovered. Many bandits were known to have been mortally wounded, and to have crawled into the impenetrable jungle to die, but these were not listed. Within each Commando an inter-Troop scores list was maintained and when a kill had been confirmed a red star would be proudly added to the Troop flag. The Brigade 'league' was published in *Commando News*, a weekly publication circulated throughout the Brigade giving both military and world news, and it is to the unit's credit that Four Five headed this list for long periods. On 29 June, 1951, the one hundredth bandit killed by the Brigade, since its arrival in Perak, was accounted for by Z Troop, when a camp near Gopeng was attacked.

One of the Marines on the patrol, Tom Power, remembers the incident well. 'It was early one morning and they were wading through a swamp when the scouts opened up on two bandits. One was killed and the other escaped into the jungle.' A brief encounter, undramatic, but nevertheless, important. The patrol was led by Lt Bob Darwall, and it is of interest that it was the same section that won a £5 prize from the Brigade Commander, Brigadier C. F. Phillips for the fiftieth kill, in March, 1951. Brigadier Phillips had assumed command of the Brigade in February, 1951, from Brigadier C. R. Hardy who was later to accompany Four Five into Suez as Commandant General.

It may be gruesome to us, detached from the Malayan Emergency, that there was intense competition, and indeed monetary prizes, for the recorded kills of bandits. It must be remembered, however, that the police and security forces were all joined in a common task, that of preventing the MRLA seizing power by force. It was an elusive enemy, and one which thought nothing of barbarously murdering innocent and unarmed civilians or sabotaging lines of communications. Kill or be killed. The successes registered by Four Five and other units would only serve to lessen the future effectiveness of bandit activities.

These sentiments were reinforced by a comment in the 3 Commando Brigade Newsletter of March 1951 . . . 'we hope that readers will bear in mind that a dead bandit is a tangible result and reward for many, many hours spent in pursuit through swamp and thick jungle, in tropical downpours and torrid heat, of many nights spent lying in ambush plagued by mosquitoes and every living thing that flies or crawls by night.'

Although the bandits could never be described as sophisticated military opposition the effort expended to break their grip over certain areas was enormous and the stiff resistance they put up meant that the jungle canopy hid many acts of individual and collective bravery on both sides. Four Five won no less than thirty-one awards for gallantry in the twenty months it spent on operations in connection with the Malayan Emergency, a most noteworthy achievement. The courage of Marine Leslie Tarbuck, in this instance not recognized by a decoration, is perhaps typical of the courage and tenacity of the average Commando. On the night of 12 June, 1951, the bandits launched a determined attack on the auxiliary police post, some 200 yards from the railway station. Two auxiliary policemen were killed and Tarbuck, on duty at the station waiting to collect mail from the night train, rushed to the sound of the firing in company with a Malay police corporal. It was pitch dark and at almost point blank range Tarbuck met a bandit who shot him with a carbine in both legs and an arm. The gang then fled but despite his terrible wounds Tarbuck recovered his rifle and painfully crawled the seemingly endless 200 yards

9. *Marine W. K. Laidler hoists the 'B' Troop flag, 'Bash On Regardless', in Osnabruck. (Imperial War Museum)*

10. *'Chow Time'; HQ Troop in the Aller Woods, 11–12 April, 1945.*

11. *Looking back over Europe. Marine Moyle standing by a silent AA gun after the final river crossing. (Imperial War Museum)*

back to the station to telephone for assistance. A member of Four Five later wrote: 'Such samples of devotion to duty were but an indication of our tremendous spirit which in Malaya was second to none.'

A week later, on 19 June, 2 Section of A Troop, led by Lt Johnny Herron, ambushed a group of six bandits in the Cameron Highlands. Three bandits were wounded but the remainder ran away. Showing customary persistence the men of A Troop conducted a 'follow up'. One of the escapees turned on his pursuers and shot and wounded Lt Herron and Cpl Ron Brierly but the chase went on with spasmodic fire being exchanged between the two parties. Eventually one of the bandit rearguard was killed and another hit (his body was found two days later). The third escapee surrendered later, giving valuable information. Thus, as a result of A Troop's dogged chasing, an enemy gang had ceased to function.

Marine R. G. Hodgkiss showed his skill as a leading scout of a patrol on 18 February, 1951, and his ability and fortitude won him a Military Medal. He was carefully following the tracks of a bandit group when he suddenly spotted their camp. Unnoticed he daringly stalked and shot the sentry, but the resultant fire pinned the rest of the patrol down. Undaunted Hodgkiss let off two smoke grenades and charged into the camp in the face of a Bren gun. The enemy fled leaving two dead behind them. This toughness led to glowing reports in the press: 'Throughout this brief encounter Marine Hodgkiss showed determination to come to grips with the enemy with no thought for himself, and it was by his determined aggressive example that what might have proved to be an inconclusive encounter was in fact a resounding success.'* 'Outstanding courage and leadership . . .' This was an extract from the citation of nineteen-year-old 2/Lt Alistair Gavin who was awarded the Military Cross on 20 July, 1951. Gavin joined the ranks of the Royal Marines in August, 1949, as a National Serviceman and was commissioned in March, 1950. When he joined Four Five in November of that year he became a

* *Singapore Standard*, 21 July, 1951.

7

section subaltern in B Troop and was, at the time, the only National Service officer in the Brigade. B Troop had many successes in early 1951, but it is 9 March that Gavin will doubtless remember for many years to come. Positive information was received of bandit activity on the Palawan Estate near Bidor, some ten miles south of Tapah. A patrol of B Troop, thirteen strong, left camp in transport that afternoon under the command of 2/Lt Gavin. They left the vehicles some distance from their objective and moved from the road through abandoned tin tailings into the edge of the rubber plantation where the suspects were thought to be hiding. A cover party consisting of a Bren gunner and two marines was placed on an embankment to act as a cut-off in case the bandits broke back. A thorough search of the plantation was made without success, and on the way back, 2/Lt Gavin decided to check the area surrounding some nearby labour lines. Right in front of one of the huts stood a man dressed in khaki and holding a Sten gun. Recognition between the leading scout and the bandit was instantaneous. The patrol fired the first shot, but the bandit rushed round the corner of the hut and made for the rubber, closely followed by 2/Lt Gavin's section. When the patrol got to the back of the hut they found the bandit racing towards the widely spaced rubber trees accompanied by four of his comrades. Shots were exchanged between both parties and for about ten minutes there was a running battle between the two groups over a distance of some three hundred yards. Gavin bravely led his men through the open ground, raked by automatic gunfire, and charged the bandits down. Of the original five only one got away unscathed. Three were killed outright and one other, although wounded, managed to escape into the dense undergrowth. The haul for the operation, which had lasted barely three hours, included a Sten gun, a rifle, two grenades, large quantities of ammunition and the arrest of ten suspects from the labour lines. The *Singapore Standard* of 21 July, 1951 gave glowing praise to this gallant National Service Officer: 'There is no doubt that the losses inflicted on the enemy before they reached the cover of thick jungle were directly due to 2/Lt Gavin's fine leadership, perseverance and determination and that if it had not been for his *élan* and example few of the bandits would have been caught.'

Four other Military Crosses were awarded to Four Five for exceptional gallantry during this campaign; Capt Nick Carter (B Troop); Lt Bob Darwall (Z Troop); Lt Pat Griffiths (X Troop) and Capt David Hunter (X Troop). Capt Carter was also Mentioned in Despatches during the same period. Likewise the Second-in-Command, Major Jack Richards, who had led many Headquarters patrols and operations, received two awards for bravery in Malaya; an MBE and a Mention in Despatches. Major Richards was later to command Four Five in Cyprus.

Perak was, at one stage of the Emergency, described as the 'most troubled State'. As we have already witnessed bandit activity was high and although the number of incidents had been admirably contained by the Commando Brigade it is probably fair to say that considering the size of the State the forces were too widely dispersed. Four Five's area was more than busy and on occasions reinforcements were called from other Commandos to give assistance for specific operations. This meant that there was a risk of a deteriorating situation in areas temporarily denuded of troops and at times the desirable permanency of some security measures could not be maintained. To meet the required intensifying of operations an extra battalion was moved in to the Brigade area. Therefore the 1st Battalion, the Gordon Highlanders was transferred from Pahang and assigned to Perak in August, 1951. The Gordons assumed responsibility for the South Perak district, whilst Four Five moved some twenty miles north to their new base at Batu Gajah, the move being completed by 25 August.

Departures from areas of military responsibility are often sad occasions, and this one was no exception. A strong bond of friendship had grown up between Four Five and the citizens of Tapah, and the glowing letters of appreciation bear testimony to this. Lim Cheng Chuan on behalf of the Chinese community wrote, 'Though we have known you for only one year, we have learnt to admire your courage, exemplary conduct and, not least, your true sense of sportsmanship on and off the playing field. During your stay in Tapah, you have added further lustre to the already glorious record of the Marine Commandos, and we, as members of the civilian population, owe you all a debt of gratitude for coming all the way from your homeland in your effort to restore peace and prosperity to Malaya.'

The District Officer Mr J. A. Craddock, added: 'In particular, I should like to refer to the part played by your unit in establishing a number of squatter villages. The morale of these villages is still better than any others in this area. . . . Your record of killing and capturing bandits is also an imposing one, and we feel honoured in having had your assistance in this area. We regret your departure but feel sure that you will go on to even greater successes in your new area.'

The Batu Gajah district was little more than half the size of the South Perak region. It was, however, the largest tin mining area in Perak, and in consequence contained much swamp and low lying ground. Three Troops were based with Commando Headquarters at Tyrone Camp, Batu Gajah, but Four Five still maintained responsibility for Kampar (X Troop, Major Allenby) in the former district. B Troop (Capt Carter) was detached to the Sitiawan district, fifty miles away and bordered by the sea, but separated from Batu Gajah by an inpenetrable swamp and river complex. Their stay here was a quiet one as they killed a bandit on the first patrol in the district!

The move of locations also afforded an opportunity for the Troops to have a two week rest and retraining period at Minden Barracks in Penang. The combination of weapon training, parade work, sea bathing and, of course, the bright city lights, made a welcome break from the constant strain of patrolling and living in isolated locations. At the time the average length of a tour in the Commando Brigade was two and a half years. Each rank was entitled to a fortnight's leave a year, and in addition to these retraining periods the majority of the personnel were able to get away and spend their well-earned

183

eaves either in Singapore, Ipoh or Penang, the latter being the most popular.

The departure from South Perak was also marked by presentations both from and to the Commando, at a special parade on Batu Gajah Golf Course on Trafalgar Day, 21 October, 1951. Lt-Col Leathes presented a shooting shield to the South Perak Police Circle. In return, on behalf of the Police, Mr Goldsburg presented a silver bugle inscribed with the Corps Crest. Then Mr Alex Rodgers, the Chairman of the Tapah District Planters Association, presented a shield, on which was mounted two 300-year old Malayan *kris** surrounded by small silver shields representing the rubber estates in the area. Both these trophies and two other *kris*, presented by the Kampar Police to X and Z Troops, are still proudly displayed within the Commando.

The redeployment did not mean that there could be a respite. Bandit activity had been checked but not suppressed. In the *Tiger Times*, the Commando's own weekly newsheet, the Commanding Officer commented, after leaving Tapah, 'We can feel justly proud of our achievements. So much for the past. We now go on with the same task in a new area. The task is, in its simplest terms, that of making this country safe for decent citizens to go about their work and recreation without fear. . . .'

The aim was straightforward. It could only be fulfilled through the maintaining of the same unrelenting pressure.

The *Tiger Times* fulfilled the dual role of acting as the Commando's weekly newspaper and newsletter. One of its earlier pioneers was Sgt 'Abdul' Harvey, BEM of the Orderly Room (later a frequent contributor to the *Globe and Laurel* under the name of 'Sandpiper'). Despite the difficulties of production and distribution, the editorial staff in Headquarters managed to maintain regular publication. The contents were varied and lively, and in addition to coverage of internal events, items of Brigade and world interest were included for the benefit of those in outlying locations.

* A two-edged Malay dagger having a wavy blade.

Another feature of everyday life in the Commando, and indeed most units out in Malaya at the time, was the contractor. Four Five's was an exuberant Pakistani by the name of Hamid Gul. It was Mr Gul's responsibility to provide the unit's amenity staff such as tailors, laundrymen, barbers, charwallahs and other sundry tradesmen. The charwallahs were seen most frequently and it was their proud boast to be able to provide, at virtually anytime of day or night, fried egg sandwiches and hot coffee to sustain Marines after long operations or late 'runs ashore'. It has been recorded that 'tick' was usually available on the days preceding pay day (pay for the Marine was £2.27½ per week), but that the charwallahs' photographic memories enabled them to pounce on their victims soon afterwards!

With leave and retraining completed, the Troops returned to their task of intensive patrolling.

Bandits were not the only enemy for the Marines. On occasions snakes were mistaken for jungle creepers, with frightening results, and Marine Milne of Support Troop had a fortunate escape on 18 September, 1951. A patrol was crossing a bamboo bridge where a water buffalo was wallowing below. Suddenly the animal became violent and pinned Marine Milne against a barbed wire resettlement fence and then tossed him on top of it. Lt Colin Walker, the Mortar Troop Commander, dashed to the rescue and finished the buffalo off with his carbine. Milne escaped with shock and bad cuts.

One of Lt Walker's next patrols proved to be equally as eventful. On 31 October, 1951, near Pusing, elements of Support Troop were returning from an arduous two day patrol, when the leading scout spotted an alien face in the lallang. The patrol took prompt action and within seconds two bandits were killed, one wounded and the remaining eleven or so fled. The enemy were in a well prepared camp with slit trenches when they were first seen and they left weapons and equipment behind them. A follow-up patrol from Support Troop injured a further bandit, but dusk brought the chase to a close.

Altogether three of Four Five's patrol were wounded, but, perhaps the luckiest escape was that of the signaller, Marine Roy Lunn, whose '68' set was riddled with bullets, but he himself was unharmed.

As a result of the concentration of Troops at Batu Gajah we now enter the phase of large operations involving the major part of the unit which were mounted during the latter part of 1951 and early 1952. One of the first of these was 'Operation Rimau' lasting for a week in early November, 1951, and mounted near Tangong Tualang by E and A Troops. The aim was a drive against the Communist 27th Platoon led by Chai Soo and on the first day of the operation one of E Troop's sections, commanded by Sgt Funnell, contacted a party of seven bandits, and immediately opened fire. The patrol then seized packs and food supplies and it was learnt later from a captured bandit that three of the terrorists, on a food supply mission, had been wounded and had subsequently died. This was a remarkable achievement as fire had to be opened up at a range of some 400 yards due to the swampy nature of the ground. A Troop (Lt Johnny Herron), operating in the same area, had similar successes on 3 November, 1951. One patrol leader, after a bandit was seen to have been hit in the chest by a burst of Bren, was keen to claim a kill, but as no body could be found he suggested that 'the two halves ran separate ways, the top half on it's hands!' This patrol then discovered a camp nearby thought to be the headquarters of an important District Committee.

The next operation to be mounted was 'Operation Springtide' which was staged in two phases between 1 December, 1951 and 2 January, 1952, with a short break for Christmas. This was the longest operation so far mounted within the Brigade area. The force was a large one and included, in addition to Four Five, two Troops each from 40 and 42 Commando, two companies from the Gordons and a detachment from the Lancers. The area of the operation was the mountainous region between Gopeng and Kampar where the 27th Platoon had fled to after 'Operation Rimau', and the main aim was to drive the enemy group into ambushes on the jungle fringes. The first success of this operation was scored by Commando Headquarters, which was deployed in an offensive as well as a command role. On 5 December, after an all night vigil, a small party from Tactical Headquarters under the Second-in-Command, Major Jack Richards, was waiting in an ambush near a mining kongsi. Information had been received that an enemy 'visit' was likely. The report proved to be true and all four bandits that walked in to the ambush were killed. The hero of this battle was Marine Timms, on the Bren gun. Within a thirty-second period he changed magazines on two occasions to fire a remarkable total of nearly seventy rounds at the enemy.

'Springtide' continued with two more successes ensuring that the 27th Platoon was well and truly broken up. A Sakai bandit was killed near Gopeng on 18 December by an A Troop patrol, and on Christmas Eve Sgt 'Ozzie' Want's patrol from X Troop accounted for two more bandits. An official report later laconically described what must have been a drama-filled incident. '24 Dec. Over 3,000 feet up in the Kampar Hills a patrol of X Troop being guided by a surrendered bandit contacted the tail of a gang of eighteen bandits. The leading scouts opened fire, killing a female bandit and wounding a male bandit who ran away. He was caught within 100 yards and killed'. It was Sgt Want's speed and dash which spelt disaster for the bandit who was chased through the thick undergrowth. It appears that banditry was not purely a male domain, and throughout the tour in Malaya there were several instances when patrols clashed with uniformed members of the opposite sex. It was naturally difficult to identify these women at long range and the fact that they were dressed the the same as their male counterparts and carried arms was ample proof that their duties were not purely domestic. On 15 August, 1951, a Z Troop patrol had opened fire on two female bandits— not 'bumped two popsies', as someone had suggested, and a pistol and thirty-six rounds of ammunition were found on one of the bodies. Sentiment could not enter this type of warfare.

Four Five's last big operation in Malaya was codenamed 'Broderick' and this meant that the Commando was on full deployment almost up to the day of departure. The operation was directed by Brigade Headquarters and was the longest ever carried out by the unit in Malaya, lasting nearly seven weeks from early January until the end of February, 1952. 'Broderick' took place in lower Perak, an area normally the responsibility of the Gordon Highlanders but which was well known to those of the unit who had served at Tapah before the move to Batu Gajah. The aim of the operation was: 'To disrupt the terrorists of 39 Independent Platoon MRLA, together with its associated Min Yuen organization, to such an extent that they remained ineffective for a considerable time.' The platoon was about eighty strong and led by the well known guerilla leader, Yong Hoi. It was hoped that the enemy would be located by saturating the area with troops whilst the police tightened up on food and movement restrictions by imposing curfews and establishing check points. The unit operated mainly in the Pasir Panjang Ulu area and in the Kroh Forest, both of which were regions of appalling terrain—miles of swamp and mangrove jungle and acres of lallang and thick beleukar.

The Intelligence Officer, Lt John Richards, remembers that Commando Headquarters was situated in a dilapidated rubber kongsi north of Batu Sembelas and the Troops were dispersed throughout the featureless landscape in locations nicknamed 'Kensington', 'Haymarket', 'Whitechapel' and 'Bloomsbury', all of which bore absolutely no resemblance to their more famous counterparts.

'Sandpiper' later recalled what life was like for Troops in that fearful swamp: 'Their only contact with each other was through wireless sets carried from camp to camp with who knows what exasperation, submerged often in oily swamps, dried out and carried yet further. Their supplies and almost sole contact with the outside world came when a twin-engined Dakota circled an appointed rendezvous every fourth or fifth day, discharging its precious cargo of corned beef, tinned beer, cigarettes and ammunition. Pack up and move on again, fighting atrocious country and a burning sun by day and clouds of mosquitoes or torrential rain by night.'

Sgt Want again distinguished himself as patrol commander. On 8 February his section, of X Troop, was approaching a camp, south of Gopeng, when a bandit sentry suddenly opened fire. Despite the enemy fire Sgt Want led his men in a quick charge through the camp, which resulted in the deaths of three out of the four fleeing Min Yuen. Sgt Want was later awarded the Military Medal for his outstanding action.

Apart from Min Yuen only three bandits were accounted for on 'Broderick', two by B Troop on 17 January and one by E Troop on 2 February. This latter kill was the result of a long chase by the Troop. On 21 January ten uniformed armed bandits had been spotted briefly in an area to the west of Tapah Road Station. These were successfully stalked and seen to be collecting food in a cultivated area. The stalking party, only four men, opened fire and the bandits scattered, taking two wounded with them but leaving their section commander dead, shot by Cpl Didcock. This encounter was the prelude to a long follow up, but the enemy eluded capture despite the discovery of several resting places containing blood-soaked bandages. At the conclusion of 'Broderick' Four Five was able to look back at a three-month period during which the Commando had spent virtually the entire time away from base operating as a complete unit.

We thus draw near the end of another chapter, indeed an epic one, in which it has been possible to mention but a few of the outstanding events. Since 1950, Four Five had spent eight months on resettlement work and fourteen on full time operations. The Commando topped the Brigade kills list with a total of seventy-six bandits for the loss of one officer (Lt Paul Budgeon) and ten other ranks, who either died or were killed on active service. In addition ten bandits were captured and fifty-four rifles and automatics recovered. Thirty-one awards for meritorious service and gallantry were won by members of the unit during this tour. Also, for the record, it is noteworthy that the Mortar Platoon fired 20,000 rounds at the unseen enemy, and on one occasion created a 'first' by scoring a direct hit* on a bandit patrol, killing one and wounding six. Successes were not confined to the battlefield. The Commando's shooting teams achieved many excellent results too. QMS Newport, X Troop's sergeant major, won the individual championships of Malaya in October, 1950. In 1951 Four Five topped the list of ten teams in the Perak Police Shield competition at Ipoh, and in the Malayan championships that year recorded one first, one second and one third place in three out of four team events. All remarkable results considering that the Commando was fully employed on operations throughout this period.

Before the Commando left a Service of Remembrance was held on the lawn of the Rest House at Batu Gajah on Wednesday, 12 March. The Chaplain, the Rev Dick Thornley, addressed the unit and doubtless the minds of all present were filled with poignant memories of the families of the men who would not be returning.

Four Five's operational tour in the Federation ended on 15 March, 1952, when the unit handed over to the 2nd Battalion, the Malaya Regiment. At noon the troop train drew slowly out of Batu Gajah Station to begin the four hundred mile journey to Singapore. The Brigade band struck up *Auld Lang Syne* and as the last three coaches moved past a shower of spare coins was tossed out by the cheering occupants. The unfortunate bandsmen were almost inundated with hordes of local urchins diving for the money, and for a few moments both their composure and musical offerings were completely lost!

At Tapah Road Station another big reception awaited the Commando. The association between Four Five and the local population had been a close one and as a result the platform was packed with members of all communities including miners and planters. One of the old friends of the Commando, Mike McConville, was present at this departure. He had been transferred to Four Five from 43 Commando, at the end of the

* 22 November, 1951.

war and had then served in Hong Kong. Mike McConville had taken a close interest in his old unit in subsequent years, which included a hitch-hiking trip across Europe to visit Four Five, then based in Malta. He was now in Government service in Malaya and had been a visitor, and liberal host, on many occasions.

Musical accompaniment on the platform was provided by the pipe band of the Gordon Highlanders and two Chinese bands. The kind citizens also saw to it that the troops, facing a long and tedious journey, would not go unrefreshed and liquid sustenance, in the form of seemingly inexhaustible crates of beer piled high on the platform, was passed round all on board the train. The scene at Tapah Road, however, was dominated by a large hand-painted notice. Bandits had recently burnt down the station at nearby Kampar and the inhabitants of Tapah did not wish to suffer a similar fate at the hands of Four Five. The words of friendly warning read as follows: 'Please don't burn our station down, give us time to pay!'

As Four Five left Tapah, before spending a fortnight in Singapore, the thoughts of all those who had survived the rigours of those last two years can probably best be summed up by the words of the Commanding Officer, Lt-Col Reggie Leathes:

'Throughout its time in Malaya the Commando was never in any doubt that it had a purposeful role to play, and this was reflected in the high morale of all the unit which sustained all activities from start to finish.

Four Five stood firmly between the ordinary people of Malaya on the one hand and the forces of oppression that sought to dominate them on the other. The unit helped to curb this terrorism without gain to itself except that of a job well done.

The building of new communities was an achievement in itself and the men were able to see for themselves the queues that used to await the arrival of the unit's doctor (Surg-Lt John Houghton) and his equally dedicated assistants as they went about their unofficial rounds. As Four Five left Malaya all ranks realized that they, in their own small way, had helped to restore order where before they had found turmoil.'

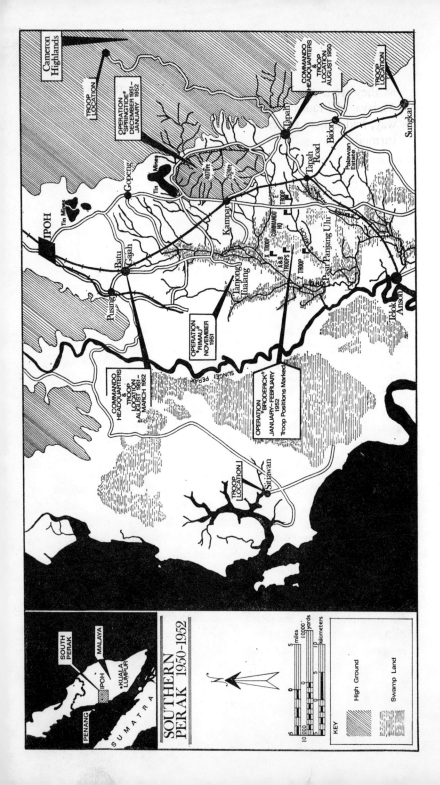

Cameron Highlands

TROOP LOCATION

OPERATION "HELSBY" DECEMBER 1951–JANUARY 1952

COMMANDO HEADQUARTERS & TROOP LOCATION AUGUST 1950

TROOP LOCATION

Sungkai

Tapah

Bidor

Tapah Road

Palewan Estate

IPOH

Gopeng

Tin Mines

Tin Mines

470 ft

1524 ft

Kampar

TROOP

TROOP COMMANDO HQ

Pasir Panjang Ulu

Batu Gajah

Pusing

Tanjong Tualang

TROOP C

TROOP B

TROOP A

OPERATION "RIMAU" NOVEMBER 1951

SUNGEI PERAK

Telok Anson

COMMANDO HEADQUARTERS & TROOP LOCATION AUGUST 1951– MARCH 1952

OPERATION "BRODERICK" JANUARY–FEBRUARY 1952 Troop Positions Marked

TROOP LOCATION

Sitiawan

SOUTH PERAK

MALAYA

PENANG

IPOH

KUALA LUMPUR

SUMATRA

SOUTHERN PERAK 1950–1952

miles
yards
kilometers

KEY

High Ground

Swamp Land

CHAPTER 9

The Mediterranean and Middle East 1947–1960— An Active Decade in many trouble spots

It has been the privilege of the Royal Marines to provide the spearhead units in almost every theatre in which Great Britain has had a military involvement since World War II. In 1947 the immediate post-war problems centred on the Far East, but these seemed to recede as world strategic and political attention shifted to the Middle East. The Jewish-Arab conflict, caused by the emergence of Palestine, was beginning to smoulder. Other countries in the Mediterranean, previously content with Britain's attentions, were starting to show signs of dissatisfaction. The deployment of 3 Commando Brigade as mobile reserve for the Mediterranean and Middle East was an indication of how serious the situation might become in the years ahead. Initially Britain's aims in the area were largely strategic— the maintenance of the Suez Canal and other military bases— but as time progressed this emphasis changed to one of peace-keeping.

At the outset there were seven particular areas of direct

British interest in the Mediterranean; the Canal Zone, Cyprus, Egypt, Gibraltar, Libya, Malta and Palestine. Only Gibraltar, the fortress captured by the Royal Marines in 1704, was to escape serious unrest during this period.

Four Five disembarked in Malta from HMT *Strathnaver* after the trip from Hong Kong, on 10 June, 1947. The Commando's home for the first five months was the chiefly tented camp at Ghadira, in Mellieha Bay, some thirteen miles from Valetta. The distance from the capital was compensated by the excellent bathing facilities on the nearby beaches. Ghadira, in fact, was only a temporary home as Four Five then moved to St Patrick's Barracks, in the main cantonment at Pembroke Fort, but not before the autumn rains which made life under canvas particularly unpleasant. For these months the unit concentrated on training, limited by the fact that large tracts of the island were under cultivation and compensation rates, were exorbitant, and ceremonial duties—Governor's Palace Guards at Valetta. In addition to its strategic commitments the Brigade also had other tasks which were described, on arrival, by the *Times of Malta*: 'For the first time, Royal Marines are to take over the island's garrison duties in their entirety, replacing British infantry who, along with the Royal Navy, had come to be regarded as "Britain's Ambassadors-at-large".' This move also created another 'first'—the accompanied tour—and by the end of October some twenty-eight families of ranks serving in Four Five had come out to join their husbands. 'One is reminded very much of home, to see all the married ranks, complete with small cases of what-have-you, travelling to and from their homes in various parts of the island.'* One of the first visitors to Four Five was Major-General 'Lucky' Laycock, the retiring Chief of Combined Operations, who inspected the unit in late June. It was Major-General Laycock who had been closely associated with the Commando in the early months leading up to D-Day and was to renew these ties, in Malta, in the years ahead.

The move up to St Patrick's Barracks took place on 17

* *Globe and Laurel*, 1947.

November and shortly afterwards the Commandant-General, Lieutenant-General R. A. D. Brooks, inspected Four Five on Tuesday, 25 November, 1947. The parade was commanded by the Second-in-Command, Major Alan Newson: 'Green berets, khaki battledress and white accoutrements stood out against the light coloured square, the whole set off by the Mediterranean blue background.'*

Four Five was not to remain out of the operational limelight for long. During the winter months the unit, now commanded by Lt-Col E. C. E. Palmer, had been making preparations for a move to Cyrenaica, the eastern sector of Libya. The task was to act as bodyguard to the four-power United Nations Organization Commission which was in Libya to discuss a new constitution, as the country was still under British military administration. Trouble was expected and the advance guard of Four Five arrived on 23 March, 1948 and, after much delay, the main body on 24 April. The unit was split between Benghazi and Derna, 200 miles apart by road. Headquarters were established in a derelict Italian barracks in Benghazi, and the only interesting item remembered in an otherwise featureless area seems to have been a 'large pornographic painting splashed on the shower bath wall'.

Whilst the Commando was concentrating on settling in at Derna and Benghazi the situation at the eastern end of the Mediterranean worsened considerably. The British Mandate in Palestine was due to end on 15 May, and the evacuation through Haifa due to be completed by 30 June. In this six week period it was estimated that some 70,000 personnel and 5,000 police and civilian officers plus 210,000 tons of stores and other unit equipment would have to be taken out.† To achieve these results it was thought that several different routes of withdrawal would have to be employed, taking into consideration the unsettled internal situation at the time. For much of

* *Times of Malta*, 26 November, 1947.
† *The Evacuation of Palestine*, Lieutenant-General G. H. A. MacMillan, CB, CBE, DSO, MC. *Journal of the RUSI*, November, 1948.

this period British troops had found themselves in the unenviable position of keeping the rival factions apart, in addition
to carrying out this massive move of men and equipment. Serious
outbreaks of fighting had already broken out in Jaffa, Haifa and
Jerusalem, on 12, 21 and 24 April respectively. As more
violence was anticipated reinforcements were called for. These
were to include Four Five and 42 Commando, of the Commando Brigade. 40 Commando had already been in Haifa
since earlier on in the year, guarding the docks.

At half-past nine on the night of 29 April, 1948 Lt-Col Eric
Palmer recalls being 'hauled out of the cinema' by the Assistant
Adjutant, Capt Derek Pounds, and being told that he was to
report to Cyrenaica District Headquarters to be warned of a
possible move, within the next few days, to Palestine. At half-
past three the next morning (30 April) another summons
came. This time the notice was shorter. The Commando was
to be flown to Haifa in Dakotas in two lifts of 200 men—the
first ever operational air move of a Commando unit. The first
flight was due to leave Benghazi at eight o'clock, which left the
Adjutant (Capt John Parsons) only five hours in which to
prepare for what was virtually a completely new venture for
Four Five. It was now a question of 'panic stations' and the
next period is left to the reader's wildest imagination!

Fortunately the time of emplaning was put off until ten
o'clock, that morning, but even so time was short and every
man had to be ready for battle immediately on landing. At
this stage the Commanding Officer had been given no intimation
as to what Four Five would have to do on arrival, or even
precisely where it was going, and he wisely decided to prepare
everyone for the worst possible occurrences when they got
there. In the event these precautions were not put into practice.

The first lift from Benghazi was airborne just before midday,
and the Intelligence Officer, Capt Bob Loudoun, without maps
or other briefing aids, recollects following the route to Palestine,
along the coastline, with the only means available, the open
pages of a school atlas! This first lift eventually stepped out of
the aircraft that evening at Ramal El David Airport, fifteen

miles from Haifa. It was a considerable anti-climax to find everything relatively calm and peaceful. The Dakotas were doing sterling work and after a brief refuelling stop flew back to Benghazi with relief crews to pick up the remainder of Four Five. They returned to Haifa by midday on 1 May (six hours before schedule), and thus the unit accomplished a fitting 'first' and one which was to become a far more frequent feature of strategic operations in the years ahead.

Under command of the 1st Guards Brigade the Commando rapidly settled in to its district of Haifa where it was responsible for security in the area of Mount Carmel. Duties for the next few days consisted mainly of manning road blocks and observation posts and patrols in the streets. It was not a particularly eventful period as the tension was beginning to ease, but there was one exchange, overheard at a road block, worthy of repetition. A large civilian vehicle containing four fierce-looking armed men had just drawn up at the barrier. The Marine on duty bent down and asked the driver to identify himself and his companions:

'Haganah,'* was the reply.

'Haganah? Who are they and what do they do?'

'We are soldiers of God,' said the driver, drawing himself up in his seat proudly.

'Well, you must be a long way from your barracks then!'

On 12 May, despite the heartfelt representations of the Commanding Officer, it was time for Four Five, after such a short stay in Palestine, to depart again for Benghazi in HMT *Empire Test*. The British Mandate was almost at an end, and it had always been the intention to withdraw the reinforcement units first as soon as the tension began to ease. In any case, a larger number of troops than was really necessary could easily have caused the situation to deteriorate again.

After the quick moves and activity of the previous fortnight,

* 'Official' Jewish Army.

Benghazi was relatively quiet. The UNO Commission had left, and it was just a question of waiting for three weeks for the return to Malta on 8 June, 1948.

The next six months saw the final transition of Four Five from wartime (Hostilities Only) to regular and National Service ranks. The last of these—the 'Rajah Draft', which had sailed for Hong Kong some two and a half years previously— returned to the United Kingdom, and a busy time followed training the reinforcements, culminating in a six week work-up in Tarhuna, Tripoli, beginning in August. Command also changed in this period. Lt-Col Eric Palmer was unfortunately invalided home in July and his place was taken by Lt-Col P. L. Norcock for the next five months, until Lt-Col Charles Ries returned to Four Five, the unit which he had formed some five years previously.

The latter part of 1948 was punctuated by several 'move' scares, including a minor disturbance in Malta Dockyard on 15 December. These, however, came to nothing, but in January, 1949, Four Five was on its travels again. In the true spirit of the Brigade, whenever trouble was brewing in the Middle East, one of its units was usually summoned to the scene. Tension was now mounting in the Canal Zone. The Israelis had shot down a British aircraft on 7 January, and in addition King Farouk's attitude to our forces was becoming increasingly aggressive. It had already been planned that Four Five should relieve 42 Commando, in the Canal Zone, but the dates of this *roulement* were advanced and the Commando sailed from Malta on the 7th. The Commanding Officer and the Adjutant, Capt Leslie Marsh, flew out on the same day.

The Commando's first base was the tented camp at Port Tewfiq, some four miles from Suez, but at the end of the month the unit moved up to Moascar to patrol the lengths of Royal Signals underground cable that linked Port Said and Suez. The cable was made out of valuable copper coil and thieves were removing lengths of up to 9,000 yards nightly and loading them upon vehicles which were quickly driven away to the local black market. The 'wogs' seemed adept at this sport and the cable joiners had many sleepless night repairing the damage.

Between February and April all the Troops of Four Five carried out long night patrols in this featureless area checking the cable, setting up road blocks and laying ambushes. Such was Four Five's skill that within two months some forty thieves had been accounted for and the stealing virtually stopped, thus easing considerably the burden of the cable layers.

On one patrol Z Troop (Capt Bengie Keen) surprised a gang who were trying to remove a section of oil pipeline with the aid of a camel. The thieves were arrested and the camel confiscated. The next morning Z Troop decided to do a victorious ceremonial entry into Moascar camp. The camel, ridden by Keen 'Pasha' and sporting the Troop colours, was triumphantly 'towed' along the main road into camp by a jeep to the accompaniment of a bugle fanfare and the cheers of the Marines lining the route. The camel took fright and broke loose, heading at great speed towards the camp exit, unseating its rider. The jeep, brought to the rescue, succeeded in re-capturing the 'ship of the desert', whose presence within the unit lines became increasingly embarrassing as the days wore on. Rumour has it that the camel was resold to the thieves after they had completed their prison sentence! During this time at Moascar the Commando's longest serving rank, Capt Bob Armstrong, left for civilian life. Capt Armstrong had been with Four Five since formation, a record of continuous service that is unlikely ever to be surpassed within the unit. Capt Armstrong joined A Troop, with which he landed on D-Day and then subsequently became Administrative Officer. There was very little that this redoubtable officer was 'unable to lay his hands on' to keep Four Five supplied with operational stores and equipment.

Having successfully checked the thieving of cable the Commando was soon to be on the move again to another place where trouble threatened. This time it was to Aqaba. In April, large elements of the Jewish Forces had concentrated on the

Trans-Jordanian border with the apparent aim of occupying the strategic port, the only usable one at the head of the Red Sea. A force which included Four Five was rushed to Aqaba and the unit established a defensive position to the north east of the airfield in some derelict buildings. For over two months, up until the end of June, 1949, Four Five was to occupy these sparse desert positions in the uncomfortable and intense summer heat. It was reported to be so hot (115°F) that TSM Mendham was reputed to be able to fry eggs on aluminium plates in less than twelve minutes without the use of a fire. Not unnaturally, with traditional guile, the unit enthusiastically set about improving its surroundings. A *Globe and Laurel* article describes how: '. . . we actually do possess a village of mud brick houses, but we are rather wary of inviting guests to the location, for the houses are roofless, windowless and doorless, and in many cases lack the requisite number of walls to justify the name. In the village Arab builders may be seen at work repairing gaps in the structure, fly-proofing windows where none previously existed, and installing simple but effective drainage systems. "Starlight" roofs, although a very healthy measure, do not account for sandstorms, so they have been replaced by tentage, and even this we hope to be only a temporary arrangement until roofing materials become available. Imagination and initiative amongst all ranks have resulted in some excellent *objets d'art*. The Regimental Aid Post, which houses our Medical Section under Surg-Lt Hugh Walters, is known to its occupants as Navy House. This has been very well finished and is our *pièce de résistance* to be shown to all visitors. Headquarters is a veritable rabbit warren and in order to find the Adjutant one has to wind one's way through tents and side-screens and gaping walls. A subterranean tunnel leads to the Headquarters "priest-hole", the dug outs and command posts essential to our task. We also have cause to be grateful to Sgt Stelfox of the Regimental Institute (responsible for the unit's recreational and entertainment activities) who has opened up a very successful canteen in one of the more respectable derelict buildings.'

The quick reaction of our force meant that the tension lessened considerably and the Commando was able to concentrate on routine desert training, which included long range desert patrols. By now news was reaching Aqaba of a move to an altogether different theatre of operations, the Far East. Generally this was popularly received by all except the married ranks, who had only been able to spend a few months with their families in Malta—a hazard of accompanied overseas tours. The evacuation from Aqaba was not without incident as the LCT carrying the transport and some ranks for repatriation to Suez, around the Sinai Peninsula, was forced by heavy seas to take shelter in a convenient bay. The vessel was feared lost until located some days later by a Royal Air Force search aircraft. On board the LCT food and supplies were low and everyone was overjoyed to receive new stores from a relief ship. The LCT eventually arrived at Suez two weeks behind schedule. The trip of the main body from Aqaba to Suez in LST *Reginald Kerr*, on 21 June, 1949, was comparatively uneventful and lasted for only two days. In Suez the next month was spent in preparing for embarkation to Hong Kong, after an absence of two years, in HMT *Georgic* which having left Malta on 21 July, was due to pick up Four Five at Suez so that the entire Brigade could sail to the Far East to face the threat from mainland China.

It was not until 1952 that the Commandos were eventually able to return to the Mediterranean and in that year, on 21 March, it was Four Five that was the first unit of the Brigade to return to Malta from Malaya. For the next eight years this Mediterranean isle was to form the base, but not for long periods the permanent home, of the Commando. It seemed that whilst Four Five disembarked in lighters from HMT *Devonshire* at Valetta, at the start of its second phase in the Mediterranean there was a slight clue, unknown at the time, as to future events. The Commando diarist recorded '. . . The Mediterranean Fleet left for Athens as we arrived led by the aircraft carrier *Theseus* and cruisers *Euryalus* and *Glasgow*. . . .'

It was HMS *Theseus* in four years' time, that was to take Four Five on a historic mission to evolve important new tactics in modern warfare.

Four Five's first home in Malta was only a temporary one—St Andrew's Barracks. When the remainder of the Brigade returned to the George Cross Island the Commando moved to the north west, where it was split between Ghadira and Ghain Tuffieha camps, on 25 June. For the next few months the unit enjoyed a respite from the operations of the preceding two years. Normal garrison duties, including Governor's Palace Guards and swimming on the idyllic Mediterranean shores were the order of the day. Command changed during this period. On Saturday 25 July, 1952, Lt-Col R. C. de Mussenden Leathes, whose coolness had successfully steered the unit through the troublesome days of the Malayan Emergency, departed. His place was taken by Lt-Col F. A. Eustace, a legendary figure whose apparently outspoken military exterior hid a warm and ready sense of humour. It was Lt-Col Frankie Eustace who described his two years in command of Four Five as 'the best of my service career'. He also remembers jovially that when he joined the Commando both the Second-in-Command, Major Charles Price, and the Adjutant, Capt John Owen, were in hospital: 'luckily they soon recovered from the surgeons' knives and carried the Commanding Officer!'

As the bright summer turned into autumn the Commando began preparations for the big ceremonial event of the year—and indeed of the Commando's history—the Presentation of the Colours which was due to be held on Floriana Parade Ground on 29 November. The Colours were to be presented to all three units of the Brigade, 40, 42 and 45 Commandos, by HRH Prince Philip, Duke of Edinburgh. (Later, on Coronation Day, 1953, to be appointed Captain General, Royal Marines.) This was the first occasion on which Colours had been presented to the Royal Marines Commando units since their formation. The rehearsal period for the parade took some six weeks. The first fortnight of this was, for Four Five, spent at Ghain Tuffieha, a difficult task as the parade was by no means large enough for major ceremonial rehearsals. For the next four weeks the drills were perfected at either Floriana or St Patrick's Barracks and the final dress rehearsal was held on Tuesday, 25 November in pouring rain. This meant that great efforts were required to clean the blanco which had dripped from the helmets and belts on to the best blue uniforms. An even greater mishap occurred a couple of days later at St Patrick's Barracks where the Colour Parties were completing their rehearsals. Tradition was broken when the Colours were 'uncased' so that the officers could 'get the feel' of these weighty items. A strong wind was blowing at the time and some of the Colours were damaged, necessitating frantic stitching to restore these valuable emblems to perfection for the big parade.

Fortunately Saturday, 29 November, 1952, dawned bright and clear. The *Times of Malta* correspondent sets the scene:

'The day was warm, the sky almost cloudless, the dark blue uniforms of the Royal Marines showed up their slick precise movements against the dust of the parade ground. The white helmets, belts and rifle slings gave a clean, spick and span look to the ceremonial and the varied colours of the ladies' dresses all helped to make a memorable and brilliant scene. Spectators were amused by the antics of a brown and black dog who seemed to think he had every right to wander over the parade ground. He was chased the length of the square by an athletic Marine until the police took over and the animal took cover among the crowd.'

Each Commando on parade was represented by four strong guards, each of three officers, four senior NCOs, and seventy-two rank and file.* It is of interest to note that two officers were on parade who had formerly served with Four Five at Montforterbeek; Lt-Col Ben de Courcy-Ireland (Commanding Officer 42 Commando, RM) and Major Bunny Kirby (Staff Officer to the Brigade Commander).

* See Appendix F for a list of those of Four Five holding key appointments on the parade.

The parade formed up as the Colours were being consecrated by the Chaplain of the Fleet, The Venerable Archdeacon F. N. Chamberlain, in St Paul's Anglican Cathedral,
Valetta. This ceremony was divorced from the presentation in
observance of the religious laws of the island. His Royal
Highness then arrived at Floriana at ten o'clock accompanied
by Sir Gerald Creasy (the Governor), Earl Mountbatten of
Burma (Commander-in-Chief, Mediterranean Fleet), Lieutenant-General Westall (the Commandant-General) and Major-
General Hemming (GOC, Malta Forces) and the parade, under
Brigadier J. L. Moulton, followed the prescribed ceremonial
sequence; the inspection in line; the troop of the Massed
Bands;* the presentation of Colours after the units had
formed hollow square; the address by the Duke of Edinburgh
followed by the Brigade Commander's reply; the re-forming
of line; the forming up for the march past in column of guards;
the march past; the reforming of line, and the advance in
review order and finally a Royal Salute followed by three
cheers.

In the true tradition of the Royal Marines it had been a
faultless display witnessed by many thousands, both official
visitors in reserved seats, and many others watching from
balconies and other vantage points. The Colour Officers from
Four Five on this historic occasion were Lt David Alexander
(Queen's) and Lt Mike Bull (Regimental). Major-General
C. F. Phillips, a noted historian of the Royal Marines who
witnessed the parade, reported: 'As far as we can discover, the
only previous occasion on which new Colours have been
presented to a Royal Marine unit was 142 years ago. The 1st
Battalion Royal Marines left the United Kingdom for the
Peninsula in November, 1810, and were presented with new
Colours by the British Envoy in Roscio Square in Lisbon the
following month, on 17 December, 1810.' Formerly Colours
had only been presented to the Royal Marines Divisions, but

* The Massed Bands and Drums of 3 Commando Brigade, HMS
Glasgow, HMS *Ocean*, and HMS *Tyne* under the direction of Major F.
Vivian Dunn.

sometimes battalions proceeding overseas had been lent Colours by the Divisions or been provided with old stands still retained by the Royal Marine Office.

Concurrent with the rehearsals for this spectacular parade the Brigade was also planning a full display of Commando training for his Royal Highness on the following Monday, 1 December, showing the great versatility of the Corps. Many of the ranks, who had been drilling smartly in blue uniforms during the previous week, now donned the more familiar green berets and denim smocks for this second demonstration on the south-west coast of the island; 'remember a Royal Marine Commando is always expected to achieve the impossible'. Four Five's contribution started with a judo display under Sgt Alan Downton (a Physical Training Instructor in HQ Troop) followed by A Troop (Capt Mark Nunns) crossing a steep inlet by various methods including rope bridges and rafts made of ground sheets. The Mortar and Machine Guns Troops, under Lt David Alexander, then engaged targets out at sea, and finally, in complete contrast, Z Troop (Capt Charles Watkins) showed the painstaking preparations and tactics employed on night raids.

Desert training in Tripoli for the first two months of 1953 provided a sharp contrast to the ceremonial of the previous year. The 200-mile sea journey from Malta was notable for the fact that a total of nine days elapsed before Four Five was complete at its destination, an old Italian barracks at Tarhuna where, ironically, RSM Albert Rendall had been a prisoner of war. The passage out was complicated by the fact that a variety of craft was used and one unfortunate LST had to make three separate journeys. Also the departure of one ship was delayed until 'certain ladies of easy virtue had been awakened and put ashore'. The Commanding Officer continued, 'Needless to say the Padre (Rev Dick Thornley) was travelling in this craft!' The training period ended in a fifty mile return march at night back across the desert to Tripoli. On this march B Troop (Capt Richard Fairrie) decided to conform to local custom and at the end of the last leg were seen to arrive bare-foot, will all their boots tied on to a rather doleful looking camel!

For a long time now the internal situation in Egypt had been worsening. A military coup in July, 1952, had resulted in the deposition of King Farouk and General Neguib had taken his place as 'titular leader of the revolution'. One of the major bones of contention between Egypt and Britain was, of course, the British presence in the Canal Zone, and in early 1953 negotiations were started on the subject. These talks were complicated on the one side by the Egyptian domestic struggle for power and differences of doctrinal policy between Neguib and Nasser, and on the other by Britain's reluctance to change its strategic policy towards the Canal. One author* describes our stand as follows: 'The Canal Zone base, quite apart from undoubted strategic importance, was regarded by the right wing Tories rather as a medieval baron might have regarded a chastity belt, since it guarded the integrity of the "imperial life line" and prevented the Arabs from getting up to any serious mischief'. A settlement was eventually reached in July, 1954, but not before the talks had broken down (in May, 1953) and strong British reinforcements had had to be rushed to the Zone. As mobile reserve for the theatre this task naturally fell to 3 Commando Brigade.

Four Five, now in St Patrick's Barracks, first heard of the news at seven-thirty on the morning of 12 May, when the General Assembly was sounded on the bugle and Lt-Col Eustace 'cleared lower decks'† and warned the unit that it was at twenty-four hours notice to move—destination unknown. The Commando was given the codeword to embark early on the morning on the 13th and by ten o'clock was alongside Manoel Island, in Sliema Creek, ready to board the destroyer depot ship HMS *Ranpura*. The transport travelled in HMS *Dieppe*. 'The Navy, though only given a few hours to prepare,

* John Marlowe in his *Arab Nationalism and British Imperialism*, Cresset Press, 1961.
† Naval terminology for addressing all ranks on board ship.

rose nobly to the occasion and made us very welcome. We slept on camp beds in every conceivable corner, ate our meals on the same camp beds and between times did a little PT, weapon training and—sunbathing.'

HMS *Ranpura* docked at Port Said on 18 May, 1953, without incident, although a warning of things to come was given to one unfortunate driver from Brigade Headquarters when some 'nimble fingered and footed native' lifted his kitbag only minutes after landing! Four Five started its second tour in the Canal Zone by being installed at the Base Ammunition Depot at Abu Sultan, having to squeeze into accommodation designed only for two infantry companies. However, operational tasks soon preoccupied the minds of the majority as the base stretched over an enormous area and patrols had to be on the constant alert to prevent the large scale pilfering which had been carried out by night intruders, despite the presence of strategically placed minefields. 'On one occasion,' wrote Lt-Col Eustace, 'the Intelligence Officer (Lt Denis O'Kelly) reported that the enemy had infiltrated the minefield walking backwards, judging by the footprints in the sand. The enemy had not. It was B Troop going out on patrol with their longing for bare feet, which they were convinced would not set off a mine— neither did they!'

After a month's stay at Abu Sultan, which included a full Coronation Day parade and service—ceremonial even found a place under active conditions—Four Five moved to Port Fuad, where facilities, although still rudimentary, were a great improvement. Duties consisted of guards on the Moascar Filtration Plant and other depots and manning road blocks and customs posts. In fact it was a long and tedious period which stretched intermittently until August, 1954. The monotony of internal security and guard was relieved by two exercises, one in Crete ('Weldfast') and one in Milos ('Med Convex'), which both ended in a very welcome 'runs ahore' in Athens. Another visit to Greece, this time unscheduled, took place on 15 August, 1953 when HMS *Gambia*, with a party of Four Five on board, was diverted from Malta to the island of Zante, recently struck by a devastating earthquake. Four Five's party was commanded by Capt Richard Onslow (formerly of X Troop) and QMS F. W. Selby (A Troop). TSM Selby later wrote a detailed account of the relief work carried out by those on board HMS *Gambia*:

'The ship was within half an hour's steaming from Zante when we saw the smoke and later, as it drew nearer, we saw the shattered buildings and the source of the smoke, which was a large fire in the centre of what had been the town of Zakinthos, the capital of the island. . . . From the ship we could see two buildings which appeared undamaged, in fact they were the only buildings we could see, they stood out amongst the rubble.'

For three days the party, working with the ship's detachment and sailors, helped clear a road through the ruined town, erect a fire break (despite two more earth tremors), put up a tented camp for the homeless and distribute food to the stricken populace. A busy time for Capt Onslow and his team, proving one has to be prepared for anything—even on a routine trip back to Malta.

When not on guard or other duties in the Canal Zone Four Five found time to carry out extensive exercises in the training areas south of Suez. During one of these training periods, on 16 March, 1954, Lt-Col Eustace found himself confronted by an irate Egyptian Border Patrol officer, escorted by Lt Jeremy Arnold (Z Troop), who arrived at the unit concentration area, right in the middle of the desert, in a battered American-type taxi 'in great need of paint'. The officer appeared convinced that Four Five was about to march on Cairo as it was approaching the Erskine Line.* He was soon persuaded, however, that the unit wasn't going any further west and in any case had no live ammunition! Seemingly satisfied the Egyptian departed, muttering that he hoped the Anglo-Egyptian settlement would soon be reached.

In March, 1954, there was another warning that Four Five

* The border between Egypt and the Canal Zone.

would be required to carry out ceremonial duties whilst on active service. A royal visit to Malta was scheduled for May and the Commando had to furnish guards totalling 185 men. Major Peter Spittall, the Second-in-Command, broke this 'welcome' news and it was soon noted that there was a sudden improvement in personal drill and bearing in Port Fuad in order to impress the selectors! A combined force from all three Commandos and detachments from HM Ships was formed under Lt-Col Eustace (later awarded an OBE in the 1954 birthday honours) and carried out guards, street lining and a Ceremonial Review. One special feature of the second day of the visit was an invitation given by the Captain General that he would like to meet 'his officers and their wives for drinks that evening'—a royal cocktail party was duly arranged in the Union Club at less than six hours notice. Having been welcomed by Brigadier Moulton, Prince Philip was reported to have thoroughly enjoyed an informal evening, and several stalwart Marines were required afterwards to clear a path through the dense throng outside so that the royal car could get away.

As the hot summer wore on there were signs that headway was at last being made over the political talks in Egypt. An agreement was arrived at in July, 1954 which provided for the evacuation of British troops within eighteen months. Thankfully, Four Five left the Canal Zone by sea on 16 August and on the 19th the unit was happily unpacking and settling in to Ghain Tuffieha and Ghadira again, having been based in the desert for nearly fifteen months.

Several noteworthy arrivals occurred in Malta in the latter part of the year 1954. The first of these was RSM Jimmy Baines, who joined on 3 September. Small in stature, Mr Baines was a greatly respected character and every Marine's ideal of a regimental sergeant-major. Baines' connection with Four Five had been a long and historic one. He had joined the Commando in late 1944 as a sergeant and was wounded in the left leg by shrapnel at Montforterbeek whilst in B Troop. He then became Sergeant-Major of C Troop (later to become

X Troop) and served in Hong Kong and Malta. In December, 1948, he received the British Empire Medal for outstanding service and was subsequently awarded the Military Medal and the United States Bronze Star for his bravery whilst serving with 41 (Independent) Commando, Royal Marines, in Korea in 1951.

Another long association was revived on 28 September, when General Sir Robert Laycock became Governor of Malta. Command of the unit also changed in this period, on 28 October, when Lt-Col N. H. Tailyour took over from Lt-Col Frankie Eustace. Lt-Col Eustace's last duty was a ceremonial Trooping of the Colour on St Patrick's Parade to celebrate the Corps Birthday. He recalls that 'as the troops marched off Norman Tailyour was invited to halt them as it was after twelve o'clock and he was in command. Being well disciplined troops they would otherwise have marched into the sea!'

The early part of 1955, after a visit by the Captain General on 17 March to watch the Brigade training in Malta, was eventful for amphibious training which took place in conjunction with French forces at Arzew, some thirty miles east of Oran, in Algeria.* A strong bond of friendship was soon built up between Four Five and the French Forces—Marines, the Foreign Legion, and the Deuxième Zouaves. After the first part of the exercise, '*Bon Marché Un*', a week was spent in local liaison. Z Troop (Capt Don Michell) combined with the Brigade band at the celebrations of a local festival. The band, leading the detachment, got hopelessly lost in a maze of back streets and the Drum Major marched past the saluting base, it was reported, on no less than three occasions! 'A fourth attempt found them marching the wrong way past the dais—and the crowd loved it!'† To cement the association between the Brigade and the French troops the Brigade Commander, Brigadier I. H. Riches, and Lt-Col Norman

* The French forces were commanded by Vice Admiral Barjot who was to be the Deputy Allied Commander-in-Chief for the Port Said landings in 1956.

† *Globe and Laurel*, 1955.

12. *Four Five's mortars in action in Malaya, 1951.*

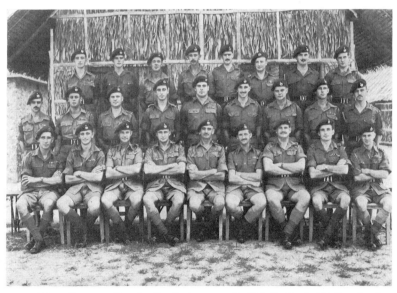

13. *The officers at Tapah, Perak, in 1951. Lt-Col R. C. de M. Leathes is
fifth from the left, front row.*

14. Tapah Station, 15 March, 1951.

15. Marine E. P. Lynn, a veteran of N.W. Europe, keeps a wary eye on a Cypriot village, 1958.

Tailyour were honoured by being invested as Honorary
Corporal and Private First Class of the Deuxième Zouaves.
The ceremony was performed in the French Officers' Mess to a
background of popping champagne corks.

Later on in the year longer periods were spent in Malta and
Four Five was able to show its prowess in the sporting world.
Z Troop (Capt Don Michell and QMS J. F. Jones) proved to
be particularly outstanding in this sphere and won no less
than seven sports trophies including the island's Water Polo
League, winning all eight matches and scoring sixty goals without reply. Fitness is an important feature of Commando life
and where possible all facilities are fully utilized. Others too
made their contribution and the Commando fielded a very
useful polo team doubtless well conditioned by days spent on
camel, and horseback, during gymkhanas in North Africa!
Donkeys also featured in these events and it was here that
Four Five acquired one of its first mascots entered in the books
as 'Probationary 2/Lt Ernest' with a ration of fifteen carrots per
day. Ernest's career was both chequered and brief and a few
months later he was reported absent, later amended to desertion,
having broken out of his paddock!

These carefree diversions could not last for long and beginning in September, 1955, the eastern end of the Mediterranean
was plunged into grave political turmoil, and Four Five found
itself in its rightful place as the spearhead of our operational
forces. The unit was committed to the majority of this period
both in Cyprus and at Port Said and accounts of these important campaigns have been included separately. During this
time only relatively brief spells were spent in Malta either
for rest and re-training or in preparation for the next bout of
active service.

Later on, in 1958, Malta too had its share of trouble and the
most serious incidents occurred in April when the Prime
Minister, Mr Dom Mintoff, resigned, and a General Strike was
called. Four Five was then training in Tripoli, but was rushed
back on 14 April for internal security duties. Political observers
at the time were beginning to forecast another Cyprus and

slogans of 'Independence' and 'British Go Home!' were being shouted with increasing vigour. From 19 April, at least one Troop of the Commando was at immediate notice. Incidents were beginning to become more widespread and several ugly scenes took place outside the Governor's Palace. The General Strike was due to take place on 28 April, and as the date drew nearer, tension mounted. On the day, X Troop (Lt Ray Frost)* was the first to be despatched, soon after midday, when it was sent to protect the Royal Navy Boom Defence Depot and vessels at the Marsa Hard area of Grand Harbour. When X Troop arrived it found an angry crowd of some 200 on the scene who greeted the Commandos with a hail of rocks and stones. Lt-Col Jack Richards visited the area later on in the afternoon, at five past three, and chose a particularly bad moment as the stoning was at its height. The windscreen of his vehicle was smashed, injuring the Post Corporal, who was on his daily run to pick up mail, and he had to have five stitches in his chin. Reinforcements were called and E Troop (Major Desmond Dillon) arrived soon afterwards, but by then the crowd had decided to move on. The Maltese appeared to have vented their feelings adequately and the disturbances soon petered out. More trouble was expected after a May Day meeting at the Empire Stadium. This was poorly attended and the meagre gather soon drifted away, allowing the troops to be 'stood down' at five to one. Relative political calm settled on the island once again, although Four Five was alerted during the following year when Mintoff demanded further action after the British Government's refusal to revoke the Malta Government's Constitution. The first stand-by was on 3 February, 1959, and another on 26 March, when the Naval

* For much of the period 1957–59, both in Malta and in Cyprus, X Troop was commanded by the legendary Capt Hamish Emslie. A tough and wiry officer he was later described as 'undoubtedly the best leader of a Company/Troop that the Corps has produced since the end of the Second World War'. Although a hard taskmaster, Capt Emslie always got the best results and his Troop's morale was always high. He was later ambushed and killed in Oman in 1966, while serving as a contract officer with the Sultan's Armed Forces.

Dockyard was due to be handed over to Bailey's. As the 26th was the last Government pay day, riots were expected, but the presence of our troops obviously had a salutary effect, and everything passed quietly.

The final year in Malta was a most settled one. Lt-Col Billy Barton was able to plan a regular programme of exercises in Libya and in Italy, and other training. As 1959 wore on the 'buzzes' that Four Five would be on the move again increased. Eventually these were confirmed, on 16 October, when the Commanding Officer was able to tell the unit that it would be leaving the now relatively peaceful Mediterranean and going to Aden in the following April. To mark its departure from the island, after an association which had lasted for over a decade, Four Five decided to lay on a farewell tattoo at Mtarfa Barracks, the Commando's last home on the island, at dusk on 20 February, 1960. The programme was an ambitious one and was produced by Capt Jimmy Wild. Items included drill and ceremonial, under the watchful eyes of the Adjutant and Regimental Sergeant-Major—Capt Alastair Donald and RSM J. R. McDonnell; Physical Training under Lt Jim Golds-worthy; Motor Transport and a March Past of the entire unit with its various weapons and equipment. Band displays were also on the agenda plus light relief provided by Z Troop who re-enacted the legend of St George and the Dragon. For this act Sgt 'Wat' Tyler was mounted on an immaculate white police charger which had to face, and subsequently chase, an amazingly realistic fire-breathing dragon built by members of the Troop under Sgt Chilcott. This performance delighted the 2,000 or so schoolchildren who attended the dress rehearsal and the 'official' audience for the final show. Local press reports later hailed the performance as both 'impressive' and 'spectacular'—indeed a fitting finale before the unit's departure.

The Mediterranean period again proved the mobility and strategic importance of the Commando Brigade. Its quick response and presence in many political and military crises doubtless helped to contain situations which would otherwise have deteriorated rapidly. These critical years fully tested the alertness of Four Five, and we have seen how reaction times to calls for action were reduced considerably by air reinforcement —a notable 'first' for the Commando. Amphibious strategy, too, was developed and Four Five was able to show how admirably this could be combined with the helicopter assault, a most significant step forward in modern warfare.

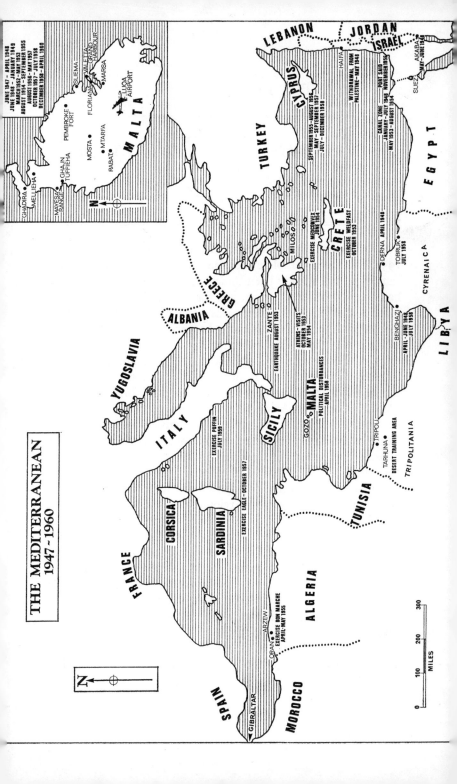

THE MEDITERRANEAN
1947~1960

JUNE 1947 - APRIL 1948
JUNE 1948 - JANUARY 1949
MARCH 1952 - MAY 1953
AUGUST 1954 - SEPTEMBER 1955
AUGUST 1955 - MAY 1957
OCTOBER 1957 - JULY 1958
DECEMBER 1958 - APRIL 1960

MALTA

GHADIRA
MELLIEHA
MAYSE RANGE
GHAJN TUFFIEHA
PEMBROKE FORT
SLIEMA
VALLETTA
GRAND HARBOUR
MARSA
MOSTA
MTARFA
RABAT
FLORIANA
LUQA AIRPORT

SPAIN
GIBRALTAR
MOROCCO
ALGERIA
ORAN
ARZEW
EXERCISE BON MARCHE
APRIL-MAY 1955
FRANCE
CORSICA
SARDINIA
EXERCISE EAGLE - OCTOBER 1957
EXERCISE PUFFIN
JULY 1959
ITALY
YUGOSLAVIA
ALBANIA
GREECE
SICILY
GOZO
MALTA
POLITICAL DISTURBANCES
APRIL 1958
ZANTE
EARTHQUAKE AUGUST 1953
ATHENS - VISITS
OCTOBER 1953
MAY 1954
MILOS
EXERCISE MEDICONVEX
JUNE 1954
CRETE
EXERCISE WELDFAST
OCTOBER 1953
TUNISIA
TARHUNA
DESERT TRAINING AREA
TRIPOLI
TRIPOLITANIA
BENGHAZI
APRIL - JUNE 1946
JULY 1958
DERNA APRIL 1948
TOBRUK
JULY 1958
CYRENAICA
LIBYA
TURKEY
CYPRUS
SEPTEMBER 1955 - AUGUST 1956
MAY - SEPTEMBER 1957
JULY - DECEMBER 1958
LEBANON
JORDAN
ISRAEL
HAIFA
WITHDRAWAL FROM
PALESTINE - MAY 1948
PORT SAID
JANUARY-JULY 1948
NOVEMBER 1956
CANAL ZONE
MAY 1953 - AUGUST 1954
SUEZ
AKABA
MAY - JUNE 1949
EGYPT

0   100   200   300
MILES

CHAPTER 10

Cyprus—The Battle against the EOKA Gangs

As so often happens, the first move to Cyprus, in 1955, came as a complete surprise to Four Five. The terrorist campaign had already been under way for some time and this had sparked off civil unrest, but for the marines of the Commando back in Malta there was little to suggest that there would soon be an emergency. In early September routine training was the major preoccupation and the unit was busily engaged in preparing to embark in the Amphibious Warfare Squadron for an exercise in Benghazi. On 3 September, the day before the planned embarkation, the move to North Africa was placed in abeyance. An operational deployment, to a destination yet undisclosed to the majority of the Commando, was pending. Stores were hastily re-packed and although married ranks were allowed home, the unit remained on full alert. At two-thirty on the morning of the 6th Lt-Col Norman Tailyour was awakened and given the executive order to move. Such was the speed of the recall that one sergeant rejoined the unit dressed in pyjamas! By six o'clock that morning Four Five started to embark in HM Ships *Striker*, *Reggio* and *Meon* 'with commendable tidiness and speed'. Those embarked were briefed in detail on their destination and on the following morning the BBC was able to announce to the world that a 'Commando force of over 600 Royal Marines was on its way to Cyprus', an island that was to be in the headlines for many years to come and is still the centre of bitter controversy.

The fame of Four Five was to spread abroad quickly because the Unit Instructor Officer, Instructor Lt-Cdr Lionel Jenkins, on leave in Athens at the time of the announcement of the move, was able to pick up the local newspapers and see big coloured cartoons emblazoned across the front pages depicting the 'Herculean monsters of 45 Commando invading Cyprus'!

Trouble in Cyprus had been anticipated for some time and the first serious threats had been uttered by General Grivas in Athens some two years before he had landed in Cyprus, in November, 1954, to begin the struggle for ENOSIS (Union with Greece). The preamble to his 'General Plan' read as follows and formed the basis for all subsequent operations:

'THE OBJECTIVE. To arouse international public opinion, especially among the allies of Greece, by deeds of heroism and self-sacrifice which will focus attention on Cyprus until our aims are achieved. The British must be continuously harried and beset until they are obliged by international diplomacy exercised through the United Nations to examine the Cyprus problem and settle it in accordance with the desires of the Cypriot people and the whole Greek nation.'*

The ENOSIS slogan had been shouted for over twenty years and in the early years of evolvement had been actively supported by both the Greek Orthodox Church and the local Communist Party. The Hierarchy was removed from the Greek Orthodox Church after its involvement in anti-government disturbances in 1931. The Hierarchy was restored after the war and since 1950 had been held by Archbishop Makarios. The Church had used its organization and funds to set up an island-wide movement for ENOSIS, complete with National Youth Clubs and other bodies. The contribution made by the communists was not nearly so comprehensive, but nevertheless ENOSIS provided an eminently suitable platform for their propaganda.

The terrorism in Cyprus, as is usually the case in these internal struggles, was to last for many years and Four Five was to complete three tours of operational duty in this particular

* *The Memoirs of General Grivas*, edited by Charles Foley, Longmans Limited.

emergency, from 10 September, 1955 to 14 August, 1956; from 30 May to 28 September, 1957; and from 27 July to 14 December, 1958. The Commando also provided the personnel for an independent 'Heliforce' between 19 June and 18 July, 1958. These three years, however, could not be entirely devoted to the Cyprus problem and once more the unit was to prove its versatility and its worth by its outstanding contribution to the Port Said landings in November, 1956.

The speed with which the unit undertook its new task can be judged by the fact that within six hours of its arrival at Famagusta on 10 September, 1955, all the new operational locations had been taken over. This had already prompted the Military Commander to comment to a senior member of his staff, after Lt-Col Tailyour had carried out his initial reconnaissance, 'We have a strange Commanding Officer here who says that his troops will be out on patrol a few hours after disembarking—a previous Battalion asked for twelve days to settle in!' The Commando area was along the Kyrenia mountain range which stretches across the north of Cyprus. Headquarters were situated at Aghirda, at the southern entrance of the strategic Kyrenia Pass. The remainder of the range was divided into four areas, each with a Troop operating independently. Also under command, for internal security duties, was the Amphibious Warfare (AW) Troop, commanded by Major John Waters, composed of Royal Marines from the Amphibious Squadron.

The pattern of operations was a mixed one. The detached observer would like to think that they fell into two major categories; either internal security or anti-terrorist operations. This, however, would be over-simplifying the case, for there could often not be a clear definition of each of the separate types of incident. The emphasis in the intial period in Cyprus was on assisting the civil authorities to restore law and order, which by now had become undermined by EOKA. This meant that the Commando was employed in a police-type role, manning road blocks, removing EOKA flags, seizing pamphlets and dispersing hostile crowds in villages. The halting of civil unrest was insufficient to check the real cause of the trouble—the hard core of EOKA terrorists who were inciting the opposition. Terrorism had to be countered by long hours of patrolling and the subsequent cordoning of villages or mountain areas when positive information had been received. The aim of the village cordon and searches was to capture known EOKA supporters and suppliers, and the aim of mountain operations was to 'shoot it out' with the terrorists in their hides or camps. In all operations a village or area had to be sealed off with a cordon of troops by first light. This meant pre-dawn starts from the various locations. When the cordon was in place search parties, usually accompanied by the police or local authorities, would sweep the area. In village operations the search party would be preceded by a Land Rover with a loud hailer mounted announcing that there was a curfew confining females and children indoors and instructing males to walk to a barbed wire cage for screening and interrogation. This last process was normally carried out by Special Branch or Intelligence personnel.

The opposition used these first few months as a period to try out the strength and determination of Four Five. This they soon learnt to their cost and as a result of the Commando's policy of completely dominating the Kyrenia Range by patrolling and operations most of the hard core elements withdrew to the Troodos area and the towns. Initially one of the great problems was the gathering of intelligence concerning terrorist activities in the mountains. The duties which are now (normally) undertaken by police, Special Branch, Military Intelligence Officers and others, were carried out by unit officers, using local civil servants recruited as interpreters, and uniformed police. This improvization frequently occurs at the beginning of campaigns and although not entirely satisfactory it does at least provide some basis upon which a fully complemented organization can be later built. In the case of Cyprus it was a slow process to gather together information concerning terrorist strengths and the location of their 'hide areas'.

The first village cordon to be carried out by Four Five was

'Operation Stormsail', which started on the night of 14 September, less than five days after the arrival of the unit in Cyprus, to search the village of Mandres. The inner cordon consisted of three Troops, B (Major Andrew Halliday,* X (Capt Dan Hunt) and the A.W. Troop. E Troop (Capt Dennis Sluman) formed the search party whilst A Troop (Major Hugh Bruce) and the Machine Gun Sections patrolled strategic sectors away from the village. The first convoy of vehicles left Aghirda at ten o'clock on the night of the 14th, and by four-forty on the morning of the 15th the cordon was in position. Reveille was sounded just after five and the operation continued after that. One of the first men to be brought forward was the Mukthar (Mayor) of Mandres. The Commanding Officer interviewed him and, according to contemporary records, 'kept up a remarkable spate of questions—twenty-three in two minutes'. Even a priest was brought in for interrogation, but such was the speed of his inquisitor that he was soon caught out. 'Are you married?' 'No.' But later, 'How many children have you got?'. 'Seven! One died last year.' In the meantime the search of the village continued. Firearms were brought to the local coffee house for the checking of licences and taking no chances, the A.W. Troop searched the church to the north-west of the village, believed to be the first time that religious property was included during Cyprus operations.

Although nothing of startling importance was uncovered during 'Stormsail' it did have its lighter moments. It was usual, on this type of operation, for the unit to be accompanied by the Medical Officer, Surg Lt Guy Bradford, RN, both to treat our casualties and tend the sick in outlying villages. The intrusion of troops had usually been greeted by a typical sullenness and it was hoped that this sort of assistance would not only break down the barriers of mistrust, but also win the population to our side so that they would be more willing to

* Son of General Sir Lewis Halliday who, as a captain in the Royal Marine Light Infantry, was awarded the Victoria Cross after an outstanding contribution to the defence of the British legation during the Boxer rebellion in China, 1900.

come forward with vital information about the terrorists. After the cordon had been in position for about an hour, the Medical Officer was duly called forward to the village square and unpacked his valises, 'feeling rather like a uniformed hawker of patent medicines'. His presence was then announced by the loud hailer, 'free medical attention is available', but there seemed to be an initial hesitance on the part of the suspicious villagers. The first person to come forward was the Mukthar who muttered something to an interpreter, 'Sir— he says there are no sick'. However, the ice was soon broken after that and the doctor was still holding surgery two hours later!

It was an incongruous scene as the doctor held court in the bright sunshine. The women and children just stood and watched patiently, their faces without expression. The Medical Officer claimed that his best case was when a young girl came up complaining of earache, and he found that he had run out of ear drops. The Sick Berth Petty Officer, Petty Officer Blythe, tugged the MO's sleeve and whispered evilly, 'Don't worry sir, why not try local anaesthetic?' Surg Lt Bradford had a quick twinge of conscience, knowing that the 'cure' would only be temporary. However, the treatment was duly administered and after a short time the girl whispered something to the interpreter. A murmur of appreciation arose from the crowd. 'What was that?' queried the Medical Officer. 'She says the pain has gone', was the reply. The doctor's magical healing powers had now been witnessed by all, and the looks of suspicion now turned to smiles and friendliness.

Whilst the bulk of Four Five was engaged in 'Stormsail' the remaining Troop, Z Troop (Capt Donald Michell) was carrying out its own operation on the south of the island. The Troop's base was at Paralimni, in the south-east corner of Cyprus, and on 14 September, they moved from here to Larnaca and embarked in landing craft to carry out a coastal search and then move inland. This 'amphibious assault' was the prelude to a thorough search of buildings and caves for arms and subversive documents. The warlike appearance of the

Commandos with fixed bayonets caused some consternation and extreme fright amongst the women. Realizing that this image would only alienate relations, the Troop Commander ordered the removal of the offending bayonets. The search continued uneventfully, except for some of the ranks of Z Troop who had to rope down into wells a hundred feet deep to check for hidden arms. The pin-prick of light representing the outside world seemed many hundreds of feet above, and it was naturally with great relief that these ranks reached the bright daylight after the dark gloom below.

One amusing incident which occurred during the time when Four Five was based in the Kyrenia area was when an operation was mounted against the 'Bishopric' who were making incitement speeches and generally whipping up anti-British feeling. As a result road blocks were set up and in charge of one of these was a 'big, tough' sergeant from B Troop, who was given orders to stop and search all vehicles. A car was subsequently halted at his barrier which contained a bishop and his secretary who both refused to get out and let it be searched. After repeated requests and refusals the secretary got out and approached the sergeant to complain that 'His Beatitude did not like this treatment'. To which the sergeant promptly replied, 'I don't like his B-attitude either—get out!'

On 23 September, when the Greek appeal over Cyprus was rejected at the United Nations, sixteen EOKA detainees made a daring and spectacular escape from Kyrenia Castle prison. The unit was warned at ten o'clock that night and almost immediately road blocks were set up and search parties dispatched. General Grivas, in his book, claimed this as the 'last humiliation' for the régime of the Governor, Sir Robert Armitage, but failed to mention that seven of the prisoners were recaptured within twenty-four hours, four of these being accounted for by Four Five. Support Troop notched up their first success on this chase when Lt Alan Naylor and one of his patrols grabbed two escapees attempting to make good their getaway on the afternoon of the 24th. The trail of some of the escapees led to a monastery and although we have already heard of a church being investigated this was the first time that our troops had ever set foot in this type of building. The monks and priests, of course, vehemently denied their involvement, and this particular search caused much concern to the British authorities when it was later reported. As a result of this escape the Commanding Officer was invited to investigate the internal security of the Castle. This was done in company with Major Bruce (A Troop) who was an expert on such matters. The team found the security arrangements to be most inadequate and it is reported that a signal was sent, which caused considerable comment in higher circles, to this effect: 'Instructions carried out accompanied by Major Hugh Bruce, late of COLDITZ, who states that given twenty minutes he would have been out of the Castle himself!'

The A.W. Troop departed on the 26th after their 'two weeks' holiday' and in a farewell message to the Commanding Officer Major J. T. O. Waters begged that 'you will not withdraw our red lanyards next time we give you a wet landing'. Z Troop moved in from their outpost to assume the A.W. Troop's role.

The internal situation was getting increasingly hostile with both acts of terrorism and the distribution and display of provocative slogans and literature becoming the order of the day. On several occasions Four Five was the direct recipient of these outbursts and one typical example occurred on 2 October, 1955, when the Commanding Officer was handed a poster, written in Greek on poor quality paper, which had been found in the Commando's area. 'British Commandos. You are informed to abandon our Greek island before your blood is shed and left to us as a souvenir. . . . Signed Dighenis' (The Leader, i.e. Grivas). About this time overall security matters were being strengthened too by the appointment of Field-Marshal Sir John Harding as Governor on 25 September. It was now clear that sterner measures were to be implemented and on 26 November the new Governor proclaimed a State of Emergency. In view of this declaration the Governor, luckily as it turned out, had to cancel his visit to the annual Caledonian

Ball at the Lydria Palace Hotel. The terrorists were determined to see that the new state of affairs did not go completely unheralded. Several bombs were thrown into the ballroom—putting the lights out and severing a water pipe which subsequently flooded part of the dance floor. When the lights eventually came back on again it was discovered that the entire hotel staff had fled 'thus enabling', as one witness explained, 'the guests to enjoy free food and drink for many hours after the excitement had died down!' Field-Marshal Sir John Harding had already been closely associated with Four Five when he had been Commander-in-Chief Far East Land Forces whilst the Commando had been in Malaya and had last seen the unit in May, 1951, on a farewell tour of inspection before relinquishing his command. His first visit to Four Five in Cyprus was on 9 December, 1955, when the Commando was at Platres.

The longest operation undertaken by Four Five in its early months in Cyprus was 'Turkey Trot', which was mounted in five phases, the Commando being deployed in the field for a week. With companies attached from the 1st Royal Leicesters and the 1st Royal Norfolks the unit carried out intensive searches in the mountains near Kyrenia for terrorists and their supplies. Although no terrorists were caught, a considerable haul of arms and ammunition was made. Many hideouts were also located in the precipitous countryside, well supplied with food, stores and the inevitable literature. The EOKA were being kept on the run. On 6 November it was learnt that an EOKA 'defector' was able to give information on the whereabouts of terrorists in the mountains. Taking no chances the Adjutant, Capt Derek Pounds, set off for the village of Lapithos, a notorious local 'hot-spot', at four-fifteen in the morning to snatch the informer. The house was typical of the buildings in the neighbourhood, painted white on the outside, but primitive indoors with a hard-packed earthen floor and the all-too-familiar odour of a peasant existence which clings to the nostrils. The victim was a butcher, who had previously been a shepherd and had enjoyed the confidence of a local terrorists group led by Gregoris Afxentiou, but had tired of the rigours of life in the mountains, and had opted for a more sedentary routine in the village. After the house had been surrounded the poor unfortunate was dragged from his bed and handcuffed to the imposing figures of the Regimental Sergeant Major, RSM Jimmy Baines, and Colour Sgt Lund of E Troop. In this manner the Cypriot was taken to a waiting patrol and dragged across the mountainsides in search of the terrorist groups. The butcher's information was reliable and several caves, which had been recently occupied, were discovered containing arms and ammunition. Grivas later said that the gang had been warned beforehand, but even so admitted that it was a close shave and reduced Afxentiou from his leadership for employing a traitor. Another interesting find in the search was a forgery outfit for Cyprus two-shilling pieces—it seems that EOKA's subversive activities were widespread. Such was the skill of the terrorists at concealing hides and equipment that the forgery kit was found in a cave some fifteen feet below the north face of a peak in the Kyrenia range. The Commandos had to follow the same precipitous route as the forger, down a rope, which led on to a small ledge from which a cave ran back into the mountainside.

The hard core of the terrorists were known to be operating from the Troodos Mountains, in the south west of the island, and on Thursday, 10 November, Four Five moved by convoy, in heavy rain, along the twisting roads to new locations. The 1st Royal Leicesters assumed control of the Kyrenia area. The Troodos Mountains extend over an area of some 400 square miles, and the highest peak is Mount Olympus which rises to 6,000 feet. In some areas the mountains are covered in pine trees and thick undergrowth, but other are sparse, and the surface consists of treacherous loose shale. Lower down, the slopes are terraced into vineyards which surround the primitive villages in the valleys. The main roads in the region are asphalt surfaced, and wind along the contours, thus creating splendid ambush positions for the terrorists. Dirt tracks link the remote villages to these main roads.

The population was found to be predominantly anti-British due mainly to the medieval power of the Greek Orthodox Church which had a strong influence over its subjects. There were only a few Turkish Cypriots in the region. The problem was worsened by the fact that the majority of the inhabitants had been thoroughly intimidated by the hard core terrorists who had (until Four Five arrived) enjoyed a long period without any harassment in which to establish and organize themselves in the area.

The anti-British sentiments expressed by the villagers meant that the terrorists in their hides dug into the mountainsides, were getting full support from the surrounding communities. The villagers often gave their assistance to the EOKA campaign in the subsidiary roles of agents, couriers and suppliers. It was, therefore, difficult for the Special Branch to break into this close-knit web and plant informers, and it also meant that the plans and movements of security forces had to contain a degree of flexibility to avoid detection or prior warning.

The Troodos region was designated a Sub Area and was commanded by Lt-Col Tailyour from the base at Platres. This headquarters was situated in the Hotel Splendid, which according to a contemporary observer 'didn't quite live up to its name' and was shared with senior police and Special Branch officers. Major Ian De'Ath, who had commanded Four Five for a short spell at the end of the war, was Staff Officer Operations at this headquarters and was responsible for co-ordinating all the information from his colleagues and subsequently planning, in detail, the operations.

Platres appeared to be a pleasant town with its spacious buildings tucked amongst the trees on the rising hillside. One of the houses that will doubtless re-kindle many memories was Kosta's Bar, where many a successful operation was re-fought over a bottle of Keo beer or a glass of brandy sour. The Provost Section under Sgt Jackman found themselves keeping a watchful eye over the large prison block, which was described as bearing a close resemblance to Alcatraz. Detainees were held here for initial interrogation before being escorted to the larger centres in Limassol or Nicosia. The suspects, despite ill-founded claims to the contrary, enjoyed a sheltered existence here after their somewhat uncertain lives in the mountains, and many were reported to be reluctant to leave.

The Rifle Troops (Support acted in an infantry role) were split between the two locations of Platres and the Troodos Leave Centre. This latter was at an altitude of 5,500 feet and was reputedly 'unsuitable for heart conditions or cases of chronic kidney disease'. These limitations did not appear to effect the occupants of Troodos, A, X and S Troops.

The total strength of the forces in the area was some 800 troops which included two companies from 1st Gordon Highlanders, old friends of the Commando from the Malayan campaign, who were under command and based at Kakopetria and Pedhoulas; a troop of A Squadron, the Life Guards (later relieved by B Squadron, the Royal Horse Guards); and elements of the Cyprus Police Force and military tracker and arms recovery dogs.

Within three days of its arrival in the mountains the Commando was called out for its first major operation, the restoring of order in the village of Vouni. The village was known to be a troublesome one, 'stroppy' in Marine parlance, and had defied a request from the Assistant Superintendent of Police, Mr Lee, to remove an EOKA flag which was hoisted above the school. As strong resistance was expected the Commanding Officer decided to commit the whole unit, and gave orders to that effect at six o'clock on the evening of 13 November. The normal textbook procedure for riot dispersal in narrow streets was often inappropriate, especially in cases where open hostility and militance was being shown. The operation normally started with a pre-dawn curfew, the erection of a cage and the entry of the riot troops armed either with batons or rifles. To supplement the armoury tear gas and dye sprayers were carried. The latter weapons were used both to deter the crowd and to make the identification of ringleaders easier. Their accuracy and reliability, however, were somewhat erratic and our own side often suffered the most, many of the operators being covered in the bright-coloured liquid!

It was a crisp morning as the convoy came to a halt near the village and the cordon troops began to fan out. Warning of Four Five's arrival had been given well in advance and it appeared that most of the village had turned out at five in the morning to form a reception committee. The church bells were rung vigorously and a crowd of about 300 was assembled in front of the school. The story is now taken up by Instructor Lt-Cdr Jenkins:

'As the "Naval Acorn"* my vehicle was the Loud Hailer Land Rover in which I had a driver (a well suited ex-stock car racer), an interpreter and one policeman. We were always first into any village during cordon and search operations and Vouni was no exception. When ordered into the village we drove round a spur on to a short U-bend leading to the village. Some twenty five yards from the first houses there was a small road block of rocks erected by the villagers and facing us, where the houses began, was a large mob in the front of which were villagers armed with crowbars, clubs and axes. They started shouting and bombarded us with rocks and stones. After a quick scrabble for the one tin hat in the vehicle we did a speedy reverse out of range.'

Despite numerous requests the crowd refused to move, and as A, X and Z Troops formed up at five forty-five they were greeted with a further barrage of cat-calls, jeers and rocks. Colour Sgt Jim Pollitt, of Headquarters Troop, remembers one rather vociferous lady who was standing at a vantage point with an apron full of stones which she was hurling at the Marines to the accompaniment of shrieks of 'EOKA'. She had to be restrained forcibly.

The school, sited rather like a castle keep on a mound in the village, was being used as the last bastion of defence with pyramids of rocks piled at intervals around the crest. The

* Intelligence Officer.

building, whose only access was by two flights of steep steps, had an EOKA flag flying above it and other derogatory posters and banners placed all around in prominent positions. Lt-Col Tailyour realized that the hostile population could not be calmed down by kid-glove methods—'the women were fighting like Amazons'—and that serious injury might occur amongst his men, many of whom were already badly cut and bruised. He therefore ordered tear gas to be fired followed by a baton charge by A, X and Z Troops. Armed with truncheons and rifle butts raised the troops waded in. The confused hand-to-hand fighting continued for some time until, as the unit diarist reported, 'the crowd began to waver before the determined onslaught of the baton parties'. Injuries were inflicted by both sides. One Cypriot was wounded in the leg by a tear gas bomb which exploded when he tried to kick it away, and Sgt Robinson of X Troop sustained a broken jaw in the mêlée. One party from Z Troop found themselves cut off from the remainder and completely surrounded by villagers who were screaming for revenge. Led by the Troop Commander, Capt Donald Michell, they fought their way out and were fortunate in escaping without loss of life. The early part of the struggle was contested against the background of the steady tolling of the church bell, but this ceased after QMS Frank Collingwood, of B Troop, ordered one of his charges to go to the tower and muffle the sounds. By six-thirty, after a struggle which had lasted for nearly an hour, Four Five were firmly in control and those who had escaped arrest were in full flight. The rioters who had been caught were by now being herded together and marched under escort to a nearby café where they were held until trucks could be brought up to take them to the cages built by the Assault Engineers under the able direction of Cpl Wainwright and Marine Dunlop.

For the remainder of the day the Special Branch interrogation team screened some 300 persons, whilst the village was kept under strict curfew by B and Support Troops. At six-thirty, when the questioning was completed, thirty men and nine women were held on charges of inciting and leading the riot. By nightfall all was quiet in the village. Moderates might oppose the methods used, but after 14 November there were no more open acts of hostility towards the security forces from the population of Vouni which had unsuccessfully embarked on a trial of strength to gauge the tenacity of Four Five . . . and lost.

On 22 November, a new threat was directed at Four Five; that of the road ambush. However alert the drivers and escorts were, these attacks always seemed to come when least expected and all too quickly. On this occasion the terrorists, in a bid to capture explosives, opened fire on a vehicle driven by Marine William Stephenson, carrying sixty cases of dynamite to the Amiandos mines. The first burst of fire shattered the windscreen and wounded Stephenson's hand and forehead. With bullets still pouring into the cab Stephenson, his face covered in blood and his hand useless, stopped the vehicle, and switched off the engine, thereby preventing the truck from leaving the road and possibly exploding with its cargo. Then, with Sgt Hodges, he started to return the fire. Stephenson was later invalided out of the Service but was awarded a Queen's Commendation for this display of courage. In the meantine the escorts, led by L/Cpl Maghee, leapt out of the back in an endeavour to cut off the ambushers. Maghee was seriously injured by a burst of fire, but his prompt action and that of his two comrades scared off the attackers, who fled without any further attempts to get at the dynamite. The score was settled early on the morning of the 25th when E Troop, commanded by Capt Denis Sluman, shot and killed a Cypriot who tried to escape from an ambush that they had laid. Another ambush occurred on 5 December when one of Four Five's vehicles was on escort duty. Marine Terence Roberts, X Troop, a police constable and a Cypriot civilian were killed. The driver of this vehicle too, Marine David Walker, was decorated and awarded the British Empire Medal. His citation reads:

'Marine Walker was driving a vehicle which was escorting an ambulance on a mountain road near Troodos, Cyprus.

As the vehicles rounded a corner they were met by heavy and sustained small arms fire. Marine Walker's vehicle was hit and stopped, and as his four companions jumped out, one was hit and fell. Marine Walker immediately took charge of the situation and with complete disregard for his own safety moved the wounded man to safety. He then returned the terrorists' fire and when two more Marines were wounded, he again exposed himself in order to move them to safety. He continued to engage the terrorists single-handed until the arrival of another convoy.'

The attackers were reported to have numbered some five men with Bren guns and Thompson sub-machine guns.

These and many other attacks of violence were all part of Grivas' general offensive code-named 'Operation Forward To Victory'. We now know that Grivas himself had moved into the Troodos mountains and set up his Headquarters in well concealed dug-outs on a steep ridge overlooking Spilia.

The villages of Spilia and Khandria had been suspect for some time and early on in the morning of Sunday, 11 December, 1955, 'Operation Foxhunter' was mounted to search the villages for couriers and suppliers. The force consisted of the entire Commando plus companies from the Gordon Highlanders and was accompanied by David Burk, the Middle East correspondent of the *Daily Express*.

It was a cold, damp, and misty morning when the cordon and search parties arrived near Spilia at six-fifteen. The villagers had obviously been caught by surprise and as the search party of Gordons started their search of the villages they found a man hastily trying to dispose of terrorist plans and papers. A few minutes later the silence was broken by bursts of Sten gun fire. Sgt Jackman, the Provost Sergeant, had spotted a man dressed in a white sweater and grey slacks dashing out of the houses and trying to make good his escape up one of the ridges which surrounded the village. Despite the gunfire and ignoring Sgt Jackman's challenge, the man—later identified as the brother of the Bishop of Kyrenia—kept running. He was shot in the shoulder as the result of some expert marksmanship by Lt Bob Otway-Ruthven. So that any useful information could be extracted as quickly as possible Lt Godfrey Seager and a strong escort rushed the wounded terrorist and captured papers to Nicosia.

Grivas and his aides were by now on full alert in the hills above, but decided, correctly, that the search was only a routine one and their whereabouts was still unknown. A cordon patrol of Z Troop, commanded by Capt Donald Michell, was searching the slopes around the village. David Burk then continues: '. . . The patrol found a man carrying a British Lee-Enfield rifle, some ammunition and forty Cordex fuses—the kind used by saboteurs. He was a short man roughly dressed with grey in his thick brush of hair. When he saw the troops he started whistling and put on a great show on unconcern.' The man, Geoghiou Zavlis, was brought back to Spilia for interrogation and told his inquisitors that there was a hide-out in the hills with some fifteen men in it and that he could show the way. Lt-Col Tailyour quickly assembled a forty-strong patrol of Headquarters and Support Troops and ordered that two police dogs with their handlers should be brought along as well. The police dogs and their Metropolitan Police handlers had only arrived in Cyprus three days previously, and it was the first time that dogs had been used on this type of operation. One of the handlers, Police Sgt Beverley commented to David Burk: 'What a life. A Metropolitan Policeman on Thursday. A Cyprus policeman on Saturday. And a Commando on Sunday'. The patrol leapt into trucks and by the time it had debussed it was nearly midday. The route to the caves was a tortuous one, up and down steep slopes thick with trees and gorse and slippery with shale, moss, and rain soaked grass. The prisoner, surrounded by his captors, was in the leading group. Cpl R. V. Shellard, of Support Troop, remembers the final approach well:

'By now the mist had really clamped down and visibility was barely ten yards. Then a burst of fire from above us forced us to take cover. We returned the fire and the Commanding Officer ordered that the two-inch mortar should be fired at the caves. Due to the foliage overhead the mortar bomb exploded soon after it had left the barrel. Lt David G. Alexander, the Signals Officer, was hit in the knee, and I was also slightly wounded by the shrapnel. The rest of the patrol then dashed up the hillside and disappeared into the mist'.

The two minutes or so warning that Grivas and his companions were given was enough for them to make good their escape. The caves, which consisted of five dug-outs connected by tunnels, were neatly stocked with ample supplies of food, clothing and ammunition and were undoubtedly the main hide of the EOKA terrorists. The chase over the precipitous mountain tracks continued until dusk. Over five miles were covered in a westerly direction towards the village of Kakopetria, but the follow-up had to be abandoned when darkness fell. This had been the first every really 'hot' pursuit of Grivas, but on this occasion Four Five was denied, by a matter of minutes, the capture of the most wanted man in Cyprus and the hard core of EOKA's terrorists. This chance snatch in a routine cordon and search operation nearly led to arrests that could have altered the whole course of the future campaign. Grivas reprints in his memoirs* an account attributed to the man captured by Z Troop earlier that day:

'The British believed that they were surrounded and began to fire wildly in the mist and kill each other. The shooting went on for nearly half an hour. I lay flat behind a pine tree with a soldier who had been leading me on a rope.† Words cannot describe what was happening. Not a branch was left on a tree. The soldiers were scattered right and left, wounded and dead. Finally one of them gave a signal and they stopped

* *The Memoirs of General Grivas*, edited by Charles Foley, Longmans.

† Grivas had slightly sprained an ankle in making good his escape.

firing. Their leader had been killed: a bullet had gone through his right eye and came out at the left temple.'

Grivas later claimed, in the same book, that his position had been attacked by 700 men; Four Five had suffered fifty casualties, and the resultant chaos had disrupted the unit's organization and taken the Commanding Officer's mind off his job!

The Commando Battle Diary lists casualties during 'Operation Foxhunter' as two slightly wounded. The 'patrol leader', Lt-Col Tailyour, was unscathed in this operation and completed an oustanding career in the Royal Marines in 1968 when he retired as Commandant-General.

Christmas and the New Year were celebrated in traditional style. The pipers from the Gordons helped to make the Hogmanay festivities more realistic and although they were on 'Operation Mangol Wurzel' the next morning they were reported to be 'none the worse for wear'. The Company Commander of the Gordons, on this occasion, left Platres driving his own Land Rover with the piper seated on the bonnet playing a 'merry tune', as ordered. Another amusing departure from Platres was that of Frankie Howerd, the comedian, who had been with a Service Entertainment team giving a show to the unit. The last view Four Five got of Frankie Howerd was as he disappeared down the road from the Hotel Splendid mounted on a runaway donkey dressed as a Greek Priest!

There was little time to recover from seeing the New Year in, and those that did manage to snatch some sleep were soon awakened as the convoys for 'Mangol Wurzel' left their bases at three in the morning. The approach march took place in darkness and by dawn a massive search, with the assistance of an informer, was being mounted in the area south of Kakopetria. The Second-in-Command, Major Peter Spittal, and Major Frank Taylor led the party that found an enemy hide and soon afterwards three armed men were captured by the cordon. Five suspects were also arrested in Kakopetria, thus depriving EOKA of eight trusted men in one day. 1956 had begun in fine style for Four Five.

Musical accompaniment, of a different nature, was also provided on 28 January when Four Five was searching the villages of Pano and Kato Amiandos. The villagers were reluctant to leave the comfort of their homes because of a heavy snow storm outside, however, good relations were restored by the Brigade band which performed lustily to the population which sat huddled in the cages awaiting screening. The Greek national newspapers, however, put a different complexion to the story and claimed that 'the band was used to drown the cries of the prisoners being tortured in the interrogation cages!' They are not likely to have added that the thirteen out of fourteen wanted men were identified by 'sonny boys' (informers) and were subsequently detained as being EOKA members or supporters.

The heavy snowfalls in February provided a further test of versatility for Four Five. X Troop (Capt Dan Hunt) was supplied with skis and in addition to carrying out patrols was responsible for delivering dynamite to the Amiandos Mine. The long downhill descent was normally navigated at speed by all except for the unfortunate person selected to carry the detonators! This snow training team was led by Major Ian De'Ath and the men were soon nicknamed the 'White Ghosts of Troodos'. The snow also brought tragedy. On 9 February the recovery vehicle of the Brigade Light Aid Detachment became trapped by drifts, and the crew had to walk back. Two men arrived at Four Five's camp reporting that the rest of the crew were still on the road suffering the effects of the sub-zero temperature. Lt Peter Montgomery and a patrol of Z Troop rushed to the scene, only to find RSM Alfred Wheeler and Marine Benet Blakeway dead from exhaustion. Two other men were rescued, although they, too, were suffering from severe exposure.

Both terrorists and security forces suspended operations during the latter part of February whilst talks between Makarios and Harding were being held. The talks were eventually broken off, terrorism re-started and Makarios was exiled to the Seychelles. The first major EOKA incident in their new offensive was the ambush of an A Troop road patrol soon after midnight on the morning of 17 March. The patrol consisted of a Land Rover which was escorting a Fiat saloon driven by an interpreter. Five were wounded; Lt Bob Forrester-Bennett, Sgt Robinson (who had previously been injured at Vouni), Marines Wood and Buckingham, and the interpreter. Despite the heavy casualties the patrol fought back and killed one of the ambushers before the rest fled into the darkness. Service in Cyprus had also brought romance to Lt Forrester-Bennett just over two months previously, on Saturday, 10 January, he had married Miss Patricia Halley, a former police secretary in Nicosia, at St Andrews Church, Kyrenia. The church was searched thoroughly before the service, and during the ceremony armed sentries remained outside, but there were no incidents.

Success in operations often came only after days of waiting— an uncomfortable process in the bitter cold of winter in the Troodos mountains. Noteworthy amongst these was the capture by B Troop (Major Andrew Halliday) of a terrorist following many nights spent in ambush positions. One marine, in a cordon, had concealed himself up a tree and his initiative was rewarded when a 'suspicious character' walked underneath. The marine dropped from his perch and apprehended the startled individual who at first was thought to be of little importance. During interrogation it was revealed that he was a hard-core member from one of the mountain hides and he subsequently disclosed a vast amount of information that proved to be of great significance throughout the Emergency. Another important 'find' at the time was some reels of film which were accompanied by two rather bedraggled terrorists. When developed the photographs revealed a more than useful dossier on many of the hard-core members from the Troodos mountains. These were rapidly distributed throughout our forces who for the first time were able to identify many of their adversaries.

Throughout the spring and summer operations were intensified after the earlier lull. On 1 May, E Troop dashed into a cave at dawn and found two frightened terrorists who were only too glad to surrender. In the middle of the month Operations 'Mustard Pot' and 'Pepper Pot' involved intensive and successful searches of caves in the Paphos Forest. The 'bag' included both terrorists and caches of arms. 'Mustard Pot' also involved a search of the notorious Kykko Monastery. The cell of one monk revealed the following 'a box of airgun pellets, a pair of khaki breeches, a pair of anklets and a water bottle. Photos and letters also suggest he is an active EOKA supporter'.* In another cell the searchers were surprised to find items which one does not normally associate with those supposedly maintaining vows of celibacy! Although the monks vehemently denied involvement an earlier find in the Abbot of Kykko's quarters provides more than ample evidence of their sympathies and justifies any searches of their premises: '6 spent Breda cartridges. 6 12-bore shotgun cartridges. Several hundred empty 12-bore cartridges. 3 cartridge fillers. 1 pair WD binoculars. 1 WD water bottle. 1 stick dynamite. 2 lengths of safety fuse.'†

Before Four Five was recalled to Malta in August, 1956, for the Suez crisis, the majority of troops on the island were engaged on Operation 'Lucky Alphonse' which lasted from 8–23 June. This involved a series of massive cordons and searches combined with mortar shoots when terrorists were flushed out of their hides. Even Grivas paid tribute to the thoroughness of the tactics but, despite many reported sightings, he still eluded his captors. The vagaries of the mountain climate again hampered the security forces, but this time it was the elements of heat and wind in contrast to the snow which made Sunday, 17 June, one of the most horrifying days that eye-witnesses can ever record. Mortar fire, which had previously been laid on suspected terrorist positions and escape routes, had ignited the surrounding undergrowth. A forest fire started

* Unit Battle Diary. Friday, 18 May, 1956.
† Unit Battle Diary. Wednesday, 14 March, 1956.

and by the morning of the 17th it had got completely out of control and encircled cordon troops, which included ranks of the Gordons, the Norfolks and the Parachute Regiment. By the end of the day the fire had claimed nineteen lives. Capt Richard Meadows, who was later to lead B Troop at Suez, was awarded the MBE for 'leadership and courage of a high order' during the rescue operations. He organized the evacuation of his men to safety areas through intense heat and burning trees, and then personally carried a wounded man for a mile through the smoke-filled undergrowth to receive medical attention. When he reached the forest road, Capt Meadows found that it was blocked by a burning armoured car. Regardless of his own safety he jumped inside, removed cans of petrol, beat out the flames and released the handbrake. The vehicle was then pushed off the road, thus clearing it for other vehicles assisting in the evacuation.

Five more major operations were mounted by the unit before it left Cyprus at the end of its first tour of duty in August, 1956. Despite being on active service for nearly a year there was to be no respite for Four Five. In its nine-month absence from Cyprus the unit was to add yet another illustrious chapter to its history.

The period in Malta after Suez was again a busy one. Lt-Col Jack Richards, who had been Second-in-Command in Malaya, assumed command of Four Five from Lt-Col Tailyour, who had been wounded at Port Said, on 19 January, 1957. From 15 March to 26 April, the whole Commando underwent desert training in Tripoli and on return to Malta it was time to prepare for Cyprus. At six o'clock on the morning of 30 May, Four Five was again responsible for the Troodos area, having taken over from 40 Commando.

The helicopter, which had more than proved its worth and versatility at Suez, was introduced to the Cyprus theatre during this period and from now on was to become a regular weapon in the assault armoury. Unfortunately, as far as Four Five was concerned, helicopter operations during this tour started on a sad note. E Troop (Lt Tony Quin), within a day of its arrival in the mountains, was undergoing helicopter training at the Internal Security Training School, at Forest Park, and perfecting techniques for future operations. One of the aircraft crashed resulting in fatal injuries to the sergeant major, QMS Graham Casey, and serious wounds to Marine Miller. This accident, however, did not hamper progress in this field and 'swoops from the sky' were soon to become a regular feature of tactics in Cyprus. The first major heli-borne operation undertaken by Four Five, 'Sherry Spinner', was mounted on 24 July to cordon and search the villages of Arakapas, Pharmakas and Sykopetra, at the eastern extremity of the Troodos Mountains. A Company the King's Own Yorkshire Light Infantry, B Company, the Royal Ulster Rifles and Support Company, the 3rd Battalion the Grenadier Guards were under command. In addition to the command elements three Troops of Four Five participated. E Troop (Lt Peter Montgomery commanded the airborne section), X Troop (Capt Hamish Emslie) and Z Troop (Major Alexander Wright). 'Sycamore' helicopters were used and cordons and observation posts were rapidly established soon after the initial wave became airborne at four forty-five in the morning. Although no major arrests were made during this and the subsequent operation on 30 July, the success of this type of operation lay in the speed and surprise effected.

On the whole the military situation in Cyprus had become much quieter during the first half of 1957. Archbishop Makarios had returned to Athens from the Seychelles on 17 April and Grivas had ordered a cease-fire amongst his followers as a result. It seems probable that the motives for this reduction in hostilities were not purely political and Grivas claims that he used this respite to re-arm and regroup his terrorists.

During this tour Field-Marshal Sir John Harding paid two visits to Four Five at Platres, on 26 June and 20 September, before relinquishing his Governor-Generalship. On both occasions he proudly wore his green beret which had been presented by Brigade Headquarters. Field-Marshal Harding was greatly admired by all ranks of the Commando, not only because of very close ties which had stretched over nearly a decade, but also because of the supreme personal efforts he had made to resolve the Cyprus question both politically and militarily.

This calm period, of course, was a frustrating one for Four Five, separated from its families in Malta, and one writer, obviously pining for some excitement wrote: 'Our first five weeks in Cyprus have not been as packed full of action as we hoped might be possible.' Even so, the patrol and ambushes continued unabated and as is so often the case success eventually came the unit's way. On the night of 29 July, 1957, a section of X Troop under Cpl Haydn Davies was ordered to patrol the streets of the village of Pelendria, south of the Amiandos mines. To Marines Brian Thornton and Geoffry Salisbury it was just another routine evening. Darkness had fallen and as eight-thirty was approaching they knew that their hour long spell of guard duty was drawing to a close. As the Marines prepared to leave the village for the section base camp they noticed a car ahead which had just stopped, and then turned to go back. Shortly afterwards Salisbury and Thornton heard footsteps, and took up positions of alert. The two figures were challenged in the correct manner when they were some five yards away. The figures stopped and they were both seen to be dressed in khaki and seemed very hesitant. At first the Marines thought that the two Cypriots were possibly policemen, but Thornton's suspicions were aroused by the leading man who was carrying a Thompson sub-machine gun. As Salisbury covered him, Thornton moved forward, grabbed the loaded weapon and escorted the two men back to base. This chance encounter led to the arrest of a prominent EOKA terrorist, Costas Michael, who had a price of £5,000 on his head. His companion was Demetrakis Christodoulou and a subsequent search found him to be in possession of a haversack containing spare parts with which to make a bomb. The terrorists were later sentenced to death for carrying arms, but their sentences were reduced afterwards. Both Thornton and Salisbury received awards for gallantry for their outstanding capture.

Four Five left Cyprus in late September, 1957 and for nearly ten months was able to have a break from active operations. However, on 27 July, 1958, it was 'back to business' in the Troodos Mountains for the third and last tour. This move was preceded by a general 'dance around the Mediterranean', about which we shall hear more later, and the deployment of a special party from the unit to Nicosia. This special party, which operated from RAF Nicosia, was named the 'Heliforce' and was commanded by Lt-Col Richards. It consisted of Tactical Headquarters, X and Z Troops, and 728 (Commando) Flight Royal Navy (four 'Whirlwinds'). As on previous occasions the aim of this force was both to provide a mobile unit for snap operations and also to develop the techniques for day and night helicopter tactics. To cut down the build-up times between waves going to distant villages a system was evolved whereby the third and successive waves were sent out by road as soon as the 'scramble' order was given. The helicopters were then able to pick up their subsequent sticks from the roadside at a point much nearer the objective. Operating procedures by night, which were still in their infancy, were rehearsed on several occasions, and although the helicopter pilots won much admiration for the daring manner in which they flew into landing sites marked only by glimmering lamps, the opportunity never arose for the Heliforce to put in a night assault.

The first major operation of the 'sky cavalry' was on 10 July, 1958, when 'Operation Springtime' was mounted in the area of Akanthou, thirty miles north-east of Nicosia on the northern range of mountains. A total of seven villages were cordoned and screened in the first three days. At dawn on the fourth morning an assault on a suspected terrorist hide took place to the south of Akanthou. Ten helicopters, including 'Sycamores' with ranks of the 1st Battalion, the Royal West Kents on board, took part in the attack. The rugged countryside made landing difficult, and one of the first casualties was the Commanding Officer who was roping down from a helicopter which was hovering above a steep rocky outcrop. Lt-Col Richards made a particularly hard landing, from a considerable height, and broke his heel. Further casualties occurred soon afterwards when Sgt 'Snowy' Baldwin and Marine David Whitham, both of X Troop, were both accidentally killed by gunfire before the second helicopter wave arrived. Despite these setbacks the operation continued for another four days—but the terrorists evaded capture.

On 17 July the Heliforce was withdrawn from 'Springtime' at the start of what was to prove a very hectic ten days. After a brief stop at RAF Nicosia, the Heliforce moved to Limassol where it was told to stand by to embark to sail for Tobruk, there to rejoin the remainder of the Commando. Whilst at Limassol the Commanding Officer, although still in considerable pain, bravely 'broke out of hospital' to say farewell to his force. In the meantime the main body of Four Five had embarked at Malta (two days previously) prior to sailing for Cyprus but had since been diverted to Tobruk as a result of the worsening of the Middle East situation particularly in Libya. HMS *Tenby*, with Brigade Headquarters, then sailed for Limassol where it embarked the Heliforce, which had by now been disbanded, and returned to Tobruk where X and Z Troops rejoined the remainder of the Commando.

By now there was a rapid re-deployment of units in the Mediterranean which included bringing 42 Commando out from the United Kingdom. It was then decided, on 20 July, that Four Five and Brigade Headquarters should concentrate on Benghazi where the base was in the process of being handed over to the Libyans. All the transport, by now ashore in Tobruk, was ordered to travel the 300 miles to Benghazi by road whilst the remainder of the unit went by sea. There was no accommodation at Benghazi, but showing true Royal Marine initiative Four Five moved into a stores area, as yet unoccupied by its new owners, and was established ashore on the 22nd. Plans were changed again that morning and confirmatory orders were received for Four Five to move to its original destination, Cyprus. The Brigade's game of 'musical chairs' finally ended on 26 July when the Rifle Troops of Four Five arrived in Limassol in HMS *Bermuda* and the transport in LST *Striker*. The Commando, with traditional speed, took over operational responsibility for the Troodos area on the following day. Lt-Col Richard Crombie had by now assumed command as Lt-Col Richards had been evacuated back to hospital in England after his accident.

Fresh outbreaks of violence had broken out in Cyprus in July on Grivas' orders, mostly reprisals aimed against the Turks, and, of course, against our own military camps and installations. Within four days of arrival 'Operation Swan Vesta' was mounted as part of an island-wide search for terrorists and their associates. The unit's 'bag' after several days of screening at Kakopetria and Galata was, appropriately, forty-five detainees. On 6 August, 1958, the Turks and Greeks declared a cease-fire, and the EOKA organization switched its activities to the distribution of leaflets and general intimidation. As usual, during a cease-fire period, the terrorists used the time to re-group and re-organize. Checks and ambushes were kept on known routes and on 22 August, X Troop caught two Greek Cypriots red-handed as they were about to receive two two-inch mortar bombs from another pair, who were hiding behind a wall. The group of terrorists was also equipped with a walkie-talkie radio which was in full working order.

The lull lasted for over six weeks, until the end of September when the appointment of a Turkish Commissioner in Cyprus was confirmed—which of course caused a political, and military, outburst in the Greek camp. A week before this, however, Lt-Col F. C. Barton had assumed command from Lt-Col Crombie. Lt-Col Richard Crombie had spent over two and a half years in Four Five as Second-in-Command and had twice commanded the unit. His farewell took the form of being towed up the hill in his Land Rover from the Hotel Splendid in Platres to the 'edge of the unit's premises' were a local taxi waited to take him to Nicosia 'and an ambulance to carry the exhausted officers back to the Mess'. Another departure at this time was the popular quartermaster, Capt John Baker. Such was his reputation for 'winning' stores that the supply chiefs in

9

Cyprus were prepared to grant Four Five almost anything rather than sit through Capt Baker's explanations as to why they needed it!

As a result of the rapid deterioration in the situation Lt-Col Barton's first few weeks in command were to be ones of intense activity. There were five major incidents in the Troodos area in the first fortnight of October. The police station at Kambos and the forest station at Platania were destroyed by fire and and there were three road ambushes. Four Five lost one marine killed and the Royal Welch Fusiliers, who were under command, lost one killed and five wounded. One terrorist was killed and six other Greek Cypriots were arrested in the same period.

The ambush tactics of the terrorists were skilful, and positions were usually sited on sharp bends where vehicles could only travel at about 10 mph. Fire positions were well disguised and sited about fifteen feet above the road so that the maximum range of fire was only thirty yards. In addition, the terrorists often laid mines under the surface of the road and in overhanging trees. On 6 October a patrol was fired on as it was debussing, prior to moving off on foot. As it was a two-vehicle road the second truck stopped a hundred yards behind, and its occupants dashed up to clear the terrorists. The ambush group took flight and one of them, armed with a pistol and grenade ran into the follow up party and was promptly shot. The grenade went off and killed Marine Raymond Greening and injured two others. The terrorist was killed as the bullets ripped through his body and the pack full of bombs which he was carrying. Marine Alexander MacDougall was killed when an E Troop patrol was ambushed on 22 October, and Lt David Spurling died of wounds on 3 November, as he was leading a section which was attacking a hide near Pedhoulas, where terrorists had been spotted by one of our own observation posts. To counteract the EOKA wave of violence Four Five adopted several new measures: where possible patrols moved out on foot to minimize the chance of vehicle ambush; observation posts were set up and manned for long periods so that a careful check could be made on likely enemy routes and hides; and intensive training, starting at six-thirty every morning, was carried out concurrently with operations to improve alertness and tactics.

As November progressed the Commando began to even the score and achieve the Commanding Officer's interim target of 'six terrorists and six hides'. The first victim, a Greek Cypriot, was shot on the 19th as he tried to prevent a patrol of Z Troop from entering his house in Kyperounda which was being used to harbour an EOKA suspect. Although the hunt for terrorists continued in earnest the Intelligence Section supplied a bit of light relief two days later after they published the interrogation report of a woman suspect who had just been released from questioning. It was alleged that her husband was acting as a courier and that she had been hiding food in various parts of his clothing. When asked why she had put corn in his shoes she replied 'to feed his pigeon toes!'

The week commencing Monday, 24 November, 1958, was probably the most successful in Cyprus for Four Five. It started with a twenty-four hour general strike and Sgt John Chiplin, leading a patrol of B Troop, snatched a man at Trimiklini, on the Limassol road, who was addressing a meeting and distributing leaflets. On the 25th the observation post policy paid dividends. A post under the command of Lt Nick Wise of A Troop (Capt James Clarke) spotted an old man near Yerakies, carrying a bundle, apparently innocently exercising his dog. Suspicions were aroused when the man was seen to be looking around nervously. The man was then joined by another younger one and they appeared to be in deep conversation. The OP party approached stealthily, but as they drew near the dog started barking and the old man darted for his village. The younger man, now joined by another headed in the other direction out of sight from the patrol which then gave chase over the rough countryside. The two youths were eventually found panting under a bush, gasping 'No EOKA' to their captors. The men were later found to be hard core members of a Nicosia killer group who had committed several murders and, having found

life in the town too 'hot', had been transferred to a mountain group, with which they were just making contact when
they were spotted. A valuable capture indeed.

It is perhaps fitting that the account of the Cyprus period
should end with another successful elimination of a wanted
man, again on 25 November. The patrol was a small one and
shows that in this type of warfare the end result normally
depends on the speed of reaction of the individual and the
foresight and initiative of his leader.

A patrol of X Troop was operating in the area of Dhymes.
Lt Max Barrett had taken two marines up to an OP to watch a
nearby road and the surrounding countryside. Sgt C. H.
Youngman and Marines Cobb and Gillard remained in the
firm base with the intention of moving out that night to an
ambush position at the junction of three tracks. As dusk
approached, at about five-thirty on that chilly November
evening, the patrol, scanning the surrounding hills, noticed a
lone man in rough ground fifty yards away. The man seemed
very furtive and on one occasion stopped behind a bush and
looked around. Sgt Youngman continues with the story:

'I told Marine Cobb to stay in the firm base to act as cut off
and took Marine Gillard to where I thought the man would
appear. We scrambled over a couple of walls which were
built round the small fields and eventually took up a position
opposite a water tank at the track junction. Suddenly the
man appeared from behind a bush, closely followed by
another man, who we had not seen before. When I challenged
them the second man shouted out: "Okay, don't shoot",
but the first one turned and ran . . .'

Youngman and Gillard opened fire simultaneously at the
escapee. He staggered towards the cut off position and was
shot down as he attempted to climb a wall in front of Cobb.
In the few seconds during which the firing took place the second
man leapt behind a nearby tree and fled to safety in the
gathering darkness. Thus Grivas lost Savvas Rotsides, a man

who had been a hard-core terrorist for many years and one whom he described as a 'veteran guerilla'.

Following these successes, Major-General K. Darling, the Director of Operations, sent the following simple signal, 'Well done. Keep it up.' Major-General Darling had arrived just over a month previously and was insisting on the highest military standards to combat the latest terrorist outbreaks.

Since the Commanding Officer had announced his new policy during an address to the unit on 6 November, Four Five easily exceeded the interim figure and accounted for over seventeen men; one EOKA killed; two EOKA captured; a man guarding a hide with a suspect inside, killed; a cordon breaker shot; a man captured and 238 sticks of dynamite recovered after a robbery at a chrome mine; and finally ten suspects detained (after a swoop on a village), doubtless giving Grivas good reason to remember the Commando's last month in Cyprus.

The bandit in Malaya could be recognized both by his uniform and his whereabouts, and as a consequence the conflict in the jungle was almost purely military. In Cyprus, however, the EOKA doctrine was permeated throughout all sections of the population. The problems that arose were largely political, and as a result great restraint had to be exercised by the security forces. The jungle rule of 'shoot on sight' was not applicable here. The creditable way in which Grivas evaded capture could lead to the assumption that the terrorists gained a military victory. Admittedly their murders and killings exceeded those deaths inflicted by our own forces, but EOKA losses in terms of terrorists captured and imprisoned were far greater. Four Five's record on this score is outstanding. A total of nearly twenty-one months were spent on active service in Cyprus. During this period over eighty major unit operations were mounted and some 800 arrests were made as a result of interrogation and screening. Nearly seventy of this number were known to be hard-core terrorists or men wanted by the Special Branch.* Many of the remainder

* The figures for the first tour of Cyprus were supplied by military sources and were published in the *Times of Malta* on 21 August, 1956.

were detained or placed on restriction orders for infringing the Emergency Regulations. Three known terrorists were killed by Four Five and another two Cypriots died when trying to avoid arrest after being challenged. The Commando's own losses on Operations in Cyprus were eight killed and some twenty wounded, mostly not serious.

This praiseworthy outcome can be attributed largely to the skill of the individual; his alertness, speed of reaction and fitness to endure long marches over rugged terrain in all types of weather.

Four Five was Malta bound on 15 December, 1958. Before the Commando left Cyprus a message was received from the Governor, Sir Hugh Foot, congratulating the unit on the way in which it had carried out the exacting task of patrolling such a big, rough mountain area, but by now thoughts are switching from the past to the future, and the pleasant thoughts of a peaceful Christmas for 1958.

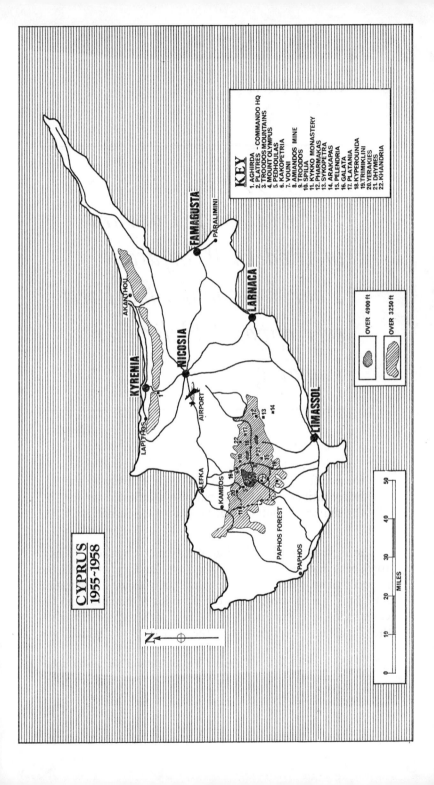

CYPRUS
1955-1958

N

| 0 | 10 | 20 | 30 | 40 | 50 |
MILES

FAMAGUSTA
• PARALIMINI

AKANTHOU

KYRENIA

LARNACA

LAPITHOS

NICOSIA

AIRPORT

LEFKA

KAMBOS

LIMASSOL

PAPHOS FOREST

PAPHOS

KEY
1. AGHIRDA
2. PLATRES – COMMANDO HQ
3. TROODOS MOUNTAINS
4. MOUNT OLYMPUS
5. PEDHOULAS
6. KAKOPETRIA
7. VOUNI
8. AMIANDOS MINE
9. TROODOS
10. SPILIA
11. KYKKO MONASTERY
12. PHARMAKAS
13. SYKOPETRA
14. ARAKAPAS
15. PELENDRIA
16. GALATA
17. PLATANIA
18. KYPEROUNDA
19. TRIMIKLINI
20. YERAKIES
21. DHYMES
22. KHANDRIA

OVER 4900 ft

OVER 3250 ft

CHAPTER 11

Suez, 1956—
A Great Step Forward
in Modern Warfare—
Four Five make the First
ever opposed Helicopter
Landing

'Suez is . . . left in a curious no man's land of time; too painful, too close to be reached effectively by the heavy artillery of history, but also a little too far for the snipers of contemporary politics and journalism.'*

The Egyptian nationalization of the Suez Canal on 26 July, 1956, was not received by Four Five, in Cyprus, with the impact that an event of this nature normally arouses. 'Operation Pool Bull' was in progress in the Troodos Mountains, and the Commando was conducting a search with the 1st Battalion the Parachute Regiment for the Lenas gang, which was

* *The Suez Affair*, Hugh Thomas, Weidenfeld and Nicholson, 1966

reported to be in the area. Night marches over the rugged countryside and intensive searches in the thirsty heat left little time for individual thoughts on international affairs. Within days, however, Four Five was soon to become involved in preparation for an operation in which it was destined to make history, and which the *Illustrated* later described as the 'forty hours that shook the world'.*

In the days that followed the nationalization, many emphatic denials were issued, by the British Government, of plans to invade Suez. Despite these announcements, 3 Commando Brigade was one of the formations earmarked for the assault. The British and French Governments did, in fact, start taking 'precautionary military measures' on 30 July, and 2 August the first indications of an impending move were evident to Four Five. Although no official reason had been given, orders were issued to mark all equipment and stores crates—something was in the air. Confirmation of the news was received the next morning, but despite this, intensive operations in Cyprus continued until the Gordons arrived, on 10 August, to assume control of the Commando's area.

On 14 August, Four Five left for Famagusta and started to embark in the carrier HMS *Theseus*. Sir John Harding came on board and gave the Commando a short farewell talk, and then at five o'clock HMS *Theseus* sailed, bound for Malta. The Governor-General later wrote to Lt-Col Norman Tailyour praising Four Five for its work in Cyprus, and said that the unit had 'maintained the highest standard and made a magnificent contribution to the security campaign here . . . it has been the greatest honour and pleasure for me to have had your Commando under my command'. HMS *Theseus* arrived in Malta on 16 August. Four Five had spent a total of eleven months and five days in Cyprus, but in spite of this the men could not rest on their well-deserved laurels. The Commando established itself in Ghain Tuffieha Camp, and after a brief respite started an intensive training programme on 20 August.

The overall military picture was still confused and whilst

* 17 November, 1956.

the unit was on its way to Malta many formations had been placed on stand-by, and a limited number of British Reservists were called up. British and French staffs conferred in London to plan the assault on Egypt, but no details, at unit level, were available. On 11 August, General Sir Charles Keightley was appointed Supreme Allied Commander of the operation, code-named 'Musketeer'—supposedly at the instigation of Lieutenant-General Sir Hugh Stockwell (Commander, Land Forces), who had a weakness for Dumas' dashing characters.* The military planners of 'Musketeer' were hampered by political requirements and the original contingency was to capture Alexandria as a prelude to an attack on Cairo. The amphibious assault was to be led by 3 Commando Brigade, commanded by Brigadier R. W. Madoc. With these original intentions in mind, the Commando Brigade in Malta concentrated its training on the seaborne assault role.

Four Five's programme included small-arms firing, assault courses, the use of scaling ladders, the development of special techniques to land in dock areas and the tactical crossing of breakwaters and hards. Throughout the training period in preparation for 'Musketeer' one of the key appointments in the Commando was held by Major Ian De'Ath, the Staff Officer Operations, his task was to co-ordinate the training requirements to meet the operational plans. A *Globe and Laurel* article later described this training period:

'We had barely time to get re-accustomed to the idiosyncrasies of Ghain Tuffieha Camp before we found ourselves in the midst of an intensive training programme. Three full-scale amphibious exercises in quick succession punctuated troop training, and two "set piece" exercises with live enemy run by the unit for each rifle troop in turn. A troop of LVs T† were living with the unit at this time and much training was done with them, although we never worked with them operationally. A Squadron, 6th Royal Tank Regiment,

* *Suez: The Seven Day War*, A. J. Barker, Faber & Faber Ltd.
† Landing Vehicles Tracked, nicknamed 'Buffaloes'.

drove up from Marsa at dead of night and spent a week on Mayesa field firing range, during which time each troop did an exercise with two troops of tanks, which was of great value. It was felt by the infantry, however, that realism had over-stepped the mark when the umpires made them wear respirators for half an hour during an uphill assault; even the fittest marine formed the opinion that a death by gassing would be preferable to drowning in his own perspiration.'

Security throughout this period was so strict, that when Lieutenant-General Sir Hugh Stockwell addressed the Commando on 27 September, 1956, to emphasize the importance of the tasks that possibly lay ahead, his visit, in orders issued two days previously, merely named him as a 'VIP'. At this stage of the painstaking preparations it had almost seemed that the much awaited landings were going to be declared 'off', but nevertheless planning continued apace and the Commandos could only wait for further developments.

Originally Four Five was designated as seaborne reserve in the event of an assault on Port Said. Then the news that helicopters were to be used in this operation was broken and this came as a tonic to the whole unit. In this plan Four Five's tasks were to have been daring ones, namely to have landed in waves and secure the railway and pontoon bridges about a mile south of the town and to establish stops to prevent the Egyptian Army escaping to the south. This plan was stopped, in London, on 25 October and was announced to the Commando on the 27th. Instead, Four Five's mission was changed to that of helicopter reserve to the seaborne assault in Phase One. The Commando's task of taking the bridges had been given to the French parachutists.

This was a bitter blow to the men in the unit who naturally wanted to be in the thick of it right from the word go.

Further orders were to be issued during the passage and Four Five's task was eventually finalized as being: 'When ordered, land by helicopter within the Brigade beach-head and support 40 and 42 Commandos as required.' This was the final disappointment to the unit's planners who had studied the seemingly more exciting alternatives such as helicopter build-up times for sorties to the bridge at El Kantara, on the canal south of Port Said, and even Suez itself.

However, in retrospect, the decision to change Four Five's task meant anything but the exclusion from the major part of the action. In future years the unit's employment at Suez was to have far-reaching and historical significance in the tactical use of helicopters.

Throughout October, therefore, Four Five continued infantry training in Malta, rehearsing co-operation with tank forces and specialized Army and Naval Units. It was not until the end of the month, when HMS *Theseus* and HMS *Ocean* arrived at Malta with 845 Squadron, that the troops could rehearse section helicopter drills and practice loading bulky equipment, such as the 106 mm. anti-tank gun. Even so, security precautions and shortage of time prevented any full scale Commando rehearsal exercise with the helicopters.

In addition to the operational training, Four Five still managed to rehearse and execute a full ceremonial parade on Sunday, 28 October, the 292nd anniversary of the formation of the Corps of Royal Marines. Although the Commanding Officer was advised that he could forego this parade in the midst of all other preparations, he decided that amongst other considerations it would help to instil discipline and *esprit de corps*, which is a factor common to both the battlefield and the parade ground. The Commander-in-Chief, Malta, Admiral Sir Guy Grantham, took the salute, and the parade was described as 'a magnificent display of faultless turn out and precision drill'. Indeed a fitting and moving prelude to a major operation.

Monday, 29 October, was declared a general 'Make and Mend'* in the Commando, but in the meantime the general alert had been given for the Suez Operation. The Israelis had already launched an offensive, and all troops earmarked for the

* Naval slang for a day off—derived from the period when ratings were given time off to repair clothing and personal items at sea.

invasion had been placed at short notice to move. Her Majesty's Government issued a requirement to both Israel and Egypt:

To cease hostilities by land, sea and air.

To withdraw contestant troops ten miles from the Suez Canal.

To allow occupation by Anglo-French forces of Port Said, Ismailia and Suez.

The Israeli attack provided the go-ahead for the initial embarkation of troops in the Mediterranean for 'Operation Musketeer'. In Four Five, the married ranks living outside Ghain Tuffieha, were warned of the impending move, and the preparation of stores and equipment began in earnest. The embarkation started on the 30th when the Commando's vehicles and heavy stores embarked in HM LCT* *Lofoten*, to sail for Port Said with the Amphibious Warfare Squadron. The Commando assault force embarked in *Ocean* and *Theseus* on Friday, 2 November, and sailed on the following day.

Embarked in HMS *Ocean* was the Joint Experimental Helicopter Unit (JEHU, the word 'Experimental' being dropped on the day of landing!) which consisted of six Mark 2 Whirlwind helicopters and six Mark 4 Sycamores (the Sycamores carried three men as opposed to the five carried by the Mark 2 Whirlwinds), Z Troop, Support Troop, Tactical Headquarters and elements of Headquarters Troop. The remainder of the Commando, A, B, X, and E Troops plus the rest of Headquarters Troop, was embarked in HMS *Theseus*, which carried 845 RN Squadron (ten Whirlwinds—eight Mark 22s which carried seven men and two Mark 3s which carried six men). This splitting up of the force, together with the lack of communications within the helicopters of those days, was a contributory factor to the rather extraordinary events of the Commanding Officer's first reconnaissance of Port Said. This resulted in his helicopter visiting an enemy held football stadium en route to the selected landing zone. The helicopter which was to fly this mission was from 845 Squadron,

* Landing Craft, Tank.

in *Theseus* and had to pick up its serial from *Ocean*, thus reducing prior liaison between pilot and passengers.

The Commander of Z Troop, Lt Jack Smith, later wrote:

'The sea passage from Malta to Port Said took three days, an intense period of briefing, rehearsal and preparation. The first day at sea was taken up with briefing and preparing loading tables. In HMS *Ocean* these were complicated because there were two types of helicopters, the Army version of the Whirlwind with a load of only five fully armed men, and the Sycamore capable of carrying three. Each man, as well as carrying his own ammunition, weapon, rations, water, respirator and spare clothing, had to carry some support weapon ammunition. All the Commando's vehicles had already sailed in the slow LST and LCT convoy a week before, and were thus unlikely to join up with the unit for some hours after landing.

A loaded Sycamore presented an extraordinary sight. The back seats, side panels and unessential fittings had been stripped to increase the lift. The three passengers sat on the floor, one hunched in the middle with six mortar bombs on his lap, and the other two with their legs dangling over the side, each holding a 106 mm. anti-tank shell about three feet long. The man in the centre was responsible for the two out-board members not falling out. The Whirlwind was a little more orthodox, but there were no seats, doors or windows. The five passengers hung on to any hand hold available. On approaching the landing zone the Bren gunner was ordered to put down suppressive fire out of the window if necessary, while the rifleman covered the area of the door. Communications between troops and pilot in both aircraft was either by shouting or tugging at the pilot's legs.

The second day at sea was devoted to rehearsing loading drills. The ship was darkened and the troops filed from their mess decks led by guides. The Commando was assembled in the forward hangar by helicopter sticks in landing waves. The after hangar was used for helicopter maintenance and for stowing the Joint Experimental Helicopter Unit's ground support vehicles.

The helicopters were ranged on crosses on the flight deck. On the order "stand by" the first wave of troops was raised in the lift and led to the sponsons on the starboard side of the flight deck. Then, on "start up", all Whirlwind motors were started. On "emplane", the sticks were led to their helicopters, emplaned, and the stick leader then tugged the pilot's leg, signifying that all was ready. The first wave could take off. A similar procedure was adopted to load the Sycamores.

During the third day there were further rehearsals, test firing of all automatic weapons, issues of operational ammunition, and inspections. The Commando was now ready to land.'

The overall political and military situation in the Middle East had by now deteriorated. Although the Israelis accepted the requirements of Her Majesty's Government, the Egyptians refused. Air attacks on Egyptian airfields were intensified and on the night of 31 October the first major incident in which Great Britain was involved took place. The cruiser HMS *Newfoundland* sunk the Egyptian frigate *Domiat*, in the Gulf of Suez, after the *Domiat* had failed to heed a warning signal and was seen to train her armament on *Newfoundland*. By now, complete military intervention was a virtual certainty, barring any major last minute political moves. The French were pressing to get the Allied operation under way, as Egyptian forces, including Soviet tanks, were building up in Port Said.

Keightley later reported that on 31 October his operational objective was Suez. He wanted to prevent the Egyptians moving their armoured forces, which were concentrated in reserve, to the Canal Zone and on to the causeway which runs from Port Said to Ismailia. By keeping the Egyptians uncertain to the last moment whether the main attack was to be at Port Said or Alexandria, Keightley hoped to minimize the deployment of tanks and thus avert the major threat. This in fact, he succeded in doing.

At eight-twenty on 5 November the 3rd Parachute Battalion Group and 16 Parachute Brigade Tactical Headquarters (some 600 men strong) began their jump on to Gamil Airfield, to the west of Port Said. A few minutes later 500 men from the 2ème Régiment Parachutistes Coloniaux (2RPC) dropped near the water works to the south of the town to capture the Raswa Bridges—Four Five's original objectives. A further 460 men of 2 RPC were dropped on to the southern outskirts of Port Fuad, to the east of Port Said. All these airborne landings were successful, and although there was heavy resistance in Port Fuad the paratroops took control.

At first the Egyptians seemed keen to surrender. The Egyptian military commander at Port Fuad, acting on behalf of the Commander of Port Said, offered to discuss terms of surrender. A cease-fire was ordered at three-thirty pm GMT, however, Cairo ordered fighting to continue and at eight-thirty the cease-fire ended. The garrison and local population were encouraged to resist by loudspeaker vans which toured the town announcing that Russian help was on the way, that London and Paris had been bombed, and that the Third World War had started. Arms were also distributed throughout the night.

It was now clear that Port Said could not be captured and cleared by the parachute force alone, and the seaborne force would have to make an opposed landing the next morning.

The Allied Commander ordered pre-bombardment by the Naval task force to be kept to a minimum so as to reduce Egyptian civilian casualties and damage to property.

Four Five was now ready for action. In HMS *Theseus* and HMS *Ocean* the troops had been up since before two am, breakfasted, donned their equipment and been given final briefings. The Naval gunfire support began at four and as the first sticks arrived on the flight deck their attention was naturally riveted to the shoreline, now some seven miles away. It was an overcast morning and the first assault wave of Commandos was streaming towards the beaches in landing craft. Over the town, a thick pall of black smoke billowed into the sky, giving a darkened effect to this memorable dawn. The roar of gunfire from the surrounding ships of the massed fleet was deafening.

At five-forty the Commando was ordered to land within the beach area already secured by 40 and 42 Commandos. Minutes later Lt-Col Tailyour and Major De'Ath took off from HMS *Ocean* in a Whirlwind of 845 Squadron to reconnoitre the landing zone (LZ). The LZ originally selected by the unit (near the De Lesseps Statue) had been rejected by higher command as it was intended that Four Five should land nearer Brigade Headquarters.

This LZ was obscured by smoke, and it later transpired that it was unsuitable because of overhead wires. The Whirlwind pilot made a quick detour and landed at the Egyptian Stadium. This incursion was resisted by enemy fire, and the reconnaissance party had to take up a defensive position in the players' entrance of the grandstand. Realizing that he had dropped his charges in an enemy stronghold, the pilot bravely landed again. Lt-Col Tailyour, his Operations Officer, and their two signallers then made a smart 200-yard dash to the Whirlwind, quickly reloaded the cumbersome wireless sets, and scrambled back on board the helicopter which, despite twenty direct hits and a slightly wounded pilot, was still able to fly. The reconnaissance group then landed safely to the west of the De Lesseps Statue, and by six am had ordered the first wave of helicopters, by now airborne, to land.

To those who landed in the early waves there seemed to be an air of unreality about the whole scene. The LZ was a large area of waste ground strewn with boulders and rubble. The shore, to the right, was lined with wooden bathing huts, built on stilts, some of them burning furiously as the result of the earlier bombardment. Alongside the sea wall once active Egyptian anti-aircraft guns lay shattered and silent.

All round the noise of warfare could be heard; the thud of mortars firing both from the beachhead and enemy held positions; the drone of fighters circling overhead followed by bursts of cannon fire as they strafed the retreating Egyptians; and the occasional crack as bullets from defiant snipers whistled past.

The helicopters approached the shore in waves, then orbited to allow each aircraft to land singly and deplane the troops. The helicopters hovered a foot or so off the ground and the troops leapt out amidst a cloud of sand and dust and 'went to ground' until the aircraft had again taken off.* It was probably not appreciated before 'Musketeer' that helicopters greatly speeded up the process of casualty evacuation, and thus drastically reduced the severity of many of the wounds. There was one instance when a marine, wounded by sniper fire on the LZ, was returned on the same helicopter wave, and was back on the deck of the carrier which he had left only nineteen minutes earlier. One Whirlwind returning with three Commando casualties ran out of fuel some 400 yards short of HSM *Theseus* and plummeted into the sea. Fortunately a launch reached them a short time afterwards, and all on board were rescued.

The build up on the LZ was rapid. By six-thirty the first wave had begun to land. This included E and Z Troop, Tactical Headquarters, Anti-tank gun detachments and an Air Contact Team.† Within ninety minutes all the Rifle Troops, Support Troop and Commando Headquarters had landed with their battle stores; a total of 425 men and twenty three tons of equipment.

Once they had landed the Troops moved inland to the assembly area near the blocks of flats that flanked the LZ. Many of these buildings bore the scars of the earlier bombardment, and shell holes were much in evidence. E Troop (Major Leslie Marsh) immediately started to clear the flats near the LZ so as to ensure that sniper fire did not interrupt the landings. Searching buildings of this size was a difficult and terrifying task as there were many hideouts for the expert gunman.

---

* This ensured that personnel were clear of the helicopter wheels on take off, and that no one would run into the tail rotor in the dust cloud.

† A small unit, commanded by Major Long, RTR, which worked with forward troops to demand and control aircraft which were providing close air support.

At eight o'clock Four Five moved off the assembly area. The Unit's task was to move to the centre of the town, clear and hold Shari El Mahrousa and the Governorate building, a large colonial-type residence, set back behind formal gardens. To reach this area the Commando advanced with E and Z Troops leading down a wide street, flanked by tall white flats with balconies on the south side, and wooden beach huts and small buildings set back on the north. The rocky, dusty soil in the middle was broken by gaunt lamp-posts, spaced at regular intervals.

Lt Jack Smith, Commanding Z Troop, had already carried out a forward reconnaissance and tied up details with the operations officer of 42 Commando, the unit on the right flank. As the rearguard Troops turned left and moved south towards Shari El Mahrousa, the advance was halted as E Troop cleared snipers which were firing from the Governorate building. Enemy movement was seen and gunfire heard from further down the street. It was clear that Z Troop was going to meet stiff opposition.

At eight forty-five, whilst the forward Troops advanced, the Tactical Headquarters approached the northern end of Shari El Mahrousa. A, B and X Troops were moving behind. Marine Ronald Jackson, the Commanding Officer's orderly, was standing beside Lt-Col Tailyour and his signaller Marine Michael Fowler, in the middle of the street. Four Wyverns, marked with 'our side' recognition bands, flew overhead. Suddenly the fourth one peeled off and headed straight at the Marines, strafing them with cannon fire. The defenceless troops dived for what cover they could find. Jackson remembers that he threw himself on the ground and 'could feel the draught of the cannon shells as they hit the ground'. The Commanding Officer was hit in the arm,* and Fowler, who subsequently died, badly

---

* One of the bullets was picked up and later given to Lt-Col Norman Tailyour as a souvenir, and several years afterwards, at a Fleet Air Arm dinner, he handed it back—suitably mounted on a plinth—to his hosts as 'returned stores'. It is not recorded whether or not a signature was obtained!

wounded. The Intelligence Officer, Lt John Weston and fourteen other ranks were also wounded. All the wireless sets in
headquarters were damaged and for a short time radio contact
was lost with the forward troops. The Medical Officer, Surg Lt
Guy Bradford, Sick Berth Petty Officer Blythe, and Sick Berth
Staff immediately rendered first aid and began evacuating the
wounded to the LZ, some in an ambulance borrowed from 40
Commando. It subsequently came to light that the pilot had
been given an erroneous map reference for his air strike target.
Even so, the streets along which Four Five were advancing
were behind our forward bombline, and neither Commando
Headquarters nor the ACT had any previous warning of the
impending strike. A quick re-organization of Commando Headquarters was now necessary. The Adjutant, Capt Derek Pounds
and the Signal Officer, Capt Jess Haycock maintained continuity
whilst the Second-in-Command, Major Richard Crombie, was
called forward to assume command. The unit Instructor Officer,
Instructor Lt-Cdr Lionel Jenkins, RN, took over as Intelligence
Officer until Lt Mick Marchant, the Unit Emplaning Officer,
came forward that evening. During the air strike Major
Crombie was back at the LZ organizing the stores and administrative area. He had landed with the Commandant-
General, Lieutenant-General C. R. Hardy, who, although not
in a position of operational command, wished to accompany his
men into battle. It was, of course, a source of great strength
to the Marines to see their Commandant-General moving
among them and giving words of encouragement.

In the meantime Z Troop was advancing past the Governorate building. The Troop report read as follows:

'Almost immediately 19 Section (Sgt Saxton) and 18
Section (Sgt Fellows) suffered casualties from snipers in a
large white building. 18 Section had Marine K. Essau
hit in the leg and L/Cpl M. T. Porter in the back. 19 Section
had Marine Cyril Goodfellow killed and Marine Smith
shot in the arm. 17 Section (Sgt Smith) had two casualties
from an enemy on the top floor, Cpl J. F. Rutherford shot in

the leg, and Marine Cowling. The luckiest escape was Marine McLeod who had the lion shot off the badge on his beret, but was unhurt . . . E Troop then moved forward from the area of the gardens to give support . . .'

The difficulty of street fighting against an enemy largely composed of para-military troops was described in the Commando battle report:

'The buildings along Shari El Mahrousa were in general seven storey blocks of concrete or brick flats. The ground floors consisting of shops, protected by steel shutters. Inside the buildings narrow stairways gave access upwards. The houses were occupied by civilians, with children. Egyptian army and police, many disguised in plain clothes, fought furiously. Some prisoners were found to have Benzedrine tablets in their possession. Many enemy wearing plain clothes fought until the last moment, and then discarding their weapons, posed as civilian refugees. In general the enemy defence was not co-ordinated, but groups of riflemen and machine-gunners hotly contested any advance. In two instances enemy snipers committed suicide rather than be captured. To offset the lack of tanks a 106 mm. anti-tank gun was set up on a borrowed carrier and used to blast a way through steel shutters and concrete walls. By this means the assault troops were able to effect an entry . . .'

At this point (nine-fifteen) B Troop (Capt Richard Meadows) had moved forward to assist the forward troops. Seven men had been wounded in the air strike. Capt Meadows later wrote:

'The Troop reformed to four sections and remained in the first block on the west side of the Shari El Mahrousa from where they shot along the streets going west, thereby covering the movement of our own troops up the main axis of advance. Z Troop asked for assistance to clear a sniper who was preventing them from evacuating wounded. Sgt Cooper's section cleared the sniper with the aid of an Energa bomb,*

* Anti-tank bomb fired from a grenade launcher fixed to the muzzle of a rifle.

which was very effective in this role, and then covered the removal of wounded.

The Troop Sergeant-Major, Kennedy, and Marine Connelly, berets on in the approved Browndown* fashion, together with Marine Galley, Morris and Watson in the Bren Group, killed a considerable number of enemy moving 200 yards along one of the roads going west from Shari El Mahrousa. The enemy were endeavouring to remove a small gun from its position in the middle of a road . . .'

By eleven o'clock the Shari El Mahrousa had been cleared and the buildings picketed to prevent infiltration. As the Troops consolidated their positions orders were received from Brigade to swing westwards to clear the blocks north of Shari Eugénie and Arab Town. This would effect an eventual link up with the 3rd Parachute Battalion who were moving eastwards from Gamil Airfield. The Commando's advance was to be supported by C Squadron, Royal Tank Regiment. Orders were given at twelve-twenty and the Troops began to move off soon after one o'clock. For the advance westward, each Troop was given a separate sector coinciding with the blocks of buildings north of Shari Eugénie, E was on the southern flank, A and Z in the centre, covering Shari Urabi. B Troop was withdrawn to act as reserve and set up its headquarters in a deserted school building, to the north of Shari El Mahrousa, in which a generous supply of arms and ammunition had been left by the fleeing Egyptians.

As the Troops moved off the air began to fill with smoke. A fire had started in the northernmost building of the Shari El Mahrousa and smoke and burning debris impeded progress. At one-twenty the welcome rumble of the Centurions of C Squadron was heard as they moved up to give their support.

Opposition varied considerably in each sector, but each group gave support to the other as the painstaking advance continued. A Troop's first objective was the Mosque El Abbasi, although not defended there were several wounded left

* The Royal Marines Small Arms Training School.

in its vicinity. All Troops reached Bound One, the first lateral road, Shari El Sherrif by two-thirty.

Z Troop had, perhaps, the busiest afternoon. After clearing the first bound they found that snipers and gunmen were still firmly entrenched in some buildings. 18 Section Commander, Sgt Fellows, and his Bren gunner gained entry into one building and started climbing a small flight of stairs. Their ascent was halted by two 36 grenades, though both of them managed to dodge the exploding metal and with the remainder of the section beat a hasty retreat amidst bursting grenades, but without casualties. The grenade thrower still resisted despite fire from 17 Section and the Support Section, who lobbed in phosphorus smoke grenades. Eventually a tank was called up and dislodged the offenders from the building by firing at point-blank range.

On the north side of the street Z Troop second-in-command, Lt Stuart Syrad, was leading 19 and 20 sections in their house clearing mission. His task was impeded by the burning surroundings and the sections not only had to dodge falling masonry but also snipers' bullets that were being fired from further down the street. These objectives were quickly secured. Lt Syrad was later awarded the Military Cross for his bravery at Port Said.

Bound Two, Shari El Ghazi Moukhtar, had been reached by four o'clock and further orders were issued for the remainder of the day.

During the afternoon the Commando's transport had been brought up to the assembly area from the fishing harbour where it had previously been landed by LSTs and LCTs. The depth of the fishing harbour, along with other intelligence matters, had been the cause of some controversy amongst the planners. No authoritative statement could be given as to the exact depth of water in the harbour. Opinions varied between four and thirteen feet, and its use was vital to the operational plan. In the event the vessels were able to enter with safety and unload their cargoes.

Throughout the day the elements of Support Troop

(Lt Tony Quin) made their valuable contribution to the Commando's advance. The medium machine gun platoon covered the waste ground to the north of Shari El Mahrousa. So accurate was their fire—they hit a running enemy at 800 yards' range—that six more ran out from one of the beach huts waving a white flag. The Assault Engineers kept close behind the forward elements setting up supply areas for the provision of ammunition and explosives. Although the mortars had a relatively quiet day the 106 mm. Anti-Tank Gun Platoon commanded by Lt Tony Richardson was kept fully occupied. Originally, each of the four detachments was allocated to a Rifle Troop. On landing, however, they combined and with carriers from the Somerset Light Infantry moved up to the Governorate area to give supporting fire. Over ten rounds were fired into buildings with great accuracy, causing considerable damage, and effectively clearing them of snipers.

When dusk fell the Troops consolidated their positions and prepared all round defence for the night. Hot food was brought forward from the administrative area near the LZ, and Commando Headquarters began to compile reports of the day's activities. Enemy casualties inflicted by Four Five were estimated to total 150, whilst the Commando had lost two dead, twenty-eight wounded evacuated, and three slightly wounded.

At nine o'clock that evening a warning was received that a cease-fire would become operative at midnight, but it was not a particularly quiet night for the unit. The fire that had started earlier that afternoon was now raging fiercely and out of control. Z and X Troops had to evacuate their positions, and the Command Post, which was smoked out, had to move back. By dawn on 7 November, the fire had burnt out, having gutted six blocks of buildings.

The remainder of the 7th was spent in centralizing captured enemy equipment and planning for a search of Arab Town on the 8th, for which Major Crombie had received orders. The search began at dawn and Crombie remembers the trepidation that he felt when hordes of hostile Arabs swarmed around his vehicle in this hutted area, honeycombed with narrow streets.

The sullen looks soon turned to smiles when the Commandos claimed that they had been sent by 'Jim Irish'. This was the name given to a legendary trader of doubtful repute who was known to Arab and soldier alike in the Middle East, and was alleged to have been able to provide or obtain anything under the sun!

By the end of the day, as tension eased, over fifty-seven three-ton truckloads of ammunition and weapons had been recovered by Four Five. However, it was believed that coastal dhows were still ferrying in more arms which were then redistributed throughout the Arab quarter.

For the next five days the Commando carried out internal security duties in Arab Town, which included clearing and searching houses, patrolling, enforcing night curfews and the control of refugees, a relatively tame period compared with the intense activity of 6 November.

On 13 November, the advance party of 1st Royal Scots arrived, and assumed control of the area on the following morning, whilst Four Five joined Brigade Headquarters and 40 Commando to embark in the *Empire Fowey*. The arrival of the troopship alongside had been delayed for three days due to congestion in the harbour. She had been ordered back to her anchorage off the coast on two occasions, and had also been rammed by a tug that had been sent out to help. Thus it was with great relief that she embarked the Commandos on 14 November and set sail for Malta, arriving on the 17th.

The political controversies of Suez will doubtless continue for many years. The combined military operation was an overwhelming success, and the order to cease fire came as a bitter blow to many of the troops, who earnestly wanted to continue and complete their task.

Naturally I have covered the activities of Four Five in isolation and detail. Barker* describes the helicopter assault as the 'most outstanding feature of the operation' and goes on to give the Commandos the well-earned title of 'instant troops'.

Although there were mixed feelings within the Commando as

* *Suez. The Seven Day War*, p. 197.

to the role that the helicopters should play in this assault, in retrospect it was a wise decision of the commanders to hold the force in reserve. This ensured that the characteristics of the helicopters could be fully implemented, and if unforeseen delays in the main assault had occurred the airborne force could have been diverted. Four Five was also able to land in an area of the beach-head previously secured. If the unit had landed on 5 November and met stiff opposition, the future of helicopter operations might have been jeopardized, and the helicopter casualty rate greatly increased.

Once ashore, Four Five was then committed to the more conventional tasks of street clearing on the left flank of the 3rd Commando Brigade advance. It was possible to drive straight through Port Said, at speed, and only sustain light casualties, but the initial beach head had not only to be consolidated but cleared of the menace of lurking snipers. This was a dangerous and methodical process for which the Commando deservedly gain ten operational awards out of the thirty awarded to the Brigade.

Brigadier Madoc, whose skilful handling of the 3rd Commando Brigade at Port Said was subsequently recognized by the award of the Distinguished Service Order, received the following signal on the 22 November from General Keightley.

'Now that "Operation Musketeer" is almost complete I would like to congratulate you and all ranks of the 3rd Commando Brigade for the brilliant part which you and all your Command played in it. The planning, training, and execution of the operation were of the highest order and I am extremely grateful for the skill, determination and courage displayed throughout.

Your Brigade has now been under my command for many operations and on relinquishing C-in-C MELF I would also like to let you know the tremendous admiration I have always had for the splendid manner in which you have done anything you were ever asked to do without complaint and with complete success . . .'

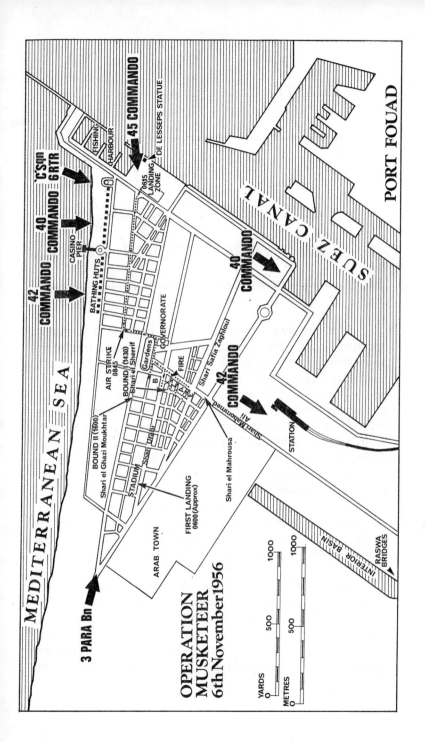

OPERATION
MUSKETEER
6th November 1956

CHAPTER 12

Aden I, 1960–1963— The Commando's Early Years in a Troubled Land

In the years preceding 1960, Four Five normally operated under direct command, or in the same theatre of operations, as Headquarters, 3rd Commando Brigade. In many campaigns after the war, the Brigade had hunted as a pack—Hong Kong, Malaya and Suez. In Cyprus too, although not always under full operational command, Four Five remained under administrative control either from the island itself, or nearby Malta. In these post-war years it has been difficult to completely isolate Four Five's activities and achievements, and in doing so one frequently neglects the comparable contributions made by 40 and 42 Commando, Royal Marines. In Aden, however, Four Five was able to carve an independent path for itself over a seven-year period, in which its actions could be closely associated with the problems which surrounded South Arabia at the time. Headquarters, 3rd Commando Brigade, moved to Singapore in 1961 but still remained, of course, the superior authority on purely Royal Marine matters.

The history of Aden is a long and involved one, surrounded by political intrigue and tribal dealings, many of which have been lost in antiquity. The British first showed diplomatic interest in this barren area, situated on the south-western tip of the Arabian peninsula, in 1802, when a treaty of friendship was signed with the Sultan of Lahej, so that Aden could be used as a safe port for our trading vessels. A new Sultan broke the treaty in 1838 and later held a ship, flying the British flag, to ransom. In 1839 a Capt Haines was despatched by the Bombay Presidency, and with the aid of the Royal Marine detachments captured Aden and annexed it to the British Crown as a Dependency under the Government of India. At the time Aden itself had virtually declined to a small fishing village but under its new masters rapidly gained in importance as a coaling station. The opening of the Suez Canal, in 1869, provided even more work for this now thriving free port which was to become a Crown Colony in 1937.

The hinterland between Aden and the Yemen had a less straightforward history during this period and the difficulties and complications which existed then were to make themselves apparent in the troubled years of the sixties. No attempt was made by the Government of India to annex the 'up country' regions but treaties of protection were later signed with the sultans and sheikhs of these surrounding provinces. This was a long drawn out process bearing in mind some of the strange and deep-rooted tribal differences. These treaties formed the basis of agreements, hastened by a Turkish invasion in the 1870s, which resulted in the formation of the Eastern and Western Protectorates. The Turkish Army again made its presence felt during the first World War and for long periods occupied territory as far south as Lahej, but after the Armistice the country reverted to its Dependency-Protectorate relationship.

A further bone of contention in this inhospitable terrain was the line of the border between the Aden Protectorate and the Yemen, which had been in dispute for many years. The Turkish influence and bitter tribal feuds had combined to complicate this issue even further. In 1934, however, a settlement was reached and the Yemen evacuated all the territory which it had occupied in the Protectorate, but even after this long tracts of the frontier still remained 'undemarcated' which did little to ease the peace-keeping problems of later years.

After Aden had formally become a Crown Colony in 1937 it and the Protectorate existed as separate, but largely inter-dependent states. Tribal differences up country still persisted and these ensured that the Aden Protectorate Levies (APL)* and the Royal Air Force based in Aden, were kept fully oc-cupied. In the 1950s political moves were in hand to bring about a Federation between the Colony and the Protectorate. These talks were carried out against a background of general unrest in the Arab world, and continuous pressure from the Yemen, who claimed her rights to the lands of South Arabia. Cairo and Sanaa Radios combined to incite the Adenis and in 1956 industrial unrest broke out in the Colony. In the following years serious Yemeni inspired incidents broke out on the border. Regular British troops were soon deployed on operational duties in the Protectorate and as a result of the Suez crisis the strategic importance of Aden grew again. In 1959 a Federation of Amirates took place. Participation was not complete, but this was undoubtedly an important step forward, and by 1960 ten states had joined the union.

The political climate in 1960, when Four Five came to Aden, was still far from settled. In the Colony the Aden Trades Union Congress was openly opposing the new franchise which gave the vote only to those born in Aden, British subjects or British-protected subjects who had lived in the Colony for seven out of the last ten years. The population was a mixed one of Arabs, Indians and Somalis. A high percentage of the Arabs were Yemenis, who had no right to vote, and their cause was being actively supported from Cairo. In the Pro-tectorate, unrest, sparked mainly from the north, continued. Russia, having one of her periodical stabs at British imperialism, ensured that the Yemen arsenals were well stocked.

This, of necessity, is only a brief summary of the major events which occurred under the British administration and it is not intended as a study in depth. Without some background knowledge of the complexities of the situation it is difficult to account for the subsequent military moves and actions.

* Re-named Federal Regular Army in 1961.

The advance party of Four Five arrived in Aden in TT *Nevasa* on 10 March, 1960. Whilst awaiting disembarkation the Commando diarist's immediate impression was, of course, the weather: 'Phew! it was really hot, even in the shade'. The high temperatures and humidity combined to make Aden an unpleasant station for the British, and it is of interest to note that Four Five were the first Royal Marines forces ever to be permanently based ashore in the Colony. The first task of the advance party, under the command of Major Dai Morgan was to take over the camp in Little Aden, leased from the British Petroleum Company, from the 1st Battalion, the Royal War-wickshire Regiment. The camp consisted of seven rows of long, single-storey huts, painted blue. The white roofs and surrounding sand combined to form a considerable glare to those unused to these elements. Each hut was blessed with an air conditioner plant but these machines, installed to serve the short term needs of the BP refinery construction teams, frequently seemed to suffer from the effects of the climate with the result that conditions inside became oppressively unbear-able. The otherwise bare terrain of the camp was broken only by two small oases of greenery—the tree-lined patios beside the Officers' and Sergeants' messes. The former had a small lawn and garden, which were, not unnaturally, the object of lavish attention. The whole scene at Little Aden was dominated by the stark mountains that rose sharply from the sand. The brown rocks had been eroded into grotesque shapes by centuries of wind and heat. At night the flickering oil-flame of the nearby BP refinery cast an eerie orange light over the entire area.

The other British forces in the Colony at the time were: an Internal Security battalion at Khormaksar; an RAF base at the nearby airfield; a cavalry squadron equipped with Cen-turions at Bir Fuqum, to the West of Little Aden; a cavalry regiment in the camp opposite Four Five's, equipped with Ferrets and Saladins. Headquarters, Middle East Command, HMS *Sheba* Naval Base, Headquarters Aden Garrison and other base installation were situated in 'Big' Aden.

The Commando's second home was in Dhala Camp, some

eighty miles north of Aden and less than ten miles from the Yemen border. Dhala lies on a plateau at an altitude of 5,000 feet, in the northern mountains. The climate is excellent compared with that of Aden because although it is just as hot by day the humidity is very much lower, and at night it gets cold enough to need blankets or sweaters. Rain in 'Big' Aden is infrequent, but is torrential when it does occur. In Dhala, however, there is a short wet season which accounts for more greenery in the neighbourhood and the terraces of cultivation which are carved into the rocky mountainsides of the deep valleys.

The camp at Dhala was built on a small ridge a mile north of the town and was originally constructed to house an infantry company. Before Four Five adopted the company organization two Troops were based there. The camp was about 500 yards long and the central road was flanked by tentage of varying sizes. In front of each tent were well kept gardens with gaily painted signs, and there was always keen rivalry between the varying sections for both neatness and originality. Possibly the most incongruous feature of the camp was the two galleys at either end constructed of corrugated iron. These buildings, invariably glinting in the sunlight, provided a sharp contrast to the dusty plain with its rocky soil and gnarled trees. In addition to the Rifle Troops a detachment of the Support Troop was permanently based here to man mortar and machine gun positions. On a similar ridge, 300 yards away, lay the larger APL Camp, and a mile away was an airstrip which had been constructed for Twin Pioneers to land on in order to bring in fresh supplies and mail.

The Dhala convoy was possibly one of the most unforgettable experiences in those days. These used to run once a fortnight to bring supplies up to the Dhala garrison and reinforcement troops. The road followed an ancient trade, military, and pilgrim route which led from the Indian Ocean to the Yemen and other important centres. For centuries the mountain tribes had run a protection racket, claiming the tolls from the passing caravans. Government traffic was exempt from these

16. *Loading camels at Habilayn to take water out to a picquet.*

17. *'Anything to declare?' Searching an Arab house in conjunction with the police.*

18. *Dhala Convoy. Dismounted troops marching up the treacherous Khuraybah Pass.*

19. *A patrol, with an Arab guide, moves down a wadi bed in the Radfan.*

tolls but even so military vehicles were sometimes considered to be 'fair game' and the tribesmen were not averse to firing off the occasional round from their lofty perches.

These convoys usually left Lake Lines, just outside Sheikh Othman, at six in the morning and this meant a four-thirty start from Little Aden. The convoys varied in size from upwards of a dozen vehicles, including scout cars, and the first one the author had the privilege of escorting consisted of nearly seventy vehicles, one of the biggest on record. The infantry escort was placed at strategic intervals along the convoy, dependent upon the size, and its task was to guard against ambush and protect vehicles that had broken down. The tarmac road petered out five miles from Sheikh Othman and after that there were frequent delays when the heavier trucks got bogged down in the soft shifting sand. Approaching Lahej conditions improved and the track was flanked by fields and fruit groves, the result of years of painstaking irrigation. After Lahej the greenery soon gave way to flat rocky desert and driving conditions improved until Nobat Dukaim had been reached. Here the road forked and the main Dhala route continued into the mountains. Rocks and boulders had to be avoided by the drivers and the troops in the back had to cling to their seats as the trucks bounced along in the dust laden air. The first halt was normally at Thumier, sixty miles and six hours driving from Aden, where the locals used to rush joyfully from their huts to offer fruit, biscuits and soft drinks at exorbitant prices to the weary drivers and escorts. The heated voices of bargaining were often intermingled with cries of 'backsheesh' and 'Nasser tamaam!!'.* The white-painted Fort Thumier was manned by the Federal National Guard, who guarded small outposts throughout the Federation and were formerly known as Government Guards.†

---

* 'Nasser good.'

† Each ruler also maintained tribal guards who owed allegiance to their ruler rather than the Federation or Government, which meant that our forces were given a greater burden in identifying friend from foe when passing through their territories.

The next twenty miles of road, after Thumier, were very rough indeed. The route followed the bed of a dried-up wadi on the line of the old Turkish road and twisted and turned for a seemingly endless distance. The scenery was truly magnificent with jagged mountains rising steeply on either side of the wadi. On some of the peaks, FNG picquets could be discerned many hundreds of feet above. The villages near the road clung precariously to the steep mountain sides and most of the houses were built as forts with thick walls and small windows as protection against small-arms fire from hostile neighbours. As the convoys passed the children would run out screaming, whilst the elders just stared impassively.

The last obstacle of the journey was the Khuraybah Pass, which rose sharply in a series of hairpin bends to the Dhala Plain. The vehicles moved up slowly at two minute intervals and as the track was so narrow, only twelve feet wide in some places, the strained drivers naturally faced some of the corners with trepidation. On several of these corners it was necessary to back and straighten up in order to get round—the evidence of those who had failed to do so was scattered in twisted heaps at the bottom of the precipitous ravine. Whilst the vehicles negotiated the track the escorts proceeded up a footpath, in case of accidents, and surveyed with relief the Dhala Plain and the camps in the distant haze. The eighty miles often took over ten hours and it was hardly surprising that the four-wheel drive Bedford three-ton trucks needed a new set of tyres after a round trip.

Aden, unlike Malta, was an unaccompanied posting, but the married ranks, in general, did not regret this as, in the Mediterranean, long periods of separation on active duty disrupted home life considerably. The average length of a tour in Aden was twelve months and a continuous system of 'trickle' drafting kept Four Five up to strength. It was also usual, at this time, to organize the Rifle Troops on a repatriation basis so that only one was reforming at any one stage. Because of the climate a tropical routine was followed in BP camp. Work started at seven-thirty hours and finished at twelve forty-five, thus leaving the afternoons free for recreational pursuits or swimming at the nearby BP beach, conveniently protected by a shark net. The intense heat and humidity also affected new arrivals from the United Kingdom and at least a week of acclimatisation was necessary before ranks became fully operationally effective.

The main body of Four Five disembarked in Aden on 23 April, 1960, from TT *Dunera*, the transport having preceded them in LST *Empire Skua* by five days. The advance party had already taken over the BP Camp from the Royal Warwickshire Regiment and X Troop (Capt Pat Griffiths) had the privilege of being the first to look after Dhala Camp. They were later joined by B Troop (Capt Freddie Slater) who travelled with the main body. The early days 'up country' were relatively quiet with only the occasional shot fired at the camp by local tribesmen, probably more as an introduction to their way of life rather than in hostility.* These were countered with mortar and machine gun concentrations which normally frightened the dissidents off for a few days. The dominating feature of Dhala was the Jebel Jihaf, whose prominent finger of rock protruded for over 1,000 feet above the plain below. The Jebel formed one of the main patrol routes and it was not uncommon for the Troops to climb the five miles up to the Turkish Road (suitable only for Land Rovers) and visit the lonely FNG ouposts at Qarnah and As Saria, and then scramble down the jebel by means of the donkey track to return to Dhala via the isolated FNG fort on the mountainside at Shima.

Lt-Col Billy Barton, who had assumed command just before the EOKA onslaught in Cyprus in 1958 and whose tour had included the last days in Malta and the move to Aden, left Four Five on 13 July, 1960. His place was taken by Lt-Col L. G. Marsh who had formerly commanded X Troop in Hong Kong and then became Adjutant in the Canal Zone. In late 1961, Lt-Col Barton was appointed Commander, 3rd

---

* It was even rumoured, at the time, that the Dhala garrison would give the tribesmen five pounds on their return from the local *souk* (market) on Thursdays so that they would shoot at the camp and give the sentries something to fire at!

Commando Brigade and was thus able to renew his association with Four Five. Brigadier Barton's predecessor had been Brigadier Norman Tailyour, and of course he too had visited his old unit both in Aden and at Dhala.

The political situation in 1960, was relatively quiet although life was occasionally disrupted by wildcat strikes. Matters came to a head in August when new legislation was introduced to make strikes illegal. The ATUC were the main opponents to the new bill and introduced one hour daily general strikes, which seemed to coincide conveniently with the coffee break! The ATUC called a full general strike on 15 August, the day the bill was debated and passed by Legislative Council. The entire Commando, including the Dhala detachment, was deployed throughout the Colony and although tension increased there was no widespread violence. The strike was eventually called off on the 17th and by the 18th everything had returned to normal. Four Five's only active task was to carry out street patrols on the 16th to encourage shopkeepers to remain open. The tradesmen needed little persuasion as there were two large passenger liners in the harbour! Four Five's action was preventative rather than curative, but even so the unit helped to maintain the peace which had been lacking on previous occasions in Aden.

In general the first three years in Aden were the most settled for Four Five. Many forms of progressive Troop and Commando training could be carried out in the surrounding desert and on nearby beaches and the ten-week spells of active service duty and patrols up at Dhala added the necessary realism. The presence of the Amphibious Warfare Squadron gave variety to the training and exercises took place either in the Western Aden Protectorate or in the Persian Gulf. One of the largest of these was 'Exercise Roulade', in March, 1961, which was the biggest combined service exercise ever to take place in the theatre. This was the first opportunity to practise the Commando Ship concept since the more exacting landings at Suez and under 3rd Commando Brigade Headquarters (Brigadier Norman Tailyour) 42 Commando, Four Five and other supporting units were landed from the Amphibious Warfare Squadron, which included HMS *Bulwark*, sixty miles west of Little Aden.

The background to this exercise gives a good account of the role and possible employment of Royal Marines Commando units at the time:

'The emergence of the "cold war" in the 1950s showed the need for strategic forces in being and able to act with little notice. At the same time the possibility of denying of over-flying rights and restrictions in the use of former bases have made it apparent that such forces must be self supporting and of extensive range. The Amphibious Warfare Squadron of the Royal Navy and 3rd Commando Brigade Royal Marines have, until recently, formed the main sea-borne reserve force. In the setting of the cold war the Commandos are now able by landing in, and being supported by, helicopters, to maintain the rule of law in areas remote from the coast and to reach their objective at short notice and when heavy weather makes landing by sea impossible . . .'

For Four Five it was the Commando's first taste of operating as an entire unit in the height of the hot season and for six days the Commando had the gruelling task of 'fighting' its way back through the scorching sand to Little Aden.

For those who tired of the endless yellows and browns of South Arabia, the more pleasant greenery of Kenya was always available for both leave and military purposes. E Troop (Capt 'Lefty' Warn) was the first to train in East Africa for a six week period in October and November, 1960, and during the next year each Troop was scheduled for a similar training period, but this was brought to an abrupt halt caused by the Kuwait crisis, in July, 1961. The crisis was part of the general Arab offensive against Great Britain to which Aden, in particular, was so vulnerable and as it was significant to Four Five it has been included as a separate chapter. Suffice it to say that 'Roulade' was a fortuitous prelude to this real-life operation and both 42 and Four Five were to be employed in an 'instant reinforcement' role when peace was threatened, less than six months after the exercise.

On return from Kuwait, later that year, E Troop (Capt Peter Downs) undertook an outstanding feat of endurance on 8 November, 1961, when the Troop marched from Dhala to Little Aden. This party was accompanied by eight ranks of 145 Field Battery, Royal Artillery, who shortly afterwards were to be trained as a Commando Battery. This was the first time that the march had been attempted by British troops since before the war, and the Troop Commander's research revealed that the previous unit to do this was the Buffs, some forty years previously.

The march was code-named 'Operation Barbara' (with apologies to Dr Moore), and took a total of three days. For the first two days E Troop followed the Dhala convoy route, stopping overnight at Thumier and some ten miles north of Lahej. The APL gave great assistance throughout the entire venture and provided a guard of honour for the departing Troop at Dhala, a camp at Fort Thumier and picquet protection along the mountainous sectors. The most gruelling day was probably the third, when the tired Troop had to march thirty-five miles from north of Lahej to Little Aden. For the first part of this stretch E Troop was accompanied by the Staff Officer Operations, Major Willy Wharfe, and Mr Harry Cockerill, a great friend of the Commando's from BP, both of whom had contributed greatly to the planning of this venture. After leaving Lahej the Troop set out, with Lt John Milne-Home acting as guide, across the flat, featureless desert. The going was particularly difficult as the sand was soft and the temperatures well above 90°. The distant rocks of Little Aden shimmered in the heat on the horizon and never appeared to get any nearer, and as twilight rapidly changed to darkness the glow of the ever-burning BP flame acted as a pilot beacon. In spite of exhaustion, one of the Troop subalterns, Lt Roger Simpson, remembers that the Troop, soon before it reached Little Aden on the night of the 10th, formed up and marched smartly into the camp to a rousing and heartfelt reception from

the remainder of Four Five. This truly remarkable performance had been successfully achieved without any special
training, and it is a great credit to the fitness of the Troop
that only six had to retire to the following truck, at various
stages, for treatment of badly blistered feet.

The farewell Malta Tattoo seems to have paved the way for
future productions and Four Five continued with two more
successes. In November, 1960, an enterprising show was given
before His Excellency the Governor, Sir Charles Johnson, and
an invited audience of 500. The whole set was then stripped
down and reconstructed on the Tawahi Sports Ground in the
centre of Aden, before an estimated audience of 14,000—
memories of the soccer semi-final in Hong Kong in 1947. The
second tattoo, also a searchlight one, took place in Little Aden
in February, 1962.

Although activities in Aden, in the early sixties, could be
described as in the 'brewing up' stage, another Middle East
country, Oman, was facing far graver threats to its internal
stability. A Commando visitor described Oman as a 'forbidding
country . . . in summer it is literally oven hot, the heat bounc-
ing off the mountain rock or the gravel plain with equal intensity. There are no roads but there are motorable tracks, on
no stretch of which is a speed of over twenty-five mph enjoyable
or advisable'. The Sultan of Muscat claimed rulership, in
addition to his coastal domain, of the mountainous interior, and
styled himself the Sultan of Muscat and Oman. The Imam of
the 'mountains', Ghalib, opposed these claims but in 1955 was
deposed and his brother, Talib, fled to neighbouring South
Arabia to gather his cohorts together. Talib then returned to
Oman in 1957 to stake his claims. British assistance was called
for and in addition to an expeditionary force of the Special Air
Service, which was to achieve great success in early 1959, we
provided personnel for the Sultan's Armed Forces both in a
training and operational capacity. In the first year alone
twenty Royal Marine officers and sixty-three NCOs were
seconded to this force, several of which came from Four
Five, then based in the Mediterranean. Many distinguished

themselves, including Sgt 'Taff' Rees who was awarded the Military Medal: 'He extricated his Special Patrol Section from a battle fought at point blank range . . . his coolness under fire, personal courage and devotion to duty surprised the rebels in their own position. By his daring leadership he inflicted enemy casualties (two killed) whilst his patrol only suffered minor wounds.' Lt Jeremy Coulter, who was Mentioned in Despatches, 'showed great determination to harass the enemy on patrol and over a two-month period enabled his company to operate freely over what was previously rebel country'. This campaign tragically cost the life of Colour Sgt Jack Halford, BEM, of Four Five who had distinguished himself during the war by managing to escape after being caught during the fall of Crete, and had then served for over two years with the Yugoslav patriots.*

Throughout its many years in Aden, Four Five was to make a valuable contribution to the Sultan's Armed Forces, an association that was to be upheld even after the British troops had been withdrawn from South Arabia.

The first half of 1962 passed quietly for Four Five, now under the command of Lt-Col N. S. E. Maude. The year opened with two important visitors to the unit, Lord St Oswald, the Defence Speaker to the House of Lords, and Mr John Profumo, the Secretary of State for War. Both visitors were able to witness varied forms of training and inspect ranks and stores ready for air portability. A Commando unit, in addition to other commitments, must always be prepared in case the 'balloon should go up' and can normally be expected to undertake a move anywhere in the theatre from its base within between twelve and twenty-four hours. If there is a specific crisis then this notice is reduced and activities are limited to enable the reaction time to be met satisfactorily. Two months later, on 29 March, the Minister of Defence, the Rt Hon Harold Watkinson, visited Little Aden, and he too was able to see the high state of readiness forever maintained by Four Five. The year continued with an uninterrupted programme of

* *Globe and Laurel*, April, 1957.

exercises and progressive training but it became abundantly clear that a political crisis was fast approaching. The Peoples Socialist Party, formed as a political party of the Aden TUC, was busily inciting its members to demand a union with the new republican régime in the Yemen, led by General Sallal. At the same time as these representations were being made the Legislative Council of the Colony met in Crater on 24 September, 1962, to debate the proposed merger of the Colony with the Federation of Aden. The PSP had threatened beforehand to march on the LEGCO building during the debate and drag the ministers through the streets. Extra security measures were ordered throughout the Colony and because of these Four Five had to modify its programme, which had been prepared some weeks prior to this, for the changeover from five Rifle Troops to three companies to form the new enlarged Commando organization. The changeover was completed successfully, so that in the first week of existence X-Ray, Yankee and Zulu Companies were ready to meet the coming emergency. Although Z Company (Capt David Carrie) remained at Dhala to hold the fort, so to speak, X Company (Major Willy Wharfe) and Y Company (Capt Peter Stickley) were placed on immediate alert in Little Aden. On the morning of the 24th, as the threat of violence had not subsided, Y Company was deployed by six o'clock over a large area. Company Headquarters and 4 Troop (2/Lt Graham Evans) were based at Maalla Police Station, 5 Troop (2/Lt John McGregor) were at Sheikh Othman and 6 Troop (2/Lt David Young) were at RAF Steamer Point. Crowds of over 3,000 advanced on the LEGCO and the Armed Police had a busy time that morning breaking up mobs with the use of tear gas and batons. X Company moved down to the King's Own Scottish Borderers' Barracks at Waterloo Lines that afternoon after the battalion had been deployed, but for Four Five the day was mainly a monotonous one, with the Troops sitting in stifling and dusty buildings waiting for orders to move. Activity quietened down in the siesta hours but that evening the Armed Police had to suppress some of the more militant elements who started damaging property and set fire to some printing presses and two cars. The police killed one and wounded three in these skirmishes. In Little Aden, CS gas was used for the first time against a riot in the Colony. The crowd of about a hundred quickly dispersed and nearly fifty were reported to be still in bed twenty-four hours later! Those arrested were seen to be extremely ill while in the custody of the police. That evening patrols from Four Five were out guarding strategic points in the Colony but although the Companies remained deployed throughout the period of the debate there were no further disturbances.

The newly formed Republican Government in the Yemen was by now hurling out a torrent of anti-imperialist propaganda and this prompted Federal rulers to ask for stronger British action. The external and internal threats were now becoming apparent. There had already been one serious incident near Dhala when, in July, the Commanding Officer of the 4th Battalion Federal Regular Army, Col Thomas, had been attacked with a *jambia** by an unfriendly sheikh. The Emir of Dhala, who was accompanying Col Thomas, claimed the right to shoot the offender but the Political Adviser, Mr Godfrey Meynell, himself an ex-Royal Marine officer and great friend of the Dhala Detachment, intervened and the sheikh was brought to justice the next day before a Federal Court and imprisoned for ten years. This incident shows just how volatile the situation in the Border States was and how ancient tribal laws still prevailed. It was this type of situation that the Yemen was so eager to exploit.

Exercise 'Hollow Laugh' dominated the latter part of 1962, through it was not really an exercise at all. It was mounted on 11 November at four days notice as an operational patrol to Lodar, some one hundred miles east of Aden just a few miles from the Yemen border. The internal events of the Yemen had increased the desirability of such a show of force, and this was coupled with the knowledge that dissidents had been active in the Lodar region. The force consisted of over 1,000 troops and in addition to Four Five included a squadron of Centurions of the Royal Scots Greys, a troop of the 9th/12th Lancers, D

* A curved Arab knife.

Battery, Royal Horse Artillery and other supporting units. An exercise amphibious landing was made at Shuqra and then the entire force became operational for the fifty mile journey up to Lodar. A full scale of ammunition was issued. There were over 150 vehicles in the convoy and the twisting track was even worse than the Dhala road. Whilst Four Five picqueted the rocky mountain heights, the dust-covered tank crews of the Royal Scots Greys sweated to keep their prized vehicles going through the sweltering heat below. The track in some places was so narrow that the sections of 34 Independent Field Squadron, Royal Engineers, were frequently brought into use to widen and straighten the surface. The men of the repair and recovery sections, 52 Command Workshops, Royal Electrical and Mechanical Engineers, moved up and down the convoy carrying out their vital task of keeping trucks and tanks service-able and could be seen, stripped to the waist, working all hours of the night to repair the numerous breakdowns. It took nearly two days to reach Lodar, at midday on 13 November, and that morning the ground troops were supported by Scimitars and Sea Vixens from HMS *Ark Royal*. Although these aircraft were not required in an offensive role they screamed past the convoy, often at heights of only a few feet, and could not have failed to impress friend and foe alike.

It is significant to note that on the 13th, whilst Four Five were engaged in 'Hollow Laugh', the House of Commons was debating the political aspects of South Arabia and voted not to recognize the Republican régime in the Yemen but to continue to support the Federation of South Arabia and the plans to merge the Aden Colony into it.

This force was the biggest military one ever to visit the area and contact was made with the FRA so that the inhabitants could see Commando and native troops working together. The force left Lodar that afternoon, as scheduled, much to the delight of Radio Sanaa who claimed that Four Five, with tank support, had reached the Yemen border but had now turned and raced back to the sea in full flight!

The merger of the Aden Colony (now to be known as

Aden State) with the Federation finally took place on 18 January, 1963, and this heralded a year of increased tension. Again, for the first few months of the year, the political problems did not interrupt Four Five's activities and on 11 May the unit commenced to fly to Kenya for an exercise appropriately named 'Winged Marine'. The two-week training period in lush parkland provided a sharp contrast to the sands of Aden and in addition the bright lights of Nairobi supplied extra relief. The last three days in Kenya were spent on Exercise 'Tame Baboon' and the climax of this exercise was the Commando attack on an airstrip. As the unit was moving up a gully to the start line, Marine T. G. Cuthbertson of X Company, was twice bitten by a puff adder. Many other members of the Company had already crossed the same piece of ground, but it was Cuthbertson that this venomous snake chose as his victim. Fortunately, the company Sick Berth Attendant, Docherty, who was rushed to the scene, recognized the symptoms and gave the correct serum treatment. The Sick Berth Petty Officer at Commando Headquarters, Booth, was also standing by as the patient was rushed back. To complete the chain of good fortune a Beaver aircraft was shortly due to land with the General Officer Commanding, Major-General Sir Richard Goodwin, who was to witness the final part of the exercise. The injured man was hurried on board and the pilot, Major S. W. Whitehead, AAC, radioed Nairobi for a helicopter to take Cuthbertson from the airport on the last leg. That evening he was sitting up cheerfully in his bed in the British Military Hospital, fully recovered from his ordeal.

The next episode, back in Aden, does not have such a happy conclusion. The British Government had been forced to break off direct diplomatic representation in the Yemen and as a result relationships between the two countries had deteriorated. These were further worsened on 22 June, 1963, when an adventure training party from Middle East Command, including women, accidentally strayed across the Yemen and was ambushed. Four of the party were killed, one of these being L/Cpl Reginald Jeffery, attached to Headquarters Middle

East Command from Four Five. Four servicewomen in the party and the bodies of the four killed were handed back by the Yemenis, but they held eighteen of the group captive. Some twenty members of the group had already managed to escape. The news did not reach Four Five until the afternoon of Sunday, 23 June. The nearest point to where the incident had taken place was the FNG fort at Tor Al Bahr, fifty-five miles north-west of Aden, and X Company (Major Peter Thomas) was alerted to move up to the fort, 2,000 yards from the border, to create a firm base. The confusion on a Sunday afternoon can well be imagined as troops had to be collected from the surrounding beaches. Anyway, by a combination of Beaver aircraft, Belvedere helicopters and a road convoy, X Company was concentrated at the fort by two o'clock on the morning of the 24th. The incident soon reached international proportions and Tor Al Bahr became the base for a signals link through which official reports were passed for an increasing army of pressmen.

Initially, it was thought that firmer action might be necessary and Y Company was stood by at immediate notice for a move from RAF Khormaksar. This was, however, cancelled and political negotiations continued. The Commando's Medical Officer, Surg Lt Allistair Thom, bravely crossed the border on two occasions to the fort at Mabak, where the prisoners were being held, a mile inside Yemeni territory. On the second visit the Medical Officer remembers that he had to spend the night in the fort where the prisoners were sleeping under tarpaulins spread from their trucks in the courtyard. Next morning, Thom was allowed to bring two of the captives, suffering from heat stroke, back to Tor Al Bahr, but not before he had seen the remaining sixteen being led away at pistol point by Egyptian officers, en route for the Yemen city of Taiz. X Company was withdrawn after three days and the prisoners returned ten days later. This incident merely added fuel to the Yemeni 'Imperialist' claims and worsened the situation considerably. In addition, movement in the Federation was greatly restricted, and the newly formed Reconnaissance Troop (Lt Anthony Langdon) had to take their first steps only in the immediate area of Little Aden. The Troop was formed basically from the Machine Gun Troop whose Vickers had been superseded by the General Purpose Machine Gun, issued to all sections.

Lt-Col T. M. P. Stevens assumed command in mid-July and during his tour Four Five was to see the transition in Aden from isolated incidents to full scale military involvement. In Taiz, the Egyptians had formed the National Liberation Front and the organization, later in the year, pledged itself to militant measures, i.e. the overthrow of the Government in South Arabia. On 10 December an assailant threw a grenade at an official party at Aden Airport. Mr George Henderson, GM, an official, pushed the High Commissioner, Sir Kennedy Trevaskis, aside and bore the brunt of the explosion. Mr Henderson died a fortnight later and during the incident an Indian woman was killed and fifty-three others, including officials and Federal Ministers, were injured. Four Five was brought to an immediate state of internal security readiness as a result of this outrage. As Mr Henderson was very popular amongst the tribes up country more trouble could be expected. In addition, it was noted in the unit Newsletter of December, 1963, that there had been increased dissident activity in the Protectorate, particularly at Thumier on the Dhala Road.

The pattern of things to come in Aden for the next three years was by now becoming apparent.

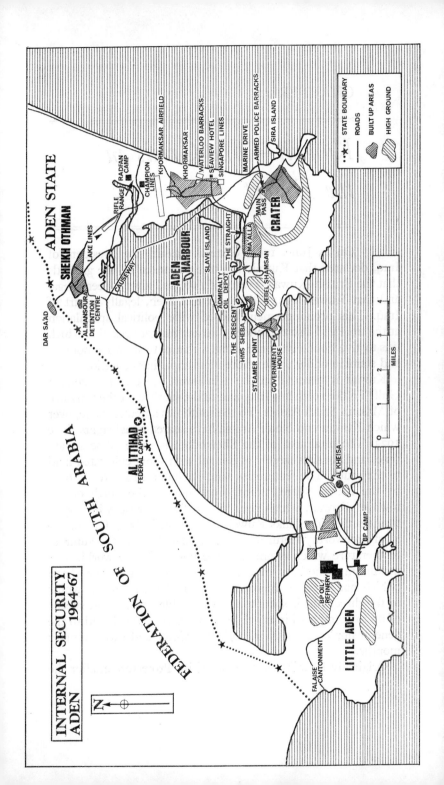

CHAPTER 13

Kuwait—The Crisis in the Desert

On 25 June, 1961, General Kassim, the President of Iraq, declared that Kuwait was to be annexed on the grounds that the British–Kuwait Treaty of 1899 had always been illegal and that Kuwait was, and always had been, legally a part of Iraq. This pronouncement caused wide political speculation at the time and also demanded a strong military reaction which was to give Four Five, once again, a chance to show its mobility and stamina under some of the most appalling conditions.

Kuwait is situated on the north-west coast of the Persian Gulf. To the north lies Iraq, and to the south-west the province of Masa in Saudi Arabia. To the south lies a neutral zone, over which Kuwait and Saudi Arabia have shared equal rights since 1923. The total area of the Sheikhdom is some 5,800 square miles and consists largely of desert, with some cultivated land to the south. The featureless sand in the north is broken only by the Mutla Ridge, twenty-five miles to the north of the town of Kuwait, which rises to 400 feet. A road which runs through the ridge links Kuwait with Basra in Iraq. One of the most noteworthy features of this sparse land is the summer temperature which is amongst the hottest in the world. The maximum sometimes exceeds 115° Fahrenheit in the shade (which one observer reported was very hard to find!), whilst in the direct sun it soars to an unbearable 170°. Wind speeds of up to 30 mph whip up violent sandstorms, which add to the general unpleasantness, in both the winter and early summer months.

Originally Kuwait had been a British Protectorate, after the signing of the 1899 Treaty, but this was formally ended on 19 June, 1961, after an Exchange of Notes. Kuwait then became a fully independent sovereign state, though at the same time the British Government reaffirmed its undertaking to support the Amir on request. This support was soon to be needed in the light of the threats from the north which sparked off an international crisis. The demands of Iraq were taken seriously by the staff in Headquarters Middle East Command at Aden and a quick assessment revealed that the Kuwait Army Frontier Force numbered only some 1,200 ranks, the Security Force and Police could have added a further 3,000, whilst the strength of the opposition included a complete Iraq infantry brigade plus armour based at Basra, a few miles north of the border, which could attack without warning, plus an additional battalion further to the south at Shuaiba. These could all be quickly reinforced by rail from the capital, Baghdad, 300 miles away.

The reports of General Kassim's speech were not received in Aden until 26 June, and on the following day the Amir of Kuwait formally appealed to the United Kingdom for military aid. It was clear that speed was going to be an integral part of this operation right from the very outset. The Amir's request was agreed to immediately—Kuwait was an exceptionally important nation in our eyes. The rich oil fields accounted for an enormous income and the *Economist* had calculated that Kuwait's sterling reserves in the Bank of England accounted for about one third of the total British sterling reserves.

Throughout the 28th preparations for a mammoth military reinforcement were being made, although at this stage no executive orders were given to the 'teeth' units. The current plan in Aden for intervention in Kuwait was 'Vantage', then under revision, and a new plan was being prepared. In the event the Commander-in-Chief Middle East, Air Chief-Marshal Sir Charles Elworthy, gave instructions that 'Vantage' should be 'restudied, reviewed and brought up to date where necessary' in order to implement the impending mobilization of forces. This had the effect that much of the operation was mounted on verbal orders.

Early in the morning of Thursday, 29 June, Lt-Col L. G. Marsh was summoned to Headquarters Middle East Command. At eleven-thirty he stepped out in to the sweltering bright sunlight. Four Five was at twelve hours notice to move. On the far side of the Arabian Sea more activity was taking place. Half an hour previously 42 Commando had sailed 'with dispatch' from Karachi, bound for the same trouble spot, in the Commando Ship HMS *Bulwark*. Again the Corps was going to be first in.

The Commanding Officer's first task was to concentrate Four Five in Little Aden, the unit being spread out in the Protectorate. Late that afternoon a fast convoy of Royal Army Service Corps vehicles was despatched to Dhala to bring back the detachment consisting of A (Capt L. P. F. Edwards) and B (Lt J. M. Coleby) Troops plus the Machine Gun Platoon. The convoy arrived at Dhala at five o'clock in the morning after an all night journey along this treacherous and inhospitable route. There was little time for rest at the camp and, disregarding their intense fatigue, the drivers made a quick turn round and dashed back to Little Aden, completing the journey by two o'clock in the afternoon of 30 June. Another party of twenty-five men under Capt D. L. A. Ware was more difficult to locate. They had set off four days previously on a trip to the Hadramaut area in the east of the Aden Protectorate. Signals for their recall had to be passed along a complicated and tenuous communications system and they were eventually traced to Shuqra on the return trip. They did not join up with the Commando until after the unit's arrival in Kuwait. This party contained a large proportion of the Mobat anti-tank gun crews and these weapons were considered to form an imporant part in the desert defence positions, as intelligence had assessed that one or possibly two regiments of medium and heavy tanks had been moved up to Basra by the Iraqis. Tanks were an ideal weapon for the flat and featureless country, and would, it was assumed, lead any thrust into Kuwait. The absence of these vital Mobat crews could have seriously impaired the Commando's operational effectiveness, but with typical speed personnel arrived back at Little Aden, including some ranks who had just arrived out from the United Kingdom and who didn't sport the traditional Aden tan, were hurriedly trained as additional anti-tank numbers ready for any emergency. Later, on the 30th, notice to move from Little Aden was reduced to two hours, which caused the Commando to form up on the open sandy space to the north of the camp with its hastily packed and marked stores. The long period of waiting was about to begin. The order was finally given to move to Khormaksar airfield, in Aden, at nine-thirty on the morning of Saturday, 1 July. Again there were to be further delays and the Commando had to remain patiently for several hours in the sticky heat of the tented transit camp near the airfield.

'Chalks' (or flights) were planned and assembled by a planning team consisting of the Second-in-Command (Major R. J. McGarel Groves) and the Staff Officer Operations (Major F. D. M. 'Lefty' Warn) who worked some thirty six hours non-stop on this project. Once the chalks had been gathered together they moved off to the edge of the airfield to join a mixture of Beverley, Hastings and Britannia aircraft. Due to the necessity for speed and the different types of aircraft an 'ad hoc' system of dispatch resulted in a 'first come first served' arrangement. This had two unfortunate effects on Four Five. Firstly, due to the difference in speed and range of the various types of aircraft, chalk numbers arrived in a different sequence to that in which they had taken off; secondly, if an aircraft went unserviceable, the poor chalk—which had probably been waiting for more than a day by now—was delayed further until that aircraft was ready to fly once more. A further factor which was eventually to cause repercussions at the Kuwait end was the arbitrary decision to unload certain heavy items of the Commando's freight at Khormaksar, with the result that vital items such as radio sets, charging engines for their batteries and mortar base plates were considerably delayed in arriving. In fact, some of these operational stores never arrived at the 'sharp end' at all. The general effect of these changes was the negation of the Commanding Officer's carefully worked out fly-in plan and the creation of an enormous sorting-out problem at Kuwait International Airport. Neither did the difficulties end here. The International Airport was still in the final stages of completion and such was the heat that the Britannia aircraft were sinking through the newly laid tarmac of the dispersal areas and required towing to extricate them, so they could return to Aden with all haste for the next lifts. There was also a lack of unloading equipment for the Britannias and Hastings; as a result some of the stores which did arrive were damaged by being thrown out bodily by over-enthusiastic unloaders—these included one of the all-too-precious Mobats. Fortunately, the Commanding Officer had ordered that the fighting troops should take as much of their battle equipment as possible with them and every weapon had with it a limited quantity of ammunition so that the unit was fully capable of going into action immediately on arrival, should the need arise.

Despite these frustrations the advance party, consisting of about fifty ranks of Tactical Headquarters and X Troop (Lt M. D. Cavan), departed in two Beverleys on the morning of 1 July. They were closely followed by E Troop (Capt B. A. Franklin) in a move described by Headquarters Middle East as one of 'high priority'. The aircraft staged through Bahrein where the cramped Commandos were able to refresh themselves with a quick wash and a meal. They arrived in Kuwait in the late afternoon in a sandstorm having travelled some 1,600 miles that day. The new airfield had already been secured by 42 Commando, who had flown off HMS *Bulwark* earlier that day. The first wave of sixteen Whirlwind helicopters had taken off shortly before noon, but, like Four Five, they had encountered a sandstorm and visibility had become restricted to less than a mile. However, the delays were not to be for long and skilful navigation, plus some 'enlightened guesswork', by the senior pilot of the squadron, ensured that the airfield was located and the occupation was then carried out with swift precision—reassuring proof of the speed and flexibility to be gained by deployment from the Commando Ship.

Soon afterwards, the build-up of military forces began.

First on the scene, later that afternoon, were ten Hunters of No. 8 Squadron, Royal Air Force who, directly on arrival, assumed an immediate state of readiness. These were followed by Brigadier D. G. T. Horsford, the Commander of 24 Infantry Brigade, who were based in Kenya, who was to assume command of the land forces. At the same time other units continued to move by both sea and air.

The first impression that Four Five's Advance Party gained on landing was that of intense heat and glare, even by Aden standards. The men had been warned by the Medical Officer (Surg-Lt C. J. M. Maxwell, RN) to drink plenty of water both to combat heat exhaustion and because there would be very little 'up the road'. There was an immediate rush to the 'lolly water' stand only to find that the drink was too hot to have any thirst quenching value at all! The Marines then turned their thoughts to the question of transport. The answer was soon provided. A motley collection of Kuwait Oil Company vehicles had been earmarked for the operation and these were now lined up nearby, waiting to take the first arrivals to their defensive position out in the desert. The vehicles ranged from two huge ten-ton articulated lorries to smaller trucks and trade vans. The final destination was to be a location, known as the Arhaya position, which was in the heart of the desert and over twenty miles away. The route to Arhaya was later vividly described by the 1st King's Regiment the battalion which was to relieve Four Five.

'Leaving Kuwait we pass through an incredible scene, a mixture of skyscrapers and large American cars, and dirty Arab houses and scruffy children, hovels with a new Oldsmobile outside. The further from town the more truly primitive are the people, flocks of goats and the odd Bedouin with their camels.' After leaving the main road near Al Jahara the journey continues: 'This area is bleak in the extreme, we are in a wilderness. We follow a winding twisting succession of tyre marks, marked at intervals with a little sign post; in some places the going is over a hard solid surface, in others we gather speed to plough through deep cloying, clinging sand. We bump, bang and nearly stop, only a four-wheel drive vehicle could make it. The wind is savage and hot, and goggles to protect the eyes are a necessity. All we can see are distant folds and twists of sand and the bright haze strains the eye. Finally we turn a corner and head towards low hills. They become a ridge and a separate hill as we approach, and here the Battalion is positioned.'

Four Five had to pioneer this route, so let us now return to the advance party setting out in their assorted vehicles. They reached Al Jahara without mishap just before dusk, and then branched off into the desert as the last rays of sunlight were spreading over the broad expanse of sand. Soon afterwards the convoy halted at a prearranged rendezvous where the bodyguard of a local Sheikh was waiting to act as guide—those maps which were provided were extremely hard to follow, in addition to being of doubtful accuracy. Lt-Col Marsh then went forward, in the darkness, with his Machine Gun Officer (Lt Tayler) to reconnoitre the position ahead. The Arhaya position was some twelve miles south of the Kuwiat–Iraq road which formed the main axis for the defence of the country. Other defensive positions had already been established out ahead—42 Commando already occupied the Mutla Ridge and some of the Kuwaiti forces were forming a screen nearer the border.

The Advance Party had to wait for two hours until the recce group returned. This was a welcome break and the enforced period of quiet came as a sharp contrast to the continuous activities of the past thirty-six hours. The stillness of the night was soon shattered as the vehicles revved up, at half-past nine, to continue their journey. This next part of the trip was, to put it mildly, a nightmare. On the way to the objective the unwieldy trucks soon became bogged down in the soft ground and a violent sandstorm, whipped up without a moment's warning, did little to make life easier. Eventually, later that night, the position was reached and digging-in started straight away, not with shovels but with mess tins and bayonets . . . the trench digging tools were still being off-loaded at the airfield.* Digging in dry sand is never easy at the best of times as the dust soon begins to seep into the trench, which has to be shored up all the time, but this formidable task was described by one marine in X Troop as 'rather like shovelling coal with a teaspoon'. As the men on the Arhaya position kept up their long vigil and attempted to get their defences dug the other fighting Troops and supplies started to arrive at the Kuwait airfield. Z Troop added another notch to their bow by claiming to be the first passengers in a Britannia ever to attempt a night landing at this airport. A later account of the operation stated '. . . a rather jittery Troop descended from the aircraft more quickly than was necessary!'

The first night out in the desert position was a short one. By four o'clock everyone had to stop their makeshift digging and stand to. First light was approximately twenty minutes later and by this time absolute readiness was required because, similar to dusk, this was the most likely time of possible attack. Soon after stand down the monotonous process of digging re-commenced, but this was brought to a temporary halt by another blinding sandstorm. The sand, driven before a hot wind, not only made things uncomfortable but painful as well. Visibility was reduced to such an extent that air recces to the front of the positions, vital on this first morning, were not possible. The conditions in the front line during this crisis are hard to imagine but one correspondent, serving in the 2nd Battalion the Parachute Regiment, who were in a position north of Al Jahara at the eastern end of the Mutla Ridge, gives his impressions of life during those early days.

'The heat in early July is difficult to describe: it was the hottest time of the year in one of the hottest place in the

* It was the policy during air moves of this nature for sharp trench-digging tools—picks and shovels—to be packed in bundles and carefully wrapped, otherwise the protruding edges of these tools, normally attached to the back of the troop's equipment, could have caused serious damage to the fuselage of the aircraft.

world . . . this means that your eggs arrive hard boiled and you can make Nescafé with water out of a jerrican. For the first forty-eight hours there was no shade other than slit trenches with blankets over the top. Thirst was intense and an average of twenty pints of fluid was drunk daily, and was needed, by each man during the first week.'

In Four Five's area plans were being made for the construction of strongly defended locations. Positions were consolidated and the all-too-limited supplies of water and rations distributed. The Mobats (Lt Hawkins) with their newly trained crews were brought forward to dig the broad pits for their long, low weapons—the 'regulars' were not to arrive for another two days. This first day on the Arhaya ridge was a gruelling one. Supplies were scarce and there was little material to provide cover for the trenches apart from the hessian strips which the men, with their Aden experience, all packed into their cape carriers. These sand-coloured strips were just wide enough to stretch over the tops of the slits and keep the worst of the harsh sun off, although the heat inside was still, of course, intense. In addition to the shortage of stores the appalling conditions prevented the bulk of the troops getting forward. Only four-wheel drive military trucks could negotiate the soft sand and these were in short supply during the initial stages of the build up. One of the Troops to learn of the problems of movement in the desert was Z Troop (Capt Carroll). After its arrival in the Britannia the men spent the night in the airport trying to get what rest they could in the stifling heat. The Troop account continues:

'The transport which took us into the desert next morning was a ninety-seater articulated bus, so over a hundred of us squeezed on board with our kit, wondering how on earth we would get out again. We rolled along merrily over tarmac roads and then turned into the desert. Then we stopped rolling, stopped moving. We were stuck. Two-wheel drive vehicles do not perform well in the desert. When they hit soft sand they do not perform at all. If when trying to push such vehicles, the worst sandstorm for twelve years descends upon you, the wind hits you like a hot blast from a furnace, you are short of water and you haven't slept for two days, then life can be very trying indeed. When darkness spread that night (2/3 July) the Troop was scattered. If the Iraqis had attacked . . .

Another day dawned and there was no attack. With the aid of three-tonners, lent to us by our opulent neighbours, 42 Commando, we arrived at the ridge—our ridge, God's Little Acre, the only rise in miles of desert, only thirty feet high. It was strategically important and 45 Commando were to defend it against the enemy mustered at the border. As we dug into the soft sand and prepared our defences, we thought of the training on Woodbury Common* and of all the exercises since, and we realized that they had prepared us for an occasion such as this—an interesting and sometimes gruelling experience, but we wouldn't have missed it.'

By now the seriousness of the threat could be judged by the intensity of movement at Kuwait Airport. Aircraft were pouring in men and equipment from all parts of the Common-wealth—Kenya, Cyprus, Aden and the United Kingdom. This also helped to ease the supply problem out in the desert and by 3 July the situation in Four Five's sector had improved immeasurably. 42 Commando, based further north along the Mutla Ridge, loaned Four Five six of their four-wheel drive three tonners and a water bowser, plus some petrol and large camouflage nets which could provide increased and more effective shade. Helicopters from HMS *Bulwark* also came to the rescue with more supplies, including the much-needed picks and shovels. The supply route across the desert was also re-opened with the arrival of Z Troop, who had taken twenty-four hours to complete their thirty mile journey, and the build-up of all the other Rifle Troops continued that afternoon. 42 Commando had also broken some useful ground in another direction in the form of an arrangement with a local Sheikh

* One of the major training areas for the Royal Marines at Lymp-stone in Devon.

who owned an ice factory. The Sheikh agreed to supply 42 Commando with ice and 'lolly water' on signature each day and this valuable information was subsequently imparted to Four Five. Each day the Second-in-Command had to sign ever-increasing supply notes for the Arhaya position, but was greatly relieved at the end of the operation to hear that the Amir of Kuwait had generously undertaken to redeem all these chits as a token of gratitude.

By now a more co-ordinated administrative 'chain' had been established within Four Five. B Echelon under the Quartermaster (Capt Tom Houghton) was set up alongside that of 42 Commando at Mina al Ahmadi, which was south of the town of Kuwait, and its task was to transit stores and personnel to A Echelon just outside Al Jahara, commanded by Major R. J. McGarel Groves. Al Jahara, where the main road met the desert track, acted as the forward staging post to the Commando, which had by now moved forward to occupy the whole Arhaya Ridge as all the Troops had arrived. Also in residence were the Centurion tanks of C Squadron 3rd Dragoon Guards and 'Sphinx' Battery, Royal Horse Artillery, who had arrived to add their support and make this a formidable position.

The next period can be described as a war of nerves. Ground and air recces confirmed that there were no Iraqi troops on Kuwait soil but that movement of enemy forces had been reported in the Basra—Shuaiba—Umm Qasr areas. It was also believed that some Iraqi Centurion tanks, which had moved forward from Baghdad, were now in the front zone. These moves, however, were considered to be precautionary and no immediate aggressive threats were in evidence. In spite of General Kassim's apparent reluctance to carry out his promises the need for constant vigilance under these scorching conditions was paramount, and this was highlighted by the daily routine which was adopted. We have already described the dawn stand to. This was followed by breakfast at six o'clock after this, when observation sentries had been posted, the remainder would work continuously throughout the morning in order to develop and improve the position. This was a never-ending process because maintenance was always necessary, and after a few days some trenches would have to be completely resited following the collapse of the dry soil. During the afternoons the heat and wind usually made work impossible and as much as possible the local custom of 'siesta' was observed, and in general activity restarted at about five o'clock and lasted until supper time. The evening 'stand to' at seven o'clock did not close the day, however, as a high degree of alertness had to be maintained throughout the night in case of a sudden attack. Although the Iraqi threat still persisted the situation took a somewhat different turn on 5 July, when Intelligence reported that 'digging and mining of tank traps was evident on the Iraqi side of the Kuwait border' and, on the following day, 'the deployment of an anti-aircraft unit around Baghdad'. It seems that the Iraqis were preparing, in depth, for an attack or counter-attack by ourselves, and their leaders were doubtlessly telling their citizens that we were the 'imperialist aggressors'.

Conditions in the line gradually improved but the great heat by day made life very trying and several ingenious methods were developed to stave off the inevitable boredom. One popular pastime was a form of desert draughts making use of dried donkey and goat droppings as counters. Others, more scientifically inclined, built desert fridges, using the principle of cooling by evaporation, and thus could keep small supplies of cool beer and soft drinks. One of the greatest problems was shipping ice across the desert. At first, A Echelon's efforts met with little success as most of the precious blocks had reverted to liquid form many miles before Arhaya, but as the days slipped by the 'quantities of unmelted ice that arrived at the location increased'. Water, too, posed many difficulties and as a result washing had to be severely restricted. One enterprising Troop Commander found a way round this and built a desert bath out of groundsheets, which he and his Troop used until the water became too rich for further use! However, the washing problem was soon solved and after a time a rota was set up allowing those in the front line trenches a night out of the position aboard HMS *Bulwark*, where all had a good night's sleep in air conditioning after the first shower for many a day—a great morale booster. Marine Kelly of Support Troop (Capt D. L. A. Ware) found another way of solving his particular water problems. The story starts with Sgt Andrews, who had been sharing a slit with the Machine Gun Platoon Commander, who was given a rude awakening one night by a donkey braying at close quarters. The donkey was hastily caught and was pressed into service by Kelly, who was given the title of 'muleteer' and had to drag this unfortunate beast around the defences laden with jerricans of water.

A Troop had their excitements as well. The formalities of one of their orders groups were suddenly interrupted by the Troop Commander's orderly, Marine Taylor, whose shout of 'Still' was interpreted by some as the first warning of an enemy attack. In fact it was Sgt Williams who was about to come under fire for, as he leapt into the air, a long sand viper slid gracefully away from underneath the seat on which he had been sitting only seconds beforehand. Cpl Small of the same Troop also joined the league of 'weirdy watchers'. He used to while away the many anxious hours waiting for his golden salamander to appear out of its hole again! Needless to say its persistence was greater than that of our forces and 'we had to leave the desert and Kuwait before it did'. Others, more successful, discovered that the flesh of the salamander on either side of the tail was no bad substitute for chicken and supplemented their evening rations accordingly.

These somewhat bizarre diversions were put in the background with the arrival of the 1st Battalion the King's Regiment (Manchester and Liverpool) on 7 July. The King's had been flown in from Kenya and, after two days of preparation in Kuwait, had moved into the forward positions on the Arhaya Ridge. Although Four Five remained in some of its original locations the unit was, in effect, now in reserve. Around this date there was sufficient time to do a fuller reconnaissance of the area and it was discovered that it would be possible to move A Echelon to within half a mile of the Arhaya Ridge and thus cut out the twelve-mile drive from Al Jahara. This also straightened out the slightly illogical situation of A Echelon, although partly protected by the troops on the Mutla Ridge, being somewhat closer to Iraq than the Commando itself. This move certainly was to make the eventual withdrawal from the Arhaya position much easier.

It was with considerable relief that the hot and tired men of Four Five learnt that they were to be pulled out on 17 July, after nearly three weeks in this featureless ocean of sand. The Iraqi threat was by now becoming almost purely academic and the vigil could afford to be relaxed. The night of 17 July was spent in the Technical College and on the 18th the fly back to Aden commenced. This bit of desert was far more preferable than the Kuwait variety.

The Kuwait operation still poses many 'ifs' and 'buts'. The Iraqi threat of attack never materialized and it is arguable as to whether in fact they ever intended to implement it. The speed of reaction by British forces, the hasty airlift and the fortuitous presence of the Commando Ship, doubtless made the would-be aggressor reconsider his plans. In addition the wholehearted assistance by the Kuwait authorities and other organizations enabled this deployment to progress quickly, unencumbered by local differences of opinion or friction.

Four Five returned from this crisis, as did all the other units, with credit. A high morale and sense of humour enabled a constant state of readiness to be maintained, under the most severe climatic conditions, for a long period. Doubtless desert training and previous acclimatization in Aden stood the unit in very good stead and helped to keep the cases of heat exhaustion to the barest minimum. It was inevitable, considering the speed with which the operation was mounted, that some of the vital equipment and stores were unavailable during those early days but by some judicious improvization the Commanding Officer ensured that the Commando would be ready to do battle whenever called. Although the need never arose Four Five constructed a defensive position which would have given any attacker a bitter lesson. In this case prevention was surely better than a cure.

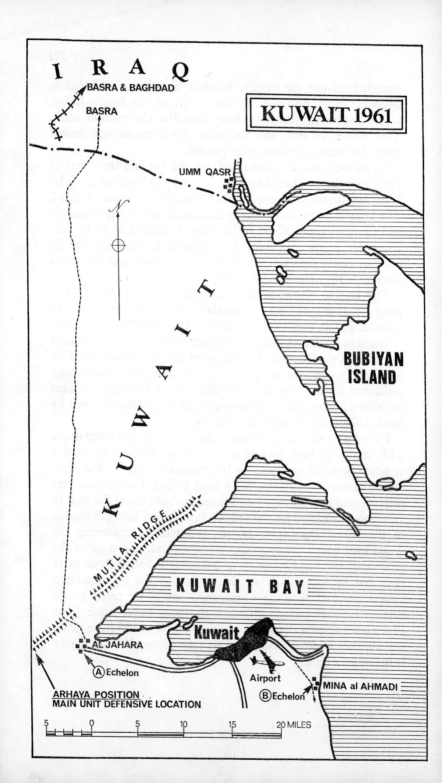

KUWAIT 1961

I R A Q

BASRA & BAGHDAD

BASRA

UMM QASR

N

BUBIYAN ISLAND

K U W A I T

MUTLA RIDGE

KUWAIT BAY

AL JAHARA

Ⓐ Echelon

Kuwait

Airport

Ⓑ Echelon

MINA al AHMADI

ARHAYA POSITION
MAIN UNIT DEFENSIVE LOCATION

5   0   5   10   15   20 MILES

CHAPTER 14

East African Interlude

There are times when our forces are called upon to undertake tasks which are not only military but are of vital international political importance as well. This following account admirably demonstrates the versatility of the commanders and the individuals of Four Five and how they were in complete military control of a nation whose stability was threatened. This operation also shows the delicate balance between military intervention on the one hand and the support of a country in turmoil on the other.

At the beginning of 1964, serious rioting had broken out in Zanzibar and as a result of this Four Five, in Little Aden, was alerted to be at three hours notice for a possible move. This was subsequently lengthened to twenty-four hours and it was assumed that the scare had died down. Routine training recommenced, stores were unpacked and life in Little Aden returned to normal. It was merely the calm before the storm. The situation in East Africa further deteriorated with the expulsion of British personnel, seconded to the Tanganyikan Rifles, from their posts. Local officers, including some newly promoted, had seized command without the authority of President Nyerere and armed conflict was threatened. It was feared that these mutinies might spread and some of the less optimistic were forecasting a new 'Congo' in East Africa. Britain had troops based in Kenya but not in Tanganyika and thus a special problem had arisen.

Early on the morning of 20 January, Lt-Col Paddy Stevens was summoned to the large colonial-styled buildings of Headquarters, Middle East Command, in Aden. The Commander-in-Chief, Lieutenant-General C. H. P. Harrington, gave orders for the Commando to embark in HMS *Centaur* which had speedily been diverted from passage to Gan, in the Indian Ocean, and was now awaiting the arrival of Four Five. Right from the outset the unit had been virtually sent into the unknown. The Commanding Officer's instructions were especially brief, just a 'get cracking Paddy!' The ultimate destination and aim, if any, at this stage had not been clarified. Lt-Col Stevens later wrote:

'It was dramatic. We knew nothing at all about what we might be required to do until we received the final signal (before landing). We had been pitched on board a strange ship, which was neither designed nor trained in our particular games. There was no precedent for an operational landing from an unconverted strike carrier with its full range of aircraft embarked—indeed it had been described as impossible. We, Commando and ship, solved these enormous problems, working under immense pressure for four days.'

As HMS *Centaur* was a strike carrier there were few facilities for a large embarked land force. The following days were to prove that an operation of international importance would be carried out with unprecedented success, despite the numerous initial problems. This was due largely to the willing co-operation of all those on board, and a high degree of flexibility.

In Little Aden feverish activity began to prepare the Commando for its impending move. Z Company was away from camp carrying out field firing exercises in the desert, and as there was no immediate radio contact a vehicle raced out to give the Company the warning order which was to gather them back into the fold. Whilst Z Company was returning, the advance party, composed of X Company, started to embark in the late afternoon. Their job was to load Four Five's heavy stores and assist with as much preparation as possible for the reception of the Commando. In addition to the 486 ranks of the unit, a troop of the 16th/5th Lancers was also embarked, plus

20. *L/Cpl Tilley, one of Four Five's snipers, in an OP above Crater, 1967.*
(Beaverbrook Newspapers)

21. *Marine Cox (right) perched high on a mountain in the Radfan.*

22. Lt-Col Paddy Stevens confers with Brigadier C. H. Blacker on Cap Badge. May, 1964.

23. Lt Ian Martin disarms a mutineer at Colito Barracks. 25 January, 1964. (United Press International (UK))

Belvedere helicopters and their aircrew from 26 Squadron, RAF.

The loading of HMS *Centaur* was a major operation in itself. The first troops and stores arrived at five o'clock that evening, and soon after midnight a total of 592 officers and men, fifty tons of stores, petrol, ammunition, two Belvederes, five Ferret Scout cars and thirteen Land Rovers had been embarked. Ship's boats and other service craft operated a shuttle service with the Commando equipment and vehicles. The Captain of HMS *Centaur*, Capt O. H. M. St J. Steiner, had one anxious moment just before dark when severe winds of up to thirty knots were forecast within the hour. This would have meant that HMS *Centaur* would have had to seek the shelter of the outer harbour of Aden, thus causing serious delays in the loading programme. These winds did not materialize and due to the necessity of embarking Land Rovers, which were considered to be essential for land borne operations, the Captain decided to take the risk of remaining at his original position until embarkation was complete. At one o'clock on the morning of 21 January, *Centaur* slipped her moorings and proceeded 'with dispatch' to Dar-es-Salaam. A Naval force of five other smaller vessels was also standing by in other parts of the Indian Ocean to join *Centaur* when she neared her objective.

The scene on board ship was a chaotic one. To provide living space for the Marines, Sea Vixens, which comprised half the ship's aircraft, had to be parked on the flight deck. There was no room for the unit stores below, so they were sorted into dumps amongst the aircraft above. The sight of jerricans of petrol for the Land Rovers horrified the ship's officers, as fire precautions on board were naturally stringent. A compromise was made and a space was found for the jerricans surrounded by fire extinguishers and sentries.

The hangar was to be the home of the majority of the Commando for the next five days. Camp beds, loaned by HMS *Centaur*, were packed side by side, and in many cases the sleeping occupants were only separated from their nearest neighbours by a matter of inches. The quarterdeck, normally a sanctuary for those officers wishing to take a stroll on warm tropical evenings whilst at sea, was hastily converted to provide sleeping accommodation for the senior NCOs. One witness later reported that 'the one outstanding thing about the trip was the sight of the Ship's Commander on the Quarter Deck, weighing off his defaulters with a SNCO's dhoby flapping in his ear—Nelson is still turning'. The attached Lancers found themselves bedded down in the Schoolroom. The RAF remained loyal to their helicopters, and the Belvederes on the flight deck provided ample cover for them.

After the first night at sea, joint activities carried out between the ship's company and the Commando began to bring about an efficient and operational working relationship. The unit Second-in-Command, Major David Smith was a specialist in planning combined operations, and later proved to be invaluable. Three joint planning teams, Assault, Communications and Intelligence, were set up.

The aim of the Assault Team was to adapt the organization within the strike carrier to enable it to fulfil its primary rol concurrent with mounting a full Commando assault. Firstly, in the event of a fly-off, plans had to be made for the clearing of hangar space of personal living accoutrements, secondly, the provision of guides from members of the ship's company, and finally a helicopter landing plan (stick orbat). This orbat is a plan which enables a unit to be transferred from ship to shore by helicopter in tactical sequence. A numbered white card is made out for each helicopter load, giving either the names of the passengers or a description of the stores to be carried. Once these cards have all been made a completed table is published giving a serial number to each load. As a result, all ranks know their load number and can be called forward to their assembly area prior to being checked for take-off.

The provision of guides is always a necessity. A fly-off would be seriously delayed if fully laden troops were either lost on their way from accommodation to assembly areas, or blocking passageways and preventing the movement of vital stores.

One of Lt-Col Stevens' first dilemmas was to produce a

suitable 'batting order' so that the landing plan could be worked out by the Assault Team. The traditions of the Second World War, still in vogue in many circles, favoured the issue of cast iron plans. In this case, as the unit did not known yet what it was going to be required to do, the thinking had to be altered drastically and a highly flexible landing plan developed. In the event Major Smith was given the following order to work on: Company Group (including Support weapons elements) with the Landing Zone Team (to control the helicopters); Tactical Headquarters; Company Group; Company Group; Specified Headquarters elements. In case this sounds too straightforward the Commanding Officer added another proviso:

'This plan was based on a conventional landing—The Tanganyikan Army was reported to have had armoured cars. On the other hand we might have had to land to form riot squads and I issued orders to the effect that I might wish various Support elements to be dropped out and Support Company landed as a Rifle Company.'

Major Smith therefore had the enormous problem of producing this landing plan, bearing in mind all the possible contingencies.

The Communications team was making plans for the radio control of helicopters whilst airborne and for controlling the intial stages of the shore battle. In addition, provision had to be made for the Commanding Officer to control the initial stages of the land battle from the ship until his headquarters were firmly established ashore.

For the first two days on board the Intelligence Team, to whom the Assault Team and others were constantly looking to for current information, had very little to offer apart from the standard background material. Official channels seemed unable to provide recent reports, although the ever-faithful BBC was able to give some news of value! It was considered at the time that the most likely employment in Tanganyika would be the protection of British residents in the Oyster Bay area north of Dar-es-Salaam, as a prelude to more extensive rescue operations.

All reports of possible helicopter landing sites, places of tactical importance and airfields in the area were studied in detail and upon this information rough plans were drawn up which were discussed at the daily co-ordinating meetings which were presided over by the Commanding Officer and the Commander (Air).

Hopes that the situation ashore would be clarified on 23 January when Lt-Col Stevens, the Intelligence Officer (Lt Tony Hazeldine), plus a representative from HMS *Centaur*, flew ashore to Mombassa, were soon dispelled. Although the officers of 24 Infantry Brigade, from Nairobi, were able to provide air photographs, essential maps and some more useful background information, they could not provide the vital, up-to-date intelligence. It seemed that there was a blanket of silence and uncertainty surrounding Tanganyika.

The anticipated launching area, Dar-es-Salaam, was reached on the morning of 24 January and the final touches were made to the alternative landing plans. This news received from ashore that day seemed less dramatic and the Colonel later reported that 'generally there was a feeling of anti-climax. All seemed quiet in East Africa, and we assumed that we would soon be on our way back to Aden'.

However, one problem did arise on the 24th that could have put even the best-laid plans in jeopardy. In the rush to leave Aden some of an incorrect type of ammunition had been loaded and this fact was not discovered until three days after sailing, when final checks were being made. The ammunition in question differed from that of the Commando's basic weapon— the Self-Loading Rifle—carried by the majority of the men and rapid adjustments had to be made to ensure that each man could land in a battle-ready condition despite this setback. These adjustments included the sparing issue of the SLR ammunition held for HMS *Centaur*'s Royal Marine Detachment to the bulk of the unit, and the issuing of older type rifles from ship's sources to one of the Companies—suitable for use with this other ammunition. Fortunately there was not any heavy firing when Four Five eventually got ashore, but even so this incident gives an example of the last minute problems that often crop up before an operation and the rapid alternatives and improvisations that have to be adopted.

Soon after midnight the situation which had up to now seemed much quieter changed drastically. HMS *Centaur* was ordered to 'close Dar-es-Salaam with all despatch to support the Tanganyika Government in putting down the mutiny of the Tanganyika Rifles'. Orders were also received for an unknown VIP to be brought out clandestinely from a jetty at Dar-es-Salaam.

At two-five in the morning of the 25 January, Brigadier Sholto Douglas, former commander of the Tanganyika Rifles arrived on board in true James Bond fashion. He was accompanied by a member of his staff, Major Marciandi. A motor boat, armed specially for the occasion, had gone inshore from HMS *Centaur* to pick them up from their secret rendezvous. Whilst the Commando slept on, the Brigadier gave his briefing to the Captain and Lt-Col Stevens in a small office just below the bridge. Although he had been in hiding, he was able to maintain some contact with the Tanganyikan Government. Even so, there were some understandable gaps in his knowledge.

This meeting in the middle of the night was to be an historic one. The Commando's first task was to disarm the 1st Battalion Tanganyika Rifles at Colito, a few miles north of Dar-es-Salaam. News was also received that another battalion, the 2nd Battalion, had also mutinied at Tabora some 400 miles to the west of Dar-es-Salaam—giving an indication of the immense size and distances Four Five had to face in order to solve this problem. Overall command of this operation lay with Capt Steiner, the Captain of HMS *Centaur*. Lt-Col Stevens had command of the operations ashore, but he in turn was to come under the operational control of Brigadier Douglas after the initial landing. Having heard the latest intelligence the Commanding Officer, in order to quell the mutiny of the 1st Battalion, had decided to land in helicopters on the football pitch to the south of Colito Barracks soon after first light on 25 January. Lt-Col Stevens recollects that soon after he had given his judgement, 'it was an awful moment when they turned to me and asked if we could do it. Going "straight down the chimney" was against all the accepted conventions of helicopter landings, unless you had plenty of helicopters and detailed intelligence. We had neither. The accepted United States Marine Corps practice at the time was "hit 'em where they aint".' Although the football pitch was alarmingly close to the barracks it was agreed that the element of surprise gained would reduce the possibilities of armed resistance. The maxim throughout the operation was to be the use of 'minimum force'. A pitched battle fought between the barracks and a more distant landing site might well have resulted in heavy casualties.

Brigadier Douglas himself decided to accompany the first Company, Z Company, to try and address the mutineers, and it was agreed that the remainder of the Commando would land at the same site as well. A switch landing site, further south, was earmarked in case of trouble. After this daring plan had been confirmed the officers of Four Five, plus representatives of the Air Branch and helicopter squadrons, assembled to receive their orders for this momentous landing.

The Marines in the hangar were unable to go to sleep until after midnight on the night of the 24th/25th as the after lift was being used for a film show. Soon after two in the morning the men, cramped side by side in their camp beds, realized that something was afoot. The whisper 'we're going in' was quickly passed round. The Tannoy in the background added urgency to the situation, 'D'you hear there. D'you hear there. Call the hands. Call the hands. Call the hands.' By now the tempo in *Centaur* was increasing. In the hangar Marines were clambering over beds in a rush to get to the bathroom before queues formed. Officers, fresh from Company briefings, came in to locate their scattered troops and issue hurried orders. Breakfast for the men about to be launched into the unknown was a luxurious one; fried eggs, spaghetti, coffee and hot fresh rolls. Luckily the night's baking had just been completed, and Four Five reaped the benefits.

By now ammunition and weapon stores had been opened and the issuing and preparation of grenades and rocket launcher bombs was continuing in earnest. H-hour was fixed at soon after six o'clock. In the next hour and a half the hangar had to be completely cleared of camp beds and personal baggage so that the Wessex helicopters could be raised to the flight deck, and the Gannets, which were already down there, moved back into the hangar to allow more space. In order to 'darken ship' at night whilst at sea, all bright lights, visible from the outside of the ship, were extinguished, and those in passageways leading to the outer decks substituted by dull orange or red bulbs. These gave an eerie light as men, by now fully clad and armed, moved around at five-fifteen to form up for their assault stations. Short delays occurred at this stage due to technical problems encountered with Belvedere helicopters and the task of clearing the hangars below.

The first indication that the inhabitants of the northern sectors of Dar-es-Salaam had that anything was afoot was the sound of the helicopters roaring in at low level. Soon after dawn, as the populace looked seawards, they were able to see the grey silhouette of HMS *Centaur* which had crept in silently and unobserved during the hours of darkness. By skilful navigation, Capt Steiner had brought the carrier close inshore in Msasana Bay between the headland and an offshore island, in a depth of seven fathoms. His aim was to get as close as possible to Colito Barracks in order to achieve a quick Commando landing and swift turn round of helicopters. At six-ten (first light) four Wessex helicopters were launched in pairs, carrying thirty-three assault troops to the selected landing site on the playing fields to the south of Colito Barracks.

It was a dull dawn, typical of the overcast ones which are common in the tropics. Low cloud and rising mist on higher ground made it seem somewhat unreal. The green grass and neat settlements contrasted sharply with the barren sandy wastes to which the Commando was accustomed. To the casual observer it could have been mistaken as English parkland with small shrubs and eucalyptus trees breaking up the long, uneven coarse grass. Colito Barracks, with its trim white huts and red roofs, soon loomed on the horizon. The main road, with deep monsoon ditches on either side, ran along the western perimeter of the camp. On the southern side was a large expanse of playing fields separated from the barracks by another monsoon ditch. The eastern side was dotted with more coarse grass and shrubs. Above the roar of the helicopters the dull thud of the 4.5-inch shells fired from one of the supporting destroyers, HMS *Cambrian*, could be heard in the distance. The gunfire was pre-arranged to commence at six-twenty, coinciding with the first assault wave. Shells were planned to burst at a height of 500 feet in a safe area over the sea and land to the north of the barracks. The aim of this firing was to add to the general noise level, create confusion in the barracks, and deter any opposition.

Major David Langley, Z Company Commander, disembarked from his Wessex with Brigadier Sholto Douglas on the southern edge of the playing fields area. Brigadier Douglas also carried a loud-hailer which he was soon to use to address the mutinous 1st Battalion. Seven Troop, commanded by Lt Ian Martin, took up positions in the monsoon ditch to the west of the road. Company Headquarters remained near the landing site. 2/Lt Steven Weall (Nine Troop) led his section towards the eastern perimeter. Weall, who had only joined the Commando two weeks previously, had just completed officers' initial training, and now, for the first time, found himself leading Marines into action.

The plan was for the Troops to take up immediate assault positions and for Brigadier Douglas to encourage the mutineers to lay down their arms and surrender peacefully. The surprise and surrounding noise appeared to leave the *askari** in confusion, for there was little response from the barracks. Intermittent and sporadic firing was also opened up from the guardroom area. Brigadier Douglas addressed the mutineers in Swahili through the loud hailer and gave them two minutes to surrender. After one minute he started a countdown and as there was no response Major Langley ordered the 3.5 rocket

* A Swahili word for soldiers, having only the plural form.

launchers of the two Troops to go into action and launch their rockets over the trees, 400 yards to their front, which separated the barracks from their present position. At the time it was not apparent where the rockets were landing and soon the askari and their womenfolk were seen to be running out of the huts. In the meantime, Seven Troop moved stealthily down the monsoon drains towards the guardroom area. It was at this stage that Marine Priest of Seven Troop was ordered to fire a rocket launcher bomb into the guardroom. He took up his position to the rear of Company Headquarters and his first shot, which hit telephone wires by the roadside, landed within a few yards of Major Langley and his radio operator. Company Headquarters scattered rapidly for cover, at this initial sign of inward opposition. The second shot had the desired effect and demolished part of the overhanging roof of the guardroom, killing one of the occupants, wounding others and sending the remainder fleeing outside in terror.

Marine Priest was later asked in a stern voice by his Company Commander, 'Why was the first shot a mistake and off target?' The reply was given in a flash with typical Royal Marine humour—'What makes you think it was a mistake, sir!'

By now, events were moving quickly in favour of Z Company. Seven Troop advanced in tactical arrowhead formation, crossed the open space, and the three sections split up to enter the southern perimeter. Eight Troop, under Lt Tim Ricketts, made their entry through the southern and eastern sectors. The magazine and armoury to the east of the guardroom were quickly cordoned off and open ground between these two buildings was used as a casualty evacuation area and collection point for the mutineers.

The time, by now, was nearly seven o'clock. Y and X Companies were beginning to land, and also the Commanding Officer with his tactical headquarters. Y Company were to block off exits to Dar-es-Salaam and cover the high ground to the west, whilst X were ordered to cover the eastern approaches. In addition elements of Y were used in conjunction with the helicopters as an airborne mobile reserve. They flew over the bush on the perimeter of the barracks, cutting of those askari who decided to flee. This was most effective, and indeed terrifying for the escapees, as helicopters swooped low over them, only to hover a few yards away to allow time for marines to rope down and accept their surrenders.

Number two on the rocket launcher in Nine Troop was Marine Brown, who was of Nigerian descent. He was the only coloured Marine in Z Company. His professional training ensured, at the outset of the operation, that his thoughts were unemotional. However, he later confessed that the sight of so many askari, some of them openly showing fear, brought a twinge of pity from him.

Initially, the askari had thought that the Commandos had come to rape their womenfolk and loot their buildings. When events turned out to be completely the opposite, mutual co-operation and goodwill was relatively quickly established. Some of the 1st Battalion were merely private soldiers doing two years national service 'for the glory of their country'. Others were professional men caught up in the speed of events and with no desire to cause further trouble. In many cases they were deeply ashamed of what had happened around them. As the ringleaders and mutineers were escorted into the open by Z and X Compaines the scene was hardly reminiscent of that of a military establishment. At times there appeared to be more women and children milling around than uniformed askari. A count was made of no less than seventeen women emerging from one hut, to be followed by one solitary and sheepish African. As the askari were made to sit down in the open with their hands on their heads under careful supervision of the armed Commandos, it was noticed that one frightened individual, who was shaking all over, was covered from head to foot in a painful army of red ants. He was so scared to move that he did not dare to admit his plight. When his discomfort was discovered, he then had the presence of mind to admit that he was not an askari, but merely an outsider visiting his brother for the night. His joy was complete when he was rapidly sent on his way to freedom through the main gate!

At about this time the Commanding Officer of the 1st Battalion, newly-promoted Lt-Col Nyirenda, presented himself to Major Langley. As is often the case when our troops are called into Commonwealth countries old acquaintances find themselves on opposing sides. Nyirenda had, six years previously, been an officer cadet at Mons under Langley and was described as 'a delightful man but caught up in an awful turmoil'.

The process of clearing up Colito began in earnest. The Commando had the task of not only escorting and guarding the ringleaders, but providing guards for all military groups and sending out patrols to scour the bush land for any further escapees. One civilian Englishman showed total disregard for his own personal safety, when he brought back one frightened askari, fully armed and festooned with ammunition and grenades, to the guardroom. Despite his menacing attire, the askari was only too delighted to surrender in return for the safety of his camp and regular food.

During the next few days the administrative requirements of disbanding the battalion were left almost entirely to Major Langley, who came in initially as conqueror and found himself overnight in the position of counsellor. Coaches and trains had to be booked, documentation for the dispersal completed. It was no small measure of Z Company's handling of the situation that when the coaches left carrying the departing askari, loud cheers could be heard in salute to the Marines.

By nine it was evident that most of the mutineers were being rounded up without resistance. Three companies were now ashore, and the Belvederes were lifting in some of the Commando's Land Rovers. Lt-Col Stevens turned his attention to Dar-es-Salaam. Helicopter reconnaissance reported no signs of military activity in the town but some armed men near the airfield. At ten o'clock, X Company, commanded by Major Mike Banks, was despatched by helicopter to secure the airfield. This they did without opposition. The Company also checked that vital points, the Broadcasting Station and a large arms dump, were in safe hands.

Y Company, commanded by Capt Gavin Hamilton-Meikle, was then sent into Dar-es-Salaam in the unit Land Rovers (which had been flown in as underslung loads beneath the Wessex helicopters) and requisitioned vehicles from the 1st Battalion, with the task of securing certain key points in the town. This was designed to be a two-pronged advance, with X Company's move by air. However, similar to events later on in the day, it thankfully turned out to be a parade rather than an opposed attack. The European, Asians and many Africans gave the Commandos an unexpected and tumultuous welcome as they thronged the pavements. Elements of Y Company secured Army House whilst the remainder carried out local patrols, which resulted in the capture of eight deserters. After a short visit by Brigadier Douglas to see the Acting High Commissioner, Mr F. S. Miles, the decision was made to send troops to Tabora to deal with the other battalion there. The Second-in-Command, Major Smith, was called forward to take command in Dar-es-Salaam. Z Company were to remain at Colito and Support Company, under Capt John Lloyd, were landed soon after mid-day near Army House. The Royal Marine detachment from HMS *Centaur*, under Capt Freddie Slater, landed by lighter with the Ferrets of the 16th/5th Lancers, who were commanded by Capt M. Brooks. A show of force was made through the town where again they received a great welcome and certain key positions were patrolled safely.

Tabora is some 400 miles west of Dar-es-Salaam and the 2nd Battalion which was stationed there had already mutinied. The only reports had been received by telephone; these indicated that hearing of events at Colito they had agreed to hand in their rifles; and all was quiet. This, however, was not confirmed and there was a distinct possibility that they would break out again and secure the airfield. Lt-Col Stevens did not want to risk another outbreak of violence nor inflict any further loss of life. Y and X Companies were earmarked for this task. In addition four Sea Vixens, armed with 2-inch rockets, were attached from HMS *Centaur* to provide air cover should the landing at Tabora airstrip be opposed. Personnel of Y Company accompanied the Commanding Officer with his tactical headquarters in a DC 4 aircraft. They arrived at Tabora at five-fifteen, after a flight of just over two hours. Lt-Col Stevens remembers his arrival at Tabora as one of light comedy. He was deeply concerned at the possibility of armed opposition but as the DC 4 came in to land, an Argosy appeared at the other end of the runway with the same intentions. The Argosy won and the DC 4 hauled off to land a few minutes afterwards. The Argosy contained an Air Commodore and some men of the RAF Regiment who had flown from Nairobi. They naturally considered themselves one up. However, honours were soon shared as it was later discovered that the Argosy had damaged its undercarriage on landing. Subsequently, the Commando was able to borrow not only the Argosy, but a Pembroke which flew in on the following days with spares!

In addition to the local officials, Mr Bourn, a representative of the British High Commissioner, was there to meet the party. Their advice was emphatic. The Commando should go nowhere near the barracks, seven miles away, as all was peaceful and quiet and the arms had been handed in. The Battalion's Commanding Officer, Capt (later Brigadier) Sarakikya was also in the party. However, there were still ringleaders in the barracks and the arms were merely locked in the guardroom— a fierce reception committee could have awaited the Commandos. At six-fifteen that evening, in the gathering dusk, Beverleys arrived with the remainder of X and Y Companies. The Colonel took a representative of each company to reconnoitre the town and the barracks. All was quiet. Brigadier Douglas, who had remained at Army House, was phoned for instructions. He ordered that the arms and ammunition should be secured that night. Local Public Works Department vehicles and some police Land Rovers were used to ferry the two Companies to within two miles of the barracks.

It was a somewhat mixed party which arrived at the guardroom of the barracks in the small hours of the morning. In the front was a Volkswagen containing Capt Sarakikya and Major Mike Banks. This was followed by a police Land Rover with a Royal Marine escort and the remainder of the convoy in the various PWD trucks. It was an uneasy period as the approach was an open one and Major Banks was keen to secure the guardroom before the remainder of the camp was aroused. When they got near their destination X Company leapt out of their trucks and moved on foot over the final distance. With great rapidity the guardroom and weapons were secured and the Marines started to load the contents of the stores and magazines into their vehicles. Meanwhile Y Company was called forward and with a Troop of X Company cordoned off the sleeping quarters. Things appeared to be going easily, all credit due to Four Five, and the next stage of arousing the sleeping Battalion—unaware of what was happening—was embarked upon. This task fell to Capt Sarakikya and with a bugler and escort he marched into his lines. The general assembly was sounded after which the men were told that they were surrounded and they were ordered on parade. Everyone fell in quietly. The ten ringleaders were called and marched off under escort to be deposited later at Police Headquarters. Lt-Col Stevens returned with X Company to the airfield and reported the successful completion of the operation to Brigadier Douglas.

On Sunday the 26th, plans were made for X Company to remain at Tabora, whilst Y Company would return to Dar-es-Salaam, in preparation for a move on the following day to Natchingwea, 220 miles to the south. A company of the 2nd Battalion was stationed there, and although it was reported that the weapons had been surrendered to the local police, Lt-Col Stevens decided again not to take any risks. Y Company in Beverleys, supported by four Sea Vixens, touched down soon after one o'clock. The mutineers had been 'advised' that the Commando was going to land by helicopter behind the barracks—to keep their eyes away from the airfield. This ruse worked and the arms and ammunition were soon recovered, and having arrested the ringleaders, the Company arrived back at six o'clock that evening with their captives. A quick and efficient Commando operation.

By now Four Five had been found a more 'permanent' home and back in Dar-es-Salaam, for Major Smith was now busy supervising accommodation in the National Stadium. The offices and other buildings were hastily adopted as living quarters whilst the arena area took on a new look with stores and supplies neatly piled up in the centre.

Looking back, the whole operation, from take off on 25 January to completion of Natchingwea had gone extraordinarily smoothly. The Commanding Officer later wrote:

'The things which I had stressed above all others from the time I took over Four Five were rapid deployment, rapid regrouping, and rapid action by Companies to deal with events in their area—coupled with clear and precise reporting back. This paid off in Tanganyika. While we were still clearing up Colito we were regrouping for Dar-es-Salaam (where armed bands of soldiers were reported). While still sorting out Dar-es-Salaam we were regrouping to go to Tabora. At Tabora we had a short rest, but then rapidly planned and executed another operation. The tempo of these few days was extraordinary. As an illustration, I had some nine hours sleep in ninety six hours. The rest was "all go".'

The final days were spent in consolidating positions and restoring the confidence of the Tanganyikan population. The Royal Marine band from HMS *Centaur* was landed and completed a heavy programme which included marching through the streets, concerts, and recording for subsequent broadcasts. Local dignitaries and ministers were invited on board to be entertained and to witness a flying display by *Centaur*'s aircraft and helicopters.

On the 28th, Capt Steiner and Lt-Col Stevens were taken by Brigadier Douglas to State House to be received by the President of Tanganyika, Mr Nyerere. They were presented with ebony and ivory fruit bowls and signed photographs of

322

the President. The President was to state later that 'the Royal Marines had served as the greatest ambassadors of Great Britain'. This historic sentence was indeed high praise for the Commandos. The operation, which was described as a classic by the then Chief of Staff of the Royal Marines, Major-General R. A. Pigot, had been a resounding success. Capt Steiner later wrote that he found 'the whole affair a most stimulating experience from start to finish'. Four Five had virtually assumed military control over a country the size of Britain with a population of six million, in some twenty hours. The only casualties inflicted were four killed and seven wounded at Colito Barracks. The use of 'minimum force' had been amply justified, and by quelling the mutiny all forces had won the admiration and affection of the resident population.

41 Commando flew out from the United Kingdom on Thursday, 30 January, to relieve Four Five. HMS *Centaur* had sailed for Mombasa on the previous day, and the Commando embarked in HMS *Victorious* to be transferred nine days later to the Commando Ship HMS *Albion*, prior to disembarkation at Aden later on in February.

Before the transfer to HMS *Albion*, Lt-Col Stevens wrote as a footnote to his report: 'With our transfer to *Albion* imminent, it is being reported that we wear out aircraft carriers at the rate of one a week. We are wondering where the next one is coming from!'

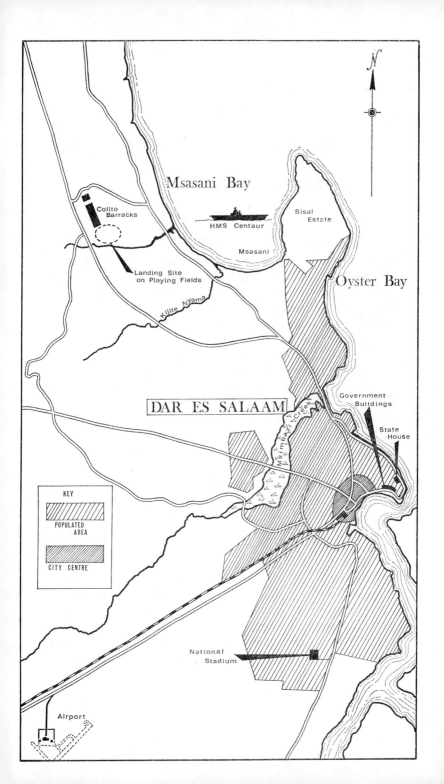

N

Msasani Bay

Colito
Barracks

HMS Centaur

Sisal
Estate

Msasani

Oyster Bay

Landing Site
on Playing Fields

Kilite Nyama

DAR ES SALAAM

Msimbazi Creek

Government
Buildings

State
House

KEY

POPULATED
AREA

CITY CENTRE

National
Stadium

Airport

CHAPTER 15

Aden II—The First Year in the Radfan

The bomb attack on the High Commissioner in Aden on 10 December, 1963, which perhaps heralded the new wave of terrorism, was followed by quick action by the Federal Government. The Yemen border was closed and some 280 Yemeni 'undesirables' were deported. In addition, fifty members of the PSP were arrested. The Federal Government then backed these measures up by declaring a State of Emergency throughout all South Arabia, including Aden State. Four Five played little part in these initial weeks of the Emergency, for the unit was busy coping with the Tanganyikan Army mutinies in East Africa, but on return had to rapidly re-adjust and carry out training and consolidation in preparation for its contribution in the attempt to bring peace to Aden.

During the last four years in Aden there were, broadly, two main campaigns which faced the politicians and military forces at the time. Both were Yemeni inspired but the theatres of operation were different. Firstly up country, in the Radfan, where a hard core of dissidents was inciting the local tribesmen to disrupt the economy and revolt in defiance of the Federal Forces. These operations were carried out by conventional warfare means. Secondly, in the state of Aden where acts of terrorism, directed at Government officials and the military and their respective buildings and installations, were becoming increasingly widespread. Operations in Aden State could be classed chiefly as Internal Security and started in earnest in late 1964, when concerted terrorist attacks and outrages became more significant. From this date campaigns in both theatres were mounted concurrently and I have included Four Five's participation in these as separate chapters to avoid confusion.

The area of the Radfan covers some 400 square miles and lies to the east of the Dhala Road from where the road enters the mountains and passes up through Thumier. Lt-Col Paddy Stevens later described the Radfan tribes as: '. . . a xenophobic lot. Every man had been brought up from boyhood with a rifle in his hands, knew how to use it, and not infrequently did so if an argument could not be settled or if there was any reasonable excuse. The arrival of the Army, whether British or Arab, was considered a reasonable excuse, an intrusion upon the sovereignty of the area, and anyway good target practice.'* These tribesmen were excellent soldiers and held in high regard by our troops, and were adept at sniping at targets from well-concealed sangars and then slipping away along tortuous mountain tracks. In campaigns of this nature the gathering of timely and accurate intelligence is always difficult and precise assessments of the enemy's strength were never possible. It was, however, estimated, that the five main tribes totalled between 35,000 and 40,000 persons, with a potential fighting strength of about 6,000. The hard-core dissidents were believed to number some 200 men, but again this figure was only an estimate. These dissidents were actively supported from the Yemen receiving supplies of ammunition and weapons from their masters north of the frontier, and in addition to being well trained and disciplined, could inflict maximum disruption with relatively few numbers.

The first operation in the Radfan, in January, 1964, code-named 'Nutcracker' was mounted by the FRA and achieved success. The military objectives were attained and a road was built through the Rabwa Pass in to the Wadi Taym. The FRA could not remain as a garrison in the Radfan indefinitely as this meant that the Yemen border would be relatively unprotected and they were subsequently withdrawn. The dissidents re-occupied the Rabwa Pass and destroyed the road, and thus regained their supremacy. In addition the rebels returned to

* *Journal of the RUSI*, 1965, 'Operations in the Radfan—1964'.

their old stamping ground, the Dhala Road, and renewed their activities of mining and ambushing passing vehicles. It was therefore decided to mount a new operation using British troops.

We are now entering what could possibly be called the 'break-in' phase of the Radfan campaign. Our troops were getting ready to penetrate deep into the heart of dissident-held territory and settle the matter from there. This new body was formed rather like an expeditionary force in the colonial wars of old and was assembled in mid-April, 1964, under the Commander, Aden Garrison, Brigadier R. L. Hargroves. The force was roughly of brigade strength and the operation was to be mounted from the base at Thumier. Training during April was aimed at preparing Four Five for the forthcoming operation and, towards the end of the month, the unit at Little Aden was joined by B Company, 3rd Battalion the Parachute Regiment (Major Peter Walter), who had come from Bahrein. B Company subsequently came under command for the operation. In this training period particular emphasis was placed on physical fitness, helicopter training with Belvederes, night movement over the hills of Little Aden, shooting and observation.

This period of preparation was an interesting one because from it were evolved tactics that were to become most significant in the first phase. The speed with which this initial study had to be carried out can be judged by the fact that the force commander had to submit his plan within three days and be ready to start in eleven days.

The Radfan was mountainous and rough and extremely difficult for troops to operate in, particularly against tribesmen adept at this type of guerilla warfare. Bearing in mind the hot climate many observers thought that it would be impossible for British troops to compete with the local experts on their own ground by day; traditionally, even the tribes and the FRA seldom, if ever, operated by night in the inhospitable region. Thus the earlier proposals were that Four Five should achieve its objectives by helicopter assault—hence the special training. However, there were not enough helicopters in the theatre, especially if the operation became a protracted one requiring logistic helicopter support. Also the treacherous terrain and insecure landing zones made this type of approach too hazardous.

The Commando, suspecting that it might one day be invited in to the Radfan, had already studied this problem and Lt-Col Stevens remembers that he had decided that the best prospects lay in deep penetration by night. This gave us the advantage of surprise, prevented the dissidents from observing the advance from the all important high ground and thus checking progress, and finally gave us a more than even chance of gaining the mountain tops by dawn. These tactics, of course, bring back memories of No. 1 Commando Brigade's classic sorties during the war, and Lt-Col Stevens also revived this idea from a similar operation whilst he was serving in No. 4 Commando Brigade. These methods were successfully rehearsed again by Four Five in small exercises and the Commanding Officer proposed to Brigadier Hargroves that this technique should be adopted. The Brigadier agreed and these proposals were incorporated in the overall plan. Night infiltration, new to the Radfan because of the terrain and climate, was to become the basic tactic on which the success of the early campaign was to be founded.

The plan was based on the necessity to hold the big rocky hill feature nicknamed 'Cap Badge' which dominated the village of Danaba, believed to be the main dissident stronghold. Cap Badge divided the Wadi Taym and Danaba basin, a fertile area some three miles wide and nine miles long, flanked by forbidding mountain ranges. The ridge to the north of this basin was nicknamed 'Rice Bowl'. There were two lines of approach into this area from Thumier. The first, and most direct, was the Wadi Rabwa which was already blocked and held by the rebels and led into the plain from the south-west. The second was the Wadi Boran, which was much rougher and longer and led into the plain from the west between two features nicknamed 'Coca Cola' and 'Sand Fly'. Initially 'Rice

Bowl' was going to be the target of the helicopter assault but this, it will be remembered, was modified and the advance was now going to be made on foot. In order to capture Rice Bowl a diversionary approach was to be made up the Wadi Rabwa whilst Four Five did a left hook march through the Wadi Boran, dropping Z Company (Major David Langley) at Sand Fly to secure the re-supply route. Meanwhile B Company (PARA) was to drop by parachute in the Wadi Taym and take Cap Badge by first light on 1 May, after the DZ had been marked by A Squadron 22 Special Air Service.

Four Five's approach through the Wadi Boran was carefully worked out between Lt-Col Stevens and Brigadier Hargroves. One of the problems was that of water. The night march, under relatively cool conditions, would help to conserve the precious supplies, but even so more would be required on the waterless Rice Bowl the following morning. Due to the limited helicopter lift only a certain amount of water could be flown in and therefore the occupation force of this feature was limited to two companies. In the end each man took three water bottles (six pints) and in addition to their normal equipment some men carried mortars and Vickers machine guns and their associated ammunition. Lt-Col Stevens decided that these support weapons might be useful because the Commando would be at the limits of the artillery support which was to be established in the Wadi Rabwa. To carry these Vickers some members of the Recce Troop (Lt Anthony Langdon) were allotted to Companies whilst the remainder of the Troop acted in its normal pathfinding role.

The Commanding Officer went up to Thumier ahead of the Commando, followed shortly afterwards by the company commanders so that they could carry out their final planning and reconnaissances. Four Five then travelled up in a convoy of sand-coloured vehicles on 29 April, 1964. The stop over in Thumier camp, recently and hastily constructed by the 1st Battalion, the Anglian Regiment, was a short one. The next afternoon, after briefings and final checks, the unit was on the move again to the 26th Milestone of the Dhala Road.

The operation was about to begin. When the trucks came to a halt a total of 400 men silently got off the track and hid in the surrounding hillsides. For this operation Lt-Col Stevens decided to leave behind the traditional green berets, and instead everyone wore their desert 'floppy hats'—normally used for field training. It was not considered politic to let the dissidents know that Commando troops were being introduced and it was hoped that the force would be mistakenly identified as other British troops who normally operated from Thumier. There was time for a quick brew-up and then a patient wait until the shadows began to lengthen across these rocky wastes. The long snake of heavily-laden men moved up towards the Wadi Boran in the fading light. As darkness set in all the Marines could see was the black masses of the mountains towering above the boulder and scrub-strewn floor of the wadi. Z Company (Major David Langley) peeled off at a prearranged point to make its way independently to the summit of Sand Fly. There was still some distance to go before the Wadi Boran was reached and X (Major Mike Banks) and Y (Capt Gavin Hamilton-Meikle) Companies could branch off to Rice Bowl. At about ten thirty-five, just as Z Company was breaking off, a distorted message was received from Force Headquarters, but as Four Five was still in low lying ground transmissions were intermittent and only part of the text got through. Then the column was halted for a seemingly endless time. X Company, in the lead, had reached the 'puddle', so named after its appearance in the air photographs. Although the water was only two and a half feet deep, there was a sheer drop of several feet before the obstacle and two unfortunate Marines had already tumbled in. The rest of the snake then had to traverse the puddle along the vertical side of the wadi. By midnight the going became faster and the moon rose to silhouette Coco Cola against the starry night sky. It was then, when higher ground was reached, that the full text of the Force Commander's message was received. The parachute drop had been cancelled and instead Four Five was to go firm on Sand Fly and Coco Cola. This decision was made after 3 Troop, A

Squadron, 22 SAS, who were going to mark the DZ, had been discovered and throughout the day (the 30th) the ten-man patrol had bravely warded off a superior number of dissidents. They then had to fight their way out of their position under cover of darkness, but not before the Troop Commander and the radio operator were killed. The force going up the Wadi Rabwa had also met spirited opposition and did not reach its objective before two-thirty.

By now Four Five had infiltrated some distance into enemy-held territory undetected, although some sightings were reported en route but were not confirmed. In the meantime B Company, whose parachute drop had been cancelled, came straight up to Thumier, arriving at about two am, on 1 May. Lt-Col Paddy Stevens now had the unenviable and formidable task of re-assessing the situation, the original plan having been altered. Coca Cola was some 1,500 feet higher than their present position and the climb had not been studied in detail. Z Company was already well on the way to its target and so the details for X and Y had to be hastily revised. Under the light of carefully shaded torches the steep route up Coca Cola was scrutinized on the air photographs. Major Mike Banks of X Company was himself an expert mountaineer, but even he, at this impromptu council of war, viewed the prospect with some trepidation, especially as some of the men were so heavily loaded with mortars and machine guns.

Two wide wadis and then a steep ravine had to be crossed before the final and long ascent could be made. Major Banks and his pathfinder party picked their way stealthily up the rocky face. This side of the mountain was in shadow from the moon and the climb was made in the darkness, punctuated only by the occasional muttered curse and falling rocks. Then, before the summit was reached, a steep section had to be negotiated with the aid of ropes. The tired men hauled them-selves up, and at last the ground levelled out. Four Five was on Coca Cola ridge at four o'clock, two hours before dawn. X Company moved a mile down the ridge and Y Company remained at the near end. An hour before dawn Lt-Col Stevens triumphantly reported Sand Fly and Coca Cola secure. As dawn broke the weary men of Four Five looked out from their lofty perches. The Danaba Basin, with its belts of cultivation, and Cap Badge stretched out to the east; the Wadi Rabwa was to the south. A foothold in the dissident territory had been gained without even a shot being fired.

For the next three days Four Five remained in its positions with the barest essentials in the way of equipment and supplies. During the day the hot sun beat down on the ridge relentlessly and the only shade available was what the Marines could provide for themselves—usually the rolls of hessian carried by most men. The Commanding Officer had to make do with a copy of the *Times*! Otherwise the time was spent uneventfully, apart from the occasional firing of the Vickers and mortars at dissidents in the plains below.

The cancellation of the parachute drop meant that only part of the initial plan had been implemented and that Danaba and the dominating Cap Badge feature were still in enemy hands. Cap Badge was given to Lt-Col Stevens as the next objective. The feature was a difficult one to capture and there was a likelihood that the dissidents would put up a fierce resistance to defend their strongholds. Cap Badge rose some 1,200 feet above the plain. A northern approach was ruled out because Danaba had to be by-passed and the feature was almost sheer in places to the south and west. Again it was decided to adopt the same tactics—to undertake a daring night approach march. There were two possible routes up to the objective from the south-west and the south-east and these were allotted X Company and B Company 3 PARA respectively. Both routes could easily be defended by a small number of dissidents and although the south-eastern route was an easier climb it involved a march of an extra two miles round the south flank of Cap Badge. A third company, Y Company, was given the task of seizing Gin Sling, a rather easier feature to the south-west of Cap Badge, which gave the Commando the added advantage of being in possession of high ground should things go wrong on Cap Badge.

Four Five was relieved on Coca Cola on the afternoon of 4 May by the 1st Battalion the Anglian Regiment and began to make its way down to the Wadi Boran in preparation for the march of five or so miles to Cap Badge. It soon became clear, however, that Lt-Col Stevens' carefully planned time appreciation was falling behind schedule. The men of X and Y Companies were pretty tired after their stay in the open and it took longer to reach the floor of the Wadi Boran than was anticipated. The re-supply point of food and water was also further back than planned and this involved an extra round trip of nearly a mile. These delays accumulated so that the Commando was nearly two hours late in reaching the Danaba Basin from the Wadi Boran. It had been hoped to complete this leg by dusk, but instead the unit was stumbling along the steep-sided wadi in pitch darkness. It was not impossible to reach the objectives even with these timings, but it made the task more difficult.

Soon after reaching the Danaba Basin B Company, 3 PARA, moved off into the darkness on their separate route. The advance over the next three miles or so to the dispersal point was led by Y Company (Capt Gavin Hamilton-Meikle) and he and his pathfinder team were able to stick to the pre-arranged route with remarkable accuracy and skill. About a mile from Cap Badge X Company (Major Mike Banks) broke off and Y Company turned south with Headquarters for Gin Sling. Although only 1,000 feet high, Gin Sling was formidable enough and a tiring climb at night, but both Y Company Commander and his Second-in-Command (Capt Ted Goddard) were experienced climbers and the summit was reached an hour before dawn.

X Company had similar adventures. Like Y Company, a village had to be skirted. Suddenly dogs started barking and the anxious Marines waited for several patient minutes lest the game should be given away. The villagers, however, slept on and progress continued. Cap Badge was a more difficult climb—sheer in places—but Major Banks was more than equal to the task, and as dawn was beginning to streak across the eastern horizon the Troops of X Company fanned out to search their objective. The only sign of the enemy was empty, but well-used sangars. In the dark valley the assessment that the dissidents usually left their hill-tops at night had been proved to be correct, although Lt-Col Stevens had thought that this time the enemy might have heard them and expected that Four Five would have to fight for it. In fact the observant sentries of X and Y Companies had already reported seeing flickering lights lower down on the mountainside. These sightings were discounted at the time but were to prove significant later on.

Nothing had been heard from B Company, 3 PARA, since it had passed south of Gin Sling. Radio contact had been screened by the surrounding hills and Lt-Col Stevens had assumed that at first light the Company would be on the lower slopes of Cap Badge, making its ascent from the south-east. As the light increased the Commanding Officer remembers reflecting with satisfaction that the objectives had been taken without opposition. His thoughts were checked abruptly. Gunfire broke out from the direction of Cap Badge. The meaning of the flickering lights, which had been seen earlier on, was now fully realized. It was the dissidents making their way to their daytime positions, the sangars, from their villages. Four Five had arrived in the nick of time. X and Y Companies in their secure positions were not bothered by the dissidents' firing but the sounds of battle from the east of Cap Badge, invisible from Gin Sling, indicated that B Company, 3 PARA, was now in action.

B Company had had the most difficult time of all. Its approach march was much longer and it had to contend with a steep and treacherous descent in to the Wadi Taym. The fast pace caused two heat casualties and the rear platoon had to slow down to accompany these. To add to the frustration, direction had been slightly lost on a couple of occasions in the difficult country and also the column had to be completely halted twice as dissident parties, with their flickering lights, passed uncomfortably near down the Wadi Taym. Dawn found the Company still in open low-lying ground to the south-east of Cap Badge. Lt-Col Paddy Stevens had already given instructions to the

Companies if this predicament should occur; they were to fall back under Gin Sling, but if they were unable to do that they were to 'kick' their way into a village. The parachutists had the misfortune to choose Habil Sabaha, which was the nearest settlement and lay about half a mile in front on the lower slopes of Cap Badge. The relative inaccuracy of the maps of this area makes it difficult to plot the precise location, but suffice it to say that the village was fairly widely spread out and consisted of a collection of mud buildings and forts. As B Company advanced, the dissidents opened up from the left and the area of the village, causing several casualties. For about an hour a determined fire-fight ensued. Major Peter Walter led one attack and cleared dissidents from one fort whilst another platoon successfully dealt with more dissidents who were trying to outflank the Company. One other platoon was detached to deal with dissidents in another outlying fort whilst the remainder of the Company attacked the village proper, accounting for several enemy. As B Company re-organized, the surviving dissidents fled to their sangars on the hillside below Cap Badge. They then opened up on the parachutists and from their commanding positions began to inflict more casualties. The Company Second-in-Command, Capt Jewkes, led a counter-attack into Habil Sabaha under cover of smoke but soon afterwards was killed, administering morphia to a wounded sergeant lying in the open.

In the meantime, Four Five moved up to see what assistance could be given. Habil Sabaha was at maximum artillery range and safety could not be guaranteed. Although mortars and Vickers machine-guns were mounted there were no obvious targets amongst the somewhat confused fighting down below. To make matters worse, the dissident sangars were tucked into the base of the sheer cliff which formed that part of Cap Badge and X Company on top were powerless to intercept. Relief had to be found for the stricken paratroopers who had had two killed and ten injured (in reply they had courageously killed six dissidents and injured many more). Army Air Corps Beavers had already braved the small arms fire and, despite one

being hit, dropped water and ammunition by parachute into the battle area.

Lt-Col Stevens decided to retain X and Y Companies in their strategic positions and asked Force Headquarters to airlift Z Company (Major David Langley) forward to Cap Badge from their reserve position on Sand Fly. Thus Z Company would be able to attack the rebels from above. The unit report continues:

'Hunter ground attack aircraft were called in (at midday) and for over an hour they circled and dived low over the rebel sangars on the slopes of Cap Badge, raking them with 30 mm. cannon and rocket fire. The remains of one sniper were found later in and around a cave which had been the impact point of one rocket attack, and others were seen to fall from fortified buildings hit by rockets. Soon after this Zulu Company was flown in by chopper from Sand Fly and moved down the feature to secure the LZ prior to casevac by Belvedere. (The wounded had spent many uncomfortable hours in the sticky heat in the shelter of buildings.) The pilot of the Belvedere must have had a few anxious moments as he was forced to wait for ten minutes while the casualties were loaded offering a large stationary target, while everyone waited for some unlocated sniper to open up. Luck was with us and at the end of ten minutes the machine lumbered away unscathed.'

As the helicopter pulled away from what was later to be known as Pegasus Village the battle-weary parachutists set off to climb 'Cap Badge'. For the next three days Four Five, until relieved, remained in its hilltop positions. An uneasy calm had settled over the Radfan.

In just over a week the enemy had been forced to withdraw from the Rabwa Pass, the Wadi Boran and Wadi Taym, and his supply routes from the Dhala Road seriously jeopardized. Four Five had achieved complete surprise by the two brilliant infiltrations. The official summing up continues:

'No less surprising to the rebels and to many others, was the ability of British troops to operate in the mountains and in the hottest months of the year. Most of our movement was done at night; but after a few days we had become more or less accustomed to the heat and learnt to live with it. . . . We moved off as lightly equipped as we could on 30 April, and until 9 May we lived in the same clothes (our packs never caught up with us), bearded and only occasionally washed.'

For the next nine days Four Five had a respite in Little Aden, but for the staff there was little rest as conferences and reports still had to be attended to. On 11 May, 1964, 39 Brigade (Brigadier C. H. Blacker) took over control of the Radfan campaign from the initial improvised 'Radforce', and Four Five came under command. The phase of operations to penetrate deep into Radfan territory, i.e. to the east and south, was to continue.

The first five days of the second tour were spent in the Wadi Taym on routine day and night searches. During this period Brigadier Blacker was concentrating on probing towards the higher mountains in the south by means of advancing down the Wadi Misrah and the Bakri Ridge. X Company was detached and under command of the 3rd Battalion, Parachute Regiment (Lt-Col A. H. Farrar-Hockley) for the latter part of this operation. 3 PARA began their move on 18 May and by 24 May had secured the entire ridge as far as the southern tip— 'Arnold's Spur'. It had been a dramatic progress against stiff opposition which culminated in a two-company attack with air and artillery support directed at the dissident stronghold village of Al Qudeishi on 23 May. On 25 May, X Company flew up to join 3 PARA on Arnold's Spur. The Wessex helicopters of 815 Squadron from HMS *Centaur* (who had flown Four Five into Tanganyika some five months previously), had by now come into the theatre temporarily to relieve the RAF Belvederes, and they had to combat formidable flying conditions which included high winds, rain and mist. Once established on Arnold's Spur Major Banks and X Company had to make final plans for the next phase of the operation, a raid on the Wadi Dhubsan.

The Wadi Dhubsan lay some 2,000 feet below the Bakri Ridge. The sides were steep and the wadi floor was broken up by subsidiary ridges. To the west of Dhubsan, and half a mile south of the Bakri Ridge, lay the Jebel Haqla, a flat-topped feature rising to over 1,500 feet, which dominated the surrounding wadis. It was known that the Wadi Dhubsan was a likely stronghold of the dissidents, and was therefore chosen as the next objective. Throughout the afternoon the sections of X Company, having been briefed, moved cautiously to the edge of Arnold's Spur to reconnoitre their routes for the following day.

At last light on 25 May the operation started. C Company, 3 PARA, moved to establish picquets on the Jebel Haqla, and A Company, 3 PARA, descended the steep escarpment to secure their area, a bowl at the western end of the Dhubsan. X Company's task was to descend into the Wadi soon after dawn and advance 1,000 yards beyond A Company to conduct a sweep as far as the village of Hawfi which lay beyond a prominent bend. After spending a wet and cold night on the Bakri Ridge X Company was glad to set off in the early hours of the 26th and move down into the wadi, 'at breakneck speed', to arrive at the bottom by eight o'clock. The picquets of 3 PARA had earlier on reported some fifty dissidents coming up the Dhubsan from the south, but the dissidents certainly did not make their presence felt and for the next 600 yards X Company progressed in eerie silence. To give added protection to the Company, Major Mike Banks picketed some of the subsidiary ridges, and this cut down the rate of advance to a very slow pace. Suddenly, one of the picquets that had been detached under Sgt William Patterson of 1 Troop spotted a group of dissidents way up on the steep ridge to the right. 3 Troop (Lt Terry Knott) was in the lead on the wadi floor. The leading sections, under command of Cpls 'Jan' Bickle and Terry Waterson took cover behind a nearby wall and opened fire, sending the armed dissidents scuttling behind a rock, dragging their wounded with them. Soon afterwards the dissidents, from the protection of their well concealed sangars, opened up from all directions to the front of X Company, who were spread out in the lower ground. Major Banks then ordered his Troops to try and get on a higher level, thus avoiding the worst of the fire. The Marines slowly picked their way up the slope, dodging from rock to rock. In these conditions it was difficult to discern precisely where the enemy fire, increasing every minute, was coming from. The battlefield noise increased as the high-pitched drone of a Scout helicopter, carrying the Commanding Officer and Intelligence Officer of 3 PARA, could be heard approaching from the rear. As it flew over 3 Troop, the Scout became the target for a strong barrage of enemy fire and was hit on several occasions. The pilot, Major Jackson, skilfully kept the helicopter under control for long enough for it to land safely in front of 3 Troop, and the Marines dashed forward to give it protection as the passengers ran for safety. Lt-Col Tony Farrar-Hockley then ordered A Company, 3 PARA (in the bowl at the western end of the Wadi), to move up on to the high ground to the north and part of C Company on Jebel Haqla, to gain the high ground on the south. Air strikes were also authorized and X Company Second-in-Command, Capt Roger Brind, and the sergeant-major, QMS A. Walton, began to lay out bright red and orange fluorescent panels in open ground, pointing towards the dissident sangars. This was a standard procedure in preparation for air strikes so that the Hunter pilots, approaching at over 400 mph, could be given a clear reference point, thus making target identification and recognition simpler. Moving out from behind cover with the the bright panels, Capt Brind soon became the target for heavy fire and was shot through the thigh and stomach. However, he had bravely completed his task and was dragged to safety, before sustaining further injury through steady sniper fire, by Marines Brownett and Robertson, and treated for his wounds by one of the Company's two Sick Berth Attendants, Williams.

1 Troop, commanded by Lt James Barr, came under the

heaviest fire. Originally the majority of the Troop was down in the bottom of the wadi near the wall where Marine Kimber with the GPMG, had been keeping up a steady rate of fire. The Troop was moving up to the south in an attempt to gain the higher ground and attracted attention from dissidents in three different positions. One of the forward sections was led by Sgt 'Nobby' Clarkson and soon after the Marines approached the top of a knoll they saw the tragic sight of Marine David Wilson, the Troop signaller, being shot through the chest by enemy fire. Wilson died almost immediately as Lt Barr began to drag him behind a rock. 1 Troop suffered another casualty shortly afterwards when Marine Dunkin was shot in the knee—his leg was later amputated. As it is customary, on these occasions, the kit of Marine David Wilson was later auctioned amongst his comrades in X Company and the proceeds forwarded to his relatives. The *The News, Portsmouth* of 18 June, 1964, reported that '. . . the Company group of 150 men raised nearly £700 in the auction. His cap badge (on his green beret) fetched £100.'

In the meantime, Cpl Waterson had moved forward with the leading section of 3 Troop and under cover of phosphorous grenades had succeeded in entering some houses on the mountainside to the south, situated before the bend in the wadi near the village of Hawfi. His section later suffered a casualty during the air strike when Marine Keswick, in an outbuilding, was terribly wounded in the head by an empty cannon shell which ricocheted off a wall.

As early afternoon approached the firing began to die down. Two Troop (Lt Richard Persse) had moved up on the northern side and forced the dissidents up there to pull back. The remainder of X Company had by now moved stealthily up to the rear of the wadi bend. Concurrently the paratroopers were advancing along the ridges ensuring that the enemy sangars were covered. The dissidents, demoralized by aircraft, mortar and artillery fire, started to withdraw. This gave Major Banks the opportunity to re-organize the Company, spread out over a large area, and the other medical orderly, Sick Berth Attendant

12

Edward Wade, a chance to treat the three badly wounded member of the Company. Wade, later Mention in Despatches for his bravery in the Radfan, had, in the true tradition of his branch of the Services, been moving about in the open visiting all the Troop position throughout the battle giving first aid to the injured.

As dusk approached two skilled REME mechanics arrived to repair the Scout. 3 PARA and X Company remained in their positions to give protection in the event of a night counterattack. The fitters, working behind a light screen, toiled throughout the night. As dawn began to filter into the deep wadi on the morning of 27 May, Major Jackson, somewhat apprehensively, started the rotors and then flew away to safety.

As 3 PARA returned to their positions X Company spent the next eight hours sweating to the top of Jebel Haqla in preparation for the return to Bakri Ridge. The mist had again clamped down, but the Wessex of 815 Squadron worked miracles to pick up the Company in this precipitous terrain. X Company was flown back to Thumier on the 28th, having been the first Company in the unit to be at the receiving end of fierce dissident opposition in the Radfan. Although pinned down in low ground the Company had held its line courageously, thus eventually forcing the enemy to withdraw with estimated losses higher than our own.

Whilst X Company had been detached the rest of the Commando had also been involved in the general advance southwards in the Radfan. It will be remembered that there were two main axes of advance, the Bakri Ridge and the Wadi Misrah, and part of the original plan had been for Four Five to clear the Wadi Misrah with 2 Battalion FRA as a prelude to gaining the high ground on Jebel Huriyah, the highest peak in the Radfan. The plan was a simple one. The FRA were to move on the western side, Y Company on the east and Z Company, now commanded by Major 'Jungle' Baizley, was to forge ahead along the wadi floor followed by armoured support, thus opening up a route into the heart of the Radfan to ease the re-supply problem. As Four Five and the FRA formed up, in the late afternoon of 25 May, the rains, which had affected the helicopter programme on the Bakri Ridge, made their presence felt on the remainder of the operation. The Wadi Rabwa, which lay across the route of advance, now became a raging torrent of water several feet deep and some members of Y Company had a lucky escape. Capt Ted Goddard, the Company Second-in-Command, and his sergeant-major, QMS Sandy MacVicar, waiting patiently for the move suddenly noticed one of the Commando's sand coloured Land Rovers in difficulty with water rising around it. Capt Goddard grabbed his rope, normally used for scaling cliffs, and with the help of the Sergeant-Major plunged into the fast flowing wadi and managed to reach the vehicle and save the two marines inside it seconds before the Land Rover was overturned. However, this was to be the only act of bravery on this part of the operation. The FRA, who had had a longer approach march, were unable to make the deadline. Their route, formerly a road, was now a river and Brigadier Blacker had to postpone the move for twenty-four hours. The next day the operation was cancelled altogether, but to make up for the bitter disappointment his keyed up men had suffered during the previous two days Lt-Col Stevens gained permission to take the unit up the wadi that night on an operational patrol. This passed without incident and on 28 May, 1964, Four Five and 3 PARA were withdrawn from Radfan operations.

The Commando had an absence from the Radfan of about a month (the third tour started on 3 July, 1964) and during this time a decisive battle had been fought by the 1st Battalion Anglian Regiment and the 2nd Battalion FRA to gain control of the Wadi Misrah and the Jebel Huriyah. This success meant that by July the dissidents, now broken up into smaller groups, were adopting harassing tactics of sniping at military convoys or mining re-supply routes. We now enter what could be broadly termed the second stage or phase of operations in the Radfan. The first was the long unit-sized marches into the heart of the Radfan—the unforgettable night infiltrations and the battle for the Wadi Dhubsan. It was now time to consolidate

these advances and we now find that the Radfan was split up
into Battalion areas. Four Five found itself operating in the
area from the Wadi Taym to the Wadi Dhubsan. The Companies were spread out on hilltop bases and the tactics in this
area were those of patrolling and ambushing. Having chased
the dissidents it was now our turn to catch them.

Throughout this time the Commando was deployed in three
locations, Y Company (Capt Paul Whitehead) was on the
Jebel Haqla, Z Company re-occupied the Bakri Ridge and
Support Company (Capt John Lloyd), acting as a Rifle Company in place of X which was detached, was on the Jebel
Widina. Re-supply to these widespread outposts was always
a great problem and in the main, food, water, ammunition and
stores were air-dropped every four or five days from Argosys or
Beverleys. Daily personal contact was usually maintained by
the Scout helicopters which flew the reconnaissance and
liaison missions.

Typical of the type of ambush mounted during this phase
was the one commanded by Sgt Jock Munson of the Recce
Troop—a Swimmer Canoeist Specialist. He tells his story:

'My tour in Four Five lasted from January to December,
1964. I was originally in Z Company but then transferred
to the Recce Troop in June. The Troop was being formed by
Capt Goddard, and tactics were based on those employed
by the Special Air Service. We did four or five weeks of
intensive training and our task was to move ahead of the
Commando, route-finding by night. I had utmost respect
for the dissidents who, of course, knew the ground well and
were excellent at shooting and camouflage.

The Troop's first success was in the Wadi Dhura'a, off the
Wadi Dhubsan. Col Stevens had left us in an empty village
with enough food and water for eight days. It was expected
that dissidents might visit this village and a Rifle Troop base
was established on higher ground to the north. After we had
been holed up inside the building for three days in the
unbearable heat I took a section out at one o'clock in the

morning of 12 July to find a lying-up position for an ambush. We moved to the north of the village and found an ideal area, a junction of five tracks with a ruined house on a hillock in the middle. In the afternoon the sentry on top of the building said he saw two armed dissidents moving carefully and tactically down the wadi. The sentry did not shoot and the enemy had passed by the ambush before he could give us warning. Fortunately the enemy didn't see us and they returned a short time later, hand in hand! Both were killed at a long range of some 300 yards, but not before one of them had returned fire, very accurately, using only one arm. I kept half the section in my position in case we were counter-attacked and sent the other half out to search and recover the bodies. It took nearly an hour to cover the rough ground and some time later a Scout helicopter came in to pick up the corpses.'

This success was a notable 'first' for Four Five for it was the first time in the Radfan that anyone had been able to recover dissident bodies after a kill so that they could be positively identified. In this instance one of the dead was a known rebel leader and the other wanted for murder. Sgt Munson had already radioed back the first 'kill' and had to repeat the procedure shortly afterwards having despatched the second dissident, who had gamely returned the fire. The following message sent in a broad Scots accent, was recorded: 'Eight zero braavo, ye can coont that tew!'

The Commando's persistence in patrolling was beginning to pay off and on 13 July, 1964, the day after Recce Troop's kill another dissident was accounted for—according to the *souk* grapevine. Seven Troop (Lt Ian Martin) and 9 Troop (Lt Phil Greig) of Z Company had been stalking a group of rebels over the Bakri Ridge. Although the Arabs fled in the nick of time a long range fire fight ensued which enabled casualties to be inflicted with the GPMG.

The numerous uses of the helicopter have already been described but on occasions these vehicles made delightful targets for the rebels—with terrifying results for the occupants. At about this time a patrol of 5 Troop (Lt Chris McDowall) which was under the command of Z Company, had been placed in an ambush position for four days in a wadi known as Pilgrim's Way. Part of the ambush, near a water hole, was spotted by four dissidents who promptly took flight. On hearing that the enemy had got out of the net Major 'Jungle' Baizley immediately requested that a Scout helicopter be tasked. When this was approved he set out with Colour Sgt Bashford and two marines, who formed part of a GPMG group, in the hope of blocking the dissidents' escape route. After doing a quick recce the Scout approached on the most likely track. Almost immediately it was hit by an explosive bullet. The dissident had scored a bulls-eye and the helicopter lurched about fifteen feet and filled with smoke. The pilot put out a May Day call and then turned to his passengers and said, in an almost final tone, 'Well, you've joined the club, I guess we're going down'. However, all hope was not lost and he decided to give the instruments a last check. The fuel gauge flickered slightly. Pressure still seemed to be registering so the pilot decided to take a gamble and limp back to the nearest landing site, Table Top, a flat plateau some four miles away. The next few minutes seemed like an eternity, and Major Baizley recalled, 'We must have said about 5,000 Our Fathers!' When the Scout eventually reached the edge of Table Top the engine literally cut out and the helicopter plunged on to the rock, fortunately only a few feet below. A later inspection revealed that the fuel tanks had been completely shot away and that the helicopter had flown on the residual vapour left in the pipes—a miraculous escape.

Although this is not an attempt to undermine the undoubted reliability of helicopter travel, the instances of mishaps are so relatively rare that they are usually newsworthy. Two more accidents occurred during up country tours involving ranks of Four Five, mercifully without loss of life. The first was in May, 1966, when a Scout helicopter, piloted by Major Greville Edgecombe, Army Air Corps, suffered an engine failure and plunged on to a small landing site in the Wadi Tiban. There was a very high-powered unit team on board which included the Second-in-Command (Major David Alexander), the Adjutant (Capt Robin Rising) and H Company Commander* (Capt Alan Downton), but fortunately there were no casualties except for the helicopter. A Wessex was called in later to attempt to recover the Scout, and an important group of service observers came in to witness this feat. Unfortunately, all did not go according to plan and the Scout had to be jettisoned into a deep wadi, where it was smashed to pieces causing many red faces! The other crash happened in February, 1967, when one of the Sioux of the Commando's own Air Troop toppled over after a particularly heavy landing. The unit photographer was on board and was able to record the scene seconds after the pilot, Sgt Blevins, had leapt from the overturned cab.

No account of this patrolling phase in the Radfan would be complete without the story of 1 Troop in the Wadi Aimaan. The operation, near the end of the Commando's third tour, shows first class ambushing techniques plus the determined efforts of the dissidents to pin our men down in the lower ground. The Troop (Lt James Barr), was under the command of Support Company on the Jebel Widina and on the night of 24 July descended into the Wadi Aimaan to lay an ambush—in conjunction with Five Troop, mentioned previously in connection with the water hole ambush. The patrol commander continues with his recollections:

'It was pitch black as we descended to the wadi floor and I had to call up Company Headquarters to fire a starshell so that we could identify the house we were heading for near the ambush position. I had two sections with me and we waited patiently until dawn. We had been told to expect two dissidents in the area and at nine o'clock on the morning of the

* At various stages during the Commando's history HQ Troop or Company was divided into two parts, 'H' comprising the executive element, and 'Q' the supply and administrative departments.

26th one enemy came into the killing ground moving rather suspiciously, I thought he might be acting as a decoy. Then another armed man appeared, I wasn't sure if there were more to come but decided to open fire as we had at least two "in the bag". Marine I. E. Deakins, with a sniper's rifle hit one at a range of over 300 yards, and the GPMG teams killed the other who was dashing to cover. Two more dissidents appeared on the scene and we injured one of them. I sent a sitrep* back on the radio and was ordered to give chase after the wounded man. I left one section back in the building and moved forward with Sgt Patterson's group. We picked our way very slowly downhill as we were in our own killing ground. After we had gone about 400 yards another group of dissidents opened up with a Bren gun from higher ground. We dashed for what cover we could find, but as we were out in the open I decided we should move back a bit and seek the rather sparse protection of a nearby cornfield. For some time the twelve of us lay amongst the corn whilst the enemy bullets ploughed into the crops around us and I then ordered Sgt Patterson to make a break and take half the group back to our original building. Fire increased and they were pinned down behind a small tree and boulder where they had a long and uncomfortable wait until darkness. I took the other Marines up a steep cliff and got out of the firing zone. The radio then packed up on us but at midday we were joined by Recce Troop who had been flown in. We stayed on this cliff all afternoon and at about four-thirty saw considerable enemy movement to our east—they were probably preparing to counter-attack. The Vickers guns, brought down to the southern tip of the Widina, opened up and a Hunter air strike was called. The dissidents dispersed but we thought it unwise to move until darkness had come. It had been an unpleasant day, but we hadn't suffered any casualties. My group then went back and joined up with Sgt Patterson. The dissident bodies had still not been recovered, but by now I had a feeling that the other enemy

* Situation Report.

were moving close and it was therefore considered an un-
necessary risk to attempt another recovery. We thankfully
set out in the darkness on the 2,000-foot climb and didn't
get into our lines until after daybreak.'

The fourth, and final, tour of 1964 lasted from 23 August to
18 September, and it was again a continuation of the patrol and
ambush policy. This time Four Five was spread out in the
plains of the Danaba Basin and the Wadi Taym. The area was
three miles wide and nine miles long, and as it will be remembered from the initial assault on Cap Badge was broken up
with deep cut wadis and deceptive little ridges. The easternmost
Company, Y Company now commanded by Capt Godfrey
Seager, which was at Blair's Field with Recce Troop, probably
had the busiest time. The dissidents took great delight in
shooting at the camp almost every night from north, east
and south (sometimes all three at the same time, or so it
seems!)

Y Company was not content just to remain in its camp to act
as a target for the rebels and frequently sent out small groups
to dissuade the enemy from carrying out his nuisance tactics.
One of these groups, led by Lt Peter Bell, was moving out to
lay an ambush at night and managed to shoot a dissident in the
dark when the two parties met unexpectedly. The ambush was
then duly laid as planned and was able to notch up another hit
the next afternoon. An official report describes the incident:

'Lying in their ambush positions on a hill top they spotted
a group of four dissidents (jungle greens, brown gym shoes and
khaki turbans) returning from a shooting competition against
Blair's Field. They had to move their ambush position, but
got to within 350 yards of them and opened up. Confusion,
the dissidents took cover, and mortar fire was brought down
on them. One dissident ran for it, and was hit by two riflemen
and didn't move again. . . . With only a small patrol of
eight men in very broken country it was risky to attempt to
recover the body.'

Success and setbacks often walk hand-in-hand in this type of warfare. In the same period Recce Troop (Capt Ted Goddard) was split up into small ambush parties in the Wadi Sha'ab. One group, held up by the broken ridges, did not arrive in its position until after daybreak and must have been spotted. The Arabs laid a decoy and as the section gave chase they in turn were ambushed, killing Cpl Edward McGrath and wounding Marine Sandvid. By now another section of the Troop had joined in and Marine Murphy bravely dashed into the open, firing his Bren from the hip at the by now fleeing rebels. Artillery fire too was brought down and it was later learnt that one dissident had died and another had been wounded. It was at least some consolation to find that the scores had been evened mathematically.

Even Dhala, manned by X Company at this time, had its fair share of excitement and similar to Blair's Field was carrying out a full ambush and patrol programme. One story, that filtered down from the hills during these months, was of the two marines who were new to Aden. They had already spotted the Motor Transport Tent (marked Dhala Taxis) and as they were not on duty so soon after arrival they decided to see the sights and went in to ask for a car to take them down to the night club in Dhala town. With great presence of mind the duty corporal sent them back to their tents as they were not wearing ties!

The fourth tour in the Radfan was to be the last for Lt-Col Paddy Stevens who was to hand over, in November, 1964, to Lt-Col Robin McGarel Groves (formerly Second-in-Command in 1961). Lt-Col Stevens' leadership had inspired Four Five in perhaps one of its busiest post-war years. Operational success depends heavily (in modern warfare) on sound administration, and in the Radfan stores and supplies, on a unit level, were fed through from both Little Aden and Habilayn (Thumier). Observers during this year are unanimous in their praise for the fine support team, so ably led by the Second-in-Command, Major David Smith, and Quartermaster, Capt John Clooney, whose untiring work in the background ensured that the men in the outposts in the front line were not lacking in ammunition, equipment, food, water and the other daily necessities.

Thus we draw to the close of the first year in the Radfan, a full one by any account, but one in which the affairs of this hostile terrain were still left very much in the melting pot. Lt-Col Julian Paget later summed up the situation and speculated for the months ahead as follows:*

'So 1964 ended up-country with the major pacification operation completed, and the dissident tribesmen ready for a settlement. The question was "What next?" would British troops be withdrawn, having proved their power and taught the rebels that they could not with impunity defy the lawful Government? Would a long-term "hearts and minds" campaign be started, in the hopes of winning over the tribes to a more effective loyalty to the Federation, so that the insurgents would no longer have freedom of movement in Radfan? Or would a British military presence be essential for some time yet, in order to counter the deliberate and persistent policy by Egypt of subversion and infiltration from the Yemen? It was to be this last course, and the British Army was not to see the last of Radfan for another two and a half years.'

These sentiments could easily be reflected by Four Five whose contribution to peace-keeping in the Radfan in the past eight months had been an enormous one. Like many other units this was not to be the last of the mountains for the Commando. The first two phases of operations had virtually been completed, that of penetrating deep into the territory and then dominating it by setting up bases and patrolling from these. In the months ahead it was going to be the turn of the dissidents to show off some of the more advanced methods which they had perfected, and then a general worsening of the situation as part of the troubles that were spreading throughout South Arabia.

* *Last Post: Aden 1964–67*, Julian Paget, Faber and Faber, 1969.

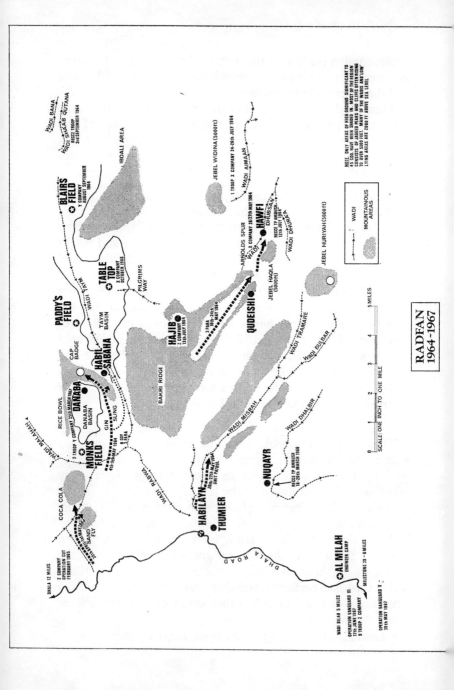

RADFAN 1964-1967

NOTE: ONLY AREAS OF HIGH GROUND SIGNIFICANT TO
45 CDO. HAVE BEEN SHADED IN. MOST OF THE REGION
CONSISTS OF JAGGED PEAKS AND CLIFFS OFTEN RISING
TO OVER 5000 FEET. MANY OF THE WADIS AND LOW
LYING AREAS ARE 2000 FT ABOVE SEA LEVEL

····· WADI

MOUNTAINOUS
AREAS

0   1   2   3   4   5 MILES

SCALE: ONE INCH TO ONE MILE

WADI BANA
WADI SHAAB QUTANA
RECCE TROOP
3rd SEPTEMBER 1964

BLAIRS FIELD
Y COMPANY
AUGUST/SEPTEMBER
1964

IBDALI AREA

JEBEL WIDINA (5000ft)

WADI AIMAAN

1 TROOP X COMPANY 24-25th JULY 1964

PADDY'S FIELD

TABLE TOP
X COMPANY
OCTOBER 1966

WADI TAYM

TAYM BASIN

PILGRIMS WAY

ARNOLDS SPUR

HAWFI
DHUBSAN
RECCE TP AMBUSH
12th JULY 1964

WADI DHURA

HABIL SABAHA

CAP BADGE

RICE BOWL

DANABA

DANABA BASIN

SLING

5 TROOP Y COMPANY 7th MARCH 1967

GIN

B COY
3 PARA

4th-5th MAY 1964

BAKRI RIDGE

HAJIB
Z COMPANY
13th JULY 1964

QUDEISHI

JEBEL HAQLA
(5000ft)

JEBEL HURIYAH (5600ft)

3 PARA
18th-24th MAY 1964

X COMPANY 26/27th MAY 1964

WADI

WADI TRAMARE

Wadi BULSAR

MONKS FIELD

COCA COLA

WADI MATLAH

WADI MISRAH

NUQAYR

WADI DHALBIR

RECCE TP AMBUSH
18-26th MARCH 1966

HABILAYN
26th/27th MAY 1967
UNIT PATROL

THUMIER

WADI RABWA

SAND FLY

Z COMPANY OPERATION CUT FEBRUARY 1965

DHALA 12 MILES

AL MILAH
ENGINEER CAMP

DHALA ROAD

MILESTONE 29 ~ 6 MILES

WADI DILAH 5 MILES

OPERATION VANGUARD VI
17th JUNE 1967
9 TROOP Z COMPANY

OPERATION VANGUARD V ·.
30th MAY 1967

CHAPTER 16

Aden III—The Closing Years Up Country

By the time Four Five returned to the Radfan in early 1965* much had happened, largely due to the initial pressure applied by British forces and the ceaseless patrolling mounted afterwards to check any resurgence. Most of the Radfan tribes had now surrendered and had given hostages to ensure that they would keep the peace. These hostages were kept initially at a special camp near Dhala guarded by the FNG and were later moved elsewhere. With the 'official end' of the preliminary up country campaign, Headquarters Federal Regular Army (FRA) had reassumed control of all operations, and had established a Commander Area West at Thumier with responsibilities for all the Western Aden Protectorate. At the same time as the FRA reassumed operational control, the Political Officers, later to be renamed Political Advisers, and who came under the British Resident at Al Ittihad, started trying to resettle the tribes and restore some form of civilian administration through local rulers and sheikhs. The Political

* There were to be nine more gruelling tours up country for the Commando. These were as follows:

Tour Five, 20 January to 4 March, 1965.
Tour Six, 22 April to 28 May, 1965.
Tour Seven, 23 June to 28 July, 1965.
Tour Eight, 24 September to 26 October, 1965.
Tour Nine, 10 December, 1965 to 28 January, 1966.
Tour Ten, 14 April to 22 May, 1966.
Tour Eleven, 14 September to 10 November, 1966.
Tour Twelve, 6 February to 27 March, 1967.
Tour Thirteen, 15 May to 26 June, 1967.

Officer at Thumier was at that time Brian Somerfield, who was later to become a close friend of the unit.

All operations carried out by the Commando were planned in conjunction with the local Political Officer and had to receive the approval of Commander Area West and Commander Federal Regular Army. With the surrender of most of the tribes it had been possible to remove the garrisons from several of the more permanent outposts. Eventually only the Mahli and Dairi tribes in the Wadi Danaba remained totally dissident, although there were still dissident members of most tribes who would not obey their sheikhs and were to be a constant source of trouble and, of course, provided fertile material for external pressure. Thus, within a few weeks of the Commando's arrival up country, the unit was left with its Headquarters and one company at Thumier, one company at Dhala and the third company split between Monks Field, Cap Badge and Hotel 10 (at the head of the Wadi Rabwa).

The company at Dhala remained under command of the Dhala battalion; thus 45 Commando Group commanded from Thumier normally consisted of two Commando company groups (with Support Company elements), an infantry company group from one of the Aden battalions, an armoured car squadron, a gunner battery, a sapper field troop and a Royal Corps of Transport composite platoon. These were, on occasions, augmented by a FRA company, a Parachute Patrol Company, a Light Aircraft Flight and various sapper specialists. This was an enormous command by any standards and the strength of the Group often approached the 1,500 mark. Externally, the Royal Air Force provided Beverleys, Andovers, Twin Pioneers, Wessex and Whirlwinds for logistic support and Hunters for tactical air strikes.

Although the initial insurgency had already been broken up the dissidents still continued with their sporadic raids on our bases. The main danger was reinforcement of the rebel cause from the Yemen, which could only lead to a further deterioration. To this end 'Operation Cut' was mounted in February, 1965, by Z Company Group (Major 'Jungle' Baizley) and provided an excellent 'opening of the batting' for the year. The Company's task was to set out from Thumier on 9 February with the aim of patrolling an area some ten miles north of the Dhala Road. It was hoped that this would stop the dissidents from moving in and out of the Radfan in this region, the Jebel Shairi. Also there was believed to be a dissident base camp in the area and this too had to be located.

After six days of ambushing and observation, Z Company moved to the top of the Khuraybah Pass, six miles east of Dhala, to begin the second phase of 'Operation Cut'. It was mid-morning and as the Company clambered out of its vehicles the local FRA Company, which was picquetting the pass, reported that four dissidents had been sighted in a sangar on the route which led in to the Shairi. Major Baizley ensured that the high ground on our side of the sangar was picqueted and then sent Seven Troop (Lt Douggie Brand) forward to secure the next feature on which stood a lone house. Major Baizley takes up the story:

'I then went forward to interrogate the Arab whose house it probably was. As usual the answers were pretty vague and ambiguous. All of a sudden all hell broke loose and Seven Troop was subjected to heavy small arms and automatic fire from three groups of dissidents, probably totalling about thirty. Douggie Brand then ran up and down the firing lines of his Troop, with enemy bullets ripping up the earth and rocks behind his heels, checking the positions and giving direction orders to his men. I then ordered Eight Troop (Lt Mervyn Wheatley), forward and told them to get on higher ground, which dominated the sangars, and so cover Seven Troop. I then called for an air strike and Lt Andy Letchford came up to the front line, still under heavy fire, to control the aircraft. Andy Letchford was in a very exposed position for the whole time and his radio, just beside him, was hit twice. The rocket and cannon fire from the Hunters was most effective, destroying one dissident house completely. Naturally we had to wait some time for the strike and the fire fight continued throughout this period. The forward troops were running pretty low on ammunition and the sergeant-major, QMS Bob Smith, later Regimental Sergeant-Major of 43 Commando, made several sorties out in the open to the front line loaded with explosives. Nine Troop (Sgt J. Rudkin) probably had the most frustrating time as at the beginning of the action they were the rear Troop, in depth. Soon after I had placed them on the high ground after an exhausting climb, I had to call them back. Our only casualty was Marine Stephenson, shot in the shoulder. His story was a particularly extraordinary as he had only been with us a month out of the United Kingdom. On his first trip up country he was blown out of a truck by a mine, he then suffered a narrow escape at Paddy's Field when a blindicide rocket exploded on a wall beside him, and now "Operation Cut"! Stephenson's only remark was "When is the next plane home?!" The air strike virtually brought the engagement to a close and after it we were ordered to with-draw.'

It was confirmed later that during this encounter three dissidents had been killed and two wounded, plus a further two villagers who were aiding the dissidents. For their gallantry in this long and exposed fire fight four ranks of Z Company, including the Company Commander, were decorated.

Major Baizley was, of course, keen to press home the victory but as the initial purpose of the operation had been achieved, i.e. the destruction of a rebel stronghold, it was decided to let matters rest there. In addition this decision was influenced by political factors because on 24 February there was to be a meeting at Thumier attended by all the loyal sheikhs of the Radfan and any cause for alienation had to be avoided—a fact not easily understood by those in the front line who still had to face the live bullets whatever the background circum-stances. The Radfan tribes had already 'taken quite a beating during the campaign'* and it was hoped that this meeting

* 1965 Newsletter.

would create common ground for unity and encourage the tribes to run some of their own affairs and return to their more peaceful agricultural pursuits.

Our troops, however, in Area West, still could not afford to take any chances and during the first seven-week tour of 1965 305 night patrols were carried out by Four Five. On the surface it seemed that things were getting quieter and this intensity of operations had the effect of reducing the number of attacks on our camps and picquets.

As it so often seems in this type of guerilla warfare, in which of necessity the enemy control the tempo of activity, a respite usually covers some more sinister development. This campaign proved to be no exception and we now enter what could be termed as the third phase of operations, that in which the dissidents became more sophisticated in the methods which they used. The policy of 'hearts and minds' was really too idealistic for the people of the Radfan, who both distrusted the Federal Government in the south and were being pressurized from the Yemen and elsewhere. It was virtually impossible to check the flow of arms and supplies from the north and these were being constantly amassed by those in opposition to the loyal sheikhs. The nuisance tactics employed by the rebels were to become increasingly significant as the year wore on. Minelaying was a popular ploy and the mines themselves were of British origin (Mark V and Mark VII anti-tank mines) which had been identified as coming from the British stockpile at Tel El Kebir, taken over by the Egyptians after Suez in 1956! As one correspondent of Four Five put it, 'although it is good to know that the British mines are effective, it is more than tiresome to be the unwilling participants in this proof'.

Four Five had to take many precautions in relation to this type of warfare and as a result all tracks used in the Radfan by vehicles and all landing sites and air strips were swept for mines daily and where possible the surface was oiled to make the detection of mines easier. The Land Rovers in Aden were normally protected with some eight hundred pounds of plating beneath the engine and fuel tanks, giving protection to the driver and co-driver only. The aim of this armour plating was to deflect the blast away from the two occupants in front and therefore, with this type of vehicle, no passengers were allowed to travel in the rear. In addition all external fittings were removed and a curved roll-bar constructed over the front to prevent the passengers from being crushed.

The damage caused by mines on Land Rovers can be judged from the following extract from a Newsletter—before these modifications were introduced:

'On the way back to Aden (from an exercise on 14 January, 1965) Recce Troop Commander's vehicle was blown up on what was probably a Mark VII mine. Fortunately no one was killed, however Marine Woodford had a badly shattered leg and has since been casevaced to UK. Marine Woodham, after nearly swallowing the microphone of his radio set, has been fitted with a smart new set of front teeth and Marine James should rejoin us shortly. Lt Martin, Recce Troop Commander, having risen some twenty feet in the air, landed almost undamaged but a little shaken.'

Lt Ian Martin recovered sufficiently to be able to assist in guiding in his own casevac aircraft, but the vehicle did not fare quite so well and was adjudged to be a complete write-off. Later in 1965, in December, another mine incident occurred when the advance party was at Habilayn. A Land Rover, this time mineplated, was 'well and truly drawn and quartered', but the protective plating bulged only slightly. The passenger merely received a bruised ankle. As a result of this incident the use of Land Rovers was restricted to camp areas only.

The Bedford three-tonners, the unit's major troop and store carrying vehicles were similarly converted. Only the driver sat in the cab, surrounded by armour plating and the floor of the back was sandbagged. Because of this additional weight the load capacity was reduced to two tons or ten passengers.

To combat mine warfare, in Four Five, the team that took much of the credit was the hard-worked Assault Engineer Troop, whose job it was to search for and disarm these fearful weapons made even more dangerous by their age and, in many cases, amateurish application. It is worth recording that during the period 1964–67 no less than six members of this small Troop in the Commando received awards for the brave and painstaking manner in which they searched the tracks and rendered harmless countless numbers on mines and booby traps. Indeed four successive Senior NCO's in the Troop, Sgts McKinley, Shellard, Moon and Mayne, were honoured for this type of work, a record for any department within the unit. Cpl Ross and Marine Healey of the Assault Engineers also received awards. The danger which these men lived with for weeks on end can be judged by the fact that Sgt Moon personally destroyed four hundred mines and blinds in the course of three Radfan tours and Cpl Ross, during one incident, had to methodically disarm a booby trap hidden in a vehicle in the full knowledge that it was timed to blow up at any second. The contribution of the other Troops of Support Company (commanded by Capt John Hardy since October, 1964) is also noteworthy. We have already heard how the heavy Vickers machine guns often had to be man-handled over this most atrocious terrain to be brought into action to give covering fire. The mortars too were a considerable load and the accuracy of their precision-trained crews was a byword in the Commando. In one incident Sgt Eric Blyth,* 'forever eagle-eyed', spotted a group of dissidents from an observation post and directed mortar fire right into the middle of them before they even had time to begin their own attack.

The dissidents' first serious assault, in this third phase of the Radfan campaign, on one of the unit's positions occurred in May, 1965, at Ad Dimnah, which at the time was the home of X Company (Major Bob Campbell) and Recce Troop (Lt Chris Ledger). Ad Dimnah was a deserted village on a hill just off the road, about eight miles south of Dhala overlooked by the mass of the Jebel Shairi 2,000 feet above. In this village there were some eighty houses of various shapes and sizes made of

* Sgt Blyth served with Four Five in the Malayan campaign and received a Certificate of Commendation.

stone blocks cemented with camel dung and roofed with tree branches and earth. This site had been occupied shortly after 'Operation Cut' and the position was now being used to patrol the Shairi tribal area in order to retain stability there. By now the tribe had surrendered to government terms and had given up its quota of hostages for good behaviour. The attack, a reprisal for Four Five's successful sorties in the region, was the first serious one launched with mortars, several bombs scoring direct hits on the location. The situation was made even more dangerous by the somewhat precarious manufacture of some of the surrounding buildings. Once the dust had subsided three casualties were brought out of the wreckage, Lt Alastair Grant and Marine David Muir, both badly wounded, and Cpl Dean, hit by splinters. The attack could not have come at a worse time as it was just before dusk so that by the time a rescue Naval Wessex helicopter had arrived total darkness had fallen. Undaunted, the pilot, Lt-Cdr John Rawlins, daringly landed guided only by torchlight from the anxious troops on the ground and remained there for twenty minutes under sporadic rifle fire, luckily without damage. Although this swift response helped to save the life of Lt Grant, Marine Muir unfortunately died from his wounds a month later.

Habilayn, throughout these months continued to be the main base for operations and always had a defence company of Four Five during the units' tours. The camp, now with somewhat improved amenities, had been renamed Habilayn after Habil Habilayn, a small hill near the camp on which stood the political officer's house and the new palace being built for the Emir of Dhala's brother who, it was planned, was to become Ruler of Radfan. The name Thumier was that of a local Qutaibi village in which there was a small FNG fort. As the Qutaibi were the leasted liked and historically the least reliable of all the Radfan tribes it was felt that any seat of government bearing a Qutaibi name was doomed. Despite the change of name, Habilayn never became the formal seat of Radfan government due to the British Government's announcement that the British Base was being given up.

To add a bit of colour to the sandbagged surroundings one of the visitors to Habilayn was Miss Muriel Hallam of the Women's Voluntary Service, a popular figure in the Commando's rest room at Little Aden. Miss Hallam had stalwartly spent three days in the operational area visiting the locations and taking orders for flowers and cards to send home to gratify the 'love-lorn'. She was reported to have 'gone round the picquets by Land Rover to boost the morale of the lads out on the limb and the cheery greetings which she received everywhere were proof enough of how much her visit was appreciated.'

Returning to operations, despite the improvement in rebel techniques, the security forces were gaining the upper hand in military confrontations. Figures released between March and October, 1965, show that sixty-seven dissidents were killed, ninety-five wounded and fifty-nine surrendered out of an estimated hard core of 450. Morale and leadership amongst the opposition was reported to be low, although this state of affairs was not to last for long, especially as the dissident was only paid £7.50 a month. The pattern for our troops in the Radfan was now becoming more regularized not necessarily headline making stuff, but nevertheless vital in containing the troubles. On the command side Headquarters Area West moved to Dhala in late 1965 and early in the following year Lt-Col Robin McGarel Groves took over as commander, being seconded to the FRA, for about a month whilst command changed.

The tempo of life, however apparently regular on the surface, could never slacken up country. In December, 1965 and January, 1966, there were twenty-six reported incidents, including the detection of five mines, in the Radfan and Dhala areas. One member of the security forces and eleven civilians were killed during this period. Eight of these died on 3 December, when a house in Dhala was partly destroyed by a dissident-inspired explosion. Information was by now beginning to creep in, but contacts were rare. Recce Troop (Lt Sandy Lade) on the night of 11 January thought that their big moment had come when movement was heard ahead of an ambush patrol. Fire was rapidly brought down by everyone, but all there was to show for their troubles was a bullet-ridden cow! A week later Y Company (Major David Quested) despatched a curfew breaker who walked into an ambush position at Habilayn. Z Company (Major James Clarke) up at Dhala had perhaps the busiest time, with over eight shooting incidents, however this did not prevent the Emir from presenting the Company with a sacrificial bull for Christmas! The favours shown by the Emir to our troops brought disapproval from the dissidents as they fired on him both on Christmas Eve, whilst he was visiting Dhala camp, and then at his palace the following day.

A frequent visitor up country, was the Commander-in-Chief, Admiral Sir Michael Le Fanu. On one of his visits in January, 1966, he accompanied Commando Headquarters during part of 'Operation Stag's Head', and later, in April, stayed with X Company in Dhala overnight. His crowded tour included tea with the Mortar section, dinner with the officers, a visit to the sentry sangars, coffee with the patrol returning at midnight and finally breakfast with the Senior NCOs before departing by air. Another visitor in early 1966 was Major-General P. W. C. Hellings, Chief of Staff to the Commandant-General,* and the opportunity was taken of getting him to present on behalf of the unit a silver statuette of a Commando to Brigadier C. G. T. Viner, Commander FRA, to mark six years of close co-operation between Four Five and the FRA in the Dhala area. Brigadier Viner, in return, presented the Commando with a statuette of a FRA soldier which now serves as a permanent reminder within the unit of this association.

By now Brian Somerfield had taken over as Political Adviser at Dhala and Godfrey Meynell, an old friend for many years at Dhala, had become Political Adviser at Habilayn. The latter had joined the Corps in the same batch as Major Rod Tuck (Support Company) but had been invalided out later on. Obviously completely recovered he appeared to make it his

---

* Later to succeed General Sir Norman Tailyour as Commandant-General.

business to walk any member of the Commando off his feet, and anyone accompanying Godfrey Meynell on one of his patrols to the outlying parts of his parish was reminded forcibly of the thirty-mile speed march of his Commando course!

The overall command of the situation by the security forces gave added confidence to the local troops and it was now pleasing to see the latter featuring more and more prominently. On 19 December, 1965, a Tribal Guard surprised six Yemeni setting up a light mortar off the Danaba Basin. The Yemeni promptly fled, leaving the primed bombs behind. A few days later a force under Major Rod Tuck moved into the Wadi Taym to secure a patrol base for Y Company. The help of the Ibdali Tribal Guard was also enlisted for this operation. That night a large dissident force attacked the patrol base, injuring Marine Atter of Support Company. As the dissidents withdrew the Tribal Guard took up the battle to hasten the formers' departure. Y Company (Major David Quested) faced a further two days of harassment until Hunter air strikes finally dispersed the rebels, killing one and wounding many more. On this occasion the dissidents were some 200 strong, but were later reported to have lost face considerably due to the open support given by the Ibdali and their failure to drive us out. The episode did not end there, however, because, as a reprisal, the house of the Ibdali sheikh was attacked on 9 January, 1966, fortunately with little damage.

It was now becoming apparent, judging by the size of the last dissident force mentioned, that hopes of peace were unlikely to be fulfilled. These words of a correspondent of Four Five more than adequately sum up the thoughts of those in the Radfan at the time.*

'Each move (up country) is easier because it has been done so many times before. You learn what is possible and what is not. You learn how to be reasonably comfortable and, above all, you become more and more philosophical about the hopelessly involved political and military situation in the up

* *Globe and Laurel*, 1966.

country states. Time passes and things do not really change much. Just when you think a pattern of dissident activity is forming, it stops. For a week or two there is a lull then some outpost takes a hammering or a vehicle goes up on a mine. Most of us take it in our stride now and when not actively soldiering make the most of the countryside and all it has to offer. The mountains tower up, magnificent and formidable, ridge upon ridge, to 7,000 feet. The heavy summer rains over thousands of years have eroded their sides and formed steep wadis. Even in the highest wadis the tribespeople scratch out a living, terracing their little fields like giant staircases and diverting the precious water into them whenever it rains.

In the lower parts the Arabs are less poor. The basins contain better soil and the fields are larger. Goat-herds wander aimlessly over the thorny, rock-strewn hills. The caravans of thirty or forty camels with their loads perfectly balanced on their flanks saunter up the Wadi Rabwa from Habilayn taking kerosene, timber, tinned food and cement to the Ibdali, Bana and Jaffa countries. A lad leads them, each camel's headrope tied to the tail of the one in front, and an old man follows on a donkey. At one check point the marine at the camel picquet jokes with the boy and passes a mine detector over the loads. It brightens the day, even though nothing suspicious is found. Not that anyone particularly wants to find anything suspicious. When you live very close to nature for long you develop a sympathy for the natives who are living similar lives to your own. Despite their scruffiness, despite their roguish nature, the Arabian tribesman has such a personality that he endears himself to even the hardest of hearts . . .'

An interesting backcloth to 1966, in which the pattern (if we now dare call it that!) of dissident activity increased alarmingly. In April a six-ton roller and excavator were blown up south of Al Milah. The *chowkidars* who were guarding this plant, were, of course, overcome by 'hordes of dissidents'. Y Company were at this time based at Al Milah camp, some four miles

south of Habilayn on the Dhala road. Their task was to look
after the Engineer Camp and picquet the sections of road still
under construction, which was being extensively used for the
re-supply of military forces as well as by civilian traffic.
Another new road was already under construction into the Wadi
Taym, from Habilayn. The job of rebuilding the Dhala road,
however, had almost been finished and much of the credit for
this achievement was due to 48 and 73 Squadrons, Royal
Engineers, based at Al Milah, who had to work under the
most appalling conditions of climate as well as being sniped at.
To add to their difficulties their home, Engineer Camp, was
reported to have had the heaviest bombardment record by
night of any Radfan location. Dhala too came under close
scrutiny and this situation report of April gives some indication
of the size of the dissident threat facing our men:

> 'Sitrep as at 292350C DHALA. FRA AND BR CAMPS
> CAME UNDER FIRE FOR 20 MINS. EN APPROX 40
> STRONG FIRED SA AND LT MOR FROM POSNS 500
> YDS TO NORTH WEST. TWO BLINDICIDE LANDED
> ON TEMPLE HILL CMM ONE 60 MM BOMB LANDED
> IN TENT IN CDO CAMP CAUSING DAMAGE BUT
> NO CAS. FIRE RETURNED WITH SA, ARTY, MOR,
> SALADIN, WOMBAT AND MMG.'

Luckily all the occupants of the tent, which was completely
wrecked were on guard in their sangar at the time.

May was to be the end of a busy twenty months for Lt-Col
McGarel Groves, for in that month he handed over to Lt-Col
F. C. E. Bye. Lt-Col McGarel Groves, his predecessor,
Lt-Col Stevens and Lt-Col Bye were all to receive the OBE
for their respective periods in command of Four Five, testimony of their outstanding work and leadership in these action-
packed years.

As 1966 progressed, there began the phase where serious
trouble was spreading beyond the Radfan and, in fact, incident
figures in this region were down on the previous year. In
February, 1966, Britain had already announced its intention of

granting independence to South Arabia and the emphasis of violence shifted from the hills to Aden State, ably supported, of course, by Cairo and Sanaa. This move of terrorist activity largely dictated Four Five's deployment and the length of I.S. tours in Aden itself grew considerably. Despite Britain's declared intentions the Habilayn camp became more sophisticated as a base. The whole complex was growing in size—it was even said that 'the tarmac road was built solely to supply the garrison and the sappers building it'. The camps had £13,500 spent on them to install a complete electrical wiring system—but such was the new demand that the generators could not cope, and failures became quite common! It seems to be the wont of British Forces to begin to think of withdrawing soon after the implementation of comprehensive improvement plans.

There was only one Radfan tour during the latter part of 1966, but like its predecessors, it was not noteworthy for its lack of excitement. The expansion in size of rebel gangs was still much in evidence and X Company (Major Donald Brewster) found itself with a lot on its plate in the Wadi Taym. This was mainly sparked off by the continuance of the private feud being carried out by the loyal Ibdali tribe against the dissident group known as the Wadi Bana gang. At times this loyalty seemed to stretch a bit too far as the Ibdali took matters into their own hands and started to build their own fort at the eastern end of the Taym, and on occasions resented interference from either side.

The first incidents involving X Company occurred on the nights of October 13 and 14, when Table Top was attacked by enemy mortar, blindicide, automatic and rifle fire. At one stage Major Brewster found that as one attack was being mounted to the front, another force was forming up in the rear. The mortar control officer, Sgt Peter Littlewood, despite receiving a direct blindicide hit on his position, switched aim of his guns through 180 degrees with commendable speed, and with the customary accuracy of the Mortar Troop. This swift action scored a bull's-eye which despatched the leader of the Wadi Bana gang and wounded five others. Three weeks later X Company, on 'Operation Cast Iron' in the Taym, was attacked in a similar manner on two more occasions. Again Sgt Littlewood excelled in his duties. Cpl Patrick McGuigan, the other fire controller, was out in front on the night of 5 November, an appropriate time, it seems, for such an action. The rifle section that McGuigan was out with was caught under heavy fire, but he managed to control a shoot which inflicted one kill and two other casualties. Major Brewster was later awarded the Military Cross and both Sgt Littlewood and Cpl McGuigan received Military Medals for the brave part which they played in these encounters.

Supporting these two operations was a detachment of 79 (Kirkee) Commando Light Battery, Royal Artillery, with their 105 mm. pack-howitzers—firing their guns in anger for the first time with Four Five. This was to be the beginning of a long association with the Commando Gunners, Commando trained at Lympstone, who were to support Four Five on many subsequent operations and deployments. In the first of Major Brewster's encounters Sgt Austin, Royal Artillery, was awarded the Military Medal for his gallant contribution. Like his comrades he was under heavy fire but he did not allow this to detract from his primary duty, that of directing his 105 mm. pack-howitzer. The rebels had moved right up to the position during one attack and Sgt Austin brought his gun into action at point-blank range with only millimetres clearance above the stone sangar in which it was emplaced.

It is also of interest to note that the Royal Marines Reserve,* as part of their annual training attached to overseas units of the Corps, served on occasions with Four Five in the Radfan. Lt Mark Hatt-Cook RMR (London) later reported 'six officers were attached to the Commando in South Arabia, and of these three qualified for the award of the General Service Medal.† I spent six weeks with Four Five—Dhala, Habilayn and acclimatization and I.S. in Aden. This attachment was

* Formerly RMFVR.
† Twenty-one days in the active service zone, in the case of Aden.

conspicuous for the enormous hospitality and tolerance of all members of the Commando'.

The pattern of operations continued for the penultimate tour of 1967. In these six weeks of February and March, Four Five carried out sixty-six patrols, mostly under the title of a series of operations named 'Bulkhead'. These were directed against five known gangs of dissidents. On one such operation, 'Sarie Marais II', Recce Troop was out waiting in ambush in the Wadi Dhalbir, near the village of Nuqayr in anticipation of a party of forty dissidents reported to be coming in from the Yemen, again an indication of the magnitude of the problem against these large gangs.

The first night was spent uneventfully but on the evening of 19 March, Sgt Knights, section commander of No. 2 Section, became very ill with sandfly fever. While Lt Terry Knott treated Sgt Knights, Sgt Strathdee selected a snap ambush position nearby from which it was also possible to protect the sick man. Marine Morgan was ordered to look after Sgt Knights. Lt Knott now continues with his report:

'At two forty-five hours we heard a body of men moving down the wadi below us. They had come round the bend north of Nuqayr and sounded about ten to fifteen strong. When the group drew opposite the village, the front member switched on a torch and swung it on the bank of the field below the village, as if looking for a path. The party then moved on to the field and headed for the houses. Three or four began laughing and talking and one man shouted 'Hinah'. When the party was in the middle of the field I detonated a Schmuley flare which was the signal to open fire. The Bren guns had already fired thirty rounds when the flare burst and the two 2 inch mortars manned by Sgt Strathdee* in our position, and Marine Morgan from the other, put down HE† and parachute illuminating bombs

---

* Sgt J. Strathdee was awarded a commendation for 'acting with resource and professional skill of the highest order'.

† High Explosive.

alternately. When the first flare burst, between seven and nine men were seen scattering in the field. . . . Afterwards two hayricks had very fortunately caught fire, the flares had run out, in the houses below us and provided reasonable light. I then directed artillery fire and during this time Sgt Strathdee directed the fire of the Troop in a very comprehensive and practical manner. Sgt Knights, detached on the flank with Marine Morgan *also* joined in the fire fight.'

The next morning one dead Arab was found in the bushes on the edge of the killing ground. This was the first occasion for a year in the Radfan in which the body of a dissident tribesman had been recovered. The Arab had killed himself with his own grenade when he had realized that his friends were unable to collect him. Heavy bloodstains suggested that a further two dissidents had been seriously injured.

A week later Five Troop (Lt David Parkinson) had a similar success in the Wadi Malahah. The Troop was without its Troop Sergeant, Sgt Pearson, who had been wounded by a member of another unit on the previous day whilst on a cordon and search operation—'they mistook him for an Arab (in a green beret and GP shirt!)'.* Within ten minutes of arriving in their ambush position Five Troop had a contact— the leading scouts of a larger patrol. Lt Parkinson's citation for the Commander in Chief's Commendation ended; 'throughout the patrol, Lt Parkinson displayed the highest standards of professional soldiering and calculated courage. His very difficult approach march† was achieved with complete surprise and his speedy occupation of his ambush position was most skilfully executed. The fine discipline of the patrol was most commendable. Finally he prevented the removal of the body and thus struck a great blow to the enemy's morale'.

Thus we see how the Commando, in spite of the increased size and determination of the oppostion, notched up several kills and seriously disrupted the enemy's plans and aspirations.

* *Globe and Laurel*, June, 1968.
† This march took three and a half hours.

Even as Four Five left the Radfan, on 27 March, at the end of the twelfth tour the dissidents still seemed to have something in store and a group of ten ambushed the down convoy about fifteen miles south of Habilayn. Reaction was swift and a Scout helicopter armed with GPMGs went into the attack whilst other helicopters lifted picquets on to the surrounding high ground.

Undoubtedly the last tour up country proved to be the most dramatic and heralded the final phase of operations— that in which serious troubles broke out in Aden and the repercussions spread throughout the country. The entire tour fought against a backcloth of the Arab–Israeli War and the mutinies within the South Arabian Army in Aden which had begun on 19 June. On 1 June the FRA and FNG had been reorganized into the South Arabian Army and South Arabian Police respectively and already had taken over bigger responsibilities in Dhala and Habilayn, and thus Four Five's role became more defensive, but still with an emphasis on quick reaction mobile operations. We will hear later of some of the fast-moving operations which the Commando successfully carried out. These were planned with the wealth of experience gained on previous tours which was gathered together by the unit for a pre-tour symposium held in Little Aden, and a resumé of this study was then issued to all commanders. This study paid great dividends and is a typical example of the operational expertize which had been accumulated at this time and which will, with certainty, be passed on to future generations.

The speed of response, so typical of the Commando in modern warfare, and the techniques that were perfected, can be judged from the following accounts of two of the eight major operations that were mounted from Habilayn. Operation 'Vanguard V' was an example of the 'crash action' system in force at the time. Early on the morning of 30 May, 1967, a NAAFI truck which was heading north was halted some fifteen miles south of Habilayn near the Wadi Bilah and the staff forced to get out. The dissidents then built up a barricade of beer crates across the road and at eight-twelve a.m. halted a convoy of 39 Field Squadron, Royal Engineers. A Saracen, one of the leading vehicles, was hit by a blindicide and two men killed and ten injured. The emergency alarm signal was raised at Habilayn at eight thirty-three—the delay was due to the fact that radios in the leading vehicles had been hit by fire, and other factors. Within five minutes of the alarm the unit Sioux, piloted by Lt Ian Uzzell, was airborne with a Forward Air Controller (2/Lt John Meardon) and within fifteen minutes Recce Troop had been despatched in a Wessex and a Scout. At this stage Hunters, on immediate stand-by, had arrived from Khormaksar and the Wessex and Scout orbited as salvo upon salvo of rockets ripped into the rebel hides. 2/Lt Meardon directed one very accurate attack on to a dissident position which was underneath the overhang of a steep-sided feature, an almost impossible target, and scored a direct hit. However, the Sioux, pierced by enemy fire, had to withdraw from the fray and limp back to Habilayn. After the air strikes Recce Troop was then able to land at nine forty-five—and their action is described in the citation of the Troop Commander, Lt Terry Knott, who was awarded the Military Cross for his courage:

'As the Wessex came in to hover over the landing point, it was plain that the selected site was in the middle of the enemy position. The pilot of the helicopter was unable to land owing to heavy rifle and machine gun fire. Lt Knott decided to deplane his Troop, who jumped out on to rugged and precipitous rocks whist the helicopter was still some ten to twelve feet from the ground. They immediately came under fire, not only from the enemy on whose position they had landed, but from other strong enemy supporting positions behind them on top of the Jebel Lahmahr. This ridge completely dominated the landing point. Led by Lt Knott the Troop killed one dissident on landing and then moved into a steep gully to avoid fire from the Lahmahr. As they did so a dissident emerged from a small cave and fired two rounds with an automatic rifle at Lt Knott at point blank

range. Lt Knott and one of his Troop fired back and the
dissident, having been hit, withdrew to a sangar in the cave.
Approaching the cave from the side Lt Knott threw in an
M26 grenade which the dissident picked up and threw back.
Avoiding the explosion which followed, Lt Knott, completely
regardless of his own safety, went into the cave and personally
shot the dissident dead.'

By now Major Alan Jukes who was acting commanding
officer at the time, and had taken full advantage of the situation,
took over control of the operation and Seven Troop (Lt Bob
Sankey) of Z Company had arrived on the scene by road and
occupied the enemy position which Recce Troop had captured.
Y Company (Major Ted Carroll) consisting of Five (Lt David
Parkinson) and Six (Lt John Parsons-Smith) Troops was then
sent down by road. After more air strikes at midday Y Company
was flown by Wessex on to the 800 foot high ridge and then
proceeded to scour the area for any remaining dissidents. By
three o'clock the search was virtually over. Three dissident
bodies had been recovered, two from Recce Troop's area and
one from the cave hit by the air strike. The dissidents had laid
and executed an excellent ambush but prompt and brave
reaction from Four Five had put the rebels to flight. Three
bodies were recovered and later reports indicated that a further
two more were killed and others wounded. An SLR carried
by one of the dissidents despatched by Recce Troop had
belonged to a Gunner of the Royal Horse Artillery who had
died in a helicopter crash in the region during the previous
December. Y Company had been sent from Little Aden, after
this accident, to assist in the search for the Sioux.

The second of these textbook operations was on 17 June,
1967, and was later code-named 'Vanguard VI'. It was policy
at the time to have observation posts scattered some distance
outside the perimeter of Habilayn to give early warning of
impending dissident attacks or other movement. At four forty-
five on the evening of the 17th a Special Air Service observation
post reported three armed dissidents in the Wadi Bilah, about

24. General Sir Norman Tailyour with officers of Four Five shortly before his retirement as Commandant-General, Royal Marines. October, 1968.

25. HM The Queen presents new Colours to Four Five at Plymouth Guildhall, 13 May, 1969. Her Majesty is accompanied by the Commandant-General, Lieutenant-General Hellings, and Lt-Col Roger Ephraums.

26. *The Earl Mountbatten of Burma with the 'Arctic Commandos'.*
Stonehouse, 23 June, 1970.

27. *The northern flank of NATO. Four Five proves its versatility during*
an exercise in Norway in early 1970.

fifteen miles south west of Habilayn. Within ten minutes the fully kitted stand-by Troop, Nine Troop (Lt Phil Robinson), was embarking in Wessex prior to heading for the scene of the sighting. Z Company Commander, Major Brian Edwards, was airborne in an armed Scout controlling the deployment and giving last minute orders. Between five-ten and five-twenty— half an hour after the initial alert, Nine Troop started to land. The Troop Sergeant, Sgt John French, takes up the story:

'We leapt out of the choppers, having placed out two picquets—in case they tried to run away—and as we got out we saw the three men dashing up a low hill about two hundred yards away. One stopped and fired at us. We were right out in the open and as there was such a din going on I blew my whistle and told the lads to adopt the kneeling position for firing. This they did and two dissidents were killed outright, a great achievement as it is a most difficult position to fire from. The third ran over the crest of the hill slap into the picquet commanded by Cpl Mc-Laughlin, and was shot at thirty yards range. Throughout the entire engagement only eighty rounds were expended, a fantastically small amount for three kills.'

At half-past five, Nine Troop re-embarked in the Wessex and by five fifty-two they were back in Habilayn with three dead dissidents—a simple story of outstanding efficiency.

This was the last occasion on which Four Five was to be able to show its outward aggressiveness in the Radfan. Much of the remainder of the time was spent in defence and for the last few days the unit was literally fighting a rearguard action. Nevertheless militarily the Commando came out of these skirmishes on the winning side and it was estimated that during these last six weeks some twenty-four dissidents had been accounted for by Four Five plus sixteen wounded. The Commando only suffered two casualties as the direct result of enemy action in this period. Many of the dissident casualties were inflicted by our friends the mortars and the Support Troop attached to Y Company deserves particular mention.

13

On operation 'Vanguard IV', between 26 and 29 May, the Troop, commanded by Lt Ian Binnie, killed two and wounded four when the Y Company patrol base camp in the Wadi Taym came under heavy attack. The troop also despatched four dissidents and wounded seven others during harassing shoots from Habilayn in this period. The Mortar section, Sgt Peter Kennedy, with Cpl Francis Brewer and Marine Bernard Quinn were all Mentioned in Despatches for their courage and skill in attaining these results.

Although the move south was expected later in the month, no definite dates had been fixed. The first base to 'fall under the axe', so to speak, was Dhala and here the news was definitely a surprise. Dhala Camp had been under heavy fire now for a long period and all the accommodation was given thick over-head sandbag protection so that the general appearance was that of a strong defensive position during World War I rather than a frontier cantonment. Some seven dissidents had already been killed by X Company group (Major Donald Brewster) outside the perimeter and by 9 June a gang of thirty rebels was keeping the camp under constant surveillance. It was considered that the presence of British troops in Dhala was only aggravating the situation, and in any case X Company was needed for another task in trouble-torn Aden. The Company was to come under command of the 1st Battalion the Argyll and Sutherland Highlanders and to hold the perimeter of Crater in the area of Main Pass before the much publicized re-entry of British troops into the town. On Sunday, 11 June, therefore, X Company was ordered to withdraw from Dhala on the following morning. Secrecy for this sudden move had to be maintained and the ranks were not told of the plan until seven o'clock that Sunday evening.

That night, as the men packed their kit and loaded the three-ton trucks in the darkness, a Shackleton flew over the nearby jebel dropping flares to dissuade the dissidents from forming up for an attack. This procedure for ground-control flare-dropping by Shackletons had already been used successfully on several previous occasions at Habilayn. The men in Commando Camp worked feverishly, with the unreal glare silhouetting the jagged mountains in the background, and as the Shackleton droned into the distance the enemy mortars opened up. The picquet on nearby Temple Hill was hit six times and another bomb hit a half-empty drum of aviation fuel, which then burned furiously, now silhouetting our own camp. X Company's mortars opened up and killed two dissidents. When dawn broke the cover plan was put into operation. The civil labour, often the first outsiders to know of a move, clocked in for work as usual, and were temporarily detained. Kitbags and packs were loaded on to a 'routine' convoy from Habilayn. The remainder of X Company then moved out of the camp in two groups, in small arms order, as if to carry out routine clearing patrols. These 'patrols' conventionally ended near the airstrip where a Beverley was waiting to fly the Company down to Aden. Surprise had been complete both in the eyes of the dissidents and in the minds of the local population.

By 20 June, 1967, all engineer work in the Radfan had been completed and it was time to begin the withdrawal of the British Troops in the Habilayn Garrison, of which Four Five was the major infantry unit. Z Company left Aden on the 21st but even its departure was contested. The Beverley flying them down country hit a mine on the end of the Habilayn airstrip and was extensively damaged. Wessex helicopters from Khormaksar had to complete the lift.

The remainder of the relief now hinged on the 9th Battalion South Arabian Army, still deployed in Aden. It was hoped to complete the change-over by 24 June, but the Beverley setback and the strife in Aden forced the issue and the date had to be put back to the 26th.

The end was now really in sight and after more than three years the last phase of a memorable campaign was drawing to a close. The optimists probably considered that the end might have come in 1965 with everyone living together in harmony and returning to their fields. Pressures from outside and age-long tribal differences ensured that the fighting did not end then and it was to be another two years before we could turn our backs on the mountains. Even then, it was just a question of holding on until the politicians released us and no really conclusive settlement had been reached. For Four Five, however, these years had not been wasted, and they were to bring out again the qualities that are latent in the majority of us. Successful tactics were evolved and the type of operations provided tough and constructive military experience for ranks at all levels, especially the junior commander. The courage of the Commando again proved to be outstanding—as is shown by the thirty-seven awards for gallantry in the Radfan and Dhala. Politics, as is right, were the master, and a longer stay would have served no purpose. The time had come to depart. It was fitting that Four Five, after its long association with the Radfan, should have been the last major British unit to leave.

As midday approached on 26 June, 1967, the convoy of 108 vehicles moved slowly out of Habilayn camp. In the background, as the men gazed wistfully at the mountains, the Beverley still lay awkwardly tipped up on its side, a reminder of the ever present threat.

'1130. Command handed over to 9th Battalion South Arabian Army.'*

All that could be seen now was a long line of trucks moving at twenty-five mph down the thin ribbon of tarmac which had been constructed so painstakingly and defended at such cost over these last few years. As the vehicles crawled away into the haze and dust of the desert below many hearts still lingered in the grandeur of this inhospitable land. We hope it was the respect of the dissidents for their adversaries that led these proud warriors of the Radfan not to exact a toll from the last convoy.

* Unit Battle Log, 26 June, 1967.

CHAPTER 17

Aden IV—Internal Security and the Withdrawal

It would be a bold understatement to merely describe the last three years in Aden for Four Five as a 'busy period of operational activity'. In addition to having thirteen operational tours in the Radfan, after November, 1964, the Commando found itself fully immersed in helping to combat the terrorism which had plunged the State of Aden into disorder. This continual change round from Internal Security to more conventional operations meant that the Commando had to rapidly adapt to new environments. However, it was readily agreed by the majority that it was always preferable to go up to the relative cool of the mountains away from the humidity, squalor and intrigue of the backstreets of Aden, although the chances of being shot at were about even! Possibly the greatest strain imposed by these continuous moves and redeployments was upon the administrative and command elements of Four Five. Any change of location nowadays is always accompanied by a seemingly growing amount of paperwork. In addition, orders would have to be produced, plans for future operations made and any specialized training carried out that might be fitted in. All this would have to be done whilst the unit was still facing an armed enemy and coping with everyday incidents. A move to another area, where new problems faced the command team, also meant the compilation of copious returns and reports of results achieved on the previous tour—an unending but apparently necessary chore.

The background events and political problems which led up to the terrorism in Aden State are long and complicated and space will only permit a brief summary here, with mention of the main terrorist factions involved and the major events. The bomb outrage at Khormaksar Airport on 10 December, 1963,* had been a warning of things to come, but for the larger part of 1964 the military effort in Aden had been directed against the dissident Radfan tribesmen. This did not mean that discontent was not fermenting in Aden State. On the contrary, although there were no notable incidents, various nationalist organizations were plotting behind the scenes to hasten the British departure and subsequently install their brand of politics. Sympathy, encouragement and material aid for these causes was readily forthcoming from the United Arab Republic. 'We in 45 Commando find ourselves surrounded by intrigue and political philanderings whilst steadily pursuing the aims of our presence here, namely, the protection of British lives and property, and our pledged support of the lawful Administration and the National Security Forces, until such time as we depart . . .'†

In order to put activities in Aden State into their true perspective let us take a brief look at the three main nationalist organizations whose aims, by some means or other, were basically to oust the British and form some state either fully independent or with strong leanings towards Egypt. In the true spirit of South Arabia the development of these groups was both complicated, and at times, illogical. It is hoped that this summary will give some idea of how difficult it was for our forces to identify the foe and for intelligence to unravel the puzzle of allegiances.

The mildest of the organizations was, perhaps, the South Arabian League (SAL) which was founded in 1951 and based on Lahej. The aim of the party was to promote a state of South

* See p. 288.
† December, 1966, Newsletter.

Arabia, separate from the Yemen. This cause attracted active support from the merchant classes, but the impetus began to dwindle as the Trades Unions gained more power in the early sixties.

The two 'giants' were the now-famous National Liberation Front (NLF) and the Front for the Liberation of Occupied South Yemen (FLOSY), whose initials were crudely daubed on walls all over Aden. The NLF had a reasonably straightforward development, being formed in June, 1963, with the express aims of forcing the British out and establishing a government compatible with Egyptian ambition. This view was to change later. From the outset it was by far the most militant body and its terrorist side was reputed to be well organized, the various groups being divided up into cells, as in Cyprus. Its strength was also enhanced by the infiltration of various official departments and bodies, especially the police. From the very outset of its activities in Aden the NLF seemed to place an increased emphasis on gaining its ends by terrorist rather than political methods.

The career of FLOSY, by comparison, was far more chequered. FLOSY grew out of a union between SAL and the Peoples Socialist Party (PSP) in February, 1965, and at that time was known as the Organization for the Liberation of the Occupied South (OLOS). Its ideals were based on the concept that Aden was part of the South Yemen, but unlike NLF was opposed to violence. OLOS then moved its headquarters over to the Yemen and in January, 1966, after Egyptian pressure had been brought to bear, linked up with the NLF to form FLOSY. This union lasted less than a year. SAL, which had also joined the combine, soon faded off the scene, leaving the NLF and the OLOS 'old school' to continue the struggle. The Egyptian pipedream of a united terrorist body was found to be impracticable. NLF were reluctant to accept too much control from Cairo, whilst FLOSY, on the other hand, were fully committed to Egyptian domination and if in power would have been regarded as a puppet government. The last year in Aden for the British was, therefore, dominated by a power struggle between the militant NLF and the more moderate FLOSY. The Egyptians stepped in during this phase as well. In order to boost up their chances with FLOSY they injected a hard-core group known as the Popular Organization of Revolutionary Forces (PORF). The outcome of all this wrangling behind the scenes was that in the latter stages the majority of terrorist attacks on Security Forces in Aden came from the NLF with PORF coming into prominence in September, 1967, to fight the NLF on behalf of FLOSY!

Let us, then, return to 1964 before the serious outbreak of terrorism had broken out in Aden State. The Nationalists had already claimed that 'revolution' was in progress—this was declared in October, 1963, and they were looking around for a political event with which to make capital to open their militant phase. This opportunity was afforded on 6 November, 1964, when the visit to Aden of the Labour Colonial Secretary, Mr Anthony Greenwood, was announced. There were signs, however, before 6 November that trouble was brewing. Immediately on return from the Radfan (on 18 September, 1964) Four Five became IS battalion and training began in earnest in preparation for likely outbursts during the elections on 16 October. Initially it was reported that 'the Companies have shown more proficiency acting as mobs than as riot squads', but each demonstration always ended with a crashing volley and many groaning casualties—just to warn the many bemused Arab spectators (who might be reporting back to the NLF) that the unit really meant business!

The Commando was deployed prior to the elections after some minor sabotage attempts. Z Company moved into the maze of narrow streets and alleys which formed the town of Crater, so named because of its volcanic origins and its encircling ring of massive rocks. Sgt Jock Munson and the Recce Troop OPs, unseen on the clifftops, combined with Z Company for this operation and managed to pick out several terrorists which they reported to the police patrols, thus enabling surprise arrests. One or two crowds began to gather but these soon dispersed. It was rumoured, afterwards, that Major

Baizley's idea of minimum force was to take a Mobat* into
Crater, but this was hotly denied! Elsewhere in Aden X Company (temporarily Capt Paul Goodlet) was based in Sheikh
Othman—the sprawling township north of the peninsula which
became the supply and dispersal point for arms and munitions
brought in from the Yemen; and Support Company (Capt
John Hardy) guarded Government House. Y Company was up
at Dhala, but a full reserve was held in BP Camp, Little Aden,
in case troops had to be rushed to a particular trouble spot.

In the event the elections passed quietly and for forty-eight
hours the constant patrolling of the Rifle Troops and the
protection given to the polling stations seemed to pay dividends.
Not so, however, in November, when violence flared up in
earnest. As always seems the case in Internal Security operations the tempo was almost entirely controlled by the terrorists
and the security forces could only react after the initial damage
was done. In the last two months of 1964 some thirty-six
incidents were reported including the firing of a rocket launcher
near Four Five's camp in Little Aden. Fortunately the bomb
landed harmlessly on the oil-hardened surface of the football
field. This threat to safety on the 'home front' was to give an
indication of the circumstances under which the unit was to
live over the next three years. The Commando routine was
governed by the Internal Security threat and the requirement
to react to meet it, day and night, at little or no notice. Indeed,
towards the end Four Five lived in amongst the people who, it
seemed, never gave up trying to carry out acts of sabotage, to
kill each other, or to turn on the security forces as if for fun.
It was like a place gone mad, with our troops ensuring maintenance of the public and other services which in turn created
the conditions under which terrorism could thrive. The whole
tone of life during these years had a nightmare quality. Pressures
from the militant organizations had virtually rendered the
police ineffective in dealing with terrorist outrages, but ironically, the force still continued with routine business and investigated traffic offences and issued learners' licences. Many

* Anti-tank gun.

traders still kept their premises open and plied their wares to non-existent tourists. Stocks were not renewed and those used to the age old system of bartering found that prices rarely dropped. A sense of apathy was fast creeping in all round. Essential services worked, thanks to the effort of our troops, but the people did not. The docks, the former lifeline of Aden, were now closed and silent apart from the loading of military stores into ships bound for the United Kingdom, the Persian Gulf and the Far East. The remaining Britons kept going as best they could on the volcanic rock upon which, for so many years, the standards of the British way of life had been so soundly built, and which were now crumbling so quickly to sand. Even so, many of the population were unkind enough to blame the presence of our security forces (who kept them safe) for their economic plight. But we must go back in time to 1964.

Lt-Col R. J. McGarel Groves took over during November of that year and was given a warm welcome to Aden by the terrorists who, on his first night of command, exploded two large bombs within 200 yards of his residence in Ghadia (Little Aden). Lt-Col McGarel Groves' first two major operations took place in early December. Both of these proved highly successful and were mounted in the Sheikh Othman area against the arms smuggling organization. In the first of these Y Company (Capt Godfrey Seagar), in a blinding sandstorm, provided the cordon for the arrest of four suspects and a quantity of ammunition. The next week X Company (Capt Bob Campbell) captured five weapons and large supplies of ammunition in the village of Da Sa'Ad near Sheikh Othman (in Lahej State and outside Aden State territory), in an outstanding snatch which lasted barely fifteen minutes.

These steps were dwarfed later in the month by two murders which brought the grim reality of terrorist tactics out into the open. The first was the death of the sixteen-year-old daughter of a senior Royal Air Force officer (out for the Christmas holidays) after a bomb had been thrown into a quarter whilst a teenage dance was in progress. The second atrocity was on the following day (Christmas Day) when an Arab Special Branch Officer was shot in Crater. This was a prelude to the systematic elimination by the terrorists of members of the Special Branch in an attempt to shatter local confidence in the forces of law and order. This 'Black Christmas' meant a quiet one celebration-wise for Four Five, as a ban was imposed on gatherings of twelve or more people. Even so, 'each Company managed to have its own party'.

The threat was becoming widespread; cafés and bars used by servicemen, quarters, cinemas and important installations all suffered. To combat this Four Five had a duty Company deployed each night in Aden and another one standing by in Little Aden some forty minutes away by road. On the report of a bomb incident road blocks were normally set up at pre-determined spots to act as a cut-off to the terrorists, who often used cars to make fast getaways.

The unit ended 1964 in Aden with another oustanding arms raid, 'Operation Tadpole'. Mounted again in Da Sa'Ad, Sheikh Othman and Crater, some thirty-four weapons were seized with 78,000 rounds of ammunition, including many of the fearful 'dum-dum'* type of bullets. The search of Da Sa'Ad was not quite as fast this time—a large area of the village consisted of harems and only women could enter these! The haul itself probably seems incredibly large, but the existence of these arms in Da Sa'Ad was well known as this small frontier village, in Lahej State just on the Aden Colony boundary, had no less than eight arms dealers licensed by the Sultan of Lahej, and the sign outside each could be clearly seen from convoys going or returning from up country. It had been customary from early colonial days to pay rulers, sheikhs, and for that matter any one who had done the Government a service, in rifles and ammunition and these came from

* A rifle or pistol bullet with notches cut in the head (causing it to split into pieces on impact), or having the tip filed flat, causing the lead to 'mushroom', inflicting terrible wounds. A .45 bullet of this types makes a .45 entry hole and anything up to a 3-inch exit hole.

Government stocks. It was not, therefore, surprising that many of the rifles seized and about half the ammunition were of British origin. Although it was illegal to possess arms in Aden Colony it was perfectly legal to do so in the Protectorate. As every man up country carried a rifle from about the age of ten, arms were big business and a man's status could be judged by his weapon, therefore the arms dealers carried arms and ammunition from the 1860 muzzle-loader to the latest Russian sub-machine gun. 'Operation Tadpole' partly brought an end to this lunatic situation by putting the arms dealers out of business, but the ease with which the NLF and FLOSY appeared to acquire arms later showed that all that had been done was to make it more difficult for them.

Throughout 1965 the pattern of selected murders against the Special Branch and Government officials continued. Grenade and bazooka incidents increased, and although usually inaccurate their nuisance value was considerable. As Little Aden camp could have been considered a prime target all places where large numbers assembled, such as the cinema, were guarded and the long perimeter was wired in and kept out all unwanted visitors. This was effective except for the dogs, which could still squeeze through! One of the dogs, which was later to take up a more permanent residence with Four Five, was Oscar. Oscar is a black dog and could probably be described as 'mainly Labrador'. At the time when he first came on the scene, in December, 1965, he was a battered and bleeding pup, some eight months old. Oscar was taken into Z Company's (Major James Clarke) lines and nursed back to health with generous scraps smuggled out of the galley. One of the ranks who took pity on him was L/Cpl Barrie ('Noddy') Dunn who has since, on many occasions, become known as official dog handler in Four Five. Such was Dunn's attachment for Oscar that some five years later he had to request a change of posting from 41 Commando. Although the request was approved the drafting authorities added, rather testily: 'It is suggested that, in future, it would be easier to cross-post the dog, OSCAR, to 41 Commando RM, unless OSCAR is part of the 45 Commando RM Trophy Account. The necessary DORM* would be issued on request.'

Oscar's exploits were many and Dunn describes but a few. 'Up in Dhala, when the dissidents were about to attack Temple Hill, the dog barked to warn us to "stand to". Up country he also went out on village and medical patrols. Down in Aden he accompanied us on Company cordons, but his main delight was in Crater when he was kept in the back of a three-tonner and was sent out if the golly prisoners got cheeky!' In 1967, when it was time for Four Five to leave Aden, Z Company was not in a position to raise the £100 required for the return fare and six months' kennelling fees, and one marine summed up the Company's feelings, 'I think we would rather shoot Oscar than leave him behind'. The *Daily Mirror*, who described Oscar thus, 'the dog that became a hero has won a place in the hearts of the Marines, and the Nation',† stepped in and with the aid of the Public Relations Officer at the Infantry Training Centre, Lympstone, launched a public appeal. The money soon poured in and on 19 September, 1967, Oscar, having been fortunate enough to travel by BOAC, duly arrived at Heathrow Airport to be met by a battery of Press and TV cameras—a hero's welcome indeed.

Back now to the more serious duties of patrolling in Little Aden in 1965. The NLF tactics at this time consisted mainly of hit-and-run grenade attacks, and although some terrorists carried weapons these were largely confined to either the hard-core members or imported professional killers. Many of the local terrorists were pretty poorly trained with little or no practical experience. To combat these tactics and to gain the initiative we employed what is known as the mobile patrol. Every night in Little Aden, Four Five would send out patrols consisting of two Land Rovers, travelling sixty yards apart, each with six men. The GP machine gunner would stand in

* Drafting Order, Royal Marines. As an official mascot, Oscar has his own service documents, Ration Allowance and even a miniature General Service Medal for operations in Aden!

† 8 August, 1967.

the back, with his gun resting on the canopy bar, acting as sentry:

'The duty lasts from about 1800 hours to midnight, working from a base at the Little Aden Police Station with two, and sometimes three, patrols on the move in the area. It needs a resolute man to throw a grenade if he does not know whether a patrol may drive round the corner on to him. Certainly the record of only a single incident in one month points to the fact that this is a worthwhile, if individually unrewarding, policy.'*

Politically, 1965 proved to be an unsettled year in Aden. There was continuous friction between the Aden State Government and the Federal Government—regarded as a British 'puppet' by many nationalists. On 23 February, the Chief Minister had resigned and he was succeeded, on 7 March, by Abdul Mackawee, an outspoken member of the People's Socialist Party. His frequent outbursts did little to smooth the troubled water, and in fact largely encouraged the NLF cause. He was dismissed in September, 1965, and the High Commissioner (Sir Richard Turnbull) took over direct rule. In the meantime Emergency Regulations had been declared (6 June), and the spate of selected killings went on unabated. These included Supt Arthur (Harry) Barrie, a British Special Branch Officer well known to many in the unit, shot in Crater on 29 August. Three days later the Speaker of the Legislative Council, Sir Arthur Charles, was also shot. Another policeman was killed soon afterwards and a grenade thrown amongst a party of school children, about to depart to the United Kingdom, assembled at Khormaksar Airport. As a result of these incidents a curfew was put on Crater. Another curfew was placed on Ma'alla—a mile-long stretch of tall flats occupied largely by service families, and nicknamed 'murder mile'— after several more grenade incidents directed at British dependants. To help deal with these commitments Four Five had to supply a second company for guard and patrol duties in

* *Globe and Laurel*, Christmas, 1965.

'Big Aden' whilst still retaining responsibility for its home parish.

One of the Commando's trickiest tasks was to assist in the staffing of the Al Mansoura prison, which, in November, 1965, held some eighty political detainees. (The Emergency Powers enabled the High Commissioner to detain suspects without trial for up to six months). The job of the Company attached to the staff was to be deployed to prevent rescue attempts from outside. An observer in the Commando described the main hazard of the prison as 'the ever present crowd of disgruntled wailing womanhood—relatives of the detainees. They block the entrance to the prison and sometimes throw bricks. The situation is always rather tense.'

The skill, forbearance and tact of Four Five are probably best amplified by a brief study of 'Operation Wink' which took place in November, 1965. The operation was commanded by Lt-Col McGarel Groves in conjunction with the Little Aden Police (sixy ranks) under command of Supt Jack Crossley. The aim was to cordon and search the Arab village of Al Kheisa in Little Aden, thought to be a refuge of NLF terrorists. Four scout cars and military police were included in the force, plus Gemini raiding craft to patrol and seal off the coastline. The village, which had been built by BP to replace one displaced during the building of the Little Aden refinery, consisted of long rows of symmetrical huts spread out in the baking sand. The cordon and cage were speedily placed out before dawn and at seven o'clock screening of all the male population between fifteen and fifty years of age (a total of 635) began. The men were led in front of Land Rovers, in which informers were hidden, five at a time, and several suspects were picked out. As local nationals were beginning to come forward too it was hoped not to antagonize the populace and Four Five's motto for the day was 'firmness with a smile'—a particularly apt one which could be applied to many of its deeds throughout the years. However, the unit's kindness was not really appreciated at first especially when the victualling staff arrived with urns of tea to give to those waiting in the cage. This act was regarded with hostility and suspicion by some of the Arabs, but the ice was soon broken and eventually the dissenters somewhat sheepishly shuffled up to join the ever growing queues, whilst the guards of Four Five just watched impassively with their fixed bayonets. As a footnote to 'Wink', and to show that there was no ill-feeling, Four Five played Al Kheisa at football a few days later, on the soccer pitch that had previously been the cage, and diplomatically held the village team to a three-all draw.

The pattern of operations in Aden State up to 1965 had been mainly small preventative patrols, the setting up of routine and snap road blocks and cordons and searches based on all-too-infrequent information. This action had been sufficient to combat the terrorist-inspired incidents so far, but in the following years, when the figures rose alarmingly,* more ambitious measures and tactics had to be adopted. For the Commando these first two years or so of Internal Security, apart from unit cordons or major deployments, had largely consisted of innumerable small patrols and tedious guard duties in the oppressive and unrelenting heat. Each Company, Troop or Section undoubtedly had its own story to relate. In brief, however, the type of activities carried out by the Commando as a whole at this time are well summarized in a *Globe and Laurel* article:

> 'We've maintained a guard over an open air cinema and heard the audience applauding a newsreel about Nasser. We've hidden down a side street, ready in the background to protect a policeman due to meet an informer. We've guarded families† and had to comfort a boy of six left alone

* IS incidents in Aden State: 1964, thirty-six; 1965, 286; 1966, 480; 1967, 2,908 (approx).

† Four Five was an 'unaccompanied' unit for its seven years in Aden and for men away from their homes this was not always a popular task especially as Service dependants were often the targets for terrorists' grenades. 'The announcement that no more families will be arriving after December, 1966, should relieve some of the strain on IS tasks. The Service dependants are the prime cause of the Security Forces being overstretched. . . ." (*Globe and Laurel*, August, 1966).

in a house while his parents went out to a party. We've cordoned and searched houses, and picked up leaflets scattered by terrorists in the streets. And we've worked side by side with Military Police on Checkpoint Delta at the Little Aden end of the Causeway.'

The political haggling over the fate of South Arabia throughout 1966 gave renewed vigour to the terrorist cause, especially as the end, for them, was coming into sight. As experienced up country, they pressed home their claims using a greater sophistication of weapons and with more success than hitherto had been experienced. The situation in the Radfan had quietened considerably and when Lt-Col Bye assumed command in May, 1966, the first news he was able to give Four Five, assembled in BP Camp, was that the role of the unit was beginning to change and that in future more time was going to be spent on Internal Security than had been the custom in the past.

The Defence White Paper of February, 1966, announced that South Arabia would become Independent by 1968; 'two more generations of Marines in 45 Commando will have to sweat it out in the sand and the heat before the last British battalions leave, and their barracks turn into squatting places for Arabs and their livestock'.* So for the next two years in Aden our troops were to undertake the thankless and dangerous task of keeping peace in a hostile land, knowing that death or serious injury might confront them at any moment in a cause that had already been given up as lost by their political masters.

During the first three weeks of February, Four Five had the responsibility of Little Aden, and its vigilance resulted in only one minor incident. On the 22nd the Defence White Paper came out and on the 27th the Commando foud itself responsible for the northern half of the Aden peninsula (Ma'alla, the Crescent shopping area and Steamer Point). Ironically, the newly formed FLOSY chose the 27th as the date to begin its spring offensive and started off in fine style with a spate of

* *Globe and Laurel*, June, 1966.

accurate grenade attacks. One of the most dramatic of these incidents was on 1 March. A quarter-ton vehicle driven by Cpl Farlie was on a mobile patrol at about seven in the evening. It was dark, and the vehicle was making a sharp turn moving into a backstreet in the maze of buildings behind the Crescent. The other three passengers were all members of the Intelligence Section, which proves that even members of Headquarters can find themselves right in the front line. Lt Andy Moreland, the Intelligence Officer, was sitting in the front and Marines Gordon Griffin and David Surridge (radio operator) were in the back. Griffin continues with the story:

'Soon after we rounded the corner I heard something hit the tailboard of the vehicle. I looked down and saw that it was a 36 grenade which was smoking.* I kicked it out of the back and shouted "Grenade". Surridge, who was watching the roofs, dived for the floor. I hung over the side for protection. Cpl Farlie jammed hard down on the accelerator and the truck lurched forward. The grenade rolled away and exploded in front of a crowd of local nationals milling on the pavement outside a couple of cafés.'

This reaction on the part of the patrol undoubtedly saved their lives. But the locals were less fortunate, nineteen were injured and, as was often the case, FLOSY inflicted more harm on its own supporters than on its opponents. The scene was a chaotic one. The relatively peaceful street of minutes ago was now a mass of screaming Arabs and Somalis with the Marines crouched in positions of defence around their vehicle. Lt Moreland bravely moved forward, despite the fact that the attacker might still be lurking nearby, and administered first aid to the more seriously wounded. Most of those injured were later interviewed but the majority conveniently had their backs to the street and 'saw nothing'. It was yet another case of 'investigation closed'.

* Four seconds elapse between the removal of the safety pin and the explosion of the grenade.

The following night Lt Andy Moreland was again in action. The same area was being cordoned in a search for the grenade thrower—without result. It was nearly eight-thirty and the cordon was being withdrawn. As the Marines were moving towards their trucks a party of children approached, jeering and cat-calling. These were, in fact, being used in the most cowardly manner as a 'front' for a grenade thrower lurking behind. The grenade landed six feet away and exploded as Lt Moreland shouted a warning. Cpl Webster, Marines Surridge (of the previous night's incident) and Conway all received multiple shrapnel wounds, and several local nationals were hurt, in addition to one who was killed. Those of the patrol who were not injured opened fire at an Arab disappearing down a murky side-street, and although a hit was claimed, he made good his escape.

The tension and the alertness required often sparked off false alarm scares, many of which had amusing results. In March a little Arab boy was seen to place a satchel full of 'explosives' in a block of flats in Ma'alla (still occupied by service families). A host of vehicles soon screamed on to the scene. The duty emergency Troop leapt out of the three-tonners and emptied the building. Finally an ammunition expert arrived to inspect the satchel, still untouched. It was crammed full of—textbooks!

The most famous false alarm was that in which Marine Coxon of X Company played a leading role, in July, 1966. A patrol was searching some local nationals in a narrow street of Crater. Coxon was acting as lookout, scanning the windows above. Suddenly he saw a figure appear at a window and throw something down into the street below. Coxon fired off four rounds from his sub-machine gun and the rest of the patrol took cover in case the 'grenade' should explode. The figure from upstairs hastily disappeared from view as the bullets thudded into the frame beside him. Two other Marines dashed inside the building and grabbed a very shaken Arab, who afterwards admitted to an interpreter that he was merely disposing of the remains of his fish supper in the street below! The Arab

Four Five came to Crater against a backcloth of fast fading political confidence in Aden. Aden State completely rejected the Federal Government and Amnesty International was trying to stir matters up by accusing our troops of brutality against prisoners. Although the charges were refuted and proved to be largely unfounded this type of 'sniping' had an unsettling effect on our men. The unit's correspondent later added some very poignant remarks to Amnesty International's allegations: 'We are simply doing what we have done for so long; guarding the interests of others and ensuring peace and stability. The Marine and the Soldier work on, weapon in hand and eyes alert, but with that perennial smile and self-restraint in the face of provocation that have earned goodwill in every corner of the world.'

The terrorists were now becoming much better prepared and in early June, Intelligence assessed the threat in the Commando's domain of Crater as 'individual cells that were organized into groups of grenadiers, assassins and demolition teams, ready for further violence'—a formidable foe indeed.

During the unit's stay in Crater, in July, 1966, there were some nineteen incidents. Eighteen of these involved hand grenades and the other a home-made bomb. Seventeen marines were listed as slightly injured (many others too collected bits of shrapnel which did not merit an official casualty report, so there are still several members of Four Five carrying around spare pieces of metal inside them!) and the local nationals suffered two killed and twenty-two injured. On the second of these incidents a party of vehicles in which the Commanding Officer, Lt-Col Clifford Bye, was travelling had two hand grenades lobbed at it. Fortunately the grenades exploded twenty yards away and none of the occupants was hurt, although one local bystander was killed and another two wounded.

Despite being mainly responsible for Crater, the Commando still had many other commitments to meet and as a result was widely dispersed throughout the State. Main Headquarters was at Little Aden with the administrative elements; Tactical Headquarters was at Waterloo Barracks, near Khormaksar; one

Company acted as Guard Company for installations at Steamer Point, the other of course was based in Crater, whilst the third was held in reserve, ready for immediate deployment. This wide dispersal obviously created many headaches but shows the diversification of tasks with which Four-Five had to cope at the time.

The type of tactics adopted by us in Crater were largely dictated by the terrorists, whose favourite ploy was hit-and-run grenade attacks with the grenadiers disappearing up side streets or seeking refuge in mosques. In order to check this, to some degree, a series of walls were constructed in the alleyways connecting parallel main roads. These walls, constructed from 'attractive breeze blocks', were some ten feet high. The wishes of the local residents were observed as much as possible and much on the spot bargaining would take place before the final siting was agreed. Needless to say, these walls had to be carefully guarded until completed otherwise, the Arabs merely removed the blocks at night before the mortar had dried out!

The systematic elimination of Special Branch Officers led to another new development during this period. To supplement the over-stretched intelligence agencies each unit formed its own Special Branch Section. Four Five's was commanded by Lt Malcolm Macleod and consisted of eight men divided into two teams. Their task was to gather local operational intelligence available for use mainly at Commando level. The teams, moving more often than not at night, drove around in plain clothes in disguised Land Rovers or smart private cars, either trailing patrols or carrying out snap raids, with armed sections, on receipt of information. In spite of being an acutely dangerous task, this Special Branch concept had its successes and provided details on which three unit operations were subsequently mounted.

Two of these operations were nicknamed 'Cottage Pie' and 'Golden Guinea' and took place in July, 1966. Both these operations were mammoth undertakings which involved several different cordons being mounted simultaneously, thus creating a considerable command and control problem. Scout cars from the Recce Squadron, 1st Royal Tank Regiment, were in support in each case to provide a covering force and a mobile reserve in the event of incidents. The aim of 'Cottage Pie' was to search ten youth clubs in Crater at the same time. Regrettably, things got off to a bad start as the police constables ordered to assist the cordons failed to arrive at the rendezvous. The Armed Police kindly 'stepped into the breach' and lent the appropriate number of constables. The Motor Transport Officer (Lt James Bartlett) and the Intelligence Officer (Lt Alastair Cook) then spent a hair-raising hour delivering the policemen to their various targets. A Land Rover, cornering on almost two wheels, followed by a three-ton vehicle full of policemen hanging on for all they were worth almost brought the traffic in Crater to a complete standstill!

'Golden Guinea', a fortnight later, got off to a smoother start, but even so the Arabs seemed to have 'got wind' of the searches to be conducted in Ma'alla, Tawahi and Crater and warned the faithful by wailing from the Mosques outside the normal prayer period!

Security was becoming a major problem, especially with so many different units and forces involved and Lt-Col Bye recalls instituting several 'tightening up' measures. By now, a full unit operation was taking place in Crater once a week during Four Five's stay and every precaution possible had to be taken to achieve any degree of surprise. Some reinforcements had to be smuggled in from Little Aden in routine ration trucks and others brought in gradually into areas which already had existing concentrations of parked vehicles. Full advantage was also taken of the silent hours and many a darkened convoy moved surreptitiously out of Little Aden and into Waterloo Lines. Communications also afforded opportunities for leaks and the Little Aden telephone exchange was monitored by an Arab speaking officer whilst other general restrictions included those on briefings and the use of radios and telephones. These innovations soon paid off and 'Operation Hard Tack', on 2 August, 1966, caught many Arabs unawares as the stealthy

Commandos moved into fifteen separate areas of Crater at five in the morning.

By now the political background, at the best of times difficult to follow, became even more complicated when the Federal Government closed the border with the Yemen for a period beginning in August, as a reprisal for the murder of Rahman Basendwa, the Aden representative on the Federal Council. In addition to closing the frontier, some 150 Yemeni undesirables were deported. These measures aroused strong local feeling for, in addition to alienating the Yemenis, it successfully checked the import of *qat*, which was grown in the Yemen, and whose red stems were chewed as a form of stimulant by the majority of Adenis.

Four Five next found itself on duty in Big Aden in December, 1966, and shortly before Christmas a young officer under training, Lt Anthony Turnbull, gave the apt description of 'four more throwing days before Christmas' in a published article. The Commando spent less than three weeks in its new area of Ma'alla where fortunately terrorist activities were quiet as it was Ramadan* and NLF and FLOSY were using the time to regroup and retrain their members. In these weeks five cordon and search operations were carried out, one of which gained positive results. In IS it is considered that even success in one operation in five makes the waiting and frustration of the others well worthwhile. The Special Branch team again proved its worth and seven terrorists were subsequently arrested, with a sizeable haul of arms and ammunition.

The final eleven months of British rule in Aden State were, perhaps, the most tragic of all, with a sharply rising number of terrorist incidents, reflected up country as well. It was now just a question of conducting an orderly withdrawal based on both political expedience and the time to be taken to move the military personnel and the heavier equipment which could most economically be made use of in other theatres. These months in Aden State were also clouded by mutinies in the South

* The ninth month of the Mohammedan year, an occasion of holiday and feasting.

Arabian Army, which had wide repercussions at the time, and inter-factional feuds between NLF and FLOSY, now split up.

Four Five's first major appearance on the Big Aden Internal Security scene was in late March, 1967, prior to the arrival of the United Nations Special Mission, which was due on 2 April. It was hoped that the three-man Mission (with a Venezuelan as chairman and representatives from Afghanistan and Mali) might produce some solutions to the problems which so far had beset the State. In preparation for the visit a full alert of the Security Forces was called but this was almost entirely forgotten when, on 1 April, Aden suffered its worst downpour of rain for some fifty years. Life in the State came to a virtual standstill and widespread flooding followed. Part of the road between Aden and Little Aden was washed away and Y Company (Major Ted Carroll) guarding a wireless station found themselves with the additional commitment of directing traffic round gaping holes in the main highway, which ran through an otherwise featureless desert.

NLF and FLOSY, now vying at each other with increased hostility, each declared separate general strikes to show their protest against the Mission. Only the virtually ineffective SAL was willing to discuss the problems of forthcoming independence, but it was not afforded the opportunity. It soon became apparent, even to the most casual observer, that the Mission's actions were exceptionally obstructive. They refused to deal directly with the Federal Government and would only negotiate through the British authorities. The visit rapidly developed into an overplayed theatrical farce and the Mission spent the majority of their five days in Aden encaged in the closely guarded Seaview Hotel on Khormaksar Beach.

The Commando spent all this time on full alert in Little Aden, where for two days the strike was fully effective and production at the BP Refinery brought to a complete halt. Seven Troop of Z Company were acting as emergency riot squad at the time and their services were soon required when the police in Little Aden found themselves unable to cope with large crowds of demonstrators. On this occasion, however, the

Troop's arrival on the scene of trouble was not as immediate as one might have hoped. As Seven Troop, supported by armoured cars, swung out of BP Camp and travelled down the road which ran along the perimeter of the Refinery, they found the routes to Little Aden barred by oil drums and barriers. The Refinery workers had obviously taken the opportunity of enforced days off to purloin oil drums and other rubbish, which they set fire to with great delight. It took X Company (Major Donald Brewster) much of the remainder of the day to clear up the debris, and in all some ten three-tonner loads of oil drums and dustbins were removed!

During the visit of the Mission the most serious disturbances took place in Sheikh Othman where it seemed that the terrorists were trying to gain complete control. The 3rd Battalion the Royal Anglian Regiment (3 RAR) was responsible for this area at the time with the aid of scout cars of the Queen's Dragoon Guards. Sheikh Othman, with a population of some 140,000 crammed into a square mile or so, had always been regarded by the terrorists as the gateway to the Federation and subsequently to the Yemen. Now, with fresh troubles breaking out in the township, reinforcements had to be called in. While 3 RAR concentrated their efforts on the centre of the town an extra Company from Four Five was called in to look after the suburban communities of Al Qahira and Al Mansoura. Both these areas were in sharp contrast, Al Qahira consisting mainly of *kutcha* huts and slums crammed together, whilst Al Mansoura was more spread out and contained the homes of the wealthier Arabs.

This responsibility lasted from 17 April to 20 May, with each Company doing an eight-day tour of duty. The honour of being first in fell to X Company who entered Sheikh Othman at about nine-thirty on the morning of the 17th. Their first job was to carry out familiarization patrols in the centre of the town before moving out to the suburbs. Within ten minutes the leading Troop was in action—a grenade thrower had injured two. The terrorists were obviously testing the new arrivals.

2/Lt John Parsons-Smith (Six Troop, Y Company) later

gave an account of a patrol which he commanded during this period:*

'Apart from a centre tarmac strip, the narrow streets are sandy and confined on either side by tall houses. The latter, luxurious by local standards, appear squalid and shabby to the western eye. The total lack of drains and town hygiene cause a dinstinctive reek that hounds the nostrils. These surroundings and the constant hubbub create an unforgettable impression of this Arabian town.

In Sheikh Othman, on foot patrol, no man moves unless he is covered by another. One darts forward to a new position whilst the other watches the rooftops and windows. The system of pairs establishes great comradeship and trust; for no one conceals the fact that the life of the man who is moving depends on his partner. The concentration and alertness required by each man restricts the length of each patrol to about one and a half hours.

My patrol was in two parts, one on foot and the other circling the immediate area in Land Rovers. By now we are approaching the market whose reputation as a dangerous area is only equalled by the mosque beyond it.†

Veterans say one can never be fully prepared for an incident but when, at eleven-eighteen, a hand-grenade landed at my feet we were already flat on the ground. I had shouted "Grenade!" before I knew it. Then, cocking our weapons as we ran, we sealed the area, using a well-practised drill that required no further orders.

. . . I checked the cordon and supervised the searching of all the Arabs caught within it. The patrol, with fixed bayonets and a strange look in their eyes, coolly scanned surrounding blocks. At this point a follow-up impact grenade

---

* *Globe and Laurel*, October, 1967.

† Terrorists frequently used mosques as a refuge after attacks, but on 6 April, 1967, permission was finally granted to allow security forces to enter these buildings in pursuit or if special authority was given.

exploded and again we dived to the ground. Up again, weapons ready, all eyes watching their allotted arcs.

Two shots from my left, followed by five more. At a glance I saw two of my patrol watching their shots drop two fleeing figures. No other casualties were reported and the personnel search continued. Hurriedly my radio operator sent my report back to Compay HQ. The two men we fired on were confirmed as the grenadiers and were dead.

Two men to one grenade doesn't figure and a search produced another unexploded grenade that had cracked on impact with a wall. The ambulance took away the dead Arabs and an explosives expert finished dealing with the unexploded grenade. The men allowed a tight grin to touch their faces, for this was the climax of many hours training. Success was sweet to us all.'

It may be of interest, at this juncture, to digress slightly and examine briefly the tactics of the opposition. We have already learnt that information in this type of situation was always hard to come by, but frequently the best source was from the terrorists themselves picked up by the Special Branch or the unit Special Branch team after operations in the front line.

Six Troop's patrol proved how determined and accurate these grenade attacks were becoming. The grenadiers were either full-time professionals or employed on a more casual one-time basis. They would often work in pairs and wait until a suitable target presented itself. One terrorist was later reported to have waited in a given area for three days before releasing his missile! This meant that the grenadier would have to stand around with the grenade well concealed, either on his body or wrapped in a handkerchief or brown paper. His accomplice would remain nearby, either mingling with the crowd or sitting at a pavement café acting as lookout and reporting back casualties and damage to his headquarters. These tactics, however, were never too rigid as in the last incident we examined both men seemed to be employed as throwers. It was also common practice to make a thorough reconnaissance of likely escape routes before the raid, although on one attack, outside Sheikh Othman Police Station, the terrorists merely sat chewing *qat* beforehand, lobbed their grenades over a wall, and sat back—to resume chewing their *qat*!

Apart from the grenade another frightening addition to the terrorists' armoury was the drainpipe mortar which meant that almost every outdoor pursuit was in continual danger from this long range weapon. These mortars were home made and consisted of pieces of steel pipe, about thirty inches long, having one end welded over with a hole drilled in it. The barrels were partly buried in the sand and a lead through the hole in the base led to a battery with a timing device. In addition, to keep the dust out, a wooden tampion was fixed to the mouth of the barrel which was subsequently blown out by the bomb. These mortars were usually fired at night and had an incredible range of over 600 yards. The attacks were usually launched in Big Aden, but on one occasion Four Five at BP Camp was on the receiving end. The target was a concert party, but fortunately some bombs fell short and many more were blinds, otherwise the results could have been quite gruesome.

Four Five's brief stay in the outskirts of Sheikh Othman soon produced results. The speed and alertness of its patrols stabilized the situation until eventually, when the third Company were committed there, they were confronted with no incidents at all.

15 May, 1967, saw the main body of the Commando moving up country for its final tour, leaving X Company behind to cope with IS—and ceremonial. On 16 May, Sir Richard Turnbull, the High Commissioner, left Aden to be succeeded by Sir Humphrey Trevelyan (now Lord Trevelyan). Observers at the time thought that this change at the helm might weaken the British position in an already fast-deteriorating situation. Sir Richard had been a firm friend of the Security Forces, but his successor was soon to prove that he would continue in the same vein and was determined not to let things get worse, yet at the same time clearly briefed to ensure a punctual and peaceful withdrawal.

When Sir Richard Turnbull arrived at Khormaksar Airfield on the 16th he was greeted by a full Guard of Honour provided by X Company (Major Donald Brewster), 'immaculate in full ceremonial order', after only a few days of rehearsal. In addition to X Company, the band of the 1st the Queen's Dragoon Guards provided the music and the 1st Regiment Royal Horse Artillery fired a seventeen-gun salute. The RAF provided a finale to the farewells and Hunters based at RAF Khormaksar flew past in formation before Sir Richard boarded his aircraft to return to the United Kingdom. As proof of Four Five's extraordinary flexibility during this period, X Company found themselves back on IS duties, patrolling the streets of Sheikh Othman, at two o'clock that same afternoon.

The day after the departure of the High Commissioner Four Five had its first taste of the terrorists' murder tactics when Marine Calway (who was attached to the Port Security Force at HMS *Sheba*)* was killed with a Naval comrade by gunmen in Bohra Bazaar, a street in the shopping area behind the Crescent. Bohra Bazaar was typical of the narrow lanes in this neighbourhood which ran up from the tree-lined Crescent and then ended abruptly at the steep rock covered mountainside behind. The flat topped buildings, mostly with 'NLF' crudely painted on the outside, were built with double doors on the ground floor which were opened in the daytime to reveal a multitude of wares. During the afternoon Calway and his friend, both dressed in civilian clothes and unarmed, had visited a photographic shop on a corner. It was then that two assassins struck and committed a motiveless and senseless murder.

June proved to be the unhappiest month of this troubled year in Aden. The Arab–Israeli war had cast its shadow over the entire Middle East and with reports that Britain had backed the Israelis being rife at the time some ill-feeling crept in between the British and Federal forces in Aden. To add to

* Four Five was responsible for providing some of the manpower for a detachment based at HMS *Sheba* which patrolled Aden Harbour, the dockyards and warehouses in the port area.

this the FRA and FNG had now been amalgamated and re-organized on a South Arabian basis and inter-tribal jealousies over promotion were becoming apparent. The reliability of the Armed Police was also suspect. They had been partly penetrated by the NLF, and although they could not have been classed as disloyal, they were under strong pressure from both sides and were unsettled, to say the least of it.

Trouble started on 16 June, 1967, when four SAA Colonels were suspended from duty after complaining about promotion matters. On the 19th unrest increased and an attempt was made to break into a SAA armoury. Disturbances finally flared up on the 20th when a rumour started that the four Colonels had been hanged (probably a faulty translation from English to Arabic of the word suspended). Riots then started at a SAA camp near Sheikh Othman, and shots were fired. The South Arabian Police (SAP) mistakenly thought that the British were attacking Arabs and manned their defences. The outcome of this was a tragedy of the greatest magnitude. A truckload of British troops, innocently returning from a rifle range, was fired on at close range—killing eight men and wounding eight others. Shortly afterwards a Public Works Department official and a British officer were also slain. With great restraint and courage British troops eventually restored order in this area, but not before more casualties had been suffered.

A common feature of life in the Middle East is intrigue and rumour and the events of 20 June proved to be no exception. Whilst the troubles in Sheikh Othman continued the Armed Police in Crater heard through the grape-vine of a 'British plot against all Arabs'. They too manned the defences of the Armed Police Barracks and in an incident similar to that of earlier on in the morning a combined recce patrol of the Royal Northumberland Fusiliers and the Argyll and Sutherland Highlanders was fired on at point-blank range, killing all except one. Another four-man patrol suffered a similar fate shortly afterwards and by midday the situation in Crater had reached serious proportions. Saladins of the QDG were unable to return to recover the bodies without the use of their main armament,

28. A marine of Four Five silhouetted against a burning building in Belfast, 26 June, 1970.

*29. 11 Troop sandwiched between two rival mobs in Butler Street, Belfast,
26 June, 1970.*

*30. Past and present commanding officers, May, 1969. Back, l to r: Lt-Col
R. D. Crombie, Lt-Col J. C. C. Richards, Col J. I. H. Owen, Col T. M. P.
Stevens, Col F. C. E. Bye, Maj-Gen F. C. Barton. Seated: Gen Sir
Norman Tailyour, Col W. N. Gray, Lt-Col R. J. Ephraums, Lt-Col
E. C. E. Palmer, Maj-Gen R. C. de M. Leathes.*

and although the Armed Police seemed to have quietened down and realized the errors of their ways, the terrorists took advantage of the troubles and manned positions on several rooftops. As a correspondent of Four Five later put it: ' . . . the aim was pacification, and that meant the least possible force.' Higher authority decided to evacuate our troops from Crater—perhaps the most difficult decision of the campaign. There is little doubt that we could have easily assumed control again by force, but it was thought that in the long run this might have caused an even greater deterioration in the already strained relations. The Commander-in-Chief, Admiral Sir Michael Le Fanu, issued the following signal after this tragic period: 'There must be other difficult days ahead. But the resolution, good humour and professional skill that have been demonstrated during the past week show that we have nothing to fear. Well done all.'

The troubles in Aden State had hastened the withdrawal of X Company from Dhala and on 20 June it was acting as reserve in Little Aden. Crater had been sealed off and tactically the most important feature was the Main Pass to the northwest of the town, now held by terrorists who had occupied positions in the strategically placed old Turkish forts. X Company came under command of the Royal Northumberland Fusiliers on the afternoon of the 21st and was ordered to gain control of the Pass, or, as the Press later reported, 'Commandos storm the heights of Crater'. The QDG and RNF gave first class support in providing additional covering fire. At this stage our own GPMG was called in to suppress the rebels' fire and Major Brewster recalls that:

'To get to their post the two Marines had to dash some forty yards across open ground, carrying their GPMG and two liners of ammunition, whilst under fire from terrorists on the high ground to the south (such was the intensity of the engagement at this stage that it was necessary to change gun and crew after the expenditure of only two liners to prevent overheating) . . . I am sure that the men concerned will claim that there is nothing extraordinary in what they did, but their brave efforts were up to the highest traditions of the Corps.'

This covering fire enabled the rest of the Company to pick its way up the rocks of the northern side of this 'airless and oven-hot' volcanic rim. Amongst the leading elements was the Support Troop which, since the up country days, now formed an integral part of each Company group as opposed to acting as a centralized Company.

As the men advanced slowly upwards the terrorists kept up a lively rate of fire from their lofty perches, but the resistance began to dwindle as the Commandos got closer to their objectives. One more resolute hide, in a house at the bottom of the Pass still held out. One, just one, Carl Gustav* round demolished the building and silenced the sniper. Three Troop was given the task of securing the southern side of the Pass and a party under Sgt Moran soon found itself in a deserted emplacement, recently vacated by the rebels. The Pass was now in our hands.

After the events of 20 June, contingencies were being made for a more forcible foray into Crater. The Argylls, who had now arrived in strength and were more than eager to avenge the massacre of their comrades, were to play the dominant role in this attack, along with Four Five. However, politics prevailed and the plan was shelved. In the event the Argylls were able to make an unopposed entry into Crater on 3 July, with Y Company holding the high ground in case of trouble.

For the fortnight leading up to 3 July, each Company of Four Five spent four days manning the Pass. A checkpoint was set up to stop the passage of arms and known undesirables. This proved to be an enormous task as some 6,000 people (not including goats and sheep!) passed through daily. The most noteworthy feature of this period was the Commando's snipers, perched in the fortifications above. Typical of these snipers was L/Cpl Tilley, who was described as 'a man who never releases

* Section anti-tank gun.

a shot until he knows exactly where it is going to land.' During these two weeks the terrorists were fighting it out amongst themselves for supremacy of this volcanic bowl, but the accuracy of the unit's snipers soon made the rooftops untenable. Four Five accounted for no less than fifteen terrorists in this manner, a brilliant achievement as only twenty-four rounds of ammunition were expended. The snipers' top marksman was Marine M. C. Harrison, who later received a Commendation, with eight hits to his credit. Such was his skill that terrorists feared to come out during the daylight hours to fire at our positions.

Another favourite pastime of the terrorists during these weeks was the firing of blindicides. Sometimes the terrorists came off worst, as on one occasion when the firer of a blindicide crouched in front of a particularly solid wall—forgetting the lethal back-blast effects! The most serious blindicide attack took place on the night of 29 June. Five Troop, Y Company, was in one of the Turkish forts overlooking the two carriageways of the Pass. It was the first day in command of the Troop for 2/Lt Nick Hall and for most of the day the observers kept their sights on a couple of buses on the Crater side of the Pass, which had been parked across the two lanes so as to provide cover for the terrorists crossing with ammunition for their friends. The Troop remained on full alert after dark and the only activity, apart from the buses, had been the odd bullet whistling harmlessly overhead. Suddenly, at about nine o'clock, a terrific explosion shook the fort. A blindicide had scored a direct hit on the outer wall, sending noise reverberating round the interior. Cpl Kernan and Marines Hewitson and Burgin were all temporarily deafened, and had to be evacuated, but apart from these injuries there was no other damage.

For the next month, Four Five remained in Little Aden, responsible for the IS in that area. Politically, things were getting worse, with the Federal Government losing more ground and having to bow to NLF pressure in most States. In Aden itself NLF and FLOSY were still fighting for supremacy. By now it was time to make preparations for the phased withdrawal which, at that time, had been designated 20 November, 1967. All British troops had been withdrawn from permanent bases in the Federation and the next on the list was to be the cantonments of Falaise and Little Aden. The blue hutted BP Camp, which had been Four Five's home for seven years, took on a desolate air as the unit began to transfer itself to RAF Khormaksar. Even this process was not entirely without danger as the stores convoys often came under fire from the Al Mansoura area before they crossed the Causeway. This move provided an opportunity for many of the Commando to send unwanted items of kit back to the United Kingdom and the Quartermaster's baggage compound and the Post Office soon filled up with an assortment of boxes and parcels. Whilst BP Camp was being cleared up the Rifle Companies and Tactical Headquarters started to move in to the new operational zone, Ma'alla Straight. During this period RAF Khormaksar was to be used purely as the administrative base and rest area for the off-duty Company. Conveniently these elements were housed next door to RAF Air Movements—in case of the need for a quick getaway!

By 12 September all was ready to hand over the camp in Little Aden, 'home' for seven years, to the BP authorities and at nine o'clock the Union Jack was struck outside the guard-room for the last time in the presence of Major John Richards, the Second-in-Command.

In Ma'alla the Companies were located in the recently vacated tall blocks of flats (some even had the remains of a hurried last meal before departure) and the Marines soon ensured that most of their quarters contained air conditioners. Headquarters were appropriately situated in a building called 'Treetops', although there was hardly any vegetation in sight! Four Five took over the area, which consisted of two Company sectors (east and west), from the South Wales Borderers on 8 September. One of the first major tasks was to put sandbag defences both round the ground floors of the flats and the many rooftop OPs. To meet this requirement within a few days each man in the unit had to fill at least ten sandbags a day and this policy was characteristically led by the Commanding Officer, Lt-Col J. I. H. Owen, who had arrived in July just before the withdrawal from Little Aden.

The main feature of life in the Ma'alla area was the Observation Post. Up to sixteen were manned at any one time and these were constructed so that the observer could dominate the area and keep it, particularly the Straight, free from terrorist interference. OPs were occupied on a permanent basis or intermittently, or at peak 'trouble periods'. Some were even set up by clandestine methods to keep watch on a given sector for a specific operation or after information had been received concerning a particular area.

The static OPs were solidly built with sandbags and had overhead cover enabling them to withstand grenade, mortar or blindicide attacks. Each OP was manned by a team of four men so that every rank could rest one day in four. The daily routine was a gruelling one and varied from post to post, although the longest watches were two hours on, with four hours off. In addition to watching his arc continously through binoculars, the man on duty in the OP had to be prepared to answer a field telephone, operate a GPMG, as well as keep a listening watch on a radio set. Each position had maps and panoramic photographs with ranges marked on them so that an incident could be plotted instantly. The OPs were the eyes and ears of the Commando.

Much of the initial assessment of the incidents lay solely in the hands of the Marines. Only experience could teach a man what to report back. At first any sudden movement appeared to be the prelude to an outburst, but intimate knowledge of one's sector soon enabled the observer to differentiate between a scare and the real thing. Incidents would occur in a flash, and in those moments the Marine would have to decide whether to open fire (and face the consequences if innocent people were hurt), help direct a ground patrol to the scene, or report back to the Operations Room. The reporting process was an accomplished art, and the system evolved worked because it had been proved in the fire.

Four Five operated a regimental radio net. On it were, in addition to Commando Headquarters and Company Headquarters, the OPs and Mobile Patrols. At some times over thirty-six out-stations were manned. In this way, any incidents could be reported back verbally in quick succession by those involved, who would have been able to work out a compass bearing and an estimated range. The Company Commander in whose area it was, would react at once with his stand-by Troop and the whole operation was monitored by Commando Headquarters, where the duty officer would alert reinforcements and inform Brigade Headquarters. The Commanding Officer would be called and the 'battle' would then develop. All too frequently little happened, but the occasional success made the continuous state of alert and the hard discipline of watching and waiting worthwhile.

The responsibilities of the junior leader at this time were particularly heavy. There was a steady stream of instructions from London which gave frequent changes of emphasis, even policy, which in turn affected the man 'on the beat'. Lt-Col John Owen recalls one occasion when the men were following one set of instructions, he had just finished briefing his Company Commanders on another and was attending a conference at Brigade Headquarters, receiving a third! Hence the jingle evolved in Four Five at the time:

> Shoot 'em on Monday,
> Don't on Tuesday,
> Withdraw on Wednesday,
> Smile on Thursday,
> Don't on Friday,
> Shot at on Saturday,
> Crisis on Sunday.

It was not to be long before the grimness of anti-terrorist operations in a built-up area became apparent to Four Five. One night, during the first week in Ma'alla, 2/Lt Danny Moir, on his first tour abroad in a Commando, was leading a patrol of

X Company. His group was moving towards a building in the notorious honeycomb of the kutcha huts district, known to be a terrorist stronghold, when fire was opened at close range. He fell mortally wounded and was later buried at sea.

Moir's death, shortly after a reported NLF/FLOSY 'cease fire', prompted the *Daily Express* to demand, two days later, 'Get out . . . Now!' but it was another two months before this became a reality. In the meantime, on 11 October, the garrison was to be further strengthened by the arrival of 42 Commando, Royal Marines. 42 Commando, at the time, were based in Singapore and landed from the Commando Ship HMS *Albion*, dressed in their distinctive Far East olive greens, to cover the final withdrawal. This period was marked by a rising tide of incidents sparked off by the internal power struggle and in the first three weeks in Ma'alla there were over thirty-four reported outbreaks of violence in Four Five's area. Two of these, however, ended in success for the unit.

On 17 October, after five mortar bombs were fired at a road block, Lt Terry Knott (Recce Troop) was leading an investigating patrol. Watching its progress were a couple of local nationals, lying on beds on a verandah. L/Cpl Roy Pennington and Marine 'Speedy' Lawson both spotted one figure jerk. 'Grenade!' A burst of fire came from the patrol and the grenadier dropped dead. His accomplice, whose grenade failed to explode, ran into the building but was soon captured. A subsequent search of the house revealed the April edition of the *Globe and Laurel*—open at the page describing Four Five's previous tour in Ma'alla!

The other notable success was three days later when Marine Philip Miller of X Company found himself involved in a vehicle chase in broad daylight. Miller was vehicle commander and was ordered to follow a 'camouflaged Land Rover' with no number plates. The Land Rover driver, realizing that he was being followed, increased speed and made several sharp turns round the back streets of Ma'alla, until he came to an abrupt halt—having crashed into a car at a road junction. Miller and Marine Richard Steele gave chase and shot the man.

In both cases, although obeying the current regulations, all those involved had to undergo exhaustive inquiries—proof of the ever-present strain of such operations.

On 2 November it was announced by the Foreign Secretary, Mr. George Brown, that British troops would be withdrawn by the 'end of the month'. Even then, Whitehall was not prepared to be too specific! There was much speculation as to the actual date of the final withdrawal (W Day), but this was not confirmed until 14 November, when the troops were told that the 29th was to be the day.

The first two weeks of November, therefore, were ones of uneasiness and doubt for Four Five, and the terrorists had the additional spur of independence with which to settle their differences. One incident which occurred in this period almost ended in tragedy. On 5 November Lt Terry Knott and some of the Recce Troop were manning a clandestine OP on a hillside overlooking a strong NLF area when automatic rifle fire was opened on them from a group of houses they were observing. Cpl Dick Todd's binoculars were struck and it seemed as if he had been wounded in the eyes. In addition, Lt Knott's rifle barrel was bent by a bullet. Todd was unconscious and bleeding profusely and Knott, fearing the worst, called for an air casualty evacuation. Lt-Col Owen decided to mount a quick rescue operation with Y Company (Major Pat Mann), the unit's Ferrets, and the Saladins and Saracens of the Queen's Own Hussars. This was successful and the terrorists fled, having left two dead behind after their house, a suspected arsenal, had exploded. However, a follow-up patrol spotted three of them sitting in a mosque. At that time entry to mosques was still restricted. Lt-Col Owen, seeing an Aden police corporal standing nearby thought up a ruse. He called him over, made him stand to attention and ordered him sharply to tell everybody in the mosque to leave at once. Instinctively (a little British discipline still stuck), the policeman obeyed and the three were collared as they came out. These locals, all staunch NLF, later claimed that they had been firing at FLOSY, confirming a suspicion, rife in the Commando, that Recce

Troop were FLOSY orientated! Luckily, Cpl Todd escaped with two lovely black eyes only.

Inter-factional fighting mainly highlighted the last weeks in Ma'alla, although the previous episode was one of sixteen separate attacks which took place on our positions in the first week of November.* Ma'alla was split into two geographical sectors. The east, consisting of a contrast of tall flats and a squalid mass of kutchas huts, was considered to be a FLOSY stronghold. The west, more spread out and dominated by the enormous storage tanks of the Admiralty Oil Depot, was NLF territory. By 10 November, after heavy fighting, NLF took over political control of the entire area, although Four Five, of course, remained firmly entrenched in their locations despite the attacks. One of these attacks was made on Commando Headquarters where a newspaper correspondent was staying, covering the last weeks in Aden. An Arab had opened fire from a moving car and aimed his shots at a ground floor room where a film show was in progress. The gunner was killed seconds later when he tried to run the gauntlet through a road block. Soon more firing broke out:

'The roof-level firing had come from an Arab settlement of kutchas huts, a filthy rabbit warren of cardboard hovels on the mountainside looking down on Ma'alla. Other Arabs had fired from a nearby rubbish dump.

Any excuse will make the Arabs join in a shooting incident. The firing spreads . . . and the grip of terror sets in.

At any moment a bullet could hit you. It could be well-aimed sniper's fire. It could be a freak ricochet . . .'†

We can now see that although W Day was approaching fast Four Five still had a full operational commitment, and the detailed planning of the move had to be carried on despite the

* Six terrorists were killed in these attacks, while Four Five suffered no casualties.

† *Chronicle and Echo* (Northants), 8 November, 1967. Article by Don Morley.

constant distractions of incidents and the occasional outbursts of firing.

In outline, the overall plan for the withdrawal was to move the majority of troops out through Khormaksar, whilst the equipment went out by sea. The privilege of being the last troops out was accorded to the Royal Marines. Fittingly, Four Five was to be the last major unit of the permanent garrison to be withdrawn, whilst 42 Commando held the airfield, and then they too would be withdrawn to the Naval Task Force (the largest one assembled by this country since Suez). This phased withdrawal was planned to be fully tactical as the danger of inter-factional fighting or a full scale onslaught on our positions was ever-present.

The detailed planning, within Four Five, started in early August, 1967, whilst the Commando was still based in Little Aden. During the withdrawal from there most of the individual heavy baggage was sent home by sea plus items of heavier, and unwanted, equipment. The unit alone sent 686 crates of stores back by sea, and another 300 with 23,000 lbs of stores went out in the airlift. Another problem was that of manpower. All drafting to Four Five had been on a twelve-month cycle but with no firm date of W Day the brakes were eventually applied on 28 October, with the promise that the Commando could call men forward at seventy-two hours notice if the situation worsened or the stay was prolonged. This uncertainty caused many headaches for the Royal Marines Drafting authorities at Portsmouth because a proportion of the unit was due to leave before the Commando arrived at Plymouth, and replacements had to be waiting so that Four Five would be up to full operational strength in preparation for strategic reserve duties in early 1968. This constant state of flux is typified by the Commanding Officer's opening paragraph in a letter to the Director of Drafting: 'I have been awaiting the most appropriate moment to write to you on a number of matters, but the situation changes so fast that it is difficult to judge. Today is as good as any other day.'

By mid-November the withdrawal from Aden of other

personnel and equipment was fully under way. This imposed extra work on Four Five who, in addition to operational tasks, had to provide guards and escorts for VIP's and man services which had now been run down. A good example of this was the intelligence and interrogation set-up—normally the responsibility of higher echelons. This highly skilled and specialized aspect of security operations now became part of the heavily burdened Intelligence Section's daily routine and Lt Peter Whittaker and Instructor-Lt Tony Carne found themselves dealing with as many as eighty suspects at a time. Another distraction, during this time, was looting. There were over 1,000 empty flats on Ma'alla Straight and with traditional guile the local population soon found that the unoccupied buildings contained a lot of profitable furnishings. Some even took to removing contents in gaily coloured wagons—a common feature of the local scene. If the drivers weren't in possession of Government or SAA permits then noisy scenes would follow on the road blocks with disgruntled Arabs then being escorted back to the dwellings to unload their cargoes!

As the date of withdrawal from Ma'alla drew nearer (the night of 24/25 November) Four Five began to man its last line of defence in the area, in case of trouble. This was nick-named the 'Owen Line' and consisted of the Turkish forts on the volcanic rim between Crater and Ma'alla which dominated the area. The task of manning the Owen Line fell to X Company (Capt Alisdair Murray) and as darkness approached everyone stood to, their eyes strained for tell-tale signs of violence below. Down at Commando Headquarters in Treetops final arrangements for the hand-over to the 3rd Battalion SAA were now being made. At one-twenty-five on the morning of the 25th all was complete and Four Five was free to drive through the hot Arabian night back to RAF Khormaksar. The last vehicle, the Commanding Officer's Land Rover escorted by a Saladin of the Queen's Own Hussars, crossed into the perimeter twenty-five seconds late—'not bad after 139 years!', quoted the *Globe and Laurel*.

For the next four days it was a question of getting ready for the fly out. 42 Commando was now responsible for Steamer Point and the Owen Line and in addition was preparing defensive positions in Khormaksar to cover the last airlifts out. Up till now the Royal Air Force had been working at full stretch moving troops and stores between Aden and Bahrein with aircraft arriving every half hour. The IS situation had fortunately remained calm—possibly attributable to first rate security on all levels.

As ever, the final withdrawal to those who participated in it seemed an anti-climax. The sense of history was only apparent to the large number of journalists recording the events.

Shortly before midnight on the 28th the first chalk of Four Five's thirteen was airborne to Bahrein. There was little cause for sentimentality as the men passed through the slick and well-executed routine of air movements—passports, documents, checking of baggage. Throughout the morning of the 28th the outward flights took away the remaining members of the fast dwindling Aden Garrison. By twelve-thirty the last Company, Y Company (Major Pat Mann) had been relieved by elements of 42 Commando who, up till then, had been holding the 'Pennine Chain' between Khormaksar and Sheikh Othman. Overhead the Wessex helicopters from HMS *Albion* maintained a constant shuttle service from the airfield to the Task Force.

Then followed the formalities as the High Commissioner, Sir Humphrey Trevelyan, and the Service Chiefs left.

Afterwards a brief farewell took place between Lt-Col John Owen and Lt-Col Dai Morgan of 42 Commando—who was destined to be the last British servicemen to leave Aden and who, incidentally, had brought Four Five's advance party to Aden over seven years ago.

Soon after one-thirty on 29 November, 1967, chalk 69 had been embarked in its Hercules, which was preparing to taxi. The last to board were, symbolically, the Commanding Officer of Four Five (Lt-Col Owen), the Commanding Officer Royal Air Force Khormaksar (Gp Capt Browne), the Commander Aden Brigade (Brigadier Jefferies), the Brigadier General Staff,

Middle East Land Forces (Brigadier Dunbar) and the Senior
Air Staff Officer, Middle East Air Force (Air Cdre Sowrey).
The baking heat of the airfield gave way to the cool interior of
the aircraft. Outside, the perimeter was still being guarded by
42 Commando, C Company of the King's Own Royal Border
Regiment and 8 (Alma) Light Commando Battery, R.A. The
Hercules sped down the runway and took off, starting its climb
to 25,000 feet. As the aircraft banked the nineteen ranks of
Four Five, the last of Aden Garrison to leave, craned their
necks for a last glimpse of this Southern Arabian Territory.

Another era for Great Britain and indeed, Four Five, had
now closed.

CHAPTER 18

Return to Europe

It is, perhaps, tempting to cover the most recent years, which have been chronicled most thoroughly, in greatest detail. However, as these have been times of peace, this would put the numerous deeds of action and bravery, recorded in the previous twenty or so years, out of perspective. Nevertheless, since Four Five has returned to these shores there have been many examples of the traditions of courage and spirit that have made the history of Four Five such a brilliant one. In addition, these last years have seen great changes in Britain's overall defence policy and in aspects of this Four Five has been privileged to play an important pioneering role.

On returning to the United Kingdom in 1967, after being based abroad continuously for twenty-two years (the Commando had sailed from Chatham for Hong Kong on 31 January, 1946), we could almost say that the full cycle had now been completed. The Commando's new home was to be the historic barracks at Stonehouse, which were originally opened in 1783 and had formed the base for the Plymouth Division of Marines. The buildings, constructed of typical West Country grey stone around a parade ground, provided a noble, if at times a somewhat severe, backcloth for the new arrivals. The interior of these barracks now contrasted sharply to the ancient exterior. A 1,000,000-pound modernization programme, recently completed, had ensured that the accommodation and amenities were completely up to date without detracting from the fine external characteristics.

The Colours* were officially marched through the lofty portals of Stonehouse on 5 January, 1968. The Commando was

* The Colours had been returned to the United Kingdom on four previous occasions. Twice for ceremonial parades, the Freedom of the City of Portsmouth (14 May, 1959) and the Tercentenary Celebrations (July, 1964), and twice for repairs, December, 1962 and December, 1966.

now in residence. The advance party had arrived some months previously and in the meantime had been making detailed preparations for the move and reception. Since leaving Aden the majority of Four Five had gone on foreign service leave prior to being posted to other Royal Marines units or rejoining the Commando at Plymouth. The last unit at Stonehouse had been 43 Commando and, as a result of defence cuts, was due to be dispersed later in 1968 and had been moved in reduced strength to the Royal Marines Barracks at Eastney. The Commanding Officer of 43 Commando at this time was Lt-Col Derek Pounds, formerly a Troop Commander and Adjutant of Four Five. A similar state of affairs as existed at the end of the War was now experienced and many ranks of Four Three remained at Stonehouse to link up with the now depleted numbers of Four Five.

The Commando had little time in which to settle in. Within days, detailed preparations were in hand for the taking over of commitments as 'Spearhead' Battalion for the Strategic Reserve in seven weeks' time. The requirement for this task was to have one company and a tactical headquarters ready to emplane for operations anywhere in the world within twenty-four hours, and the remainder of the unit ready within forty-eight hours. Concurrent with this all companies, with new men to train, had to prepare again for active duties. Field exercises were severely hampered by the Foot and Mouth epidemic and for a time the only training areas available were the football pitch and a small range within the Barracks!

'Spearhead' passed quietly and the early summer months were spent in preparation for 'Exercise Polar Express' for which the Commando was to be embarked in the Commando Ship HMS *Bulwark* for training in Northern Norway some fifty miles from the Finnish border.

The unit left for Norway on a sorrowful note for only two days before the embarkation, on 29 May, 1968, three ranks, Cpl Michael Coleman and Marines Percival Newland and Michael Perry, all of Z Company, were tragically drowned at night in a boating accident off Cawsand Bay at the entrance to

Plymouth Sound. This made a sad start to the subsequent exercise.

'Polar Express' provided yet another milestone in the history of the unit, for it was the first introduction to training in connection with Britain's increased commitments for assistance in the defence of the northern flank of NATO. It appears that the Royal Marines are usually in the vanguard when the nation's defence strategy swings to a new front, and in this instance Four Five proved to be no exception to the rule. Only time can tell what effect on efficiency and morale the less tangible duties of participating in the Cold War will have compared with active involvement in peace-keeping operations in our fast-dwindling Empire. However, as the political priorities change, so must our military outlook. The NATO concept has been growing rapidly in recent years, under close international scrutiny, and it has been Four Five, probably more than any other unit, which has had to adapt and study for the implementation of this new role.

The exercise took place in the Tromso area of north Norway and for four days and nights the Commando acted as part of 'Orange' Force (enemy) against a NATO force comprising of Norwegian, British, Canadian, Italian and supporting units from the United States. The Commando, in an area of 3,000 square miles, carried out some twenty-four independent unit or sub-unit tasks during the exercise period. These consisted of long range helicopter sorties aimed at disrupting supply lines and creating delaying actions on regular advances. The exercise took place in continuous daylight, in low temperatures and weather which included rain, sleet, snow and fog, and Four Five proved conclusively that an embarked force on the northern flank of NATO can play havoc with land based units hampered by mountainous terrain and poor communications. The unit's fine display prompted Desmond Wettern of the *Sunday Telegraph* to write in the July (1968) edition of *Navy*:

'A final word on the Commandos. As usual they surprised the opposition by the speed of their deployment—in some cases arriving hours before the umpires expected them. A reconnaissance troop did a mountain crossing in a night's march—Norwegian liaison officers said it could take three days. Above all, they proved that conventional forces with armour and artillery have much to fear from a highly mobile, helicopter-borne force which takes advantage of the awful and rugged terrain in this part of the world rather than regarding it as an obstacle.'

Despite the peacetime conditions two stories emerge from 'Polar Express', one of bravery and the other of remarkable resourcefulness and initiative.

At about five-thirty in the morning of the fourth day of the exercise, 14 June, a Norwegian truck left the road over a small bridge and crashed into a fast flowing river. In the back of the truck was a Wombat anti-tank gun and jerrycans of water. The lorry turned over several times before coming to rest in an upright position some forty yards downstream in about seven feet of water. There were four Marines of the Anti-Tank Troop in the back and they were badly injured by the stores that had been thrown about. Capt Simon Down, a Royal Marine helicopter pilot, was a passenger in the cab and he describes the subsequent events:

'Shortly after the accident Cpl John Eley of Reconnaissance Troop arrived on the river bank. He attempted to swim the distance of twenty yards out to the truck but was swept a hundred yards down the flooded river. A rope was then thrown out to the stricken vehicle and after we had secured it Cpl Eley inched his way out and immediately administered morphine to a man in great pain with a broken leg. The Unit's Medical Officer, Surg-Lt David Trash, and Medical Assistant Leonard Young then came out on the rope, and despite being wet and frozen to the skin rendered aid in the most professional manner . . .'

Cpl Eley was later awarded the Queen's Commendation for Brave Conduct, and Surg-Lt Trash and Medical Assistant

Young both received the Commandant-General's Commendation.

Cpl Gil Jackman and Marine Ron Brown, both of the Recce Troop, provided perhaps one of the biggest upsets for the exercise control staff, whose moves were always being contained by Four Five, much to their annoyance! The ruses adopted by these two Recce Troop members would have graced any wartime epic. The two Marines were carefully injected into the 'friendly' forces after exhaustive preparations had been made between the Commanding Officer, Support Company Commander (Capt Terry Knott), and the Intelligence Officer (Lt Gareth Noott). The plan was most ingenious and from the outset Jackman and Brown, in an appropriately disguised Land Rover, posed as a Royal Corps of Signals monitoring team. As well as being dressed for the part, they mingled freely with the Somerset and Cornwall Light Infantry, part of the NATO 'friendly' forces, with whom they were eventually to land. They nearly came to grief on the long journey out to Norway as there were some Marines embarked in the same vessel who were unaware of the plot, but fortunately any episodes which might have proved embarrassing were carefully avoided. Once on land, the 'signals team' was able to bluff its way around all the NATO locations and built up a complete plan of positions. The 'spies' then drove eighty miles north to pass on the information to Four Five, which was subsequently able to mount a heli-borne ambush on a large convoy passing through some crossroads. Eventually a British officer became rather suspicious of his 'Royal Signals' aides and their identity cards were checked. It was here that the only flaw in the whole operation was discovered. The serial numbers that the two ranks had been given were those corresponding to the Royal Corps of Transport and not the Royal Signals. As a result of this disclosure Jackman's and Brown's true identity was soon uncovered and Four Five had to rely on more formal methods of gaining intelligence in future.

Four Five employed a similar ruse on its next major exercise, 'Exercise Swap', which took place in Northern Ireland in

October, 1968. This time the undercover men went over as ordinary hikers with radios hidden in their rucksacks. The three-man team soon landed in deep water and was arrested as probable IRA agents. Their release was eventually secured after several frantic phone calls!

In fact there was considerable doubt beforehand as to precisely what elements were going to constitute the attacking force. The assault ship, HMS *Fearless* was planned to lead the naval group, but had been rushed to Gibraltar, only a few days previously for the Prime Minister's talks on the Rhodesian situation. Fortunately she returned in time for battle to be joined, and such was the speed of Four Five's advance inland that the exercise ended two days ahead of schedule.

Ealier, in October, Four Five had bidden farewell to one of its most distinguished past Commanding Officers; the retiring Commandant-General, General Sir Norman Tailyour. During this, his last official visit to the unit he had led in Cyprus and at Suez, General Sir Norman proudly wore his old red lanyard. His send-off was equally appropriate and he departed through the arches of Stonehouse in clouds of suitably coloured smoke —supplied by phosphorous grenades. Another departure, in December, was that of Lt-Col John Owen who had been at the helm during the politically stormy and hectic days of the Aden withdrawal and through the calmer, but possibly busier, waters of soldiering in this country. Lt-Col Owen's successor for the next three months was Lt-Col John Richards, formerly Intelligence Officer during much of the Malayan Emergency, who was promoted from Second-in-Command.

It is easy to imagine that a United Kingdom-based Commando leads a relatively static existence, but a quick glimpse of Four Five's deployment in early 1969 will soon dispel this thought. All three Rifle Companies were dispersed in different countries over a total distance of 7,000 miles, a feat of considerable administrative and operational merit. Z Company (Capt Rod Tuck) spent nearly six weeks in the cold wastes of Norway testing arctic clothing and equipment. In sharp contrast, X Company (Capt Ken Buckingham) flew out to the warmer climes of the Bahamas, albeit for a shorter period, for 'Exercise Ounce'. Although this was a routine contingency move there was an operational objective as well. The Island of Andros, in the Bahamas group, had been a favourite hiding place for illegal organizations mounting operations against the Cuban Government. For over a week the force of some 160 men searched the intricate web of cays, islands and mangrove swamps of Andros in Gemini and other small craft. No terrorists were found but X Company's presence undoubtedly deterred any would-be trespassers. To complete Four Five's global moves, Tactical Headquarters and 'Yankee' Company (appropriately under Major 'Buckie' Sykes of the United States Marine Corps) embarked for two months in the Assault Ship HMS *Fearless*, for 'Exercise Sun Trap'. Parliament had directed, in late 1968, that Britian would increase its military contribution to NATO. To this effect it was decided to maintain a continous presence in the Mediterranean—the 'Southern Flank'—to counter an increase in Soviet maritime forces operating in these waters. It is significant that Four Five was the first unit to be chosen to implement this policy. The proven skill and ability of Commandos to operate as 'instant troops' and be landed to fight in mountainous terrain makes them eminently suitable for this particular role, which is likely to continue for a considerable time. This first Mediterranean deployment included landings in Sardinia, Cyprus and Malta, but was curtailed on 18 March, 1969, when HMS *Fearless* was ordered to proceed, at short notice, to Lagos where the Prime Minister was holding peace talks. The honour of remaining on board in case required for special security duties fell to Six Troop (Lt Martin Read).

Whilst the majority of the Commando was away from Stonehouse Barracks detailed and feverish planning was going ahead for the major ceremonial event of its history. It had been confirmed that Her Majesty Queen Elizabeth II, accompanied by His Royal Highness Prince Philip, Duke of Edinburgh, Captain-General of the Royal Marines, was coming to Plymouth on 13 May to present new Colours. This was the first occasion, since 1894, that the Corps had been privileged to receive Colours from the reigning monarch. On 22 August of that year Queen Victoria had presented Colours to the Portsmouth Division on the lawns of Osborne House. The unit's old Colours were by now beyond economical repair, having suffered the vagaries of the Mediterranean and Aden climates for over fifteen years. The preparations for the parade work for such an occasion normally take a month, so the intensive programme of training for this important event began in mid-April under the eye of the new Commanding Officer, Lt-Col R. J. Ephraums. The standard of drill attained by the date of the dress rehearsal on Plymouth Hoe (11 May, 1969) was impeccable and equal to highest standards ever achieved in a Corps famed for its ceremonial parades.

The long-awaited day, Tuesday 13 May, dawned miserably. By half-past seven it was raining heavily, and at the final co-ordinating conference, a quarter of an hour later, the following weather forecast was received:

'Forecast at 0730A. Mainly dull, rather misty. Outbreaks of thundery rain, heavy at times. Rather close (59°F). Wind mainly south, 10–15 mph, gusting 20–25 mph during thundery outbreaks. A big development over N. France (downwind) more than even chance of storms between 10 and 12 o'clock. Not the weather for outdoor functions.'

With these gloomy details at hand the reluctant decision was made to cancel the outdoor ceremony on The Hoe and switch to the alternative venue in Plymouth Guildhall. The Royal train was duly informed, and the arena on the Hoe, prepared for an anticipated audience of 10,000, was left gaunt and windswept. Sullen television crews, putting finishing touches to their positions, re-packed their equipment. The bitterest blow, of course, fell on the marines of Four Five, who had rehearsed with such enthusiasm and pride for the previous month and heard the news of the change with great grief. This re-arrangement meant that only one guard out of the original four could parade within the confines of the Guildhall and the one chosen was the combined one of Headquarters and Support Companies (Number Four Guard) commanded by the youngest Guard Commander, Lt Richard Hawkins.

Whatever the private disappointments this was not a day to dwell on 'might have beens'. The organization, geared for either form of ceremony, went off with clockwork precision and the 400 or so guests were seated in the Guildhall by nine forty-five. The *Globe and Laurel* report continues:

'In a remarkably cathedral-like atmosphere the great Guildhall settled into an excited silence. There was a flurry of activity in the foyer and the Colonel (Lt-Col Roger Ephraums) brought the guard to attention. Her Majesty was wearing a yellow matching coat and hat and as she approached the dais spectators from the Corps could see, high on her shoulder, the Royal Marine brooch which Her Majesty had graciously accepted from the Corps on the occasion of the Corps Tercentenary. The ceremony which took place was a shortened version of the one which would have been followed on the Hoe. The Queen was received with a Royal Salute and to the sound of "*Auld Lang Syne*", played by as many of the band as could be accommodated on the small stage, the Old Colours marched out of the Unit dipping low in salute as they passed Her Majesty. The New Colours having been consecrated on the Corps of Drums were presented to the waiting Colour Officers by Her Majesty and received into the guard waiting at the present . . . (The Queen then addressed the parade and the Commanding Officer replied, after that) . . . Her Majesty left the dais and, as the Unit filed out of the Guildhall and those families Royal Marines and Civic Dignitaries who had been fortunate enough to watch the ceremony, moved out chatting quietly among themselves, the sense of occasion faded and silence once more descended upon the Guildhall.'

The twenty-five-minute ceremony was over.

Carrying the Old Colours were Lt Peter Whittaker (Queen's)

and Lt Peter Ward (Regimental). Receiving the New Colours were Lt Allan Berry (Queen's) and Lt John Atter (Regimental). The Chaplain who consecrated the Colours, assisted by Chaplains of other denominations, was the Venerable Archdeacon Ambrose Weekes, Chaplain of the Fleet and a former Chaplain of Four Five in Malta in 1953. Two officers were present at this ceremony who were serving in the unit at the first presentation in Malta in 1952; Major Mike Bull, who had received the Regimental Colour and Major Colin Walker who had been a subaltern in Number Four Guard.

Afterwards Her Majesty and the Captain-General carried out civic functions in Plymouth before honouring Stonehouse Barracks with a visit soon after midday. The programme started in the Sergeants' Mess, where they met some of the ranks of the Commando and their families. Lunch in the Officers' Mess followed, and later, ironically in bright sunlight, photographs were taken on the parade ground with the officers and Senior NCOs. Oscar, the hardy veteran of Dhala, was also paraded and presented, resplendent in red coat and miniature General Service Medal, with his handler, Marine Barrie Dunn. Her Majesty then left the barracks at a two-forty-five— 'It had been a very proud and impressive day for 45 Commando.'

The Honorary Freedom of the City of Plymouth was originally conferred on the Royal Marines in May, 1955 in commemoration of the 200th Anniversary of the formation of the Plymouth Division, and after the Presentation of Colours on 13 May, Four Five was to have marched through the City with Colours flying and bayonets fixed, exercising this right. This march was cancelled in conjunction with the outdoor ceremony and naturally disappointed many Plymouth citizens who were eagerly awaiting this spectacle. To make up for this the Civic Authorities invited the Commando to march through the City on 20 June. A brief parade on the Hoe preceded the march and the inspecting officer was the Representative Colonel-Commandant of the Royal Marines, Major-General R. W. Madoc, formerly Brigade Commander at Suez. Thousands of spectators subsequently lined the route on the Royal Parade and cheered loudly as the new Colours were marched past the Lord Mayor, Alderman G. E. H. Creber. Even on this occasion the weather was bad, which prompted the Commanding Officer to repeat the following words, overheard from a Plymouth deck chair attendant, 'When Four Five comes on the Hoe, it either rain or bloody blow!'

Within a week Four Five was to prove its flexibility yet again and switch its horizon from one of ceremonial duties to that of operational tasks. Major Mike Bull, Z Company Commander, had already missed the 20 June parade for urgent briefings in the Ministry of Defence from an envious past Commanding Officer. The destination, at the time, was known only to a few. Lt-Col Roger Ephraums and a small Tactical Headquarters departed from Plymouth on 1 July and part of Z Company Headquarters, Eight Troop (2/Lt Mike Todd) and Nine Troop (Lt Peter Ward) left the following day.

The reason for the hasty and secret move was the threat of disorder in Bermuda during the Black Power conference due to be held in July. The main body of Z Company arrived on the island on 5 July, having flown to Freeport, Bahamas, and transferred to the frigate HMS *Arethusa*. Secrecy was maintained so well that even the ever-vigilant press did not get hold of the story, thus precluding the publication of the 'cover-plan'. Surprise was therefore effectively achieved which led to the Black Power leader, Mr Roosevelt Brown, complaining that 'the Governor of Bermuda had brought in a hundred trained killers to the island.' Whatever Mr Brown's private views were, this rapid deployment seems to have done the trick, and the scenes of threatened violence did not materialize. Instead, Z Company returned to Plymouth after a pleasant fortnight—formal training was forbidden as it was considered to be too provocative!

Later in the year the troubles in Northern Ireland over-shadowed much of the news and as a result, in August, the unit became Spearhead Battalion at only one day's notice. Other troop movements had forced this decision and pre-planning, which normally takes some time, had to be crammed into a hectic few hours. Concurrent with Spearhead the Commando completed a helicopter display on Salisbury Plain to the NATO Chiefs of Staff and then ending one commitment rushed by road to the South Coast to embark in the Commando Ship, HMS *Bulwark*, for a second Mediterranean deployment. What would have happened if a strategic emergency had broken out during this day is anybody's guess!

On return from the Mediterranean Four Five scored another 'first'. In the presence of the Lord Mayor of London, on 18 November, the Old Colours were lodged in Stationers' Hall, London, home of the Worshipful Company of Stationers and Newspapermakers. It is believed that this is the first time that regimental colours have ever been lodged in the Hall of a City Livery Company, and this is a truly memorable precedent for the unit to have made. There had been many months of discussion as to where the Colours were to be lodged or 'laid up'. Normally, in the Royal Marines, Colours are laid up in churches or chapels within establishments or where the Corps has had a particular association. On this occasion it was decided to 'widen the net' and invite the Worshipful Company of Stationers and Newspapermakers, with whom the Corps had enjoyed a special relationship since 1949, to be the guardians of Four Five's Old Colours.

We have already noted the great changes that have taken place in British strategy in recent years and the growing contribution given to the NATO Alliance. Four Five's participation in this role became significant on 1 December, 1969, when it was announced by the Ministry of Defence that the Commando was to be designated the country's first ever specialist unit fully equipped in Mountain and Arctic Warfare for operations on the North Flank of NATO. This is the first time that a complete unit has been fully committed to this task although the Corps and other arms have carried out winter warfare training. Indeed even Four Five has operated under such conditions and one is immediately reminded of those arctic-clad men on the bitter and open spaces of Belle Isle in 1945 and the 'White Ghosts of Troodos' in Cyprus. Although by no means in its infancy there will undoubtedly still be many developments in the Artic Warfare field and one trusts that the Commando will play no small part in these.

As we enter the seventies it was, probably, assumed that the Commando's thoughts would be pre-occupied with its new role. However, this was not to be for long. The first months of training in Norway and Scotland went according to plan, and then, it happened again.

The urgent voice on the Tannoy at Stonehouse Barracks during the afternoon of 21 May, 1970, giving warning of a 'clear lower decks' was to be the prelude of another unforecasted period of action. This time it was a 'short'* emergency tour to reinforce the Northern Ireland Garrison during the General Election on 18 June and the Orange celebrations on 12 July. The General Officer Commanding and Director of Operations in Northern Ireland was Lieutenant-General Sir Ian Freeland, who had commanded the 2nd Battalion the Royal Inniskilling Fusiliers alongside Four Five in Cyprus in 1955 and had been GOC in East Africa when the unit went to Tanganyika to help quell the army mutinies. Up to now the Commando had fortunately not been involved in the sorrowful task of peace-keeping duties within our own shores. As the problem in Ulster is still with us it would be premature to comment upon the political and background events which will doubtless take a considerable time to resolve themselves. Suffice it to say, however, that in three months in Belfast (1 June–2 September) Four Five made an invaluable contribution in assisting to heal some of the existing wounds and when called upon to do so was able to show the resolve and courage that one traditionally associates with the proud wearers of the Red Lanyard.

At the outset the Commando Group consisted of four Rifle Companies; X (Capt Lol Robinson), Y (Capt Mike Weller), Support (Major Bruce Weldhen) and 145 (Maiwand) Commando Light Battery, Royal Artillery (Major Ted Burch).†

---

* Later extended from two to three months.

† Z Company was retained in England for display and Royal Tournament duties.

Headquarters Company (Capt Ben Herman), of course, carried out its normal administrative duties as well as finding itself in the front line on many occasions. The supply element of the unit, B. Echelon, under the Quartermaster (Capt Vic Henry) had a large parish to look after and they were situated in a Territorial Army training camp to the south of Belfast at Ballykinler, although they were possibly better off than most, for accommodation for the remainder was most rudimentary, to say the least, and never quite reached Hilton standards. Headquarters and the Battery lived in police stations whilst the other Companies' locations varied from hutted camps to a Royal Naval Depot Ship (HMS *Maidstone*), and gaunt flax mills and factories never designed for residence at all. Washing facilities were scarce and the visits of the mobile bath unit were always eagerly awaited. 'Home' for the average marine was a sleeping bag in a crowded room, on immediate call should trouble break out. In Headquarters some ranks fared little better and two ranks spent the entire three months virtually out in the open under the axles of parked vehicles. One more enterprising marine (Cpl Alistair Henderson, the Commanding Officer's signaller) was the victim of the Unit Public Relations Officer's (Instructor-Lt David Roberts) enthusiasm. Henderson had taken up residence in an abandoned Mini Countryman parked in the Police Station yard. The PRO, ever alert to a good story, obtained newspaper coverage of Henderson reclining comfortably in his improvised home from home. Sadly, the number plate was all to clearly visible in the photograph. Later that day the legal owner reclaimed his car and the signaller was out roughing it with the remainder of Headquarters, and with a poor opinion of publicity! However, these conditions were a vast improvement on those experienced earlier on in the disturbances and throughout Four Five's tour the 9th Para Independent Squadron, Royal Engineers, worked manfully with others to make the dwelling places more habitable. Undoubtedly the overriding memories of these months were one of confinement. Leave and evenings off were rare, and for some, never at all, and one correspondent summed it up most appropriately: 'It is ironical that perhaps the most severe curfew has been imposed on the troops themselves . . . Conditions in Malaya or Aden were rarely so restricted or depressing'.

Throughout the years, although frequently on what can be broadly termed Internal Security duties, Four Five has only rarely had to come face-to-face with bitter rioting, as experienced in Northern Ireland. Two major previous occasions immediately spring to mind and those are the Vouni incident in Cyprus, 1955, and the Malta Dockyard riots in 1958. There were, of course, crowd disturbances in Aden, but not on the same scale.

Rather than examining a week by week account of operations in Belfast let us instead take a look at what was described in the unit as 'the longest weekend'. Typical, by no means, fortunately, of everyday life but an indication of the ferocity of religious and civil strife with which the unit had to cope. The Commando's main area of responsibility in Belfast included the Crumlin Road which was flanked to the north by the Ardoyne, a strong Catholic area, and to the south by an equally predominantly Protestant district, both consisting of row upon row of dull red-brick terraced houses. On Friday, 26 June a Protestant march was due to go up the Crumlin Road and violent retaliation from the 'Ardoyne Citizens' Defence Committee' was virtually guaranteed. A stand-to was ordered and companies of old friends of the Commando, the 1st Battalion the King's Own Scottish Borderers and the 1st Battalion the Royal Scots, were placed under command. An eye witness remembers the procession as consisting of eight Lodges, each with its own band 'playing the most provocative marches they could and getting every ounce of noise out of their instruments as they approached the Catholic Ardoyne . . . A crowd of about 2,000 accompanied these bands in an awesome throng'. It was about eight-thirty in the evening and the fighting soon started, the Catholics hurling the first fusillade of stones and bottles. This initial salvo landed in the ranks of the first Orange Lodge who fortunately carried on marching, but after two

more salvoes the procession virtually came to a halt and the
two rival factions joined battle—350 noisy Catholic youths on
one side and many hundreds of Protestants on the other. In
fact the word 'joined' is not quite true, because on one of the
side streets between these two mobs happened to be Eleven
Troop of Support Company* commanded by 2/Lt Ernest
Cooke. 4-ton trucks had been drawn up broadside across the
street to act as barricades but these offered little protection for
the thirty or so men of the Troop, who had to face two crowds
totalling over 1,000 persons for the next half hour. In true
spirit they gallantly held their ground whilst the terrifying
battle raged on both sides. They were subject to stones, rocks,
ball bearings, glass marbles, rivets (catapulted), bottles, iron
piping and sheets of broken glass—viciously flung at below-
knee height. Injuries were sustained by nearly every man, not
the least of these being 2/Lt Cooke who received a brick in his
mouth at a range of five yards, but after quick medical attention,
he courageously re-assumed his place, which had to be temporarily taken over by Sgt David Carman.

Further down the Crumlin Road more fighting broke out,
on a larger scale, with 400 Commandos sandwiched between
3,000 Protestants and 2,000 Catholics. The Royal Ulster
Constabulary did sterling work in this engagement, which
lasted almost until daybreak, by holding the Protestants back
whilst Four Five restrained the Catholics. As dawn streaked
over the rock-strewn streets the defiant groups of youths finally
departed to their beds, still waving Union Jacks or Irish
tricolours depending upon their allegiance.

For the rest of the Saturday morning a tense calm prevailed
and, after cleaning up operations, 'the streets began to look as
normal as is possible in Belfast'. That afternoon (27 June) more
Orange marches took place in the Catholic Falls area outside
Four Five's area, but the effects were soon felt. Rumour in
crisis spots seems to travel fast and at four o'clock shooting
broke out in the Ardoyne area, attributed to IRA snipers.

* Eleven Troop was a composite troop of ranks drawn chiefly from
Z Company but under command of Support Company.

Marine Roland Thomas, a driver with Y Company, had the narrowest escape. He recalls that he 'was chatting quietly to a Mick at a street corner when all of a sudden shots rang out and he collapsed, dead, in front of me. I dodged behind my truck and returned the fire, letting off six rounds which seemed to do the trick'. Y Company was then deployed throughout the sector to check the firing and also there to witness the action was Capt Ben Herman, now carrying out duties as Staff Officer Operations. Capt Herman seemed to be a marked man that afternoon and his driver, Marine Peter Sims, remembers that a bullet passed two inches behind the driving seat, grazing the wireless cables, just as they arrived on the scene in their Land Rover. Shortly afterwards another bullet whistled past the Staff Officer Operations, removing the eye piece from his gas mask which was in his hand at the time! The savagery of the fighting is probably best illustrated by the dreadful treatment meted out to Petty Officer Frederick MacLaughlin of Four Five's medical staff. He had been calmly rendering aid to wounded civilians lying in the street and had then been evacuating them by ambulance. Notwithstanding the bullets aimed at him he had heroically carried on until the gunmen eventually found their mark. At the time he was inside the ambulance, clearly painted with Red Cross markings, and the shots brutally tore through the outside of the vehicle and seriously injured Petty Officer MacLaughlin in the cheek.*

The sporadic fighting continued and by now a total of five Companies had been concentrated on this section of the Crumlin Road by Lt-Col Roger Ephraums, who moved with his 'Rover Group' out from the Police Headquarters to a patch of waste ground beside the road itself. The outbursts eased off later in the afternoon but restarted at nine o'clock that evening when a bus, which had been commandeered by a drunk, crashed into a pub and gave the crowd a chance to get their own back.

* Petty Officer MacLaughlin was awarded the George Medal for his courage.

'A very angry crowd gathered and began the normal shouting of abuse and hurling missiles at Five Troop (2/Lt Charles Daniel) which was at a street junction. Five Troop, consisting of only twenty-three all ranks, managed to push a 400-strong crowd back 500 metres using CS gas, arclights and snatch squads. They made seven arrests in all, one of which had been badly injured as he had been dragged back along the ground by his friends over numerous broken bottles and his white shirt was hardly an advert for Persil.'

The crowd also included a gunman, who released about eight shots in the direction of the Troop, one of which resulted in a very fortunate escape for Marine Terence Glover. His riot shield was pierced by a bullet which then travelled on into the pouch on his belt and finally landed up in his rifle cleaning box. The mob, having been routed by the fearless Five Troop, then commenced an orgy of destruction (which included cars) and looting, and then burning a petrol station, a launderette and a tyre store. This damage was not to be the end of the day's activities. The mob then decided to pay Four Five yet another visit and marched on the police station, which housed the permanent headquarters—now very much depleted, being reduced to less than twenty men. The crowd now numbered some 300, but was no less ferocious as it had just raided a wine store. The incident gives ample evidence that even headquarters can find themselves in the front line. Capt Ian Martin, the Adjutant, led his small team in a most determined defence of the Police Station to keep the mob at bay while reinforcements were rushed in. These consisted of Three Troop (2/Lt Jim Wilson) of X Company and the crack marksmen of the Recce Troop under Sgt Gil Jackman. Four Five's return of fire soon sent the Protestants scattering and as two large blood trails were found the next morning it was assumed that someone 'got the message'. One casualty that did occur during this battle was Chief Supt Bill Ligget, RUC, who bravely went out into the crowd to try and persuade it to disperse. For his pains he

was badly injured in the face by a rioter firing a shot-gun at
him from a distance of only a few yards away.

The battle report continues:

'Sunday morning (28 June) the Crumlin Road looked like
a battleground, bottles, stones, marbles, ball bearings and
bullets were found littered all over the area and the air was
thick with smoke from burnt out cars, petrol stations and
other buildings. Yankee Company moved the bus which had
crashed into the building and used it as sleeping accommodation and the whole Commando settled down for a few hours
rest. Women from the Catholic Ardoyne brought everybody
tea and the tense atmosphere returned to near normal. Yet
again Belfast Corporation dustmen came along to sweep
up the wreckage and people started going to Church'.

That Sunday afternoon passed quietly and later that night
the 'Rover Group' was able to retun to the police station—
unknown to the Protestants who decided to have another go
to make up for the previous night's failure. This time the attackers received a severe trouncing from Four Five, by now in
no mood to trifle, and they decided to call it a day. So ended
seventy-two hours of almost non-stop rioting and outbursts.
These troubles were futile in the extreme as nothing was
achieved apart from possibly releasing pent up emotions. The
bereaved were left to mourn their dead and others to patch up
their wounds* or repair damaged property. For the Commando
the aftermath meant a long campaign to bring harmony
amongst the peoples in its district. The Medical section, under
Surg-Lt Sandy Craig did much to treat those wounded in the
bitter fighting and kept this momentum going for the remainder
of the tour. Community relations were high on the priority
list and representatives from both sides were called in to advise
on the best methods of achieving results. It was a case of
'voices rather than rifles' and carefully selected teams 'with an

* Four Five had sixteen casualties during this period, though only
one serious.

15

ability to consume vast amounts of tea' toured the area to calm the troubled waters.

The Regimental Sergeant Major, Mr. Harry King, was the general overseer on this entertainments side and one of his most successful ventures was day outings and camps for the local children at a farm near Belfast. The organizers of these trips readily admitted that they were far more exhausting than riot control! Other departments too worked manfully on hearts and minds projects including the Assault Engineers (Lt Tony Smith), who found themselves doing anything from repairing a community centre to laying a basketball pitch. The Assault Engineers also repapered and repaired the damaged house of a ninety-four year old invalid in hospital at the time, doubtless providing a welcome-home surprise for him.

Only by intensive and continuous patrolling was peace maintained. Many close and happy liaisons were established during this time; Recce Troop operated jointly with both the 17th/21st Lancers and the Life Guards, excellent help was also given by the Royal Military Police.

Thus Orange Weekend, Hibernian Day and the traditional Black Precaptory Rallies passed peacefully. The unit left Northern Ireland knowing that it had carried out a most difficult and trying job well and temporarily brought peace to a corner of Belfast where both Protestants and Roman Catholics learnt to respect and admire the green beret and Red Lanyard.

The permanent stay in the West Country was not to be as long as many of Four Five might have wished, for earlier in the year of 1970 it had been learnt that the unit was to be moved north to a new base in Scotland, a country where Four Five had first learnt its Commando skills over twenty-five years previously. This move had been necessitated by another shrinkage in Britain's foreign commitments which had caused elements of 3 Commando Brigade to return to the Plymouth area from Singapore. Four Five's new base was to be the spacious Royal Naval Air Station, HMS *Condor*, near Arbroath in Angus, an ideal position both for training and embarkation for duties in connection with the protection of the Northern flank of NATO.

This move, on 1 April, 1971, after another strenuous training session in Norway, was to have more far reaching effects for the unit. In fact it was now to change its official nomenclature to '45 Commando Group', as Four Five was joined permanently by its old friends from the Radfan days, 145 (Maiwand) Commando Light Battery, Royal Artillery, and a Troop of 59 Field Squadron Royal Engineers, appropriately named Condor Troop. 1971 was to prove as busy a year as the preceding one and as the shadows of strife and violence thickened once again over Northern Ireland later in the summer, so it was necessary for more troops to be rushed into the territory as a result of the announcement of special emergency powers taken by the Stormont Government. Four Five was moving to the scene of action again.

And so, as the Commando enters the seventies after an existence that has spanned over twenty-seven action-filled and tumultuous years, one is tempted to look both ahead into the future, and back to the past glories. Back to the days of a world war in which the tradition and spirit of Four Five was born; the assault on Hitler's Fortress of Europe; the bloody and costly battle for Merville; the bitter cold and snow of Holland; the spearhead of the thrust across Germany; a series of brilliant post-war campaigns which are now household names—Palestine, Malaya, Cyprus, Suez, Tanganyika, Aden. In all a total of some fourteen years and three months on active operations, a truly illustrious record in modern times. Now to the future, which is as unpredictable as ever. Four Five is back in Europe and although, at present, the politicians seem to put most emphasis in this continent and its surrounding waters, only time will tell whether this is where our destiny lies. History has an uncanny knack of repeating itself. Success breeds success and upon this and the military and other emergencies that may confront us at a moment's notice the Commando will doubtless thrive.

Perhaps the most appropriate way of summing up the brave

deeds of the men of Four Five is to recall the simple words written by Pericles in 430 B.C. These words will doubtless provide an epitaph for those who have gone before and an ever-present reminder to their successors of their true purpose in the Commando.

TAKE THESE MEN FOR YOUR EXAMPLE. LIKE THEM, REMEMBER THAT PROSPERITY CAN BE ONLY FOR THE FREE, THAT FREEDOM IS THE SURE POSSESSION OF THOSE ALONE WHO HAVE THE COURAGE TO DEFEND IT.

APPENDIX I
COMMANDING OFFICERS

August, 1943–June, 1944	Lt-Col N. C. Ries, RM
June, 1944–March, 1945	Lt-Col W. N. Gray, DSO, RM
March, 1945–April, 1945	Lt-Col A. L. Blake, MC, RM
April, 1945–July, 1945	Lt-Col W. N. Gray, DSO, RM
July, 1945–December, 1945	Lt-Col I. D. De'ath, DSO, MBE, RM
December, 1945–January, 1946	Lt-Col R. D. Houghton, MC, RM
January, 1946–January, 1948	Lt-Col T. M. Gray, DSO, MC, RM
January, 1948–July, 1948	Lt-Col E. C. E. Palmer, DSO, RM
July, 1948–November, 1948	Lt-Col P. L. Norcock, RM
December, 1948–August, 1950	Lt-Col N. C. Ries, OBE, RM
August, 1950–July, 1952	Lt-Col R. C. de M. Leathes, MVO, OBE, RM
July, 1952–October, 1954	Lt-Col F. A. Eustace, OBE, RM
October, 1954–November, 1956	Lt-Col N. H. Tailyour, DSO, RM
November, 1956–December, 1956	Lt-Col R. D. Crombie, RM
December, 1956–January, 1957	Lt-Col N. H. Tailyour, DSO, RM
January, 1957–July, 1958	Lt-Col J. Richards, OBE, RM
July, 1958–September, 1958	Lt-Col R. D. Crombie, RM
September, 1958–July, 1960	Lt-Col F. C. Barton, RM
July, 1960–January, 1962	Lt-Col L. G. Marsh, MC, RM
January, 1962–July, 1963	Lt-Col N. S. E. Maude, RM
July, 1963–November, 1964	Lt-Col T. M. P. Stevens, MC, RM
November, 1964–May, 1966	Lt-Col R. J. McGarel Goves, RM
May, 1966–July, 1967	Lt-Col F. C. E. Bye, RM
July, 1967–December, 1968	Lt-Col J. I. H. Owen, OBE, RM
December, 1968–April, 1969	Lt-Col J. C. C. Richards, RM
April, 1969–October, 1971	Lt-Col R. J. Ephraums, OBE, RM
October, 1971–	Lt-Col Sir Steuart R. Pringle Bt RM

APPENDIX II
REGIMENTAL SERGEANTS-MAJOR

September, 1943–June, 1944	RSM J. H. Grimsey, RM
November, 1944–August, 1945	RSM G. R. Burden, RM
August, 1945–June, 1948	RSM E. G. Edlin, RM
June, 1948–February, 1951	RSM H. F. Martin, RM
February, 1951–May, 1952	RSM L. F. Mathews, RM
July, 1952–June, 1954	RSM A. Rendall, RM
September, 1954–April, 1957	RSM J. Baines, MM, BEM, RM
May, 1957–November, 1959	RSM A. Cornish, RM
November, 1959–April, 1961	RSM J. P. McDonnell, RM
May, 1961–January, 1962	RSM G. A. Bray, RM
February, 1962–January, 1963	RSM H. E. Day, RM
January, 1963–November, 1963	RSM J. Pollitt, RM
November, 1963–January, 1964	RSM C. Swallow, RM
January, 1964–March, 1964	RSM J. Pollitt, RM
March, 1964–September, 1964	RSM F. Agass, RM
September, 1964–July, 1965	RSM W. Chisholm, RM
July, 1965–June, 1966	RSM P. S. Norris, RM
June, 1966–June, 1967	RSM H. R. Rees, RM
June, 1967–November, 1968	RSM G. E. Fordham, RM
November, 1968–February, 1971	RSM H. W. King, RM
February, 1971–	RSM R. J. Tyack, RM

APPENDIX III

OPERATIONAL HONOURS AND AWARDS

1944–1945

VICTORIA CROSS (POSTHUMOUS)
L/Cpl H. E. Harden, RAMC

DISTINGUISHED SERVICE ORDER
Lt-Col W. N. Gray, RM

BAR TO DISTINGUISHED SERVICE ORDER
Lt-Col W. N. Gray, RM

DISTINGUISHED SERVICE CROSS
Rev. R. Haw, RNVR

MILITARY CROSS
Major J. N. Rushforth, RM
Major I. N. N. Beadle, RM
Capt H. N. Smith, RAMC
Capt J. A. Tulloch, RAMC
Capt H. A. Evans (FOO att. from 1st Mountain Regt, RA)
Lt T. Thomas, SAUDF
Lt H. G. Riley, RM
Lt A. Tate, RM

BRITISH EMPIRE MEDAL
RQMS T. J. Morgan, RM

MILITARY MEDAL
TSM H. F. G. Beaven, RM
TSM H. J. Bennett, RM
Colour-Sgt J. L. Fenwick, RM
Sgt J. Brown, RM
Sgt W. J. Noakes, RM
Sgt W. Deacon, RM
Sgt R. Stuart, RM
Sgt T. Harrison, RM
Cpl J. Sykes, RM
Cpl I. Harris, RWK (att. from 10 [Inter Allied] Commando)
L/Cpl F. G. Burton, RM
Marine N. Green
Marine N. J. Patrick
Marine D. Towler

MENTION IN DESPATCHES
Major A. L. Blake, MC, RM
Capt J. E. Day, RM
TSM B. M. Aylett, MM, RM
Sgt H. A. Cook, RM
Sgt W. Skeath, RM
Marine J. Clarke
Marine J. Haville
Marine W. K. Laidler

CROIX DE GUERRE (WITH SILVER STAR)
Capt J. E. Day, RM

CROIX DE GUERRE (WITH GILT STAR)
Capt A. W. Neaves, RM

1946–1970

BAR TO DISTINGUISHED SERVICE ORDER
Lt-Col N. H. Tailyour, DSO, RM (1957 Cyprus)

ORDER OF THE BRITISH EMPIRE
Lt-Col R. C. de M. Leathes, MVO, RM (1952 Malaya)

MEMBER, ORDER OF THE BRITISH EMPIRE
Major M. J. Baizley, RM (1965 Aden)
Lt A. C. Letchford, RM (1965 Aden)
Lt I. C. Martin, RM (1965 Aden)
Capt R. F. G. Meadows, RM (1957 Cyprus)
Major J. Richards, RM (1952 Malaya)

MILITARY CROSS
Lt D. J. Brand, RM (1965 Aden)
Major D. J. Brewster, RM (1967 Aden)
Capt R. P. Carter, RM (1951 Malaya)
Lt M. G. R. Darwall, RM (1952 Malaya)
Temp 2/Lt A. D. Gavin, RM (1951 Malaya)
Lt P. Griffiths, RM (1951 Malaya)
Lt D. P. L. Hunter, RM (1951 Malaya)
Lt T. P. P. Knott, RM (1967 Aden)
Lt S. L. Syrad, RM (1957 Suez)

BRITISH EMPIRE MEDAL
Colour Sgt J. G. Buxton, RM (1952 Malaya)
QMS F. Collingwood, RM (1957 Cyprus)
Sgt A. J. McKinley, RM (1964 Aden)
Marine B. R. Thornton (1958 Cyprus)
Marine D. G. Walker (1956 Cyprus)

GEORGE MEDAL
Petty Officer Medical Assistant F. J. D. MacLaughlin, RN (1970 Northern Ireland)

MILITARY MEDAL
Sgt J. S. Aubertin, RM (1952 Malaya)
Marine D. K. Davidson (1957 Suez)
Marine R. G. Hodgkiss (1951 Malaya)
Sgt P. Littlewood, RM (1967 Aden)
Cpl P. A. McGuigan, RM (1967 Aden)
Cpl M. E. Mead, RM (1957 Suez)
Sgt W. G. B. Patterson, RM (1965 Aden)
Sgt C. T. Rees, RM (1959 Oman)
RSM R. W. Smith, RM (1965 Aden)
Sgt H. H. Tydd, RM (1951 Malaya)
Cpl T. A. Want, RM (1952 Malaya)

MENTION IN DESPATCHES
Sgt E. J. Blyth, RM (1965 Aden)
Surg Lt J. G. Bradford, RN (1957 Suez)
Cpl F. J. Brewer, RM (1967 Aden)
Marine C. J. Brown (1959 Cyprus)
Capt R. P. Carter, RM (1951 Malaya)
Lt J. J. S. Coulter, RM (1959 Oman)
Capt A. D. Crawford, RM (1952 Malaya)
Major R. D. Crombie, RM (1957 Suez)
Cpl H. Davies, RM (1958 Cyprus)
Lt R. D. G. Davison, RM (1952 Malaya)
Major I. D. De'Ath, DSO, MBE, RM (1957 Cyprus)
Sgt D. G. Dorling, RM (1965 Aden)
Major B. L. Edwards, RM (1967 Aden)
Marine N. Gibson (1968 Aden)
Capt E. C. M. Goddard, RM (1965 Aden)
Capt J. H. Haycock, RM (1957 Suez)
L/Cpl W. T. Heath, RM (1952 Malaya)
Lt J. Herron, RM (1952 Malaya)
Inst Lt-Cdr G. L. D. Jenkins, RN (1958 Cyprus)
Sgt P. W. A. Kennedy, RM (1967 Aden)
Marine W. Knowles (1952 Malaya)
QMS A. MacVicar, RM (1965 Aden)
Sgt J. A. T. Mayne, RM (1968 Aden)
Acting Cpl J. McDermott, RM (1951 Malaya)
Capt R. F. G. Meadows, MBE, RM (1957 Suez)
Lt P. J. A. Montgomery, RM (1958 Cyprus)
Lt T. Morgan, MM, RM (1952 Malaya)

Sgt J. Munson, RM (1965 Aden)
Lt-Col J. I. H. Owen, OBE, RM (1968 Aden)
Capt E. G. D. Pounds, RM (1957 Cyprus)
Marine B. A. Quinn (1967 Aden)
Major J. Richards, RM (1951 Malaya)
Lt-Col J. Richards, MBE, RM (1958 Cyprus)
Lt A. W. Richardson, RM (1957 Suez)
Marine G. Salisbury (1958 Cyprus)
Cpl T. Shemmans, RM (1951 Malaya)
Sgt E. J. Sim, RM (1957 Suez)
Capt S. D. Smith, RM (1951 Malaya)
Marine W. K. G. Smith (1951 Malaya)
Lt-Col N. H. Tailyour, DSO, RM (1957 Suez)
Sick Berth Attendant E. A. Wade, RN (1965 Aden)
Acting Sgt G. H. Walker, RM (1951 Malaya)
Marine R. Williams (1952 Malaya)

QUEEN'S COMMENDATION FOR BRAVE CONDUCT
Major R. A. Campbell, RM (1965 Aden)
Cpl J. G. Eley, RM (1968 Norway)
2/Lt C. W. J. Ledger, RM (1965 Aden)
Sgt R. V. Shellard, RM (1966 Aden)
Marine W. Stephenson (1956 Cyprus)

COMMANDER-IN-CHIEF'S CERTIFICATE OF
COMMENDATION (FAR EAST LAND FORCES)
Sgt J. C. Baxter, RM (Malaya)
Acting Sgt E. J. Blyth, RM (Malaya)
L/Cpl J. D. Drakeley, RM (1952 Malaya)
Sgt J. W. Prickman, RM (1952 Malaya)
Marine G. Weir (1951 Malaya)

COMMANDER-IN-CHIEF'S CERTIFICATE OF
COMMENDATION (SOUTH-EAST ASIA LAND FORCES)
TSM H. J. Bennett, RM (1947 Hong Kong)

COMMANDER-IN-CHIEF'S CERTIFICATE OF
COMMENDATION (MIDDLE EAST LAND FORCES)
Marine A. K. Allan-Williams (1966 Aden)
Lt J. S. M. Barr, RM (1965 Aden)
Marine J. Beech (1964 Tanganyika)
Marine J. M. Bleakley (1964 Tanganyika)
Acting Sgt J. D. Bourne, RM (1964 Tanganyika)
Sgt D. A. H. Burnham, RM (1958 Cyprus)
Sgt J. R. French, RM (1967 Aden)
Marine M. C. Harrison (1968 Aden)

Marine D. M. Healey (1966 Aden)
Cpl A. P. Hemmings, RM (1966 Aden)
Marine M. J. Hill (1966 Aden)
Lt P. A. C. Howgill, RM (1964 Tanganyika)
Major D. L. S. Langley, MC, RM (1964 Tanganyika)
Lt I. C. Martin, RM (1964 Tanganyika)
Marine B. Massey (1957 Cyprus)
Sgt S. J. Moon, RM (1967 Aden)
Sgt D. G. Newman, RM (1958 Cyprus)
Lt D. M. Parkinson, RM (1967 Aden)
Cpl J. A. Rafferty, RM (1964 Aden)
Sgt J. W. Rice, RM (1964 Tanganyika)
Cpl J. Ross, RM (1967 Aden)
Major S. D. Smith, RM (1964 Tanganyika)
Sgt J. P. Strathdee, RM (1967 Aden)
Leading Medical Assistant E. A. Wade, RN (1967 Aden)
Marine K. F. Wilson (1967 Aden)
Cpl A. F. Wrey, RM (1965 Aden)

COMMANDANT GENERAL ROYAL MARINES
CERTIFICATE OF COMMENDATION
Marine W. R. S. J. Harrison (1967 Aden)
Marine G. Lloyd (1956 Cyprus)
Surg Lt D. B. Trash, RN (1968 Norway)
Medical Assistant L. F. M. Young, RN (1968 Norway)

GENERAL OFFICER COMMANDING'S CERTIFICATE
OF COMMENDATION
Colour Sgt D. A. Carman, RM (1970 Northern Ireland)
Medical Assistant C. E. James, RN (1970 Northern Ireland)
2/Lt R. J. McConnell, RM (1970 Northern Ireland)

APPENDIX IV
ROLL OF HONOUR

1943–1945

Sgt P. Ahern, RM	25/1/45	Holland
Sgt J. Atkinson	25/1/45	United Kingdom
Marine D. A. A. Baker	6/4/45	Germany
Cpl L. Baker, RM	6/6/44	France
Cpl E. B. Beach, RM	12/6/44	France
Sgt W. B. Begbie, RM	11/6/44	France
Marine R. Bell	6/8/44	France
Marine J. Benson	12/4/45	Germany
Cpl A. Bidmead, RM	6/8/44	France
L/Cpl W. G. Boniface, RM	12/4/45	Germany
Marine G. Boothroyd	13/6/44	France
Capt M. C. Brockbank, RM	12/4/45	Germany
Cpl A. R. Brooks, RM	5/8/44	France
Marine F. Campbell	2/7/44	France
Marine B. L. Cann	7/4/45	Germany
Lt A. C. P. Caspar, RM	6/4/45	Germany
Marine R. Casson	6/6/44	France
Marine R. J. Clarke	4/4/45	Germany
Cpl R. Clark, RM	6/6/44	France
Cpl J. S. Cocks, RM	23/1/45	Holland
Cpl I. Cohen, RM	15/7/44	France
Marine A. C. Conaty	1/3/45	Germany
Marine A. C. A. Cook	24/3/45	Germany
Marine E. P. Corbyn	7/6/44	France
Marine W. Crompton	12/4/45	Germany
Marine W. Crouch	12/4/45	Germany
Marine E. C. Dangerfield	7/6/44	France
Marine G. Davidson	11/6/44	France
L/Cpl O. Davies, RM	7/6/44	France
L/Cpl K. W. J. Davis, RM	7/6/44	France
L/Cpl A. C. Dryburgh, RM	10/6/44	France
Cpl J. J. Duchan, RM	28/1/45	Holland
Marine A. J. Earl	8/8/44	France
Marine B. C. S. Fenton	13/6/44	France
Sgt W. Finlay, RM	17/6/44	France
Marine E. W. Forbes	12/6/44	France
Marine B. B. Forest	1/5/45	Germany
Cpl H. A. Gage, RM	13/6/44	France

Lt A. Gale, RM	7/6/44	France
Marine R. George	20/8/44	France
Marine E. J. Gladwin	7/6/44	France
Cpl F. J. E. Goodenough, RM	16/6/44	France
Capt E. E. D. Grewcock, RM	12/6/44	France
RSM J. H. Grimsey, RM	7/6/44	France
Cpl E. G. Gynes, RM	7/6/44	France
Marine G. S. Hall	10/10/45	United Kingdom
Marine J. Hall	25/8/44	France
L/Cpl H. E. Harden, VC, RAMC	23/1/45	Holland
Marine T. F. Harrington	20/8/44	France
Marine W. Hobbins	7/6/44	France
Marine P. L. Holmes	7/6/44	France
L/Cpl C. Johnson, RM	11/6/44	France
Marine A. J. Kemp	8/6/44	France
Lt W. E. Kennedy, Royal Fusiliers	6/6/44	France
Marine R. J. Keough	4/4/45	Germany
Sgt F. Kerr, RM	17/5/45	Germany
Marine F. Kershaw	6/6/44	France
Marine C. King	13/6/44	France
Cpl J. T. Knott, RM	7/4/45	Germany
Cpl J. H. Laing, RM	28/1/45	Holland
Marine G. Lay	12/4/45	Germany
Sgt T. M. Ledger, RM	11/6/44	France
Marine E. J. Lee	11/6/44	France
Marine L. L. Lee	9/6/44	France
Marine T. A. Lovett	8/6/44	France
Marine C. A. Lyon	23/1/45	Holland
Cpl R. McFall, RM	11/6/44	France
Marine J. McFatter	20/8/44	France
Marine N. M. McIntosh	5/8/44	France
Marine D. McKeown	20/8/44	France
L/Cpl H. McNulty, RM	28/1/45	Holland
Marine C. McPake	12/4/45	Germany
Marine L. H. Manley	7/6/44	France
Marine T. B. Marshall	24/3/45	Germany
Marine A. Mitchell	12/6/44	France
Cpl D. A. W. Money, RM	26/3/45	Germany
Marine C. Moseley	28/1/45	Holland
Marine A. Mulhall	12/6/44	France
Marine W. H. Murphy	6/6/44	France
Marine K. Musgrave	11/6/44	France
Cpl L. Myers, RM	16/6/44	France

Cpl V. G. Newman, RM	11/6/44	France
Sgt M. Nutter, RM	7/6/44	France
Marine B. K. Ord	24/3/45	Germany
Marine W. H. Pearce	6/4/45	Germany
L/Cpl A. R. Percival, RM	7/6/44	France
Marine H. Plant	9/8/44	France
L/Cpl W. Purvis, RM	28/1/45	Holland
Cpl D. W. Reed	12/6/44	France
Cpl A. W. Rogers, RM	11/6/44	France
Marine R. J. Rolson	8/6/44	France
Marine J. G. Russell	23/1/45	Holland
Cpl J. R. Ruston, RM	7/6/44	France
Sgt J. R. Smith, RM	11/6/44	France
L/Cpl F. T. Stallwood, RM	8/6/44	France
Marine H. J. Stapley	20/8/44	France
Marine D. P. Sweet	28/1/45	Holland
Marine R. L. Symes	28/1/45	Holland
Marine K. E. Thomas	6/4/45	Germany
Marine R. Thomas	6/6/44	France
Marine J. R. Timmins	28/1/45	Holland
Marine E. E. L. Tonks	24/7/45	United Kingdom
Marine T. G. Unthank	12/4/45	Germany
Marine F. E. Wales	23/1/45	Holland
Marine J. Walker	8/6/44	France
Marine J. W. Walker	12/6/44	France
Marine G. Watson	6/6/44	France
Cpl J. A. Watson, RM	7/6/44	France
Colour Sgt J. D. Wharton, RM	7/4/45	Germany
Marine F. Whitaker	6/6/44	France
Capt B. G. White, RM	20/8/44	France
Sgt R. D. White, RM	18/6/44	France
Marine R. A. Wilcox	21/8/44	France
Marine F. Wild	28/1/45	Holland
Marine R. Williams	6/6/44	France
Sgt W. A. Wilson, RM	30/4/45	Germany
Lt P. Winston, RM	28/1/45	Holland
Marine A. Wright	7/6/44	France
Lt T. D. Wright, RM	4/4/45	Germany

NB Some of the above named were listed as 'Missing Presumed Killed' and as they have no known grave the date of death has been recorded as when they were last seen alive.

1946–1969

Sgt D. J. Arnold, RM	7/8/64	Aden
Bugler P. A. T. Baker	20/11/61	Aden
Sgt D. Baldwin, RM	13/7/58	Cyprus
Lt P. K. Budgen, RM	6/6/51	Malaya
Marine D. G. Calway	17/5/67	Aden
QMS G. C. N. Casey, RM	31/5/57	Cyprus
Marine W. A. Cates	6/4/57	Tripoli
Cpl M. P. Coleman, RM	29/5/68	United Kingdom
Marine M. Cullen	15/5/46	Hong Kong
Sgt D. Davies, RM	6/7/53	Canal Zone
Marine A. J. Dunn	5/5/67	Aden
Marine D. Esseen	23/3/67	Aden
Marine M. Findlay	23/1/54	Canal Zone
Marine W. Fisher	5/5/49	Canal Zone
Marine P. D. Fordham	25/9/51	Malaya
Marine M. J. Fowler	6/11/56	Suez
Acting Sgt T. J. H. Genge, RM	11/7/51	Malaya
Marine K. R. George	22/3/46	Hong Kong
Marine C. E. Goodfellow	6/11/56	Suez
Colour Sgt N. W. Grant, RM	28/12/54	Malta
Marine R. T. Greening	6/10/58	Cyprus
Colour Sgt J. L. Halford, BEM, RM	17/6/58	Oman
Marine T. H. Hall	1/12/68	United Kingdom
Cpl J. Henry, RM	10/1/51	Malaya
QMS P. R. Howard, RM	1/6/49	Canal Zone
Marine N. W. R. Husband	16/11/49	Hong Kong
Marine R. Hydes	18/5/64	Aden
L/Cpl R. Jeffery, RM	23/6/63	Aden
Marine D. C. Keyes	14/9/50	Malaya
Marine E. Lamb	16/7/51	Malaya
Marine K. Lamb	10/3/56	Cyprus
Marine A. Macdougall	22/10/58	Cyprus
Marine W. M. Masters	6/7/53	Canal Zone
Cpl E. McGrath, RM	3/9/64	Aden
Marine L. O. Miller	10/1/51	Malaya
S/Lt D. A. I. Moir, RM	12/9/67	Aden
Marine D. A. Muir	10/6/65	Aden
Marine E. J. Nevard	14/9/50	Malaya
Marine P. L. M. Newland	29/5/68	United Kingdom
Sgt P. C. O'Hanlon, RM	7/12/52	Malta
Marine D. Parr	28/12/50	Malaya

Marine M. J. Perry	29/5/68	United Kingdom
Marine J. Pettigrew	27/1/61	Aden
Marine J. H. Pilcher	7/7/46	Hong Kong
Marine G. A. Poyzer	30/5/62	Aden
Marine S. R. Roberts	18/5/69	United Kingdom
Marine T. Roberts	5/12/55	Cyprus
Marine T. Robson	24/12/46	Hong Kong
Cpl W. N. Selwood, RM	25/4/47	Hong Kong
Marine D. Smith	24/3/52	Singapore
Lt D. N. Spurling, RM	3/11/58	Cyprus
Marine R. C. Swindell	27/7/63	Aden
Marine K. Tuck	31/1/62	Aden
Marine L. J. Turner	28/12/50	Malaya
Sgt G. Westwood, RM	10/1/51	Malaya
Marine K. N. Whitaker	20/1/65	Aden
Marine D. G. Whitham	13/7/58	Cyprus
Marine D. M. Wilson	26/5/64	Aden
Marine S. W. Wilson	20/1/46	United Kingdom

APPENDIX V

ACTION ON THE MONTFORTERBEEK
—23 JANUARY, 1945
Citation of L/Cpl H. E. Harden, VC, RAMC

WAR OFFICE, 8 MARCH, 1945

The King has been graciously pleased to approve the post-humous award of the Victoria Cross to:

No. 11006144 L/Cpl Henry Eric Harden, Royal Army Medical Corps (Northfleet, Kent).

In North-West Europe on 23 January, 1945, the leading section of a Royal Marine Commando Troop was pinned to the ground by intense enemy machine-gun fire from well concealed positions. As it was impossible to engage the enemy from the open owing to lack of cover, the section was ordered to make for some near-by houses. This was accomplished, but one officer and three other ranks casualties were left lying in the open.

The whole Troop position was under continuous heavy and accurate shell and mortar fire. L/Cpl Harden, the RAMC orderly attached to the Troop, at once went forward a distance of 120 yards, into the open under a hail of enemy machine gun and rifle fire directed from four positions, all within 300 yards, and with the greatest coolness and bravery remained in the open while he attended to the four casualties. After dressing the wounds of three of them, he carried one of them back to cover. L/Cpl Harden was then ordered not to go forward again and an attempt was made to bring in the other casualties with the aid of tanks, but this proved unsuccessful owing to the heavy and accurate fire of enemy anti-tank guns. A further attempt was then made to recover the casualties under a smoke screen, but this only increased the enemy fire in the vicinity of the casualties.

L/Cpl Harden then insisted on going forward again with a volunteer stretcher party, and succeeded in bringing back another badly wounded man.

L/Cpl Harden went out a third time, again with a stretcher party, and after starting on the return journey with the wounded officer, under very heavy enemy small arms and mortar fire, he was killed.

Throughout this long period L/Cpl Harden displayed superb devotion to duty and personal courage of the very highest order, and there is no doubt that it had a most steadying effect upon the other troops in the area at a most critical time. His action was directly responsible for saving the lives of the wounded brought in. His complete contempt for all personal danger, and the magnificent example he set of cool courage and determination to continue with his work, whatever the odds, was an inspiration to his comrades, and will never be forgotten by those who saw it.

APPENDIX VI

PRESENTATION OF COLOURS
29 NOVEMBER, 1952

Commanding Officer:
Lt-Col F. A. Eustace

Field Officers for handing the Colours to
HRH The Duke of Edinburgh:

Major C. L. Price
(Second-in-Command)

Major M. Pound
(HQ Troop)

Officers for the Colours:

The Queen's Colour
Lt D. C. Alexander
(Sp Troop)
Adjutant
Capt J. I. H. Owen

The Regimental Colour
Lt M. V. Bull
(A Troop)
Quartermaster
Lt (QM) C. C. Bolton

Regimental Sergeant Major:
RSM A. Rendall

No. 1 Guard
Capt M. R. Nunns, MC
(A Troop)
Lt J. C. C. Richards
(A Troop)
Lt J. Herron
(A Troop)

No. 2 Guard
Capt R. T. Onslow
(X Troop)
Lt P. G. Ferguson
(X Troop)
Lt I. A. McDougall
(Z Troop)

No. 3 Guard
Capt H. J. Powell, DSC
(Sp Troop)
Lt E. St V. Troubridge
(B Troop)
Lt G. B. Allen
(B Troop)

Capt R. G. J. Farrie
(B Troop)
Lt B. A. Weldhen
(B Troop)
Lt C. P. Walker
(Sp Troop)

Escort to the Colours:
QMS S. T. Kemp
Colour Sgt T. F. Tanton
Colour Sgt C. U. McLennan

APPENDIX VII

PRESENTATION OF COLOURS— 13 MAY, 1969

(Indoor Ceremony)

Commanding Officer:
Lt-Col R. J. Ephraums, OBE

Second-in-Command:
Major B. L. Edwards

Adjutant:
Capt M. Weller

Field Officers for handing the Colours to
HM The Queen:

Major C. P. Walker	Major T. E. Carroll
(Sp Company)	(HQ Company)

Officers for the Old Colours:

The Queen's Colour	The Regimental Colour
Lt P. A. Whittaker	Lt P. N. Ward
(HQ Company)	(Z Company)

Officers for the New Colours:

The Queen's Colour	The Regimental Colour
Lt A. J. Berry	Lt J. R. Atter
(X Company)	(X Company)

No. 4 Guard:
Lt R. I. S. Hawkins
Lt J. M. Watkins
QMS A. L. Hammond
Ranks of HQ and Sp Companies

Escort to the Old Colours:	Escort to the New Colours:
QMS J. J. Kelly	QMS C. T. Hazell
Colour Sgt J. French	Colour Sgt P. Kirkup
Colour Sgt R. Waterfield	Colour Sgt B. H. Hostler

Regimental Sergeant Major:
RSM H. W. King

LLIED UNIT OF THE COMMONWEALTH OF AUSTRALIA ARMED FORCES 2nd COMMANDO COMPANY (CITIZEN MILITARY FORCES)

On 4 March, 1960, the following Royal Marines Routine Order was published:

'Her Majesty the Queen has been pleased to approve alliances between the Royal Marines and the 1st Infantry Battalion (City of Sydney's Own Regiment) (Commando) and between 45 Commando, Royal Marines and the 2nd Commando Company.'

The 2/1 Australian Independent Company was raised in May, 1941, but did not see action as a Company since elements were stationed over a large area in the island chain north of Australia at the outbreak of the Japanese war. Other independent companies were raised later that year and the first unit to play an important role in the war was 2/2 Independent Company, which fought at Timor. All initial training of the independent companies was carried out at the 7th Infantry Training Centre (later the Guerilla Warfare School) at Wilson's Promontory. This promontory is the southernmost portion of the State of Victoria. Training commenced on 6 March, 1941, and this date is now considered for commemoration as their Commando anniversary. These units were disbanded after the war.

It was decided to reform commando units in 1951 and by July, 1955, two Commando Companies had been raised, one at Sydney and one at Melbourne. These are citizen military forces, with regular commanding officers, adjutants and quartermasters. Since that date the size of No. 1 Company increased, and so it was formed into 1st Infantry Battalion (City of Sydney's Own Regiment) (Commando). This unit was granted the Freedom of the City of Sydney on 10 October, 1959.

The Regimental March of the 2nd Commando Company (approved by Australian Army Order No. 37/1959) is 'The Cockleshell Heroes'.

Both units carry out intensive commando-type training and Royal Marine instructors were attached to assist in training in 1956. They wear the green beret.

The size of the 2nd Commando Company remains as a company and in 1970 was based at Fort Gellibrand, Williamstown, Victoria.

INDEX